WORLD PEACE THROUGH WORLD LAW

WORLD PEACE
Through WORLD LAW

By GRENVILLE CLARK *and* LOUIS B. SOHN

Second Edition (Revised)

HARVARD UNIVERSITY PRESS · 1960

Cambridge, Massachusetts

TO ALL THOSE
WHO SEEK THE RULE
OF LAW IN WORLD AFFAIRS

TABLE OF CONTENTS

THE PROPOSED REVISED CHARTER OF
THE UNITED NATIONS

ANNEX I. DISARMAMENT

ANNEX II. THE UNITED NATIONS PEACE FORCE

ANNEX III. THE JUDICIAL AND CONCILIATION SYSTEM OF THE UNITED NATIONS

ANNEX IV. THE WORLD DEVELOPMENT AUTHORITY

ANNEX V. THE REVENUE SYSTEM OF THE UNITED NATIONS

ANNEX VI. PRIVILEGES AND IMMUNITIES

ANNEX VII. BILL OF RIGHTS

FOREWORD

This Second Edition is made necessary by the exhaustion of the 6400 copies of the original edition, published in March 1958, and by a continued demand for the book.

However, instead of merely reprinting the original edition, the authors have taken advantage of the opportunity to make certain revisions. The purpose is in part to shorten the book, in order to make it available at a lower price, and in part to include a number of minor changes resulting from further reflection by the authors or from the numerous searching comments on the first edition received from distinguished persons in many nations.

In the interest of brevity, we have omitted the two Appendices of the first edition, containing unannotated texts of the present United Nations Charter and of the proposed revised Charter. However convenient, these did not seem essential and their omission saves one hundred seventy-two pages. On the other hand, the Introduction, containing a statement of the principles and essential features of the proposals, has been expanded to make it a more self-contained summary; and the detailed plan for universal and complete disarmament by stages (Annex I) has been enlarged by the inclusion of a set of provisions for an Outer Space Agency. In addition, a number of changes have been made in form and detail both in the text of the proposals and in the comment thereon.

The authors wish to emphasize, however, that the total effect of all the alterations is in no way to change either the *basic principles* or the *essential features* of their plan for peace. These principles and cardinal features have well stood the test of the severe scrutiny given to the first edition in all parts of the world; and the inexorable course of events has confirmed the analysis upon which the authors have based their comprehensive and interrelated plan.

The Soviet proposals for "general and complete" disarmament made in the United Nations by Chairman Khrushchev on September 18, 1959 and the British proposals for "comprehensive" disarmament made by Foreign Secretary Lloyd on the previous day give a new status to the effort for genuine peace. This is so because for the first time since World War II serious proposals for *complete,* rather than merely partial, disarmament have been officially advanced, and it is unlikely that any amount of disparagement or obstruction will be effective to suppress these all-important proposals. But even should they be temporarily suppressed, it is as certain as can be that, in view of the unwillingness of the peoples to submit indefinitely to the burdens and risks of the arms race without a real effort to stop it, the subject of total and universal disarmament and all that must go with it will soon come to the front again.

As the discussion proceeds, it will be found that, besides universal and complete disarmament, nothing less will suffice than a comprehensive plan whereby there would be established on a world scale institutions corresponding to those which have been found essential for the maintenance of law and order in local communities and nations.

Thus in the very first discussions of the Russian and British proposals, it became apparent that, apart from an effective inspection system to supervise the disarmament process from the outset, it will be indispensable simultaneously to establish an adequate world police force in order that, after complete disarmament has been accomplished, the means will exist to deter or apprehend violators of the world law forbidding any national armaments and prohibiting violence or the threat of it between nations. It will then become equally clear that along with the prohibition of violence or the threat of it as the means of dealing with international disputes, it will be essential to establish alternative peaceful means to deal with all disputes between nations in the shape of a world judicial and conciliation system. It will doubtless also be found advisable, in the interest of a solid and durable peace, to include a World Development Authority, adequately and reliably financed, in order to mitigate the vast disparities between the "have" and the "have not" nations.

The necessity will also be seen for a world legislature with carefully limited yet adequate powers to vote the annual budgets of the world peace authority (whether in the form of a revised United Nations or otherwise), to enact appropriate penalties for violation of the world law and other essential regulations concerning disarmament and the maintenance of peace, and to keep a watchful eye on the other organs and agencies of the peace authority. In addition, it will be necessary to constitute an effective world executive, free from any crippling veto, in order to direct and control the world inspection service and the world police force and to exercise other essential executive functions. Finally, it will follow as surely as day follows night that an effective world revenue system must be adopted, since there would otherwise be no reliable means to provide the large sums required for the maintenance of the inspection service, the world police force, the judicial system and the other necessary world institutions.

In short, it is inescapable that if the world really wants peace, a comprehensive and interrelated system of this general character will be required. It is doubtless because WORLD PEACE THROUGH WORLD LAW faces up to all these specific and difficult problems and proposes detailed solutions in each instance that the book has had the close attention which it has commanded in many nations. This is also the reason why the authors feel confident of widespread interest in this Second Edition, since nothing is more certain than that if disarmament and genuine peace are to be realized, there is no escape from coming to grips with the thorny problems dealt with in detail in this book.

In addition to the English version, this Second Edition will be published in Dutch, French, German, Norwegian, Spanish, and Swedish. It is also hoped that the Second Edition, or a possible Third Edition, will be published in a number of other languages,—including Arabic, Chinese, Italian, Japanese, Polish and Russian.

In order to save space, we have omitted the acknowledgments contained in the first edition expressing our appreciation of the assistance received for our work from many organizations and individuals during the past decade. We remain no less grateful to these organizations and individuals and no less appreciative also of the helpful comments which we have continued to receive from correspondents in many countries, now amounting to at least twenty-five hundred. The intense interest revealed by these comments confirms our conviction that the peoples will not apathetically stand aside at the risk of a new world disaster, but will themselves make a powerful effort to achieve world peace through universal and complete disarmament under enforceable world law.

GRENVILLE CLARK
Dublin, New Hampshire, U.S.A.

LOUIS B. SOHN
Harvard University Law School
Cambridge, Massachusetts, U.S.A.

April 1960

INTRODUCTION

By Grenville Clark

This book sets forth a comprehensive and detailed plan for the maintenance of world peace in the form of a proposed revision of the United Nations Charter. The purpose is to contribute material for the world-wide discussions which must precede the adoption of universal and complete disarmament and the establishment of truly effective institutions for the prevention of war.

At the outset, it may be helpful to explain: *first*, the underlying conceptions of this plan for peace; and *second*, the main features of the plan whereby these conceptions would be carried out.

The fundamental premise of the book is identical with the pronouncement of the President of the United States on October 31, 1956: "There can be no peace without law." In this context the word "law" necessarily implies the law of a world authority, i.e., law which would be uniformly applicable to all nations and all individuals in the world and which would definitely forbid violence or the threat of it as a means for dealing with any international dispute. This world law must also be law in the sense of law which is capable of enforcement, as distinguished from a mere set of exhortations or injunctions which it is desirable to observe but for the enforcement of which there is no effective machinery.

The proposition "no peace without law" also embodies the conception that peace cannot be ensured by a continued arms race, nor by an indefinite "balance of terror", nor by diplomatic maneuver, but only by universal and complete national disarmament together with the establishment of institutions corresponding in the world field to those which maintain law and order within local communities and nations.

A prime motive for this book is that the world is far more likely to make progress toward genuine peace, as distinguished from a precarious armed truce, when a *detailed* plan adequate to the purpose is available, so that the structure and functions of the requisite world institutions may be fully discussed on a world-wide basis. Consequently, this book comprises a set of definite and interrelated proposals to carry out complete and universal disarmament and to strengthen the United Nations through the establishment of such legislative, executive and judicial institutions as are necessary to maintain world order.

UNDERLYING PRINCIPLES

The following are the basic principles by which Professor Sohn and I have been governed.

First: It is futile to expect genuine peace until there is put into effect an effective system of *enforceable* world law in the limited field of war prevention. This implies: (a) the complete disarmament, under effective controls, of each and every nation, and (b) the simultaneous adoption on a world-wide basis of the measures and institutions which the experience of centuries has shown to be essential for the maintenance of law and order, namely, clearly stated law against violence, courts to interpret and apply that law and police to enforce it. All else, we conceive, depends upon the acceptance of this approach.

Second: The world law against international violence must be explicitly stated in constitutional and statutory form. It must, under appropriate penalties, forbid the use of force by any nation against any other for any cause whatever, save only in self-defense; and must be applicable to all individuals as well as to all nations.

Third: World judicial tribunals to interpret and apply the world law against international violence must be established and maintained, and also organs of mediation and conciliation,—so as to substitute peaceful means of adjudication and adjustment in place of violence, or the threat of it, as the means for dealing with all international disputes.

Fourth: A permanent world police force must be created and maintained which, while safeguarded with utmost care against misuse, would be fully adequate to forestall or suppress any violation of the world law against international violence.

Fifth: The complete disarmament of all the nations (rather than the mere "reduction" or "limitation" of armaments) is essential for any solid and lasting peace, this disarmament to be accomplished in a simultaneous and proportionate manner by carefully verified stages and subject to a well-organized system of inspection. It is now generally accepted that disarmament must be universal and enforceable. That it must also be complete is no less necessary, since: (a) in the nuclear age no mere reduction in the new means of mass destruction could be effective to remove fear and tension; and (b) if any substantial national armaments were to remain, even if only ten per cent of the armaments of 1960, it would be impracticable to maintain a sufficiently strong world police force to deal with any possible aggression or revolt against the authority of the world organization. We should face the fact that until there is *complete* disarmament of every nation without exception there can be no assurance of genuine peace.

Sixth: Effective world machinery must be created to mitigate the vast disparities in the economic condition of various regions of the world, the continuance of which tends to instability and conflict.

The following supplementary principles have also guided us:
Active participation in the world peace authority must be universal, or virtually so; and although a few nations may be permitted to decline active membership, any such nonmember nations must be equally bound by the obligation to abolish their armed forces and to abide by all the laws and regulations of the world organization with relation to the prevention of war. It follows that ratification of the constitutional document creating the world peace organization (whether in the form of a revised United Nations Charter or otherwise) must be by a preponderant majority of all the nations and people of the world.

The world law, in the limited field of war prevention to which it would be restricted, should apply to all individual persons in the world as well as to all the nations,—to the end that in case of violations by individuals without the support of their governments, the world law could be invoked directly against them without the necessity of indicting a whole nation or group of nations.

The basic rights and duties of all nations in respect of the maintenance of peace should be clearly defined not in laws enacted by a world legislature but in the constitutional document itself. That document should also carefully set forth not only the structure but also the most important powers of the various world institutions established or authorized by it; and the constitutional document should also define the limits of those powers and provide specific safeguards to guarantee the observance of those limits and the protection of individual rights against abuse of power. By this method of "constitutional legislation" the nations and peoples would know in advance within close limits what obligations they would assume by acceptance of the new world system, and only a restricted field of discretion would be left to the legislative branch of the world authority.

The powers of the world organization should be restricted to matters directly related to the maintenance of peace. All other powers should be reserved to the nations and their peoples. This definition and reservation of powers is advisable not only to avoid opposition based upon fear of possible interference in the domestic affairs of the nations, but also because it is wise for this generation to limit itself to the single task of preventing international violence or the threat of it. If we can accomplish that, we should feel satisfied and could well leave to later generations any enlargement of the powers of the world organization that they might find desirable.

While any plan to prevent war through total disarmament and the substitution of world law for international violence must be fully adequate to the end in view, it must also be *acceptable* to this generation. To propose a plan lacking in the basic essentials for the prevention of war would be futile. On the other hand, a plan which, however ideal in conception, is so far ahead of the times as to raise insuperable opposition would be equally futile. Therefore, we have tried hard to strike a sound balance by setting forth a plan which, while really adequate to prevent war, would, at the same time, be so carefully safeguarded that it *ought* to be acceptable to all nations.

It is not out of the question to carry out universal and complete disarmament and to establish the necessary new world institutions through an entirely new world authority, but it seems more normal and sensible to make the necessary revisions of the present United Nations Charter.

MAIN FEATURES OF THE WHOLE PLAN

In harmony with these underlying principles, the most important specific features of the proposed Charter revision may be summarized as follows:

(1) *Membership.* The plan contemplates that virtually the whole world shall accept permanent membership before the revised Charter comes into effect,—the conception being that so drastic a change in the world's political structure should, in order to endure, be founded upon unanimous or nearly unanimous approval.

The assurance of assent by a great preponderance of the nations and peoples of the world would be accomplished by the revised Articles 3 and 110 providing: (a) that every independent state in the world shall be eligible for membership and may join at will; (b) that the revised Charter shall come into force only when ratified by five sixths of all the nations of the world, the ratifying nations to have a combined population of at least five sixths of the total world population and to include all the twelve nations which then have the largest populations. The assurance of permanent membership would be provided by the revised Article 6 whereby no nation, once having ratified the revised Charter, could either withdraw or be expelled.

The practical result would be that the plan would not even become operative until active and permanent support had been pledged by a great majority of all the nations, including as the twelve largest nations Brazil, France, the Federal Republic of Germany, India, Indonesia, Italy, Japan, Pakistan, the People's Republic of China, the United Kingdom, the U.S.A., and the U.S.S.R.

Since in early 1960 there were ninety-nine nations generally recognized as independent states or likely to be so recognized within a few years thereafter, the number of nonratifying nations under the proposed ratification formula would not exceed sixteen, all of which would probably be nations with populations of less than forty million. And since, as a practical matter, the average population of such nonratifying nations would probably not exceed fifteen million, it is unlikely that the population of the maximum number of nonratifying nations would be more than 240 million, or less than eight per cent of the world's population, which we have estimated as of July 1965 at 3,172,156,000.

With so large a preponderence in the number and population of the ratifying nations, it is reasonable to suppose that within a few years after the ratification of the revised Charter, there would be no nonmember nations whatever. For it seems clear that few, if any, nations would wish to stand out when at least five sixths of all the nations of the world, having over ninety per cent of its population, had agreed to the new plan for world peace.

The likelihood that there might not be a single nonmember nation is made the greater by the proposed requirement (under revised Articles 2 and 11) that every one of the necessarily small minority of nonmember nations shall, nevertheless, be required to comply with all the prohibitions and obligations of the disarmament plan. This provision that *every* nation in the world shall completely disarm and shall comply with the plan for the substitution of world law for international violence is deemed fundamental, since if even one small nation were permitted to possess the new weapons of mass destruction, such fears and suspicions might remain as to prevent the adherence of others, and the entire plan might be frustrated.

In view of the proposed requirement that every nation would, irrespective of membership, be bound to observe the world law in the field of war prevention, and the further fact that any minority of nonmember nations would necessarily be small, it may be argued that it would be simpler and legitimate to impose compulsory membership upon all the nations without exception. The plan set forth in a preliminary draft of the present proposals issued in 1953 did in fact provide that once the revised Charter had been ratified by a very large majority of the nations, all other nations should be deemed full and permanent members, even though they might have deliberately refused ratification. In deference, however, to the view that no nation should be *forced* to accept such affirmative obligations of membership as the duty to contribute financially, the present plan stops short of *compelling* membership by any nation, no matter how overwhelming the support for the revised Charter.

Nevertheless, the practical result would be little different from that of universal compulsory membership since, as already noted: (a) the maximum possible number of nonratifying nations could not exceed one sixth of all the nations and could have no more than a minor fraction of the world's population; and (b) even this small minority of nations, although exempt from certain positive duties of membership, would be bound equally with the member Nations to comply with the world law prohibiting international violence and requiring complete disarmament. This practical result would be accomplished, however, without the element of coercion involved in requiring active membership from the relatively few nations which might choose not to ratify.

(2) *The General Assembly.* A radical revision is proposed as to the powers, composition and method of voting of the General Assembly.

Although the plan sets forth in the Charter itself all the *basic provisions* of the disarmament process and of other main features (such as the proposed world police force, the revenue system and the judicial system), it would still be true that in order to *implement* these basic provisions, the powers of the legislative and executive branches of the world organization must be considerable.

The plan calls for imposing the final responsibility for the enforcement of the disarmament process and the maintenance of peace upon the General Assembly itself, and gives the Assembly adequate powers to this end. These powers would, however, be strictly limited to matters directly related to the maintenance of peace. They would *not* include such matters as regulation of international trade, immigration and the like, or any right to interfere in the domestic affairs of the nations, save as expressly authorized by the revised Charter in order to enforce disarmament or to prevent international violence where a situation which ordinarily might be deemed "domestic" has actually developed into a serious threat to world peace.

To ensure the observance of these limitations, the delegated powers would be enumerated and defined in the revised Charter; while, as still further protection, there would be an explicit reservation to the member Nations and their peoples of all powers not thus delegated "by express language or clear implication". The delegated powers are defined in revised Article 11 and in various other provisions of the revised Charter, while the reservation of all nongranted powers is contained both in revised Article 2 and in the proposed Bill of Rights (Annex VII).

As above mentioned, the principle is followed that all the *main features* of the whole plan shall be included in the revised Charter itself as "constitutional legislation", having in mind that the nations will be more likely to accept the plan if all its principal provisions are clearly set forth in the constitutional document itself. The effect would be to bind the nations in advance not only to all the fundamentals but also to many important details, and thus to leave for the General Assembly a more limited legislative scope than might be supposed.

Since, however, the General Assembly, even with elaborate "constitutional legislation", would need to have some definite legislative powers, the plan calls for a revision of the system of representation in the Assembly. For it cannot be expected that the larger nations would consent to give the Assembly even very limited *legislative* powers under the present system whereby Albania, Costa Rica, Iceland, Liberia, etc., have an equal vote with the United States, the Soviet Union, India, the United Kingdom, etc.

The purpose is, by abolishing the present system of one vote for each member Nation, to substitute a more equitable system, and thus to make the nations more willing to confer upon the General Assembly the limited yet considerably increased powers that it would need.

The proposed plan of representation takes account of relative populations but is qualified by the important provisions that no nation, however large, shall have more than thirty Representatives and that even the smallest nation shall have one Representative. The upper limit of thirty would be imposed partly because weighted representation is not likely to be accepted by the smaller nations unless the differences in representation between the majority of the nations and the largest nations are kept within moderate limits, and also because without some such limitation, the General Assembly would be of so unwieldy a size as to be unable to transact business. At the other extreme the purpose is to ensure that even the very small nations shall have some voice.

The proposed formula divides the ninety-nine nations, generally recognized in early 1960 as independent states or likely to be so recognized by 1965, into six categories according to relative populations, with representation as follows:

The 4 largest nations........30 Representatives each....120	
The 8 next largest nations....15 Representatives each....120	
The 20 next largest nations.... 6 Representatives each....120	
The 30 next largest nations.... 4 Representatives each....120	
The 34 next largest nations.... 2 Representatives each.... 68	
The 3 smallest nations....... 1 Representative each.... 3	

       99 nations   551 Representatives

It is proposed that the populations of colonial and semi-colonial areas (i.e., the non-self-governing territories and dependencies, including territories under trusteeship administration) shall not be counted in determining the representation of the independent states but that, in order to afford equal treatment to the estimated approximately 95 million people (in 1965) of these areas, they shall be entitled to representation in proportion to population on the same average basis as the people of the member Nations. It is assumed that as of July 1965 this method would entitle these areas as a whole to seventeen Representatives. The General Assembly would allocate these Representatives among the various territories or groups of territories, taking into account their relative populations.

Of the assumed 568 Representatives, 551 would therefore represent the assumed ninety-nine independent states, while the non-self-governing and trust territories would have 17 Representatives.

The four most populous nations of the world—the People's Republic of China, India, the Soviet Union and the United States—would each have the maximum of thirty Representatives; and even the smallest nation (Iceland) would have one Representative. The 568 Representatives would represent a total estimated world population (as of July 1965) of 3,172,156,000, or an average of about 5,600,000 for each Representative.

The effect would be that, with relation to population, the smaller nations would still have a disproportionately large voice, but not nearly as much so as under the present system of one vote for each member Nation irrespective of population.

Over a period of years, the authors have studied many plans for determining representation by various formulas that would take account of such factors as relative literacy, relative wealth as measured by per capita income, etc. We have concluded, however, that the introduction of any such other factors would raise so many complications and involve such uncertain and invidious distinctions that it is wiser to hold to the less elaborate formula herein proposed.

We have also studied numerous suggestions for a bicameral world legislature in which the nations would have voting power in one house in proportion to their populations, but equal voting power in the other house irrespective of their size. Modifications of this plan in the shape of a system of double voting in a single house have also been studied. After weighing these alternatives, we conclude that the one-chamber solution herein proposed (together with representation which takes account of relative populations, but is modified by the proposed system of categories and the proposed maximum and minimum number of Representatives) is not only simpler, but also is probably as fair an arrangement as any other. However, we hold no dogmatic views on this difficult subject, the essential point being that there must be some radical, yet equitable, change in the present system of representation in the General Assembly as a basis for conferring upon the Assembly certain essential, although carefully limited, powers of legislation which it does not now possess.

As to the method of selection of the Representatives, it is proposed that a system of full popular election shall be gradually introduced. This would be done under a three-stage plan providing: (a) that in the first stage all the Representatives would be chosen by the respective national legislatures of the member Nations; (b) that in the second stage at least half the Representatives would be chosen by popular vote of those persons qualified to vote for the most numerous branch of the national legislature; and (c) that in the third stage all the Representatives would be chosen by the same sort of popular vote. The first two stages would normally be of twelve years each (three four-year terms of the General Assembly) but could each be extended by eight years by a special vote of the Assembly. The popular election of all the Representatives would, therefore, normally become mandatory twenty-four years after the ratification of the revised Charter and in any case not later than forty years after the revised Charter comes into force.

With regard to the terms of service of the Representatives, it is proposed that they shall serve for four years.

Concerning the procedure for voting in the General Assembly, it is proposed in place of the present method: (a) that a majority of all the Representatives then in office must be present in order to constitute a quorum; (b) that, except as to certain "important" and "special" questions, decisions shall be made by a majority of the Representatives present and voting; (c) that on these "important" questions which would be specifically defined, decisions shall be by a "special majority" consisting of a majority of all the Representatives then in office, whether or not present and voting; and (d) that in respect of several "special" questions, also specifically defined, there shall be even larger special majorities which in one instance would require the affirmative vote of three fourths of all the Representatives in office including two thirds of the Representatives from those nations entitled to fifteen or more Representatives, i.e., the twelve largest nations.

Two full-time Standing Committees of the General Assembly would be constitutionally provided for, namely, a Standing Committee on the Peace Enforcement Agencies and a Standing Committee on Budget and Finance. The former would be a "watchdog" committee to exercise legislative supervision over the process and maintenance of disarmament and over the United Nations Peace Force. The latter would have vital functions in submitting to the Assembly recommendations as to the amount and apportionment of each annual budget for all the activities of the strengthened United Nations.

With relation to the powers of the revised General Assembly, a clear distinction would be made between legislative powers and powers of recommendation. The *legislative* powers would be strictly limited to matters directly related to the maintenance of peace, whereas the extensive powers of mere recommendation now possessed by the Assembly would be retained and even broadened. To this end, the Assembly's legislative authority would, as above mentioned, exclude any regulation of international trade, immigration and the like and any right to interfere in the domestic affairs of the nations, save only as strictly necessary for the enforcement of disarmament or, in exceptional circumstances, for the prevention of international violence.

On the other hand, as distinguished from the power to legislate, the General Assembly would have the right to make nonbinding *recommendations* on any subject which it deemed relevant to the maintenance of peace and the welfare of the world's people.

(3) *The Executive Council.* It is proposed to abolish the present Security Council and to substitute for it an Executive Council, composed of seventeen Representatives elected by the General Assembly itself. This new and highly important organ would not only be chosen by the Assembly, bct would also be responsible to and removable by the Assembly; and the Council would serve for the same four-year terms as the Representatives in the Assembly.

Special provision would be made for representation of the larger nations, whereby the four largest nations (China, India, the U.S.A. and the U.S.S.R.) would each be entitled at all times to have one of its Representatives on the Council; and four of the eight next largest nations (Brazil, France, West Germany, Indonesia, Italy, Japan, Pakistan and the United Kingdom) would in rotation also be entitled to representation, with the proviso that two of these four shall always be from nations in Europe and the other two from nations outside Europe. The remaining nine members would be chosen by the Assembly from the Representatives of all the other member Nations and the non-self-governing and trust territories under a formula designed to provide fair representation for all the main regions of the world and to ensure that every member Nation, without exception, shall in due course have a Representative on this all-important Council.

In contrast to the voting procedure of the present Security Council, whereby any one of the five nations entitled to "permanent" membership has a veto power in all nonprocedural matters, the decisions of the new Executive Council on "important" matters (as defined in paragraph 2 of revised Article 27) would be by a vote of twelve of the seventeen Representatives composing it, with the proviso that this majority shall include a majority of the eight members of the Council from the twelve member Nations entitled to fifteen or more Representatives in the Assembly and a majority of the nine other members of the Council. All other decisions would be by a vote of any twelve members of the Council.

This Executive Council would constitute the *executive arm* of the strengthened United Nations, holding much the same relation to the General Assembly as that of the British Cabinet to the House of Commons. Subject to its responsibility to the Assembly, the new Council would have broad powers to supervise and direct the disarmament process and other aspects of the whole system for the maintenance of peace provided for in the revised Charter.

The Executive Council would, for example, decide (subject to review by the General Assembly) as to whether each stage of the disarmament process has been satisfactorily completed and, once complete national disarmament has been achieved, would watch over its maintenance. Nevertheless, the Council would always remain subordinate to the Assembly, which would have final authority to make such crucial decisions as the possible postponement of any stage of the disarmament process, and the imposition of sanctions in case of any breach of the peace or serious violation by any nation of the authority of the United Nations.

(4) *Economic and Social Council, Trusteeship Council.* These two Councils would be continued, but with a somewhat larger and different composition than under the present Charter designed to provide a wider and better-balanced representation on these Councils.

The Economic and Social Council, instead of its present membership of eighteen, would have a membership of twenty-four Representatives elected by the General Assembly from among its own number for four-year terms. They would be chosen pursuant to a formula whereby each of the twelve member Nations having the largest gross national products would be entitled to have one of its Representatives on the Council at all times, the other twelve members of the Council to be elected by the Assembly from among the Representatives of all the remaining member Nations and the non-self-governing or trust territories, with due regard to geographical distribution.

The present provisions for the composition of the Trusteeship Council would also be substantially changed. This Council would likewise consist entirely of Representatives elected by the Assembly from among its own number for four-year terms and would be chosen under a formula whereby its membership would include three groups of equal number: (a) a group of Representatives from the member Nations which are actually administering either trust territories or other non-self-governing territories; (b) a group of Representatives from the member Nations which have achieved independence since 1939; and (c) a group of Representatives from all the other member Nations, i.e., from all the member Nations not covered by the two preceding categories.

Like the Executive Council these two other Councils would be directly responsible to the Assembly. Their responsibilities would be enlarged; and their usefulness would be enhanced by reason of the greatly increased funds which would be available to them under the proposed new revenue system.

(5) *The Disarmament Process.* Annex I contains a carefully framed plan for the elimination—not the mere "reduction" or "limitation"—of *all* national armaments.

It calls for a "transition period" of one year following the coming into force of the revised Charter during which the first new General Assembly would be selected, the first Executive Council would be chosen by the Assembly, and the first Inspection Commission would be appointed by that Council, subject to confirmation by the Assembly. The plan then calls for a "preparatory stage" of two years, during which an arms census would be taken, an Inspection Service would be organized and other preparations would be made. Finally, it provides for an "actual disarmament stage" which would normally cover ten years during which there would be a step-by-step proportionate reduction in all categories of all national armed forces and all armaments at the rate of ten per cent per annum. As below mentioned, this normal ten-year period could be reduced to seven years by the General Assembly or could, on the other hand, be extended by the Assembly under certain circumstances.

The proposed Inspection Commission, the members of which would be appointed for five-year terms by the Executive Council subject to confirmation by the General Assembly, would consist of five persons, none of whom could be a national of any of the twelve nations having fifteen or more Representatives in the General Assembly and no two of whom could be nationals of the same nation. The administrative head of the Inspection Service would be an Inspector-General, who would be appointed by the Inspection Commission for a six-year term, subject to confirmation by the Executive Council, and would be removable by the Commission at will.

The Executive Council would have general supervision over the Inspection Commission with authority to issue instructions to the Commission and to remove at will any member of the Commission.

Very careful safeguards would be provided to ensure the competence and integrity of the personnel of the Inspection Service and their devotion to the purposes of the United Nations. These would include a provision limiting the number of nationals of any one nation among those performing duties of actual inspection to not more than four per cent of the total number of Inspectors; a requirement that all the personnel of the Service shall be recruited on as wide a geographical basis as possible; a prohibition against their seeking or receiving instructions from any government or authority except the United Nations; and the requirement of a solemn declaration that they will perform their functions impartially and conscientiously. On the other hand, all the personnel of the Service would be assured "fully adequate" pay and allowances and retirement pensions free from all taxation.

As a still further safeguard, the Standing Committee on the Peace Enforcement Agencies of the General Assembly would have the responsibility of watching over the proper performance by the Inspection Commission of its duties and also over the proper exercise by the Executive Council of its general authority over the Commission with full power to investigate and report to the Assembly itself.

The proposed powers of the Inspection Service are carefully defined in Annex I, and the General Assembly would be empowered to adopt further regulations to ensure, on the one hand, the efficacy of the inspection system and, on the other hand, to protect nations and individuals against possible abuses of power. While Inspectors would be given unlimited access to establishments with especially dangerous potentials, periodic inspections of less dangerous activities would be restricted to a reasonable number each year. Any additional inspection of activities subject only to periodic inspection and of places not ordinarily subject to inspection could be conducted only on the basis of a special authorization issued by one of the United Nations regional courts which would be established as explained below. Such an authorization could be granted only upon a showing to the court of reasonable cause to believe or suspect that a prohibited activity is being conducted in the place sought to be inspected. Regular aerial surveys would be provided for, subject to the limitation that no more than three regular surveys of any particular territory could be conducted in any year. Special aerial surveys could also be made, but only upon court authorization after a showing to the court of reasonable cause.

The reduction process during each year of the "actual disarmament stage" would be verified by the Inspection Commission, which would report fully to the Executive Council as to whether the required proportionate reductions had been duly carried out by all the nations. The General Assembly, advised by the Council, would have power to suspend the disarmament process for six months at a time if not fully satisfied that it was being faithfully fulfilled. On the other hand, after the first four years, the Assembly would have the power to cut in half the remaining six years, so as to achieve universal and complete disarmament in seven years from the beginning of the "actual disarmament stage".

This disarmament plan should, however, be thought of as a twelve-year plan if normally carried out without either delay or acceleration, i.e., the two years of the "preparatory stage" and the normal ten years of the "actual disarmament stage". At the end of the latter period, no *national* military forces whatever would exist; and the only military force in the entire world (as distinguished from limited and lightly armed internal police forces) would be a world police force, to be called the "United Nations Peace Force", which would be built up parallel with and in proportion to the disarmament process.

No plan for universal and complete disarmament is practicable, unless *all* nations are bound by it. It is apparent to all that if any one of the larger and stronger nations were exempted from the disarmament process, no such disarmament would be feasible. But it is equally true in this world of novel weapons of tremendous destructive power that even a small nation might become a menace to the peace of the world. The disarmament system must, therefore, cover *every* nation, whether a member of the United Nations or not; and the plan includes appropriate provisions to this end.

Under the above-mentioned ratification procedure (whereby the revised Charter would not come into force until ratified by five sixths of all the nations, the ratifying nations to have at least five sixths of the world's population and to include each of the twelve nations having the largest populations), it is possible, and even probable, that there would actually be no nonmember nations whatever; and in any event any such nonmember nations would be few in number and relatively small in size. In case, however, there should be a few nations which chose to refrain from active membership, it is essential that they shall nevertheless be expressly bound to refrain from violence on the same basis as the member Nations and to settle all their disputes by peaceful means. Correspondingly also, all nonmember nations must be required to observe the disarmament provisions. It would therefore be provided that *all* nations "shall settle their international disputes by peaceful means" and the obligation to disarm would be imposed upon "every nation in the world". Moreover, every nonmember nation would be brought into a special relationship with the United Nations through a system of agreements whereby all nonmember nations would agree to comply with the disarmament provisions of Annex I and the laws, regulations and decisions made thereunder.

The proposed disarmament plan depends also on its *simultaneous* execution by all nations. It is obvious that no nation would be willing or could be expected to disarm ahead of the others; and therefore all necessary safeguards must be established to ensure that no nation would be put in a disadvantageous position because other nations have not simultaneously carried out their part of the plan. Accordingly the Inspection Commission would be empowered not only to approve annual disarmament plans for every nation but also to supervise and to ensure their simultaneous execution.

Still further, the disarmament plan must make sure that all nations will disarm *proportionately*. The year-by-year diminution of military strength must be equal for all nations, since no nation can be expected to disarm by a larger percentage than others and since no nation should be deprived of a main source of its military strength while other nations still retain their principal sources of strength. Thus a nation strong in nuclear weapons should not be entirely deprived of them while other nations retain a large proportion of their preponderant land armies. And similarly, a nation could not reasonably be asked to abandon its ballistic missiles while another was permitted to retain its bombing planes. For these reasons a *uniform percentage* reduction year by year is provided for as the fairest and most acceptable method to achieve total national disarmament.

It would not, however, be sufficient merely to provide for uniform percentage reductions in the *total* military forces and armaments of the various nations, since a particular nation might, for example, simply demobilize a large number of foot soldiers while leaving the strength of its air force and navy unimpaired. Similarly, some other nation might limit a required numerical cut in its air force to maintenance personnel while keeping all its pilots in the service. A requirement with respect to the reduction of weapons might also be easily evaded if a nation were permitted to divide the reduction unequally between its fighter planes and long-range bombers, or between its fissionable and fusionable weapons. A really fair and safe method of reduction requires, therefore, that each nation shall reduce in an equal manner the personnel not only of each major service (land, sea and air), but also of each major component thereof. Moreover, this principle of proportionate reductions would need to be applied uniformly to troops stationed in the home territory and abroad. For example, if in a given year the ground forces of a particular nation should consist of 500,000 men of whom 100,000 were stationed abroad, a ten per cent reduction of 50,000 in that year would have to be divided in such a way as to ensure that 40,000 be discharged from the forces stationed in the home territory and 10,000 from those stationed abroad.

Fairness and safety require similar equal and proportionate reductions in each major category of weapons and in all facilities for the production of armaments. Reductions of the same proportionate size should be made, for instance, in each nation's capacity to produce various categories of weapons; for example, with respect to guided and ballistic missiles, separate cuts would be necessary in the capacity for the production of short-, medium- and long-range missiles.

With these considerations in mind, the disarmament plan includes detailed provisions requiring that all personnel reductions be distributed proportionately not only among the personnel of the major military services but also among their principal components. Similar proportionate reductions would be required among the various categories of the armaments of the various services and components and in the various facilities for armament production. The annual reduction plans of every nation would be subject to approval and supervision by the Inspection Service, and a serious violation could result in the postponement of all further annual reductions, for periods of not more than six months at a time, until the violation was remedied.

The disarmament plan also includes provision for a United Nations Nuclear Energy Authority with dual functions: (a) to assist the Inspection Service in guarding against possible diversion of nuclear materials to any war-making purpose, and (b) to promote the world-wide use of nuclear materials and processes for peaceful purposes. To these ends, the Nuclear Energy Authority would have wide powers to acquire by purchase at a fair price all nuclear materials in the world, with the obligation to have them put to use at fair rentals for peaceful purposes in all parts of the world under arrangements that would apportion the materials fairly and safeguard them against seizure. It is contemplated that this new Authority, having wider scope and membership than the International Atomic Energy Agency established in 1956, would take over the personnel and functions of that Agency.

As in the case of the Inspection Service, the Nuclear Energy Authority would be under the direction and control of a five-member Commission. This body

xxvii

would be called the Nuclear Energy Commission. Within its field this Commission would correspond to the Inspection Commission and would be subject to the same careful provisions as the Inspection Commission in respect of the eligibility of its members and the authority of the Executive Council to supervise its policies and to remove any member at will.

The administrative head of the Nuclear Energy Authority would be a General Manager appointed for a six-year term by the Nuclear Energy Commission and removable by it at will. Safeguards corresponding to those provided in respect of the personnel of the Inspection Service would also be applicable to the personnel of the Nuclear Energy Authority, and the Standing Committee on the Peace Enforcement Agencies of the General Assembly would have responsibilities in respect of this Nuclear Energy Authority corresponding to its responsibilities in respect of the Inspection Service.

A new feature of the disarmament plan, made necessary by the recent penetration of outer space and its potentialities for the future, is a proposed United Nations Outer Space Agency. The broad objectives sought are: (a) to ensure that outer space is used only for peaceful purposes, and (b) to promote its exploration and use for the common benefit of all the people of this earth, rather than for the benefit of any nation or any part of mankind.

The Outer Space Agency would, subject to the over-all authority of the General Assembly and the Executive Council, be under the "direction and control" of a United Nations Outer Space Commission. This Commission, like the Inspection Commission and the Nuclear Energy Commission, would be composed of five members appointed for five-year terms by the Executive Council subject to confirmation by the General Assembly and would be removable at will by the Council.

Correspondingly also, the Outer Space Agency would have an administrative head who would be called the Managing Director.

Moreover, as to the personnel of the Outer Space Agency, there would be safeguarding provisions in all respects similar to the above-described provisions relative to the personnel of the Inspection Service and the Nuclear Energy Authority; and the Standing Committee on the Peace Enforcement Agencies would have "watchdog" responsibilities identical with those relative to the Inspection Service and the Nuclear Energy Authority.

Provision is made for reporting any violations of the disarmament plan; for correcting such violations; for the prosecution of serious individual violators in regional courts of the United Nations; and for sanctions against nations themselves in the possible event of defiance or evasion by any government. As a still further safeguard, there would be the above-mentioned committee of the General Assembly (the Standing Committee on the Peace Enforcement Agencies) with the function of keeping a sharp eye on all aspects of the disarmament process and of keeping the Assembly informed of any derelictions or defects.

It is a basic premise of this necessarily elaborate plan for universal and complete disarmament that, while the proposed system of inspection and control could not provide *absolute* assurance against the clandestine retention or manufacture of weapons, it could and would provide highly effective protection. It would be fallacious and a counsel of despair to reject the idea of the complete abolition of national armaments, including nuclear weapons, merely because no absolute or "foolproof" guarantee can be supplied that every ounce of dangerous war material has been accounted for and that no dangerous new weapon can ever be secretly made.

It is believed that the whole proposed system of inspection, including the inspection of all means of "delivery" of nuclear weapons, would, in practice, make it impossible for any group within a nation or any nation itself to assemble weapons that would constitute a serious danger. And it is also to be remembered that a powerful world police force would always be in the background for the very purpose of deterring or suppressing any rash attempt at international violence.

The guarantees of safety to be relied upon when all national armaments are abolished lie, therefore, in the *combination* of a comprehensive and highly organized inspection system with a coercive force of overwhelming power. Not exclusively on one or the other, but on the *combined* effect of both, the world could safely rely in the abandonment once and for all of all national military forces.

(6) *A World Police Force.* The plan is framed upon the assumption that not even the most solemn agreement and not even the most thorough inspection system, or both together, can be *fully* relied upon to ensure that every nation will always carry out and maintain complete disarmament and refrain from violence under all circumstances. Moreover, it must be recognized that even with the complete elimination of all *military* forces there would necessarily remain substantial, although strictly limited and lightly armed, internal police forces and that these police forces, supplemented by civilians armed with sporting rifles and fowling pieces, might conceivably constitute a serious threat to a neighboring country in the absence of a well-disciplined and heavily armed world police.

In short, our conception is that if police forces are necessary to maintain law and order even within a mature community or nation, similar forces will be required to guarantee the carrying out and maintenance of complete disarmament by each and every nation and to deter or suppress *any* attempted international violence. In consequence, detailed constitutional provision is made for a world police, to be organized and maintained by the strengthened United Nations and to be called the "United Nations Peace Force". This world police force would be the only *military* force permitted anywhere in the world after the process of national disarmament has been completed. It would be built up during the above-described "actual disarmament stage", so that as the last national military unit is disbanded the organization of the Peace Force would simultaneously be completed.

Annex II provides in detail for the organization and maintenance of the proposed United Nations Peace Force—for its recruitment and pay, its terms of service, its maximum and minimum strength, and for its training, equipment, disposition and functions. This Peace Force would consist of two components —a standing component and a Peace Force Reserve—both of which would, save in the most extreme emergency, be composed solely of volunteers.

The standing component would be a full-time force of professionals with a strength of between 200,000 and 600,000, as determined from year to year by the General Assembly. The proposed term of service for its enlisted personnel would be not less than four or more than eight years, as determined by the General Assembly, with provision for the re-enlistment of a limited number of especially well-qualified personnel.

In respect of the composition of the standing component, assurance would be provided through various specific limitations in Annex II that it would be recruited mainly, although not exclusively from the smaller nations. These limitations would include: (a) a provision whereby the number of nationals of any nation (including any non-self-governing or trust territory under its administration) serving at any one time in the standing component shall not exceed three per cent of its then existing total strength; (b) a provision that the number of nationals of any nation in any one of the three main branches (land, sea and air) of the standing component shall not exceed three per cent of the then existing strength of such main branch; (c) a provision that the number of nationals of any nation serving at any one time in the officer corps of either of the three main branches of the standing component shall not exceed three per cent of the then existing strength of the officer corps of such main branch; and (d) a provision that not less than two per cent or more than ten per cent of the total strength of the standing component shall be nationals of the nations or nation constituting any one of eleven to twenty regions into which the whole world would be divided by the General Assembly pursuant to paragraph 9 of Article 26 of Annex I.

The units of the standing component would be stationed throughout the world in such a way that there would be no undue concentration in any particular nation or region, and, on the other hand, so as to facilitate prompt action for the maintenance of peace if and when required. Proposed specific provisions in this respect include: a direction that the standing component shall be stationed at military bases of the United Nations so distributed around the world as to facilitate its availability in case prompt action to prevent or suppress international violence is directed by the General Assembly (or in certain circumstances by the Executive Council); a provision that no such base shall be situated within the territory of any nation entitled to fifteen or more Representatives in the General Assembly, thus ensuring that no United Nations military base would be located in any of the twelve largest nations; a provision that all the territory of the world outside that of the twelve largest nations shall be divided by the General Assembly into eleven to twenty regions for the special purpose of distributing elements of the standing component between such regions, with the proviso that not less than five per cent or more than ten per cent of the total strength of the standing component shall be stationed in bases in any one of those regions, save only when the Peace Force has been duly called upon to take action.

In order to ensure the greatest possible security for the standing component, provision would be made that its units be located to the greatest extent possible on islands or peninsulas, or in other easily defensible positions.

The mobility of the standing component would be of great importance, in order that its widely distributed units could be promptly brought together into a formidable force in the event of any serious threat of international violence or serious defiance of the authority of the world organization. The equipment of the standing component should, therefore, include an ample number of large and swift aircraft for the long-distance transport of men and supplies, and in voting the annual budgets for the Peace Force the General Assembly would have authority to provide for this need.

As distinguished from the active or standing component, the Peace Force Reserve would have no organized units whatever, but would consist only of individuals partially trained and subject to call for service with the standing component in case of need. It would have a strength of between 600,000 and 1,200,000, as determined by the General Assembly. Its members would be recruited subject to careful provisions as to geographical distribution identical with those applicable to the standing component. The proposed term of service of its enlisted personnel would be for not less than six or more than ten years, as determined by the General Assembly. They would receive a minimum amount of basic training during the first three years of their term of service and some further training during the remainder of their terms, but except for these training periods would remain in their home countries on a stand-by basis subject to call.

The officers of both components would be selected, trained and promoted with a view to "ensuring an officer corps of the highest possible quality" with adequate opportunity for the selection as officer candidates of highly qualified men from the rank and file.

Specific provision would be made for adequate pay and allowances for the personnel of both components, all pay and other compensation (including retirement pensions) to be free from all taxation.

It is contemplated that the United Nations Peace Force shall be regularly provided with the most modern weapons and equipment, except that its possession or use of biological, chemical or any other weapons adaptable to mass destruction, other than nuclear weapons, would be forbidden, special provision being made, as hereafter mentioned, for the use of nuclear weapons in extreme circumstances. The initial weapons and equipment of the Peace Force would come from the transfer of weapons and equipment discarded by national military forces during the process of complete disarmament. Subsequent supplies would be produced by the United Nations in its own production facilities through a separate agency to be established by the General Assembly and called the United Nations Military Supply and Research Agency. This Agency would engage in research relative to the development of new weapons and relative to methods of defense against the possible use by any nation of prohibited weapons clandestinely hidden or produced.

With regard to the use of nuclear weapons by the Peace Force, the solution proposed is that neither component shall normally be equipped with any kind of nuclear weapons, but that some such weapons shall be held in reserve in the custody of a civilian agency for use only under the most careful precautions. This agency would be the Nuclear Energy Authority which would be authorized to release any nuclear weapons for possible use by the Peace Force only by order of the General Assembly itself, and then only if the Assembly has declared that nuclear weapons (which might have been clandestinely hidden or clandestinely produced) have actually been used against some nation or against the United Nations, or that such use is imminently threatened. While it may be argued that nuclear weapons should be part of the regular equipment of a world police force so that it could immediately crush by ruthless action any defiance of the world law, this solution has been rejected as being no more consistent with the purpose of the Peace Force than the regular equipment of a city police force with weapons whereby thousands of citizens could be killed in suppressing a riot.

It is also realized that it can be persuasively argued that nuclear weapons should not be even potentially available to the Peace Force. On balance, however, it is believed wise to make it *possible* for the Peace Force to use nuclear weapons in extreme circumstances provided that, as called for by the above-described proposals, such possible use is safeguarded with the utmost care.

The immediate direction of the Peace Force would be entrusted to a committee of five persons—to be called the Military Staff Committee—all of whom would have to be nationals of the smaller nations, i.e., of those nations entitled to less than fifteen Representatives in the General Assembly. Beyond this safeguard, however, the Military Staff Committee would always be under the close control of civilian authority, i.e., of the Executive Council. Still further, the General Assembly, through its Standing Committee on the Peace Enforcement Agencies, would exercise a general supervision over the work of the Military Staff Committee and over the Executive Council itself in respect of the organization and all the activities of the Peace Force. In short, the plan includes the utmost precautions for the subordination of the military direction of the Peace Force under all circumstances to civilian authority as represented by the Executive Council and the General Assembly.

While a world police force, well-equipped and strong enough to prevent or promptly to suppress *any* international violence is, we believe, indispensable, the danger that it might be perverted into a tool of world domination is fully recognized. It is with this danger clearly in mind that meticulous care has been taken to surround the proposed Peace Force with the above-mentioned careful limitations and safeguards, so as to make its subversion virtually impossible.

Even with these elaborate safeguards, it is realized that the danger of possible misuse of the Peace Force cannot be *wholly* eliminated any more than every *conceivable* danger of violation of the disarmament process can be eliminated. However, in order to achieve complete national disarmament and genuine peace, *some* risks must be taken. What we have attempted is to reduce these to the very minimum. On the one hand we have sought to provide for a world police so strong as to be capable of preserving peace in any foreseeable contingency. On the other hand, we propose such careful checks and limitations that there would be every possible assurance that the power of this world police would not be misused.

It will be seen that despite all the proposed safeguards this plan calls for a world police that would be a strong and effective fighting force in case of need. The idea of some people that a world peace force somewhat similar as to arms and functions to the United Nations Emergency Force of 1957-1960 might suffice is, we believe, unsound and untenable. Even in a world in which all national military forces were abolished, there would, as above mentioned, necessarily remain internal police forces of substantial strength which would probably need to possess a considerable number of rifles and even a few machine guns. In addition there would remain literally millions of sporting rifles and revolvers in the hands of private persons and thousands of nonmilitary airplanes, large and small. Accordingly, it is conceivable that, even with total disarmament, an aroused nation with a strong grievance could marshal quite a formidable armed force even if no one in it possessed any weapon stronger than a rifle. And while it is true that any such force, even of a million men, could not withstand a well-armed contingent of the world police of even one twentieth its strength, that contingent in order to suppress the aggression promptly and with minimum injury would need to be a genuine fighting force, well equipped and highly disciplined.

Moreover, there would remain a lurking suspicion for some time at least that despite the most efficient world inspection system some nation or nations had contrived to hide or might produce secretly some forbidden weapons. In these circumstances it seems perfectly clear that in order to provide the necessary assurance to obtain general assent to universal and complete disarmament, it will be essential to provide a world police of such strength and armament as to be able *quickly* and *certainly* to prevent or suppress *any* international violence. We firmly believe that on no cheaper terms can universal and complete disarmament be achieved, while it is equally clear that without total disarmament, genuine peace is unattainable. We submit, in short, that a strong and well-armed police force is part of the indispensable price of peace and that the sooner the world faces up to this conclusion the better it will be for all peoples.

(7) *The Judicial and Conciliation System.* In accordance with the conception that the *abolition* of national armaments is indispensable to genuine peace, and that if such armaments are abolished other means must be simultaneously provided for the adjudication or settlement of international disputes and for "peaceful change", provision is made for a world system of conciliation and adjudication.

In proposing such a system, recognition is given to the existence of two main categories of international disputes, namely: (1) those disputes which are capable of adjudication through the application of legal principles, and (2) the equally or more important category of disputes which cannot be satisfactorily settled on the basis of applicable legal principles.

With respect to those international disputes which are susceptible of settlement upon legal principles, it is proposed to empower the General Assembly to *direct* the submission of any such dispute to the International Court of Justice whenever the Assembly finds that its continuance is likely to endanger international peace. In case of such submission, the Court would have compulsory jurisdiction to decide the case, even if one of the parties should refuse to come before the Court.

The International Court of Justice would also be given authority to decide questions relating to the interpretation of the revised Charter; and to decide disputes involving the constitutionality of laws enacted thereunder. Compulsory jurisdiction would also be conferred upon the Court in certain other respects as, for example, any dispute relating to the interpretation of treaties or other international agreements, or as to the validity of any such treaty or agreement alleged to conflict with the revised Charter.

In order to strengthen the independence and authority of the International Court of Justice in view of these enlarged powers, it is proposed that the tenure of its fifteen judges shall be for life, instead of for nine-year terms as provided by the present statute of the Court, subject only to the possibility of dismissal if, in the unanimous opinion of his colleagues, a judge is no longer able properly to perform his functions or, as now provided, has in their unanimous opinion "ceased to fulfil the required conditions" of his tenure. The judges of the Court would be elected, not by concurrent action of the General Assembly and the Security Council, as at present, but by the General Assembly alone, from a list of candidates prepared by the Executive Council upon the basis of nominations received from the members of the highest courts of justice of member Nations, from national and international associations of international lawyers and from professors of international law. The Council would be required to present three candidates for each vacancy.

In respect of the enforcement of the judgments of the International Court of Justice, it is proposed that the General Assembly (or in certain special circumstances the Executive Council) could direct economic sanctions or, in the last resort, action by the United Nations Peace Force to ensure compliance. Any such action would, however, be limited, if at all possible, to air or naval demonstrations and would involve actual military operations against a noncomplying nation only if absolutely necessary.

With regard to the other main category of international disputes, i.e., those inevitable disputes which are not of an exclusively legal nature, it is proposed to establish a new tribunal of the highest possible prestige, to be known as the World Equity Tribunal. To this end it is proposed that the Tribunal shall be composed of fifteen persons elected by the General Assembly pursuant to safeguards and an elaborate procedure designed to ensure the choice of individuals whose reputation, experience and character would furnish the best assurance of impartiality and breadth of view. Thus no two of them could be nationals of the same nation, and it would be required that at least ten of the fifteen must have had more than twenty years of legal experience as judges, teachers of law or practicing lawyers. In addition, the General Assembly would be restricted in its choice to a list of persons nominated by the member Nations upon the recommendation of a committee in each member Nation which would have to include representatives of its principal judicial tribunals and legal associations, and of its leading academic, scientific, economic and religious organizations. Beyond this, the General Assembly would be required to pay due regard to the geographical distribution of the members of the Tribunal, so as to ensure fair representation of all the principal regions of the world.

To ensure the independence of the members of the World Equity Tribunal, they would be elected for life, subject only to the possibility of dismissal if, in the unanimous opinion of his colleagues, a member is no longer able properly to perform his functions or has ceased to fulfil the required conditions of his tenure.

In ordinary circumstances this World Equity Tribunal could not make binding decisions, as distinguished from recommendations, except with the consent of the parties. But provision is made that if the General Assembly votes by a large special majority, i.e., by a three-fourths majority of all the Representatives then in office (including two thirds of all the Representatives from the twelve largest nations), that the carrying out of the Tribunal's recommendations is essential for the preservation of peace, the recommendations of the Tribunal shall become enforceable by the same means as a judgment of the International Court of Justice.

The purpose of this important departure is to supplement other methods for settling *nonlegal* international disputes (such as negotiation, conciliation and agreed arbitration) by providing an impartial world agency of so high a stature that, under exceptional conditions involving world peace, its recommendations may be given the force of law.

Through the adoption of these proposals in respect of both legal and nonlegal international disputes, world institutions would at last exist whereby *any* nation could be compelled to submit *any* dispute dangerous to peace for a final and peaceful settlement; and the world would no longer be helpless, for lack of adequate machinery, to deal by peaceful means with any and all dangerous disputes between nations.

In order to provide means for the trial of individuals accused of violating the disarmament provisions of the revised Charter or of other offenses against the Charter or laws enacted by the General Assembly, and to provide safeguards against possible abuse of power by any organ or official of the United Nations, provision is also made for regional United Nations courts, inferior to the International Court of Justice, and for the review by the International Court of decisions of these regional courts.

The proposal is for not less than twenty or more than forty such regional courts to have jurisdiction in regions to be delineated by the General Assembly, each regional court to be composed of not less than three or more than nine judges. The judges of these courts would be appointed by the Executive Council from a list of qualified persons prepared by the International Court of Justice, with the provisos that not more than one third of the judges of any such court could be nationals of the nations included in the region of the court's jurisdiction, and that no two judges of any such court could be nationals of the same nation. Their appointments (which would be subject to confirmation by the General Assembly) would be for life, subject only to dismissal for cause by a vote of two thirds of all the judges of the International Court.

The regional United Nations courts, together with the International Court of Justice, would introduce a regime of genuine and enforceable world law in respect of all *legal* questions likely to endanger world peace, while the World Equity Tribunal would, as above mentioned, provide means for the authoritative and compulsory settlement of nonlegal situations seriously dangerous to peace.

In addition to these judicial agencies, it is proposed to establish a World

Conciliation Board which could be voluntarily availed of by the nations, or to which the General Assembly could refer any international dispute or situation likely to threaten peace. The functions of this new Board would be strictly confined to mediation and conciliation; and, if it failed to bring the disputing nations to a voluntary settlement, resort could be had to the International Court of Justice or the World Equity Tribunal, as might be most suitable in view of the nature of the issues involved.

In order to achieve genuine peace we must have more than total and universal disarmament and more than an effective world police. We must also have world tribunals to which the nations can resort with confidence for the adjustment or decision of their disputes and which, subject to careful safeguards, will have clearly defined authority to deal with any dispute which is dangerous to peace even if a nation does not wish to submit to the jurisdiction of the appropriate tribunal.

(8) *Enforcement and Penalties.* The plan envisages a variety of enforcement measures, including the prosecution in United Nations regional courts of individuals responsible for a violation of the disarmament provisions.

In order to aid the Inspection Service in the detection and prosecution of any such violators, it is proposed to have a civil police force of the United Nations with a strength not exceeding 10,000. This force would be under the general direction of an Attorney-General of the United Nations, to be appointed by the Executive Council subject to confirmation by the General Assembly. The Attorney-General, besides having supervision over the civil police force, would be responsible for making arrangements with national authorities for assistance in the apprehension of persons accused of offenses against the revised Charter and the laws and regulations enacted thereunder and for the detention of such persons pending trial. Provision would also be made for Assistant Attorneys-General of the United Nations who would be assigned to each regional court.

In case of a serious violation of the revised Charter or any law or regulation enacted thereunder for which a national government is found to be directly or indirectly responsible, the General Assembly could order economic sanctions against the nation concerned. In extreme cases the Assembly (or the Executive Council in an emergency and subject to immediate review by the Assembly) would also have authority to order the United Nations Peace Force into action. Any such enforcement action would correspond to the above-mentioned action. available for the enforcement of judgments of the International Court of Justice or of the recommendations of the World Equity Tribunal for the settlement of a dispute when the General Assembly has decided that a continuance of the dispute would be a "serious danger" to peace.

(9) *World Development.* The plan further provides (revised Articles 7 and 59 and Annex IV) for the establishment of a World Development Authority, whose function would be to assist in the economic and social development of the underdeveloped areas of the world, primarily through grants-in-aid and interest-free loans. This Authority would be under the direction of a World Development Commission of five members to be chosen with due regard to geographical distribution by the Economic and Social Council, subject to confirmation by the General Assembly.

The World Development Commission would be under the general supervision of the Economic and Social Council which would have power to define broad objectives and priorities. Since that Council would be composed of twenty-four Representatives of whom twelve would come from the member Nations having the highest gross national products and twelve from among the Representatives of the other member Nations selected with due regard to geographical distribution, there would thus be reasonable assurance that account would be taken both of the views of those nations contributing large shares of United Nations revenue, and also of the nations most in need of the Authority's assistance.

This proposed World Development Authority could, if the General Assembly so decided, have very large sums at its disposal, since the Authority's funds would be allocated to it by the Assembly out of the general revenues of the United Nations. With the large resources which the Assembly could and should provide, the World Development Authority would have the means to aid the underdeveloped areas of the world to the extent necessary to remove the danger to world stability and peace caused by the immense economic disparity between those areas and the industrialized regions of the world.

While universal, enforceable and complete disarmament, together with adequate institutions and methods for the peaceful settlement of disputes, are certainly indispensable, no solid and stable peace can be assured by these means alone. There is also required a more positive approach through the amelioration of the worst economic ills of mankind. To this end, the new World Development Authority, together with the Nuclear Energy Authority, would serve as important arms of the strengthened United Nations.

(10) *A United Nations Revenue System.* It would obviously be futile to establish the proposed new world institutions called for by the plan (including the United Nations Peace Force, the Inspection Service, the World Development Authority, the Nuclear Energy Authority, the Outer Space Agency, the World Equity Tribunal and the World Conciliation Board) unless a well-planned system is provided for their sufficient and reliable financial support. Such a system should also, of course, provide for the adequate support of the already existing organs and agencies of the United Nations which would be continued and, in some cases, would have enlarged functions and responsibilities. These include the revised General Assembly itself, the strengthened International Court of Justice, the Economic and Social Council, the Trusteeship Council, the Secretariat and the various specialized agencies already affiliated with the United Nations.

The United Nations Peace Force, with an assumed strength for its standing component of, say, 400,000 (midway between the proposed constitutional maximum of 600,000 and minimum of 200,000) and with an assumed strength for the Peace Force Reserve of, say, 900,000 (midway between the proposed constitutional maximum of 1,200,000 and minimum of 600,000) would alone require some $9 billion annually. The minimum annual amount required for the General Assembly and Executive Council, the judicial system, the Secretariat, the Inspection Service, the Nuclear Energy Authority, the Outer Space Agency and the other organs and agencies other than the World Development

Authority may be estimated at $2 billion. To this should be added a large amount on the order of $25 billion which should be annually appropriated by the General Assembly for the proposed World Development Authority in order to make a real impression on the vast problem of mitigating the worst economic disparities between nations and regions.

Upon first impression, this assumed $25 billion figure for world development may appear high, but is in fact moderate if the purpose is to accomplish a substantial change in the living conditions of the more economically underdeveloped areas of the world. This is so because before the machinery for supplying any such amount can become operative, there will probably be an increase in world population to nearly 4 billion, by which time the number of people living in poverty relative to the standards of the industrialized nations will certainly be not less than 2 billion. Accordingly, the annual expenditure of $25 billion to improve the condition of these people would represent only about $12 per capita which is little enough to accomplish any substantial improvement in their living standards.

It is apparent, therefore, that the reasonable expenses of a world authority adequately equipped to deter or suppress any international violence, to administer a comprehensive system for the peaceful settlement of all disputes between nations and *also* to do something substantial for the economic betterment of the underdeveloped parts of the world, could easily run to $36 billion per annum. And while this amount would be less than one half the 1960-61 budget of a single nation—the United States—it would, nevertheless, be so large a sum that reliance for supplying it should not be placed on a system of yearly contributions by the separate governments of nearly one hundred nations. Apart from a World Development Authority, the maintenance of a high level of efficiency and morale by the proposed Inspection Service, the Peace Force, the Nuclear Energy Authority and the Outer Space Agency would be of crucial importance; and it would indeed be folly to set up these and other vital organs without reliable machinery for supplying the necessary funds. To this end, a carefully devised *collaborative* revenue system is proposed.

A chief feature of this system would be that each member Nation would assign in advance to the United Nations all or part of certain taxes designated by it and assessed under its national laws. Each nation would undertake the entire administrative function of collecting the taxes thus assigned to the United Nations, these taxes to be paid directly to a fiscal office of the United Nations in each member Nation. In this way it would be unnecessary to create any considerable United Nations bureaucracy for this purpose.

Another important feature would be an *over-all limit* on the maximum amount of revenue to be raised in any year, namely, two per cent of the gross world product (total value of all goods produced and services rendered) as estimated from year to year by the above-mentioned Standing Committee on Budget and Finance of the General Assembly.

The General Assembly would adopt the annual United Nations budget covering all its activities, and would determine the amounts to be supplied by the taxpayers of each member Nation for that budget. These amounts would be allotted on the basis of each member Nation's estimated proportion of the estimated gross world product in that year subject to a uniform "per capita deduction" of not less than fifty or more than ninety per cent of the estimated average per capita product of the ten member Nations having the lowest per capita national products, as determined by the Assembly. A further provision would limit the amount to be supplied by the people of any member Nation in any one year to a sum not exceeding two and one half per cent of that nation's estimated national product.

Taking 1980 as an example, and assuming that the gross world product for that year was estimated at $2600 billion, the maximum United Nations revenue which could be raised would be $52 billion. And if for the 1980 fiscal year a budget of $16 billion less than the maximum, or $36 billion, was voted, it being then estimated that the United States had thirty per cent of the gross world product, the amount which the taxpayers of the United States could be called upon to supply, allowing for the "per capita deduction" would be about $12.2 billion. This charge upon the taxpayers of the United States, while substantial, would still be less than one third of the approximately $46 billion to be supplied by them in 1960-61 for military purposes alone. It follows that upon the completion of national disarmament, whereby this $46 billion item would be entirely eliminated, even the maximum possible charge for the budget of the strengthened United Nations would seem relatively small. The same would be true of any other nation with large military expenses.

In addition to the provisions for the raising of annual revenue, a United Nations borrowing power would also be provided for, with the limitation that the total United Nations debt outstanding in any year shall not (except in grave emergency declared by the General Assembly) exceed five per cent of the estimated gross world product in that year.

A more detailed explanation of this revenue plan is set forth in Annex V. It is believed that the plan would be effective to provide reliable and adequate revenues for the strengthened United Nations without involving the creation of a United Nations revenue-raising bureaucracy.

(11) *Privileges and Immunities.* Annex VI relates to the privileges and immunities of the United Nations itself and of the greatly expanded personnel (including the United Nations Peace Force) which, under the revised Charter, would be in the service of the United Nations.

For the successful operation of an effective world organization to maintain peace, a body of genuinely international servants of high morale is clearly essential. To this end, it seems advisable to provide constitutionally and in some detail not only as to the privileges and immunities of the United Nations as an organization, but also as to the rights and privileges of all United Nations personnel and the limitations thereon.

(12) *Bill of Rights.* Annex VII contains a proposed Bill of Rights having a two-fold purpose: (a) to emphasize the limited scope of the strengthened United Nations by an explicit reservation to the member Nations and their peoples of all powers not delegated by express language or clear implication; and (b) to guarantee that the strengthened United Nations shall not in any manner violate certain basic rights of the individual, that is to say of any person in the world.

The reason for the former is to make doubly sure that the authority of the United Nations shall not be enlarged by indirection, but shall be confined within the limits set forth in the revised Charter.

The latter set of provisions would not extend to any attempted protection of the individual against the action of his own government. It may be argued that the time has come for a world organization to guarantee to every person in the world and against any authority whatever a few fundamental rights,—such as exemption from slavery, freedom from torture and the right to be heard before criminal condemnation. We have not, however, thought it wise to attempt so vast a departure; and the proposed guarantees relate solely to possible infringements by the United Nations itself. Against such violations it does seem advisable and proper to have the explicit assurances which would be provided by Annex VII.

The assurances thus provided would include: guarantees, in considerable detail, of the right of fair trial for any person accused of a violation of the revised Charter or of any law or regulation enacted thereunder; a guarantee against double jeopardy, i.e., against being tried twice for the same alleged offense against the United Nations; and also a prohibition against any *ex post facto* law of the United Nations, i.e., against any law making criminal an act which was not criminal at the time the act occurred.

Provisions would also be included against excessive bail and any cruel or unusual punishment, including excessive fines; and the death penalty would be specifically prohibited. In addition, a remedy would be provided against unreasonable detention through a provision securing the right of any person detained for any alleged violation of the revised Charter or of any law or regulation enacted thereunder to be brought without undue delay before the appropriate United Nations tribunal to determine whether there is just cause for his detention.

Unreasonable searches and seizures would also be forbidden, subject to the proviso that this prohibition shall not prejudice searches and seizures clearly necessary or advisable for the enforcement of total disarmament.

Finally, it would be provided that the United Nations shall not restrict or interfere with freedom of conscience or religion; freedom of speech, press or expression in any other form; freedom of association and assembly; or freedom of petition.

The effort has been to provide protection for all the most fundamental individual rights which might conceivably be infringed upon by the United Nations without, however, going into undue detail. Necessarily, as in the case of any constitutional guarantees of the rights of the individual, there will be room for judicial interpretation and application of a United Nations Bill of Rights. This function would be performed by the International Court of Justice which, in the exercise of its proposed jurisdiction to interpret the revised Charter and to declare void any law, regulation or decision conflicting with the revised Charter as so interpreted, would gradually build up a body of world constitutional law relative to the scope and application of the various provisions of the Bill of Rights.

(13) *Ratification*. The proposed requirements for ratification of the revised

Charter are: (a) that ratification shall be by five sixths of the world's nations, including all the twelve largest nations, the aggregate of the populations of the ratifying nations to equal at least five sixths of the total world population; and (b) that each nation's ratification shall be by its own constitutional processes.

At first glance, the requirement that so very large a preponderance of the nations and people of the world shall be necessary for ratification may appear excessively difficult. But it must be remembered that it would be impossible to accomplish the main purposes of the whole plan, namely, total disarmament and the establishment of an effective system of world law, unless there is a preponderant acceptance throughout the world of the constitutional document which would provide for the necessary world institutions. In practice, this means that the eight or ten principal Powers—especially the Soviet Union and the United States—would first need to agree. But once these Powers (containing together a large majority of the world's people) had reached agreement on the essentials of a revised Charter, there can be no doubt that virtually all the other nations would, as a practical matter, give their assent. Thus the obviously desirable object of obtaining the unanimous or nearly unanimous assent of all the nations appears also to be a practical one,—once the indispensable assent of the leading Powers has been obtained.

(14) *Amendment.* The proposed requirements concerning the procedure for amendments to the revised Charter are almost as strict as those provided for its ratification. Any future amendments would be submitted for ratification when adopted by a vote of two thirds of all the Representatives in the General Assembly, whether or not present or voting, or by a two-thirds vote of a General Conference held for that purpose. In order for an amendment to come into effect, ratification by four fifths of the member Nations would be required, including three fourths of the twelve member Nations entitled to fifteen or more Representatives in the Assembly.

It will be noted that while the proposed provisions for ratification of the revised Charter would require that the ratifying nations shall include *all* the twelve nations having the largest populations, the provisions relating to the ratification of amendments would require the assent of only three fourths of those twelve nations.

The reason for this difference is that in order to ensure the necessary overwhelming support for the revised Charter in its initial stage, it is considered essential to have the prior assent of literally all the world's largest nations,— defined as the twelve nations with the largest populations. On the other hand, in the case of future amendments *after* the strengthened United Nations is functioning under the revised Charter, it seems unduly severe to require absolutely unanimous approval by the twelve largest nations. Instead, it seems sufficient to require the assent of no more than a preponderant majority of those nations.

(15) *Continued Organs and Agencies.* It should be emphasized that far from impairing the existing organs and agencies of the United Nations, which despite all obstacles have accomplished important results, the intention is not only to preserve but also to strengthen them. Thus the General Assembly would have much greater scope through having the final responsibility for the mainte-

nance of peace, through the new system of representation and voting, and through the new, although limited, power to legislate.

The Security Council would, indeed, be abolished, but would be replaced by the veto-less Executive Council, chosen by and responsible to the General Assembly. The Economic and Social Council and the Trusteeship Council would be continued, with important changes as to their composition and functions, and with much stronger financial support under the new revenue system. The International Court of Justice would be continued with greatly enlarged jurisdiction and greater authority. And as to various other organs, and such agencies as the Food and Agricultural Organization (FAO), the United Nations Educational, Scientific and Cultural Organization (UNESCO), the International Labor Organization (ILO) and the World Health Organization (WHO), the revision would not only provide for their continuance but would also give opportunity for the enlargement of their activities and usefulness.

The intention is not to dispense with anything which has proved useful, but rather to revise, supplement and strengthen the existing structure so that the United Nations will be fully and unquestionably equipped to accomplish its basic purpose—the maintenance of international peace.

WHETHER TO REVISE THE UNITED NATIONS CHARTER OR TO CREATE A NEW WORLD ORGANIZATION

We have cast our proposals in the form of a proposed revision of the present United Nations Charter, retaining the structure of its 111 Articles and supplementing those very Articles, as revised, by seven Annexes.

We have done this because it seems logical and reasonable to utilize an existing organization of such scope and experience as the United Nations; because the primary purpose of the United Nations has been from the beginning "to save succeeding generations from the scourge of war"; because the name "United Nations" is very suitable to a world authority dedicated to the maintenance of world peace under effective world law; and because the creation of a new and separate world organization adequately equipped for the maintenance of peace would necessarily overshadow the present United Nations.

Nevertheless, we do not regard this question of method as one of principle, but merely of policy. It must be recognized that if the creation of adequate world institutions for the prevention of war is to be achieved through the medium of the United Nations, numerous amendments of the Charter will be required which would together amount to a fundamental change in the structure and powers of the United Nations. And if it should develop that for technical or psychological reasons it would be more difficult to accomplish these amendments than to create a wholly new world organization to take over the peace-maintenance functions of the United Nations, we wish to make it clear that we would not object to that alternative method. In other words, a thorough revision of the Charter is merely, as we see it, the most reasonable means to the end in view and not an end in itself.

For example, it has been suggested that, while continuing the United Nations in nearly its present form, there could be separately created by universal, or nearly universal, treaty an entirely new world organization wholly restricted in its functions to those matters directly connected with the prevention of international violence. Such a world organization existing parallel with the United Nations might be called the "World Peace Authority" and, to be effective, would necessarily have to possess institutions and powers similar to those formulated in the proposed Charter revision for the enforcement of total disarmament and of world law in the field of war prevention. In that case, the United Nations could continue as a forum for the exchange of views on all matters of international interest.

The existence of a new, separate and powerful world organization alongside the present United Nations would obviously be an awkward arrangement. And yet since it would be better to tolerate some awkwardness than to do nothing effective to achieve universal and complete disarmament and a genuine regime of enforceable world law, the idea should not be entirely dismissed.

We emphasize also that while an elaborate plan for universal and complete disarmament is included in the proposed revision of the Charter (Annex I), this does not imply that the revision of the Charter must necessarily precede an agreement for total disarmament. It is quite conceivable that an agreement on the technical aspects of universal and complete disarmament will be reached first, and that a revision of the Charter would come about later as the most logical means of ensuring adequate supervision and enforcement of such a disarmament agreement.

What we wish to make crystal clear is that in casting our proposals in the form of a comprehensive revision of the present Charter, we are not dogmatic about advancing this as the only available means to the desired end; and that if it develops that some other method is more feasible, we would be very ready to adopt it in order to reach the end in view.

THE PRACTICAL PROSPECTS

What are the practical prospects for the realization of genuine peace, through universal and complete disarmament and enforceable world law, not in some indefinite future but within some such period as fifteen years, i.e., by 1975?

The question is crucial because the achievement of genuine peace will largely depend upon the persistent effort of many people and, unfortunately, only a small fraction of the human race seems capable of working persistently for a purpose, however desirable, that appears far off and uncertain. On the other hand, if convinced that the goal is attainable within a reasonably short time, they will work for it in greater numbers and with greater zeal, and by this very fact make it the more realizable.

I take a hopeful view on this question and will, in fact, venture a reasoned prediction as follows: (a) that within about four to six years (by 1965-67) a comprehensive plan for total and universal disarmament and for the necessary world institutions to make, interpret and enforce world law in the field of war prevention will have been officially formulated and will have been submitted to all the nations for approval; and (b) that within four to six years thereafter (by 1969-71) such a plan will have been ratified by all or nearly all the nations, including all the major Powers, and will have come into force.

If these things come to pass, it follows that by 1975 the process of universal and complete disarmament will be well on its way, that the new world security organization (whether in the form of a revised and greatly strengthened United Nations or an entirely new world organization) will be in actual operation and that a new era in world history will have begun.

I now summarize my reasons for this prediction, mentioning first what I conceive to be the principal forces working *against* total disarmament and genuine peace.

The most important single adverse factor I suppose to be the reluctance of the average person to make any drastic change in his traditional form of behavior. As experience shows, he will, of course, try hard to save himself from destruction when he is not only in actual and imminent danger but also comprehends that danger. Short of these circumstances, however, his tendency is to procrastinate and hold to his old ways, often until it is too late.

This deep-seated trait of human nature is very evident at the beginning of the 1960s as a grave obstacle to genuine peace. This is so because nothing is more certain than that under the conditions of our nuclear age the realization of genuine peace will require a truly revolutionary change in human thinking and behavior,—a change so drastic that human nature almost automatically resists it, no matter how clear the necessity may appear. As the historian, Arnold Toynbee, has put it, "We shall have a hard struggle with ourselves to save ourselves from ourselves."

For many centuries the units into which mankind has combined—family, tribe, town, city, national state—have been accustomed to assert or defend their interests, real or supposed, by violence or the threat of it,—culminating during our "advanced" twentieth century in the two greatest wars in history and, by 1960, in the maintenance of the most elaborate and destructive armed forces that the world has ever possessed. And yet, no matter how obvious it may be that, in order to achieve genuine peace, these forces must be abolished, along with the whole ancient method of international violence, it is foolish to ignore the strongly adverse influence of these habits and traditions and of certain special influences and vested interests created by them.

Of these special influences and interests, by far the most formidable, I judge, is that of the military profession which, in many nations, has sufficient influence to force their governments to resist rather than to aid the cause of total disarmament and the establishment of the world institutions that are essential to the settlement of all international disputes by peaceful means. Unfortunate as it may be, it is necessary to accept the fact that, as of 1960, there is throughout most of the world what has been aptly called a "vested interest in armament" on the part of the military profession, which is a constant and powerful influence adverse to the new conceptions which can alone suffice to achieve genuine peace.

In appraising the weight of this pervading military influence, it is necessary to recognize its good faith in most cases. The typical professional soldier, sailor, airman or missileman does not deprecate or oppose disarmament because he is any less humane or less civilized than the average civilian. He does so because his training and environment have irrevocably *conditioned* him to assume that his profession is indispensable. In consequence, it is simply too much to expect that the military profession as a whole will do otherwise than oppose or at least "drag their feet" in respect of all proposals for total disarmament and all that this implies. It follows that there will be no solution for the problem of world peace until the "vested interest in armament" of the military profession everywhere is firmly overruled.

A less important yet significant adverse "vested interest" is that of traditional diplomacy. It must be remembered that for centuries a principal occupation of the professional diplomat has been to deal in "power politics", that is to say, in the making of alliances or in seeking to undermine counter-alliances or in veiled or open threats of force as a means of advancing the real or supposed interests of his particular country. These habits of thought are almost as difficult to shake off as those of the professional military man; and, consequently, those who seek peace through total disarmament and enforceable world law will do well to discount the almost certain resistance of the "professionals" in many foreign offices in all parts of the world.

Another "vested interest" sometimes mentioned as an important obstacle to disarmament and peace is the presumed interest of many millions of armament workers in a continuance of their jobs and the corresponding interest of proprietors in their profits from armament contracts. But while the problem of readjustment to nonarmament work is certainly one that will call for attention and planning, this should not be regarded as a serious difficulty. What is often overlooked is that the process of disarmament would necessarily be a gradual one. At the outset there would almost surely be an interval of several years between the formulation of a comprehensive disarmament agreement and its coming into force through ratification by the respective nations, and this interval would serve as a warning period in which to plan for and partially carry out the shift of workers and materials to nonmilitary purposes. There would then undoubtedly follow a considerably longer period (ten years as proposed in this book) for the carrying out, stage by stage, of the process of actual disarmament, during which the conversion of the armament plants would be completed. Remembering also the immense tax burden which would be lessened year by year and the release of manpower and materials for such purposes as roads, hospitals, schools, urban renewal and other pressing needs even in the most prosperous nations, it seems clear that this particular obstacle to disarmament and peace will prove to be a minor one.

Far more serious is the factor of mutual fears and recriminations which as of 1960 so poison the East-West atmosphere as to bring under suspicion in the West almost any proposal coming from the East and correspondingly in the East almost any proposal proceeding from the West. This state of affairs is unfortunately deeply rooted on both sides. It has been built up over a long period and "conditions" the thinking of millions of people—East and West—who on other subjects are capable of unbiased judgment. There is little use in seeking to assess the blame which both sides must share, and we must accept this mutually poisoned atmosphere as a fact of life which cannot be got rid of for a long time. This mutual fear and suspicion is indeed a most formidable barrier to peace and we should recognize that success in the accomplishment of total disarmament and the establishment of enforceable world law will not be because this barrier will soon disappear but because it will be pushed aside under the pressure of necessity.

Apart from the just-mentioned deeply rooted obstacles, there are several others which are only less important because they are likely to be more transitory. These include the exclusion of mainland China from world councils, a lack of sufficient understanding as to the necessity for complete, rather than partial, disarmament and a similar lack of understanding of the necessity for a comprehensive and interrelated plan rather than a piecemeal approach.

Taking together all the adverse factors—especially the strong tendency to resist any drastic change, the certain opposition of the military profession and of traditional diplomacy and the mutual fears and suspicions between East and West—we have a truly formidable group of obstacles. What are the *favorable* factors which are capable of offsetting or overcoming them?

Of these favorable factors the most important single one seems very clearly to be the *steadily increasing risk* of world catastrophe resulting from a continuance of the arms race and a continuing lack of effective world machinery to settle international disputes by peaceful means.

In specifying the increasing risk of world disaster, it is realized that the likelihood of all-out nuclear war may not increase at all and may even diminish during the 1960s because of a greater mutual understanding of its destructive consequences. But more than offsetting this factor is, I believe, the rapidly mounting potentialities of destruction if a large-scale nuclear war should, nevertheless, occur. For while it may be true that the chances of an all-out nuclear war may not increase during the 1960s, it is a certainty that the potential damage from such a war, if it should occur, will steadily increase from year to year. It follows that, taking the two factors together, the real risk will, in the absence of universal and complete disarmament under effective world law, be a steadily mounting one. A greater comprehension of this fact will be, I judge, the major influence in bringing about the formulation and acceptance of an agreement for total disarmament under enforceable world law.

Concerning this increase in the destructiveness of modern weapons, the most obvious development is the constantly increasing efficiency and accuracy of the so-called "means of delivery" of nuclear weapons. From year to year there has been "progress" in compressing more and more explosive power into less and less volume and weight, resulting in startling increases in the range and accuracy of the ballistic missiles designed to "deliver" nuclear warheads.

With regard to the explosive power of the nuclear weapons capable of accurate "delivery" from planes or by ballistic missiles, a report in 1959 of the Special Subcommittee on Radiation (the Holifield Committee) of the Joint Committee on Atomic Energy of the United States Congress is significant. This report postulates that 263 nuclear weapons with a total explosive power equivalent to 1450 megatons (1450 million tons of T.N.T.) could be landed on United States territory in a single attack; and the report therefore assumes

xlvi

that the average explosive power of each of these 263 weapons would be the equivalent of about 5.5 million tons of T.N.T. This means that the average explosive power of *each* such weapon would be 275 times that of the 20 thousand ton bomb dropped on Hiroshima in 1945, and that *each* such weapon would have more than four times as much explosive power as all the bombs dropped by the Western Allies on Germany in World War II. It means also that the total explosive power of the weapons postulated by the Holifield Committee as landed on United States territory in a single major attack would equal about 72 *thousand* times the power of the Hiroshima bomb and over one thousand times the power of all the bombs dropped on Germany in World War II.

Since it is difficult to grasp figures of this sort, it may be helpful to give an illustration in terms of mass. Let us imagine a solid column of T.N.T. with a uniform size equal to that of the Washington Monument in Washington at its base, i.e., about fifty-five feet (16.8 meters) square. In order to comprise one million tons of T.N.T., that column would need to be 6416 feet (about 1956 meters) high. And in order to comprise 5.5 million tons of T.N.T. (the above-mentioned average strength of the 263 nuclear weapons postulated in the Holifield Committee's report), there would need to be *six* columns of T.N.T. each of which would be fifty-five feet (16.8 meters) square and nearly 5900 feet (about 1800 meters) high.

If we imagine these six immense columns of T.N.T. set up and exploded in London or Paris or New York or Moscow, we can easily see that even so vast a city as any of these could be utterly destroyed.

Even more important is the installation of rocket-launching sites from which it would apparently be possible even in 1960 to "deliver" weapons of appalling power over ranges of up to 8000 miles and within a mile or two of the target point. It seems clear, therefore, that even as this is written the capacity exists to land highly destructive missiles on New York or Chicago as well as on Moscow or Leningrad from sites thousands of miles distant and within thirty minutes from launching time. And if this could be done in 1960, what will be possible in 1965 after five years more of a continuing and even accelerating arms race?

Beyond this is the building of nuclear-powered submarines equipped to launch nuclear weapons from under water; the development of aircraft capable of launching nuclear weapons hundreds of miles from their targets; and, still further, the never-ceasing secret work on biological and chemical weapons.

Such facts as these are only beginning, it seems, to penetrate the general masses of the people in all nations; but it seems certain that their comprehension of the danger will increase from year to year with a corresponding increase of pressure on their governments. Their dominating motive will not, I judge, be fear in the ordinary sense but rather a growing exasperation over the rigidity and traditionalism which prevent the formulation of adequate plans to remove so obvious a man-made risk. Whatever the motive, however, it is impossible to believe that the peoples will be so apathetic and helpless that they will fail to apply a steadily increasing pressure on their governments to take the long-overdue action which is necessary to remove the growing danger.

Next in importance to the risk of appalling disaster from the increasing destructiveness of modern weapons and the increasing popular pressure on the governments to remove this risk is, I believe, an increasing impatience with the vast economic waste and burden of the arms race. In terms of money this burden as of 1960 amounts to not less than $100 billion per annum, while in terms of human energy it means the full-time employment in the armed forces of some 15 million men and of not less than 30 million civilians in the manufacture of arms and other military activities,—or a total of at least 45 million persons.

In the United States the resulting cost of about $46 billion per annum in 1960-61 absorbs more than half of the total Federal budget and about nine per cent of the gross national product, while in the Soviet Union the proportion of the national product devoted to military purposes is even higher. In many other nations the cost, although proportionately smaller, is nevertheless a heavy drain on their economies which prevents or handicaps the carrying out of many badly needed improvements. Even in so affluent a country as the United States, the vast military expenditure holds back such urgent needs as the improvement of education and of medical care for lower-income people, urban renewal and the conservation of natural resources; and in nations less economically fortunate, like India, the adverse effects of military expenditure are naturally much greater. As the years have passed, there has been a growing consciousness that the existence of these burdens is incompatible with economic and social reforms urgently demanded by the peoples of many nations. In the 1960s, this consciousness will almost certainly become a more powerful force in favor of total disarmament.

Another helpful development should be a clearer realization from year to year that it is impossible to arrive at any important political settlements in the absence of an agreement for comprehensive disarmament. There has been much ill-considered talk to the effect that the settlement of various difficult political problems—such as the problem of Berlin and German reunification, the problem of Soviet dominance in Eastern Europe, the questions of Korean and Viet-Nam reunification and the Quemoy-Matsu situation—must precede, or at least be simultaneous with, any comprehensive disarmament. The common-sense of the matter is, however, that *in an armed world* it is most improbable that any of these difficult East-West issues can be settled—for the simple reason that it is virtually impossible to settle any hard controversy between opponents of equal strength and pride when the opposing parties are armed to the teeth and, therefore, bitterly suspicious of each other. All experience shows that before such opponents can settle any important issue, they must first agree to dispense with violence and cease their mutual threats and insults.

It has taken a long time to grasp this simple truth as applied to the crucial disputes between East and West; but in the 1960s it will become more and more apparent to most reasonable men and women that an agreement for universal and complete disarmament must be reached *before* these thorny East-West issues can be resolved.

Another favorable factor will be the almost certain abandonment during the 1960 decade of the exclusion of mainland China from the United Nations and from normal relations with the United States and many other nations. The bankruptcy of this policy, which has so greatly prejudiced adequate negotiations for peace, has long been apparent and it is hardly conceivable that it can much longer survive. When China, with its more than one fifth of all the people of the earth, is admitted to full participation in world councils, an important barrier to the formulation of a comprehensive plan for peace will have been removed.

Still another encouraging sign is the increasing knowledge of the *ways and means* whereby genuine peace can be achieved. The persistent and rising *desire* since the end of World War II for the abolition of war has unfortunately been accompanied by considerable defeatism as to the feasibility of accomplishing this result. This defeatism has, however, been largely caused by an exaggerated view of the difficulty of the problem which has been due in turn to a lack of sufficient study and discussion of the concrete problems that are involved, i.e., the various interrelated questions as to the nature and form of the world institutions requisite for world order. At the start of the 1960s we can discern a marked change in this respect, in that a beginning has at last been made in a closer study of the specific problems,—not only by private persons but even by public officials. There is a definite relation between the development of this study and progress toward the desired goal. This is true because the problems involved are by no means insoluble, and as more and more people begin to apprehend how these problems can be dealt with, the spirit of defeatism will naturally lessen and the better will be the prospect for the acceptance of an adequate plan for peace.

An important result of the more intense study just mentioned will inevitably be a more general understanding that *total, rather than partial,* disarmament will alone meet the situation. In 1960 it is almost universally recognized that, in order to induce acceptance of any important disarmament, a well-organized inspection system is essential, while only a minority as yet seems to understand that *complete* disarmament is equally indispensable. For this proposition there are three main reasons: (a) because experience has shown that it is virtually impossible to agree upon any plan of any consequence for merely partial disarmament, since one nation or another is almost certain to claim, and with some justification, that the particular proposed reduction would put it at a disadvantage; (b) because even if agreed upon any merely partial disarmament would not fulfil the purpose, since in the nuclear age the retention of even a small fraction of the armed forces of 1960 would be enough to keep in existence many pernicious fears and tensions between the nations; and (c) because, although an effective world police force is clearly indispensable as a condition for disarmament, there is a distinct practical limit upon the size and expense of such a force, so that if even as much as ten per cent of the national armed forces of 1960 were retained, it would be impossible to maintain a world police of sufficient strength to ensure its capacity to deter or suppress any possible international violence. As the disarmament negotiations of the 1960s develop, it can safely be predicted that the validity of these reasons will be more and more recognized. And when it is generally accepted that total, rather than partial, disarmament is no less necessary than an effective inspection system, a long step forward will have been taken.

Along with a clearer understanding that nothing less than the abolition of all national armaments will suffice, there is badly needed a clearer realization of the necessity for a comprehensive rather than any piecemeal or partial plan. No intelligent person sets out to build an adequate house without a plan providing for all the elements necessary to make the structure fulfil its purpose. He knows from the start that foundation, sidewalls, floors and roof must all be provided and that they must be so fitted together that, with each performing its necessary function, the house will stand. It is deplorable, therefore, that even in 1960 only a small minority seems to realize that the necessity for a complete *initial* plan applies also to the structure of peace; and that, if the structure is to stand, all the basic organs necessary for the maintenance of peace must be included in that plan. A more general realization of this truth will almost certainly come in the 1960s and will be a powerful force for world order.

When the various adverse factors are put in one scale and the various favorable factors in another scale and weighed against each other, my considered opinion is that the favorable factors clearly outweigh the adverse, and that we can *reasonably* look forward to a new world order based upon universal and complete disarmament and enforceable world law within some such period as fifteen years.

Against any such optimistic view, it may be objected that it takes too little account of the factor of leadership. It may well be said: "Granted that the destructive power of modern weapons will constantly increase; granted that concern over the risks and the ultimate result will also increase; granted that there will be a wider understanding of the necessity for total, rather than partial disarmament and of the ways and means whereby complete disarmament under enforceable world law can be achieved; granted that the popular pressure for a termination of the arms race will intensify; where is the requisite leadership to come from for the formulation and acceptance of the necessarily novel and elaborate plan?"

It must indeed be recognized that, even in spite of a strong and worldwide demand for a cessation of the arms race, nothing effective can be done in the absence of vigorous and persistent leadership for a specific and adequate plan. I am confident, however, that effective leadership will develop; although it will probably need to come, in my judgment, from sources other than either the Soviet Union or the United States.

In the case of the Soviet Union, there is indeed every reason to suppose that for obvious reasons of self-interest, it will press persistently for the "general and complete" disarmament proposed by Chairman Khrushchev on September 18, 1959. The difficulty is, however, that because of the intense suspicion with which almost any Russian proposal is regarded in some quarters the leadership of the Soviet Union would be under such a constant handicap that the acceptance of Soviet leadership is unlikely.

With regard to the United States, a similar handicap will operate in view of the reciprocal suspicion with which almost any American proposal is regarded in some parts of the world. And beyond this, it is unfortunate, but true,

1

I believe, that as of 1960 the United States cannot be expected to provide wholehearted leadership on behalf of total disarmament, as distinguished from acquiescence and ultimate support. For this there are, I believe, basic reasons which include the relative geographical remoteness of the United States even in the nuclear age, and above all its relative lack of suffering from modern war in comparison with the Soviet Union, France, Britain and several other nations of Western Europe. It is, therefore, no accident, I believe, that the first proposals for universal and complete disarmament came, on the one hand, from the Soviet Union and, on the other, from the United Kingdom, both of which suffered so greatly in World Wars I and II and both of which would be subject to the most dire destruction in a possible World War III.

For these reasons I believe that the necessary leadership will proceed from the United Kingdom and Western Europe, however much in later stages it is supplemented by support from other nations.

For years I have believed that the question of complete disarmament and all that it implies would come to a head when the Soviet Union was able to install a large number of ballistic missile sites both in its own territory and in Eastern Europe from which nuclear missiles could be launched with accuracy against targets in the United Kingdom, France, Italy and other nations of Western Europe. I have long been convinced that when this came about some, at least, of these nations would say in effect: "This arms race may be all very well for the superpowers, but our very life is threatened by it and we must now insist that the concept of complete disarmament under enforceable world law be taken seriously." This conviction has now been vindicated to some extent by the important proposals of the British Government of September 17, 1959 for "comprehensive disarmament by all powers under effective international control" whereby all armaments and military manpower would be reduced to "levels required for internal security purposes only."

With the constant "improvement" in the power and accuracy of ballistic missiles, it is obvious that in an all-out nuclear war the United Kingdom would be a prime target. It seems virtually certain, therefore, that with its large population in a small area the destructive effect of nuclear war on the United Kingdom would be truly appalling; and since this fact is now becoming generally appreciated, there is every reason to suppose that *any* British Government will feel obligated to persist in the effort for complete disarmament initiated in September 1959.

Apart from this strong motivation of the United Kingdom to strive persistently for total disarmament, the high degree of civilization and the maturity of the United Kingdom make it well equipped to assume this leadership. It could confidently rely upon the early support of nearly all the nations of the British Commonwealth (Australia, Canada, Ceylon, Ghana, India, Malaya, New Zealand, Nigeria, Pakistan, etc.) so that before long the initial leadership of the United Kingdom would be thought of as that of the British Commonwealth, with all its authority and prestige.

As of early 1960, this British leadership seems to offer the best prospect. But this is not to say that it is the only promising one. Thus it is also to be hoped that a group of nations which are neutral or uncommitted as between the superpowers (such as Austria, Burma, Indonesia, Ireland, Sweden, Switzerland, the United Arab Republic and Yugoslavia) can be formed to supplement and support the British leadership if it develops, or to take its place should it falter or fail. Another useful possibility would be the formation of a world-wide group of smaller nations irrespective of their neutrality which, besides the smaller neutrals, could include such countries as Belgium, Czechoslovakia, Denmark, Greece, the Netherlands, Norway, the Philippines, Poland, Romania and Thailand, and various of the smaller nations of Latin America and Africa.

Altogether in one or the other of these ways, or by a combination of them, I have confidence that the necessary leadership will be forthcoming. The role of the Soviet Union and the United States would then be not to lead the way, but to refrain from obstruction and to do their part in the formulation and implementation of a great and sufficient plan. The same will be true of Communist China, which, in the end, will have an equally important role.

What the whole question comes down to in last analysis is whether the human race will show enough intelligence to enable it to make the required adjustment to the nuclear age. In 1960 the issue as to the future of mankind is whether the human race is sufficiently *resourceful* to formulate and accept world institutions which will once and for all abolish war and utilize the great new discoveries of science for peaceful uses alone. This issue will, however, depend not upon any *inherent* lack of intelligence but upon whether sufficient *effort* is made to make effective use of our present fund of intelligence. If the peoples are so apathetic as to permit the domination of military and old-style diplomatic thinking, they can expect nothing better than an indefinite continuance of the arms race and ultimate disaster. On the other hand, if the peoples make an even reasonable effort to comprehend the danger and the available means to remove it, it lies within their power to solve the problem and to institute an age of genuine peace under world law.

EVOLUTION AND PURPOSE OF THE PROPOSALS

This book is the work of two lawyers. One of them, the writer of this Introduction, has been engaged in the practice of law in New York or in public affairs since 1906. The other, Mr. Sohn, is a generation younger, a scholar learned in the history of past efforts to achieve peace and now a Professor of Law at the Law School of Harvard University where his courses include "United Nations Law" and "Problems in the Development of World Order".

The detailed proposals of the book are the result of an evolution over a period of years. In my own case, they took tentative form in a proposed world constitution privately circulated in 1940; and ten years later certain basic ideas of the proposals were expounded in my small book, A PLAN FOR PEACE. In the case of Professor Sohn, who came to the United States from Poland as a young lawyer in 1939, the proposals reflect twenty years of thought and teaching on the subject and his experience as a legal officer of the United Nations.

Our collaboration began in October 1945 at a conference of private citizens as to "how best to remedy the weaknesses of the United Nations Charter", which some persons even then recognized as inadequate to ensure world peace; and our association has continued ever since.

During 1949, in response to various demands for a comprehensive set of proposals for Charter revision, I resolved to undertake this arduous task and sought out Mr. Sohn who was then a lecturer at the Harvard Law School. He agreed; and the result of our collaboration was a joint document, issued in 1953, entitled PEACE THROUGH DISARMAMENT AND CHARTER REVISION, together with a SUPPLEMENT thereto issued in 1956. Both of these documents were widely circulated for comment and criticism; and were then revised and combined in the book entitled WORLD PEACE THROUGH WORLD LAW, published by the Harvard University Press in March 1958. The present Second Edition embodies certain minor revisions without change, however, in the underlying principles or main features of the authors' proposals.

The title WORLD PEACE THROUGH WORLD LAW reflects a change of emphasis, progressively arrived at, whereby universal and complete disarmament, however indispensable, is treated as one of several interrelated and equally indispensable elements of world order rather than as an all-inclusive solution. Our basic premise, however, has remained intact, namely, that if the world really wants peace, it must accept world institutions fully adequate to achieve universal and complete disarmament and to enforce world law within the limited field of war prevention. Far from being weakened by recent events, this fundamental conviction is stronger than ever.

As already stated, the purpose of this book is to provide material for the extensive discussions which will be required before truly effective world institutions for the maintenance of peace are accepted by the peoples of the world.

It is true that the authors have *attempted* to present a complete plan whereby genuine peace, in a disarmed world, would actually be secured. It is true also that we have confidence in our work which is the result of so many years of study and of searching criticism by hundreds of qualified persons in many nations. Nevertheless, it would indeed be presumptuous to assert that we have the final answers to the various thorny problems. We well know that better, or at least more acceptable, solutions may be hammered out in the process of debate. We do believe, however, that these detailed and specific proposals will serve to encourage others to discuss the many and difficult questions that are involved.

The need is not for more generalities in recognition of the necessity for world law. There are already enough of these. Rather, the need is for alternative detailed plans to furnish a basis for discussion; and our purpose has been to supply such a plan. If by so doing this book hastens even slightly the day when enforceable world law actually prevails between all nations, it will have fulfilled its purpose.

For modern man the prevention of war is not only the most important of problems; it is also one of the most difficult. During our work we have often thought of Professor Einstein's remark on this point. When asked why it is that when the mind of man has reached so far as to solve the secrets of the atom it has not been able to devise means to protect mankind from destruction by the new discoveries, he replied: "The answer is simple. It is because politics is more difficult than physics."

Nevertheless, our proposals are advanced in the firm conviction that genuine peace through total disarmament and enforceable world law is now a practical prospect which practical men can work for with reasonable hopes.

GRENVILLE CLARK,
Dublin, New Hampshire, U.S.A.

April 1960

THE PROPOSED REVISED CHARTER OF THE UNITED NATIONS

Preliminary Note. The following detailed proposals for revision of the Charter have evolved from a document issued by the authors in 1953 entitled PEACE THROUGH DISARMAMENT AND CHARTER REVISION and a SUPPLEMENT thereto issued in 1956. These documents, combined and revised in the light of suggestions resulting from their world-wide distribution for criticism and comment, were the basis for the first edition of WORLD PEACE THROUGH WORLD LAW published in 1958; and this Second Edition embodies the same basic proposals.

In respect of the 111 Articles of the 1945 Charter, the proposals are submitted in textual form with a comment discussing the proposed changes from the 1945 text. All Articles in which any change is proposed are printed in parallel columns. The right-hand column incorporates the suggested amendments, Article by Article, with all changes or additions indicated by italics. The left-hand column contains the corresponding Articles of the 1945 Charter, with the portions to be omitted or amended in italics. Articles in which no changes are proposed are printed across the page.

The proposed revision calls for seven Annexes as follows:

Annex I, entitled "Disarmament", contains a detailed plan for universal, complete and enforceable disarmament. This Annex is submitted in textual form in thirty-four Articles with an explanation of the purpose of each Article.

Annex II, entitled "The United Nations Peace Force", sets forth a detailed plan for the organization, command and maintenance of a world police force to be established parallel with the carrying out of the disarmament process. This Annex is also submitted in textual form in eight Articles with a "General Comment" on its essential features.

Annex III, entitled "The Judicial and Conciliation System of the United Nations", includes in outline form: a proposed revision of the Statute of the International Court of Justice; a proposed Statute for a new World Equity Tribunal; a proposed Statute providing for subordinate "regional courts" of the United Nations; and a proposed Statute for a new agency to be called the World Conciliation Board.

Annex IV, entitled "The World Development Authority", outlines a plan for a new United Nations organ equipped with broad powers to alleviate excessive economic disparities between different regions of the world.

Annex V, entitled "The Revenue System of the United Nations", describes in detail a proposed collaborative system between the United Nations and the member Nations to provide the United Nations with reliable and adequate revenue for the support of all the principal and subsidiary organs and agencies of the United Nations, including the United Nations Peace Force.

Annex VI, entitled "Privileges and Immunities", provides in outline for the privileges and immunities of the United Nations itself and of the greatly increased number of international civil and military personnel who would be in the service of the United Nations under the revised Charter.

1

Annex VII, entitled "Bill of Rights", relates to certain basic safeguards and guarantees whereby all powers not delegated to the United Nations "by express language or clear implication" would be reserved to the member Nations; and whereby all individuals would be safeguarded as to certain fundamental rights against abuse of power by the strengthened United Nations. This Annex is submitted in textual form in two Articles with a "General Comment" on its essential features.

CHARTER OF THE UNITED NATIONS

WE THE PEOPLES OF THE
UNITED NATIONS DETERMINED

WE THE PEOPLES OF THE
UNITED NATIONS DETERMINED

to save succeeding generations from the scourge of war, which twice in our lifetime has brought untold sorrow to mankind, and

to reaffirm faith in fundamental human rights, in the dignity and worth of the human person, in the equal rights of men and women and of nations large and small, and

to establish conditions under which justice and respect for the obligations arising from treaties and other sources of international law can be maintained, and

to promote social progress and better standards of life in larger freedom,

AND FOR THESE ENDS

to practice tolerance and live together in peace with one another as good neighbors, and

to unite our strength to maintain international peace and security, and

to ensure, by the acceptance of *principles and the institution of methods,* that armed force shall not be used, save in the common interest, and

---

to save succeeding generations from the scourge of war, which twice in our lifetime has brought untold sorrow to mankind, and

to reaffirm faith in fundamental human rights, in the dignity and worth of the human person, in the equal rights of men and women and of nations large and small, and

to establish conditions under which justice and respect for the obligations arising from treaties and other sources of international law can be maintained, and

to promote social progress and better standards of life in larger freedom,

AND FOR THESE ENDS

to practice tolerance and live together in peace with one another as good neighbors, and

to unite our strength to maintain international peace and security, and

to ensure, by the acceptance of *world law in the field of war prevention and through adequate institutions for its enforcement,* that armed force shall not be used, save in the common interest, and

3

to employ international machinery for the promotion of the economic and social advancement of all peoples,

HAVE RESOLVED TO COMBINE OUR EFFORTS TO ACCOMPLISH THESE AIMS.

Accordingly, *our respective Governments, through representatives assembled in the city of San Francisco, who have exhibited their full powers found to be in good and due form, have agreed to the present Charter of the United Nations and do hereby establish an international organization to be known as the United Nations.*

to employ international machinery for the promotion of the economic and social advancement of all peoples,

HAVE RESOLVED TO COMBINE OUR EFFORTS TO ACCOMPLISH THESE AIMS.

Accordingly, *the Charter of the United Nations adopted at San Francisco in 1945, having now been revised, the United Nations is hereby continued under this revised Charter with the structure, functions and powers set forth in the following Articles and Annexes.*

Comment. No change is proposed in the present admirable statement of the *fundamental aims* of the United Nations. This could hardly be improved upon,—the difficulty being that the means provided to fulfil these aims have, in practice, proved inadequate.

Thus, in the present Preamble, the only stated means to ensure "that armed force shall not be used, save in the common interest" are "the acceptance of principles and the institution of methods" without any specification as to the nature of those "principles" and "methods". In place of this general phrase, it is proposed explicitly to state the necessity for effective world law by substituting the words "the acceptance of world law in the field of war prevention and through adequate institutions for its enforcement".

This vital change would stress that the new United Nations would be based upon paramount world law, and must possess effective means to enforce that law. The limited field in which this world law would operate, i.e., in respect of matters directly related to the prevention of war, and the powers and institutions required for enforcement, are spelled out in detail in the revised text of the 111 Articles and in the seven Annexes. The purpose of the change is to make it clear from the start that the basic principle on which the revision is founded is that of enforceable world law "in the field of war prevention".

The other change in the Preamble is in its final paragraph. This has been revised in order to emphasize that the strengthened United Nations, notwithstanding fundamental changes in its character and powers, would nevertheless be a continuance of the original United Nations established at San Francisco in 1945.

CHAPTER I

PURPOSES AND PRINCIPLES

Article 1

The Purposes of the United Nations are:

1. To maintain international peace and security, and to that end: to take effective *collective* measures for the prevention and removal of threats to the peace, *and* for the suppression of acts of aggression or other breaches of the peace, and to bring about by peaceful means, and in conformity with the principles of justice and international law, adjustment or settlement of international disputes or situations which might lead to a breach of the peace;

2. To develop friendly relations among nations based on respect for the principle of equal rights and self-determination of peoples, and to take other appropriate measures to strengthen universal peace;

3. To achieve international cooperation in solving international

The Purposes of the United Nations are:

1. To maintain international peace and security, and to that end: *to abolish all national military forces and, through a United Nations system of inspection and a United Nations military force,* to take effective measures *for the enforcement of disarmament,* for the prevention and removal of threats to the peace, for the suppression of acts of aggression or other breaches of the peace, *and for ensuring compliance with this revised Charter and the laws and regulations enacted thereunder;* and, *through United Nations agencies and tribunals,* to bring about by peaceful means, and in conformity with the principles of justice and international law, adjustment or settlement of international disputes or situations which might lead to a breach of the peace;

2. To develop friendly relations among nations based on respect for the principle of equal rights and self-determination of peoples, and to take other appropriate measures to strengthen universal peace;

3. To achieve international cooperation in solving international

5

problems of an economic, social, cultural, or humanitarian character, and in promoting and encouraging respect for human rights and for fundamental freedoms for all without distinction as to race, sex, language, or religion; and

4. To be a center for harmonizing the actions of nations in the attainment of these common ends.

problems of an economic, social, cultural, or humanitarian character, and in promoting and encouraging respect for human rights and for fundamental freedoms for all without distinction as to race, sex, language, or religion; and

4. To be a center for harmonizing the actions of nations in the attainment of these common ends.

Comment. The only change in the above Article is in paragraph 1 where it seems best specifically to mention the principal direct means whereby peace would be maintained under the revised Charter. These are: complete disarmament of all the nations, carefully safeguarded and enforced by a United Nations inspection system and a United Nations military force (see Annexes I and II); and a system of agencies and tribunals for the settlement by peaceful means of all international disputes (see Annex III).

Article 2

The *Organization* and its *Members,* in pursuit of the Purposes stated in Article 1, shall act in accordance with the following Principles.

1. *The Organization is based on the principle of the sovereign equality of all its Members.*

2. All *Members,* in order to ensure to all of them the rights and benefits resulting from member-

The *United Nations* and its *member Nations,* in pursuit of the Purposes stated in Article 1, shall act in accordance with the following Principles.

1. *All nations shall be equally entitled to the protection guaranteed by this revised Charter, irrespective of size, population or any other factor; and there are reserved to all nations or their peoples all powers inherent in their sovereignty, except such as are delegated to the United Nations by this revised Charter, either by express language or clear implication, and are not prohibited by this revised Charter to the nations.*

2. All *member Nations,* in order to ensure to all of them the rights and benefits resulting from mem-

6

ship, shall fulfil in good faith the obligations assumed by them in accordance with *the present* Charter.

3. All *Members* shall settle their international disputes by peaceful means in such a manner that international peace and security, and justice, are not endangered.

4. All *Members* shall refrain in their international relations from the threat or use of force against the territorial integrity or political independence of any state, or in any other manner inconsistent with the Purposes of the United Nations.

5. All *Members* shall give the United Nations every assistance in any action it takes in accordance with *the present* Charter, and shall refrain from giving assistance to any state against which the United Nations is taking preventive or enforcement action.

6. The *Organization* shall ensure that states which are not *Members* of the United Nations act in accordance with these Principles so far as may be necessary for the maintenance of international peace and security.

7. Nothing contained in *the present* Charter shall authorize the United Nations to intervene in matters which are essentially within

bership, shall fulfil in good faith the obligations assumed by them in accordance with *this revised* Charter.

3. All *nations* shall settle their international disputes by peaceful means in such a manner that international peace and security, and justice, are not endangered.

4. All *nations* shall refrain in their international relations from the threat or use of force against the territorial integrity or political independence of any state, or in any other manner inconsistent with the Purposes of the United Nations.

5. All *member Nations* shall give the United Nations every assistance in any action it takes in accordance with *this revised* Charter, and *all nations* shall refrain from giving assistance to any state against which the United Nations is taking preventive or enforcement action.

6. The *United Nations* shall ensure that states which are not *members* of the United Nations act in accordance with these Principles so far as may be necessary for the maintenance of international peace and security, *and that they observe all the prohibitions and requirements of the disarmament plan contained in Annex I of this revised Charter.*

7. Nothing contained in *this revised* Charter shall authorize the United Nations to intervene in matters which are essentially within

the domestic jurisdiction of any state or shall require *the Members* to submit such matters to settlement under *the present* Charter; but this principle shall not prejudice the application of enforcement measures under Chapter VII.

the domestic jurisdiction of any state or shall require *any state* to submit such matters to settlement under *this revised* Charter; but this principle shall not prejudice *such action as may be necessary to maintain international peace and security. In particular, this principle shall not prejudice: (a) the execution of the provisions for disarmament contained in Annex I; (b) the limited authority of the General Assembly to legislate pursuant to Article 11 of this revised Charter; (c) the limited authority of the Assembly to raise revenue pursuant to Article 17 and Annex V of this revised Charter; (d) the limited authority of the Assembly, pursuant to Article 36 of this revised Charter, to refer questions relating to disputes or situations which are likely to endanger the maintenance of international peace and security to the World Equity Tribunal, the authority of the Tribunal to make recommendations with respect to any questions referred to it and the authority of the Assembly to approve the recommendations of the Tribunal; or (e)* the application of enforcement measures under Chapter VII *and Article 94 of this revised Charter. Nor shall this principle prevent the United Nations from making such nonbinding recommendations as are hereinafter authorized.*

Comment. In this statement of Principles and elsewhere in the proposed revision, the term "Members" has been changed to "member Nations", and the term "Organization" to "United Nations". These changes are made both for clarity and because of the new character of the United Nations under the revision.

8

Paragraph 1 has been remodeled in order to clarify the meaning of the phrase "sovereign equality" which is ambiguous and misleading. The two concepts contained therein—"equality" and "sovereignty"—need to be treated separately; and their proper meaning needs to be spelled out in more adequate terms.

In respect of *equality*, it goes without saying that the nations of the world are far from being equal in power and influence. It is, nevertheless, fundamental that *in the eyes of the law* every nation should stand equal with every other, in the same way as individuals are or should be treated equally by the internal law of their countries, regardless of the individual's wealth, position or status. Accordingly, the Charter of the United Nations should extend equal protection to all states, and all states should be accorded equal access to the remedies provided for them by the Charter. The proposed amendment of paragraph 1 makes explicit this meaning of the principle of equality by making it a basic principle of the United Nations that: "All nations shall be equally entitled to the protection guaranteed by this revised Charter, irrespective of size, population or any other factor".

The *sovereignty* of all states is necessarily subject to all the obligations which they voluntarily accept; and this "sovereignty" is modified by international treaties and conventions and by constantly developing rules of customary international law. The present Charter of the United Nations has similarly modified the sovereignty of all member Nations, and the extensive amendments in this proposed revision would carry the process of voluntary limitation of sovereignty much further.

Under the proposed revision, the "sovereignty" of all the nations and their peoples would be modified to the extent that: (a) certain *enumerated and limited* powers would be granted to the United Nations; and (b) the exercise of a few other "sovereign" powers, relating to the maintenance of national military forces and the making of war, would be specifically prohibited to all nations. These granted powers and specific prohibitions—all directly related to the maintenance of peace—are stated with precision in later proposals.

The proposed paragraph 1 calls for an explicit reservation to all nations or their peoples of "all powers inherent in their sovereignty, except such as are delegated to the United Nations by this revised Charter, either by express language or clear implication, and are not prohibited by this revised Charter to the nations." This language has been influenced by, but is somewhat broader than, the corresponding reservation in the Tenth Amendment to the Constitution of the United States whereby: "The powers not delegated to the United States by the Constitution, nor prohibited by it to the States, are reserved to the States respectively or to the people."

No substantial change is proposed in paragraph 2 of this Article which relates only to the duty of *member Nations* to fulfil in good faith the obligations assumed by them *by virtue of their membership,* and does not apply to the few nations which might not ratify the revised Charter.

The proposed amendments to paragraphs 3, 4 and 5 would extend to all nations, whether members of the United Nations or not, the obligation to

9

settle international disputes peacefully, to refrain from the use of force and from giving assistance to any state against which the United Nations is taking action. On the other hand, the duty, under paragraph 5, actively to assist the United Nations would continue to apply only to member Nations.

The scope of paragraph 6, which deals with the duty of the United Nations to ensure the application of the basic principles of the Charter to nations which may not become member Nations, has been extended to cover explicitly the obligation of these nations to observe "all the prohibitions and requirements of the disarmament plan contained in Annex I" of the revised Charter. While the proposed amendments do not require any state to become an active member of the United Nations against its will, it is plain that certain basic provisions of world law must apply to all nations, whether or not they have accepted membership in the United Nations. In particular, every nation of the world must be bound by all the requirements and obligations of the revised Charter in respect of disarmament, since if all the member Nations are required wholly to disarm, it is obvious that even the few nations which might choose not to ratify the revised Charter cannot be left free to arm as they please. On the other hand, there is no need to impose upon any nonmember nation certain other obligations which apply only to nations which voluntarily accept active membership—such as the obligation to contribute to United Nations revenue.

The present *unqualified* prohibition in paragraph 7 against intervention in any matters "essentially within the domestic jurisdiction of any state" is plainly inconsistent with the plan for universal, enforceable and complete disarmament contained in Annex I and with various new powers relating to the prevention of war which the United Nations would possess under the revised Charter. For example, while it is now taken for granted that a nation's right to maintain military forces is wholly within its domestic jurisdiction, this right would be entirely eliminated by the disarmament plan under Annex I, which requires not merely the reduction but the gradual *abolition* of the military forces of each and every nation in the world.

To remove this contradiction and other inconsistencies which would exist by reason of the enlarged powers for the prevention of war, it is proposed to qualify the present restriction by stating that the prohibited intervention in matters of "domestic jurisdiction" shall "not prejudice such action as may be necessary to maintain international peace and security." Without impairing the effect of this general language, it is specifically provided that the domestic jurisdiction clause shall in no way prejudice: (a) the carrying out of the disarmament plan under Annex I; (b) the new limited authority to legislate for the maintenance of peace which the General Assembly would have under revised Article 11; (c) the raising of revenue under the new system provided for in revised Article 17 and Annex V; and (d) the carefully limited authority of the Assembly, by the adoption of recommendations of the proposed new World Equity Tribunal, to impose upon the nations concerned a settlement of nonlegal questions involved in a dangerous dispute. The present qualification that the "domestic jurisdiction" clause shall not prejudice enforcement measures under Chapter VII is retained.

In addition, it has been thought wise to add the further qualification that the making of nonbinding recommendations as "hereinafter authorized" shall not be construed as a forbidden intervention in matters of domestic jurisdiction. This qualification would cover recommendations of the General Assembly under revised Articles 12-14, of the Economic and Social Council under revised Article 62 and of the Trusteeship Council under revised Article 87. The effect would be to remove any basis for the argument, often made in the past, that even nonbinding recommendations constitute intervention in the domestic affairs of the nations.

Notwithstanding these important modifications of the "domestic jurisdiction" clause, it should be emphasized that the proposed text retains the broad principle that national authority over traditionally domestic affairs is to be disturbed only when United Nations authority is clearly required to prevent the calamity of modern war. Thus, while the revision contemplates greatly enlarged powers *in matters directly related to the prevention of war,* including disarmament, it does not contemplate the creation of a supranational authority with compulsory powers to interfere in any domestic matter whatever unless, and to the extent that, international peace is endangered. In short, the purpose is to provide the United Nations with effective powers to prevent the nations from "murdering each other". It is not to confer upon the United Nations any authority to reform the political, economic or social system of any nation, no matter how beneficial such a reform might seem.

CHAPTER II

MEMBERSHIP

Article 3

The *original Members* of the United Nations shall be the states *which, having participated in the United Nations Conference on International Organization at San Francisco, or having previously signed the Declaration by United Nations of January 1, 1942, sign the present Charter and ratify it* in accordance with Article 110.

1. The *initial member Nations* of the United Nations *under this revised Charter* shall be: *those of* the states *listed in Article 9 whose ratifications,* in accordance with Article 110, *have brought the revised Charter into force; and such other states listed in Article 9 as shall ratify the revised Charter within two years from the date on which it comes into force.*

2. *Any nation listed in Article 9 which has not become an initial member Nation and retains the legal status of an independent state and any nation not listed in Article 9 which after the signing of this revised Charter achieves the legal status of an independent state shall be entitled to become a member Nation, subject in each case to its acceptance of the obligations contained in the revised Charter. Any such nation desiring to become a member Nation shall make written application to the Secretary-General who shall forthwith notify all member Nations of such application. Unless at least ten member Nations shall within thirty days from such notification file written notice with the Secretary-General questioning the legal status of the applicant as an independent state,*

the applicant shall become a member Nation at the end of the thirty-day period. In case the legal status of the applicant as an independent state is thus questioned, the General Assembly shall refer the question to the International Court of Justice for final decision.

Comment. Thorough revision of the provisions of the Charter relating to membership is proposed in order to further the universality of the United Nations. This result would be achieved by several interlocking provisions, the combined effect of which should be to assure universal or virtually universal membership.

First, it is proposed (revised Article 110) that the revised Charter shall become effective only upon its acceptance by an overwhelming majority of the nations and peoples of the world, namely upon ratification by five sixths of all the nations, these to include all the twelve nations having the largest populations, and subject to the condition that the aggregate of the populations of the ratifying nations must equal at least five sixths of the total world population.

To illustrate: If we assume that at the time the revised Charter comes into force the ninety-nine nations listed in revised Article 9 are recognized as independent states, the new United Nations would, under the five-sixths requirement, start with a membership of at least eighty-three nations (revised Articles 3 and 110). Thus the number of nonratifying nations could not in any event exceed sixteen. Moreover, by reason of the further requirement of revised Article 110 that all the twelve nations with the largest populations must ratify in order to bring the revised Charter into force, the total population of the nations which might not ratify would be relatively small.

Second, the provision of revised paragraph 6 of Article 2, imposing upon all nonmember nations the obligation to comply with all the disarmament provisions of the revised Charter, should be a powerful inducement toward universal membership. This provision is made essential by the devastating and growing power of modern weapons. That power is now so vast that if the nations generally are to disarm it is plainly necessary to forbid any nation whatever, however small, to possess any armaments, save only such limited and lightly armed forces as are required for internal order. Clearly also, the United Nations must have authority to enforce this restriction upon every nation, whether or not it chooses to accept the obligations of active membership. It is therefore to be expected that nations made subject to these obligations would wish to have the full representation in the United Nations which they could only obtain through active membership.

Third, the proposed change in the requirements for membership in this revised Article 3, whereby any nation having the legal status of an independent state would be absolutely entitled to membership, should also be a strong influence toward universality.

Under the present membership provisions (present Article 4, now merged with revised Article 3), the admission of a new member requires: (1) a recommendation of the Security Council, which calls for at least seven votes, all the five permanent members concurring; and (2) approval by a two-thirds vote of the General Assembly. Moreover, the present Charter requires that nations applying for membership must be "peace-loving" and also "able and willing" to carry out the obligations contained in the Charter. The application of these provisions has led to many difficulties, and it seems clear that both the qualifications for membership and the procedure need to be simplified.

Accordingly, the new paragraph 2 of this revised Article 3 provides that every "nation which achieves the legal status of an independent state" is "entitled" to become a member Nation, subject only to acceptance of its obligations under the revised Charter. Thus, any independent state desiring to join the United Nations would have to fulfil only one formal condition. It would merely need to file with the Secretary-General a written application stating that it has accepted those obligations; and it would not be subject to rejection because of the unpopularity of its political or social system or any other reason.

In an ordinary case, the new membership would automatically become effective thirty days after the Secretary-General had notified all member Nations of the application. No further action would be required; there would be no need for any votes by the General Assembly or by the Executive Council; and there would be no possibility of a veto.

Only in the very exceptional case of a serious challenge to the applicant's status as "an independent state" would additional steps be required. The proposal is that if ten member Nations deem it necessary to question the applicant's status, they may do so by written notice to the Secretary-General; and that the General Assembly would then be obliged to refer the matter to the International Court of Justice for final decision—unless, of course, the applicant should withdraw at that stage. By this procedure the question of eligibility would not be left to a political decision but would be determined by the highest judicial organ of the United Nations on the basis of the applicable rules of international law. Each applicant nation would thus be ensured of fair treatment; and if its claim to statehood were held valid, no political maneuvers could deprive it of the right to join the United Nations.

For the above reasons: there would be absolute assurance that the membership would include all but a rather small minority of the nations, which minority could include only a minor fraction of the world's population; and there would be a strong likelihood that in actual practice the membership would be universal or virtually so.

Article 4

1. *Membership in the United Nations is open to all other peace-loving states which accept the obligations contained in the present*

The citizens of the member Nations and of the non-self-governing and trust territories under the administration of member Nations

14

Charter and, in the judgment of the Organization, are able and willing to carry out these obligations.

2. The admission of any such state to membership in the United Nations will be effected by a decision of the General Assembly upon the recommendation of the Security Council.

shall be deemed to be citizens of the United Nations as well as of their own respective nations.

Comment. It is proposed that the present text of this Article be deleted, since the matter of admitting new member Nations is already covered by the revised text of Article 3.

The new Article 4 deals with a new subject, namely, United Nations citizenship which would be extended to all the citizens of all the member Nations and of all the non-self-governing and trust territories under the administration of member Nations.

In view of the individual rights and obligations of all these people under the proposed revision, it seems both normal and advisable that their direct relationship to the strengthened United Nations should thus be recognized. For, while it is true that the revised Charter would carefully restrict the authority of the United Nations to matters directly related to the prevention of war, it is also true that its essential powers in that limited field would need to be quite extensive and would directly affect the individual citizens of the member Nations.

For example, every individual in every member Nation would be directly bound by the revised Charter and the laws enacted thereunder, and would be subject to penalties for their violation. Moreover, many millions of individuals would, under the proposed revenue system, find themselves making payments directly to the fiscal agents of the United Nations. On the other hand, the citizens of member Nations would have the right, to the extent provided by revised Article 9, to elect their Representatives in the General Assembly and, under the proposed Bill of Rights, would be individually entitled to invoke the protection of the courts of the United Nations against abuse of power by the strengthened organization.

Under these circumstances, it seems not only appropriate to provide for United Nations citizenship but also positively advantageous to do so, in order to encourage that sense of individual loyalty to the new United Nations which is indispensable to the effective fulfillment of its task. Needless to say, this grant of United Nations citizenship would in no way imperil the national citizenship of the individual. The citizens of every nation would fully retain their status and loyalties as citizens of their respective countries, just as in the United States the fact that all the citizens of New York or Illinois are constitutionally also "citizens of the United States" in no way affects their rights and duties as citizens of their own States.

15

That this purpose is psychological rather than tangible does not lessen its importance. Men largely live by symbols, and just as a United Nations flag is helpful to the present United Nations, a common United Nations citizenship may be still more helpful to the stronger United Nations which the future requires.

Article 5

A Member of the United Nations against which preventive or enforcement action has been taken by the Security Council may be suspended from the exercise of the rights and privileges of membership by the General Assembly *upon the recommendation of the Security Council.* The exercise of these rights and privileges may be restored by the *Security Council.*

A member Nation which, in the judgment of the General Assembly, has violated any basic principle or provision of this revised Charter may be suspended from the exercise of the rights and privileges of membership by the General Assembly. The exercise of these rights and privileges may be restored by the *General Assembly.*

Comment. The proposed changes in Article 5 are closely related to the proposed fundamental change in Article 6, whereby no member Nation may either withdraw or be expelled. The very fact that membership would thus be permanent and unbreakable emphasizes that there should be some way other than expulsion to discipline a member Nation which has seriously disregarded its obligations. This is provided by empowering the General Assembly to suspend a member Nation, if found by the Assembly to have violated any "basic principle or provision" of the Charter. In view of the proposed transfer to the Assembly of the power to take enforcement measures under Chapter VII of the Charter, this power to suspend should be exercised by the Assembly alone, without the necessity of a recommendation by the new Executive Council. For the same reason, the power to restore the privileges of membership should be exercised by the Assembly rather than the Executive Council.

Article 6

A Member of the United Nations which has persistently violated the Principles contained in the present Charter may be expelled from the Organization by the General Assembly upon the recommendation of the Security Council.

No member Nation may withdraw from the United Nations or be expelled therefrom.

Comment. The present Charter not only permits the expulsion of member Nations but also contains no provision against withdrawal.

It is plain, however, that the whole purpose of the revision could be frustrated if even one of the most important nations should withdraw, thereby depriving the United Nations of essential moral and material support.

The rationale and spirit of the ratification procedure under revised Article 110 (which requires assent by five sixths of all the nations which must contain five sixths of all the world's people and must include all the twelve nations with the largest populations) are to ensure that for the fulfillment of its much greater responsibilities the revised United Nations shall have the overwhelming support of world opinion. This rationale carries the implication that the ratifying nations will continue their membership, since any important withdrawals could only result in destroying the complete or virtually complete universality of membership which is fundamental to the whole plan.

Once a truly effective organization has been formed by general consent to maintain peace under world law, it would be intolerable to permit its disintegration. In short, there is simply too much at stake to permit withdrawal under any circumstances; and it is therefore deemed essential to provide explicitly that "no member Nation may withdraw from the United Nations".

The present provision permitting expulsion of a member Nation is similarly inconsistent with the complete or almost complete universality of membership which would be realized through the ratification procedure of revised Article 110. It is also clear that the conception of enforceable world law in the limited field of war prevention, on which the entire revision is based, can be better fulfilled if every nation, once having joined the United Nations, can be required to carry out its obligations within the framework of membership.

This in no way implies that a member Nation failing to comply with its obligations should be free from discipline, which can be effectively imposed by suspension under revised Article 5. It merely implies that no member Nation shall ever be "outlawed", so to speak, through expulsion. Consistently, therefore, with the provision against withdrawal, it is proposed that this revised Article 6 shall explicitly provide that "no member Nation may *** be expelled" from the United Nations.

17

CHAPTER III

ORGANS

Article 7

1. There are established as the principal organs of the United Nations: a General Assembly, *a Security* Council, an Economic and Social Council, a Trusteeship Council, an International Court of Justice, and a Secretariat.

2. Such subsidiary organs as may be found necessary may be established in accordance with *the present* Charter.

1. There are established as the principal organs of the United Nations: a General Assembly, *an Executive* Council, an Economic and Social Council, a Trusteeship Council, an International Court of Justice, *a World Equity Tribunal, a World Conciliation Board,* and a Secretariat.

2. *There are also established: a United Nations Peace Force, a United Nations Inspection Service, a United Nations Nuclear Energy Authority, a United Nations Outer Space Agency and a World Development Authority.*

3. Such subsidiary organs as may be found necessary may be established in accordance with *this revised* Charter.

Comment. The change in paragraph 1 from "Security Council" to "Executive Council" is made because of the later proposal whereby the present Security Council would be replaced by an Executive Council responsible to the General Assembly (see revised Articles 23 and 24). The inclusion as a principal organ of a "World Equity Tribunal" is because of the vital function and independent character of this proposed new tribunal (see revised Articles 36 and 93 and Annex III). For similar reasons the proposed new "World Conciliation Board" is included among the principal organs (see revised Articles 36 and 93 and Annex III).

The purpose of the new paragraph 2 is to make formal provision for the establishment of the other most important new instrumentalities which are proposed for the carrying out of the essential functions of the strengthened United Nations, namely, the United Nations Peace Force, the United Nations Inspection Service, the United Nations Nuclear Energy Authority, the United Nations Outer Space Agency and the World Development Authority.

Article 8

The United Nations shall place no restrictions on the eligibility of men and women to participate in any capacity and under conditions of equality in its principal and subsidiary organs.

Comment. No change is proposed in the above Article.

CHAPTER IV

THE GENERAL ASSEMBLY

COMPOSITION

Article 9

1. The General Assembly shall consist of *all the Members of the United Nations.*

2. *Each Member shall have not more than five representatives in the General Assembly.*

1. The General Assembly shall consist of *Representatives from all the member Nations and from the non-self-governing and trust territories under their administration.*

2. *For the purpose of determining the number of Representatives in the General Assembly from the respective member Nations, the member Nations shall be divided into six categories as follows:*
   a. From each of the four member Nations having the largest populations there shall be thirty Representatives.
   b. From each of the eight member Nations having the next largest populations there shall be fifteen Representatives.
   c. From each of the twenty member Nations having the next largest populations there shall be six Representatives.
   d. From each of the thirty member Nations having the next largest populations there shall be four Representatives.
   e. From each of the remaining member Nations there shall be two Representatives, provided that any such nation has a population of over 1,000,000.

f. From each member Nation having a population of not over 1,000,000 there shall be one Representative.

3. The apportionment of Representatives pursuant to the foregoing formula shall be made by the General Assembly upon the basis of world censuses. The first census shall be taken within ten years after the coming into force of this revised Charter and subsequent censuses shall be taken in every tenth year thereafter, in such manner as the Assembly shall direct. The Assembly shall make a reapportionment of the Representatives within two years after each such census.

4. The non-self-governing and trust territories under the administration of member Nations shall be represented in the General Assembly in accordance with decisions made from time to time by the Assembly. In determining the total number of Representatives from these territories, the Assembly shall be guided by the principle that the number of such Representatives shall bear the same proportion to the number of Representatives from the member Nations in the Assembly as the population of these territories bears to the population of the member Nations. In allotting such Representatives to the various territories or groups of territories, the Assembly shall take into account their respective populations and the extent of their respective progress toward independent statehood.

5. Until the first apportionment

of Representatives shall be made by the General Assembly upon the basis of the first world census, the apportionment of Representatives in the Assembly shall be as follows:

a. The People's Republic of China, India, the Union of Soviet Socialist Republics, and the United States of America—thirty Representatives each;

b. Brazil, France, the Federal Republic of Germany, Indonesia, Italy, Japan, Pakistan, and the United Kingdom of Great Britain and Northern Ireland—fifteen Representatives each;

c. Argentina, Burma, Canada, Colombia, Congo, the German Democratic Republic, Iran, the Republic of Korea, Mexico, Nigeria, the Philippines, Poland, Romania, Spain, Thailand, Turkey, the United Arab Republic, the Union of South Africa, the Democratic Republic of Viet-Nam, and Yugoslavia—six Representatives each;

d. Afghanistan, Australia, Austria, Belgium, Bulgaria, Ceylon, Chile, the Republic of China, Cuba, Czechoslovakia, Ethiopia, Greece, Hungary, Iraq, the People's Democratic Republic of Korea, Malagasy Republic, the Federation of Malaya, the Federation of Mali, Morocco, Nepal, the Netherlands, Peru, Portugal, the Federation of Rhodesia and Nyasaland, Saudi Arabia, Sudan, Sweden, Switzerland, Venezuela, and the Republic of Viet-Nam—four Representatives each:

e. Albania, Bolivia, Cambodia, Cameroon, Costa Rica, Denmark, the Dominican Republic, Ecuador, El Salvador, Finland, Ghana, Gua-

temala, Guinea, Haiti, Honduras,
Ireland, Israel, Jordan, Laos, Lebanon, Liberia, Libya, the People's
Republic of Mongolia, New Zealand, Nicaragua, Norway, Panama,
Paraguay, Somalia, Togoland, Tunisia, Uruguay, the West Indies Federation, and Yemen—two Representatives each:

f. Cyprus, Iceland, and Luxembourg—one Representative each;

g. All the non-self-governing and
trust territories as a group—seventeen Representatives.

6. Representatives shall be chos-
en for terms of four years, such
terms to begin at noon on the third
Tuesday of September in every
fourth year, except that the first
Representatives chosen pursuant to
paragraph 6 (a) of Article 110 of
this revised Charter shall serve
from the date upon which they con-
vene until noon on the third Tuesday of September in the fourth
calendar year thereafter.

7. For the first three terms after
the coming into force of this revised
Charter, the Representatives from
each member Nation shall be chos-
en by its national legislature, except
to the extent that such legislature
may prescribe the election of the
Representatives by popular vote.
For the next three terms, not less
than half of the Representatives
from each member Nation shall be
elected by popular vote and the remainder shall be chosen by its national legislature, unless such legislature shall prescribe that all or part
of such remainder shall also be
elected by popular vote; provided

23

that any member Nation entitled to only one Representative during this three-term period may choose its Representative either through its national legislature or by popular vote as such legislature shall determine. Beginning with the seventh term, all the Representatives of each member Nation shall be elected by popular vote. The General Assembly may, however, by a two-thirds vote of all the Representatives in the Assembly, whether or not present or voting, postpone for not more than eight years the coming into effect of the requirement that not less than half of the Representatives shall be elected by popular vote; and the Assembly may also by a like majority postpone for not more than eight years the requirement that all the Representatives shall be elected by popular vote. In all elections by popular vote held under this paragraph, all persons shall be entitled to vote who are qualified to vote for the members of the most numerous branch of the national legislatures of the respective nations.

The Representatives of the non-self-governing and trust territories shall be chosen in such manner as the General Assembly shall determine, taking into account that the right of the peoples of the respective territories to participate directly in the selection of their Representatives should be recognized to the maximum extent possible.

8. Any vacancy among the Representatives of any member Nation shall be filled in such manner as the

24

national legislature of such member Nation may determine; and any vacancy among the Representatives of the non-self-governing or trust territories shall be filled in such manner as the General Assembly shall determine. A Representative chosen to fill a vacancy shall hold office for the remainder of the term of his predecessor.

9. The Representatives shall receive reasonable compensation, to be fixed by the General Assembly and to be paid out of the funds of the United Nations.

Comment. As to the composition of the General Assembly, Article 9 of the present Charter provides merely that the Assembly shall consist "of all the Members of the United Nations"; and although (by paragraph 2 of the present Article 9) each member Nation may have five individuals to represent it, each nation has only one vote (present Article 18, paragraph 1). The result is that all the member Nations now have equal voting rights in the General Assembly, irrespective of population or any other factor. Thus, Albania has the same vote as the Soviet Union; Costa Rica the same as the United States; and Luxembourg the same as the United Kingdom.

It was apparent when the present Charter was adopted in 1945 that under a voting arrangement of this sort substantial powers could not be given to the General Assembly, since it was not reasonable that the large nations should be bound in any important matter by the decisions of a body in which their votes had no more weight than those of nations with perhaps one hundredth of their population and power. This remains a fundamental defect in the present Charter which needs correction before the Assembly can be given even the minimum powers necessary to prevent war.

Article 9 has, therefore, been completely remodeled with the purpose of so reconstituting the General Assembly that all the nations should be willing to confer upon it the limited yet considerably increased powers which must be lodged in the United Nations under any effective plan for the maintenance of peace.

The principles governing the proposed representation plan are: (1) that every member Nation, however small, should be entitled to some representation; (2) that there should be a reasonable upper limit upon the representation of even the largest member Nation; and (3) that, subject to these provisions, representation should be apportioned by groups of nations according to their relative populations without attempting to reflect any such factors as relative natural resources, productive capacity, trade or literacy.

In harmony with these principles, the concrete proposal is that all nations recognized as independent states and, therefore, eligible for membership, shall

25

be divided into six categories, each comprising a group of nations in accordance with their populations.

As applied to the ninety-nine independent states which will prospectively exist in 1965 (including ten nations not yet recognized early in 1960 as independent states but likely to be so recognized within a few years), this plan would result in their representation as of July 1, 1965 as follows:

The 4 largest nations........30 Representatives each....120
The 8 next largest nations....15 Representatives each....120
The 20 next largest nations.... 6 Representatives each....120
The 30 next largest nations.... 4 Representatives each....120
The 34 next largest nations.... 2 Representatives each.... 68
The 3 smallest nations.......
                 (under 1,000,000) 1 Representative each.... 3
—
99 nations   551 Representatives

The reason for allotting one Representative to even the smallest nation is that it seems both expedient and just that *every* independent state which joins the United Nations shall have some voice. On the other hand, the upper limit of thirty is proposed because weighted representation constitutes an important departure from the present system of one vote for each nation and is not likely to be acceptable unless the differences in representation between the majority of the member Nations and the most populous nations are kept within moderate limits; and also because the General Assembly without some such upper limit would be so unwieldy as to be unable to transact business.

The question of the best method to solve this crucial problem of representation is recognized as one of the most difficult in the framing of an effective world organization; and the authors of these proposals have themselves wrestled with the problem for years. They have canvassed a large number of other possible formulas in which factors other than population would be used as criteria,—including economic and natural resources, productive capacity, national income, trade, and the degree of literacy of the various peoples. But after testing many plans which would take account of these and other factors in various combinations, the authors have been forced to the conclusion that all such plans present such a host of difficulties that they would be impractical in application. None of them seems to yield a result as fair and acceptable as the plan here proposed whereby: (a) all the member Nations would be divided into categories measured by their relative populations; (b) all the nations within a particular category would have a specified equal representation; and (c) every nation, without exception, would have some representation while a reasonable limit would be put upon the representation of the largest nations.

The proposed plan is avowedly a compromise as between two main factors, —the factor of relative populations and the factor of the independent statehood of the individual separate nations. It will be seen, however, that it is a compromise which gives major weight to the factor of independent statehood as demonstrated by the fact that the twelve most populous nations, with a combined population far greater than the combined population of the eighty-seven smaller nations, would, nevertheless, have a representation considerably less than that of the smaller nations. In fact, upon the basis of estimated populations as of July 1, 1965, the eighty-seven smaller nations with a combined population of 891 million would have 311 Representatives, whereas the twelve largest nations with a combined population of 2186 million would have only 240 Representatives. While it is clearly recognized that this plan results in heavy overrepresentation in relation to population of the smaller and middle-sized nations, this overrepresentation is deemed advisable in order to recognize the separate existence of the various national states, some of them very old, with their distinct histories and traditions.

It may be argued that the plan goes too far in respect of not giving weight to the population factor. A slight consideration makes it clear, however, that no plan of representation proportionate to or even closely related to population would be either practicable or possibly acceptable. For example, an apportionment of Representatives in strict accordance with relative populations would entitle the largest nation, the People's Republic of China with its estimated 720 *million* people in 1965, to have 4000 times as many Representatives as Iceland with its estimated 180 *thousand* people in 1965. And if one assumes that even the smallest nation should have one Representative, it is plain that any plan even nearly related to population would result in a General Assembly of impracticable size.

In short, while the proposed plan *takes into important account* relative populations, it would be inaccurate to say that it is based upon or is even closely related to that factor.

The plan also takes into account certain very practical considerations relating to acceptability, of which the following are the most important: (1) that it is, in practice, essential to allot the same maximum representation to the United States and the Soviet Union, for the simple reason that neither could possibly accept a plan under which the other was given a larger voice; and in this age, it is impossible to deny the same maximum representation to the two great Asian nations—mainland China and India—which by tremendous margins have the largest populations in the world; (2) that it would be unwise and unacceptable to distinguish between the eight middle-sized nations, since neither France, West Germany, Italy nor the United Kingdom would consent to a less representation than the others and, this being assumed, the same representation should not be denied to the considerably larger nations in this category, namely, Brazil, Indonesia, Japan and Pakistan; and (3) that once this principle of equal representation within each of the first two categories is accepted, it should also be applied to the other four categories.

In summary, the proposed apportionment seeks: (a) the utmost practical degree of fairness to all the nations; and (b) general acceptability in the sense that, on due consideration, all the various nations would perceive that the plan is impartially conceived without intention to prefer or prejudice any particular nation or group of nations. As in the case of proposed solutions to other thorny problems, however, the authors do not presume to say that this is the only or the perfect solution. What they can say is that the proposal is the result of years of consideration of many other alternative plans, all of which, on analysis, seemed to present more serious objections than this proposal.

The apportionment of Representatives in accordance with the proposed formula would be made "on the basis of world censuses" of which the first would be taken "within ten years from the coming into force" of the revised Charter, subsequent censuses to be taken "in every tenth year thereafter". The General Assembly would be required to make a reapportionment of the Representatives within two years after each world census.

In the meanwhile, pending the first census, there would be an interim apportionment whereby Representatives would be allotted in accordance with estimated populations at the time of the approval of the revised Charter by the General Assembly or by a General Conference, as the case might be.

The assumed date as of which the interim apportionment would be made, i.e., July 1, 1965, has been chosen in order to present a picture of the representation of all the nations under the proposed plan as of a future date when there is good reason to assume that a comprehensive plan for world peace under world law will have been formulated and, if not then adopted, will at least be under serious consideration throughout the world.

The following table sets forth the estimates of population as of July 1, 1965 upon which the interim apportionment of Representatives is made pursuant to paragraph 5 of this revised Article 9:

Member Nations	Population (Estimated as of July 1, 1965)	Rank Relative to Population	Interim Number of Representatives
Afghanistan	13,800,000	35	4
Albania	1,690,000	89	2
Argentina	23,200,000	23	6
Australia	11,200,000	41	4
Austria	7,120,000	59	4
Belgium	9,330,000	48	4
Bolivia	3,800,000	71	2
Brazil	76,700,000	8	15
Bulgaria	8,150,000	51	4
Burma	22,400,000	24	6
Cambodia	5,180,000	64	2
Cameroon	3,620,000	74	2
Canada	19,300,000	27	6
Ceylon	11,100,000	42	4
Chile	7,600,000	56	4
China, People's Republic of	720,000,000	1	30
China, Republic of	12,200,000	38	4
Colombia	16,200,000	31	6
Congo	15,200,000	32	6
Costa Rica	1,320,000	93	2
Cuba	7,610,000	55	4
Cyprus	628,000	97	1
Czechoslovakia	14,300,000	33	4
Denmark	4,780,000	66	2
Dominican Republic	3,060,000	76	2
Ecuador	4,790,000	65	2
El Salvador	3,000,000	78	2
Ethiopia	12,800,000	36	4
Finland	4,620,000	67	2
France	46,800,000	12	15
Germany, Federal Republic of	54,000,000	9	15
Germany, Democratic Republic of	18,900,000	28	6
Ghana	5,340,000	63	2
Greece	8,780,000	49	4
Guatemala	4,400,000	69	2
Guinea	2,700,000	81	2
Haiti	3,880,000	70	2
Honduras	2,250,000	83	2
Hungary	10,600,000	44	4
Iceland	180,000	99	1
India	456,000,000	2	30
Indonesia	98,300,000	7	15
Iran	27,300,000	19	6
Iraq	7,300,000	58	4
Ireland	2,870,000	79	2
Israel	2,800,000	80	2
Italy	51,300,000	11	15
Japan	102,000,000	6	15
Jordan	1,820,000	86	2

Member Nations	Population (Estimated as of July 1, 1965)	Rank Relative to Population	Interim Number of Representatives
Korea, Republic of	24,600,000	22	6
Korea, People's Democratic Republic of	10,100,000	46	4
Laos	1,750,000	87	2
Lebanon	1,830,000	85	2
Liberia	1,370,000	91	2
Libya	1,340,000	92	2
Luxembourg	331,000	98	1
Malagasy Republic	5,900,000	61	4
Malaya, Federation of	7,980,000	52	4
Mali, Federation of	6,450,000	60	4
Mexico	39,600,000	13	6
Mongolia, People's Republic of	1,160,000	96	2
Morocco	12,100,000	39	4
Nepal	10,500,000	45	4
Netherlands	12,350,000	37	4
New Zealand	2,572,000	82	2
Nicaragua	1,710,000	88	2
Nigeria	36,800,000	14	6
Norway	3,700,000	72	2
Pakistan	102,500,000	5	15
Panama	1,200,000	95	2
Paraguay	1,900,000	84	2
Peru	11,800,000	40	4
Philippines	27,200,000	20	6
Poland	31,200,000	18	6
Portugal	9,520,000	47	4
Rhodesia and Nyasaland, Federation of	8,730,000	50	4
Romania	19,600,000	26	6
Saudi Arabia	7,490,000	57	4
Somalia	1,380,000	90	2
Spain	31,300,000	17	6
Sudan	10,900,000	43	4
Sweden	7,730,000	54	4
Switzerland	5,470,000	62	4
Thailand	25,600,000	21	6
Togoland	1,250,000	94	2
Tunisia	4,600,000	68	2
Turkey	31,400,000	16	6
Union of South Africa	17,000,000	30	6
USSR	234,000,000	3	30
United Arab Republic	35,090,000	15	6
United Kingdom	52,400,000	10	15
United States of America	192,000,000	4	30
Uruguay	3,050,000	77	2
Venezuela	7,830,000	53	4
Viet-Nam, Democratic Republic of	17,900,000	29	6
Viet-Nam, Republic of	14,200,000	34	4
West Indies Federation	3,685,000	73	2
Yemen	3,170,000	75	2
Yugoslavia	20,200,000	25	6
Total (99 member Nations)	3,087,156,000		551
Trust and non-self-governing territories	95,000,000		17
Grand total estimated population as of July 1, 1965..	3,172,156,000		568 Representatives

The population figures in the above table are taken from the United Nations publication entitled "The Future Growth of World Population" (1958) with some minor adjustments resulting from certain territorial changes, etc. since 1958. The table is based upon the assumption that the ninety-nine nations therein listed (all of which will presumably have the status of independent states when the revised Charter comes into force) will become member Nations. In the possible event that one or more of these nations should not ratify the revised Charter, there would, of course, be no Representatives from such nation or nations.

The nations listed in the foregoing table include all except two present Members of the United Nations, namely, the Byelorussian and Ukrainian Soviet Socialist Republics which cannot be said to have a truly independent status. In accordance with the agreement reached at Yalta in 1945, they were permitted to become original members of the United Nations in order to provide additional representation to the Soviet Union. They are now omitted because, under the proposed plan of representation, the Soviet Union would have the maximum number of thirty Representatives which it could distribute at its discretion among all its component Republics, including the two above mentioned.

The ten prospective member Nations, namely, Cameroon, Congo, Cyprus, the Malagasy Republic, the Federation of Mali, Nigeria, the Federation of Rhodesia and Nyasaland, Somalia (Somaliland under Italian trusteeship), Togoland, and the West Indies Federation are included in this table in anticipation of their attaining the status of independent states by the time the revised Charter comes into force.

The estimate for France of 46,800,000 includes 45,900,000 for continental France and 900,000 for her "overseas departments" but does not include Algeria or other parts of the French Community. The estimate of 56,300,000 for the Federal Republic of Germany includes 54,000,000 for West Germany proper and 2,300,000 for West Berlin. The estimate of 18,900,000 for the German Democratic Republic includes 17,700,000 for East Germany proper and 1,200,000 for East Berlin. The estimate of 12,350,000 for the Netherlands includes 11,800,000 for the Netherlands proper and 550,000 for the self-governing territories of Surinam and the Netherlands Antilles. The estimate of 194,-500,000 for the United States includes 192,000,000 for the United States and 2,500,000 for Puerto Rico.

The matter of representation for areas that have not attained independent status presents a separate and difficult problem. As to this, it is proposed that the population of all colonial and semi-colonial territories (every non-self-governing territory and dependency, including territories under trusteeship administration) shall *not* be counted in determining the representation of the independent states. The estimated population of these colonial and semi-colonial areas as of July 1, 1965 is about ninety-five million; and it is proposed that their combined representation shall bear the same relation to their aggregate population as the total representation of the member Nations bears to the aggregate population of those nations. On the basis of the July 1, 1965 estimates, this principle would entitle these areas to seventeen Representatives whose allocation as between the territories or groups of territories would be a function of the General Assembly taking "into account their respective populations and the extent of their respective progress toward independent statehood."

It may be objected that a General Assembly of 568, which might soon increase to 600 Representatives through the recognition of new independent states, would be too large for a legislative body. But when it is remembered that this Assembly would represent all the people of the world, such a number does not seem excessive. Most national legislatures are certainly much larger relative to the populations represented, a well-known example being the Parliament of the United Kingdom which in 1960 has 630 members to represent only about fifty-two million people.

It should be noted that the effect of the proposed plan of representation would be that, while the smaller nations would still have a disproportionately large voice relative to population, this disproportion would not be nearly as great as under the present system of one vote for each member Nation irrespective of population. Nor would the disproportion be as great as under a bicameral system whereby every nation, however small, would have an equal voice with the largest nations in one of the two houses. Nor again would the disproportion in

30

favor of the smaller nations be as great as under a double-voting system in a single house whereby any measure, in order to carry, would need approval not only by a majority vote of the Representatives voting individually, but also by a majority of the delegations, with each delegation casting a single and equal vote.

On the much-discussed issue as to whether a General Assembly with much greater powers should be *unicameral or bicameral*, the authors have concluded that the balance of advantage lies in this instance with a unicameral system.

This conclusion has been reached only after the most careful study and in spite of the traditional use of the bicameral system in most federations. In order to test the relative advantages, a detailed proposal for a bicameral plan was, in fact, prepared with the following main features: (1) There would be a Senate whose concurrence would be necessary for all decisions; it would be composed of one Senator from each member Nation, with the proviso that this Senator shall be either Chief of State, Prime Minister or Foreign Minister unless a particular nation should choose to elect its Senator by popular vote or by vote of its national legislature. (2) The other house—to be called the Chamber of Representatives—would be composed on a plan similar to the above plan for a unicameral General Assembly, but with a somewhat greater spread between the representation of the smaller and the larger nations.

It has also been proposed that any world legislative body be composed of three chambers. The first chamber, it is suggested, could be similar to that provided for in this revised Article 9; the second chamber could consist of delegates from member Nations appointed by Governments, either on an equal basis or varying from one to six delegates on the basis of categories similar to those proposed in paragraph 2 of this revised Article 9; while the third chamber could be composed of about 200 members elected in a joint session by the first two chambers from among properly qualified individuals (former Presidents of the General Assembly, elder statesmen, etc.). The function of the third chamber would be to resolve possible deadlocks between the first two chambers; in particular, if a law or regulation should be approved by the first chamber but rejected by the second, it would come into effect if approved by the third chamber.

On balance, however, it is thought that neither these nor other plans calling for more than one legislative chamber would be as workable and effective as the proposed unicameral system. In saying this the authors recognize that, despite the more cumbersome slower procedure under a bicameral or multicameral system, such a system might sometimes produce better-considered decisions. Nevertheless, after weighing the relative advantages, the authors prefer the *unicameral plan* because: (a) it is easier to create an equitable plan of representation within a single house than to achieve a well-balanced apportionment where the problem is complicated by the necessity of allotting representation in two or three houses; and (b) a General Assembly composed of one chamber can, as a practical matter, function more promptly and effectively.

As to the *terms of office* of the Representatives, the proposal is that they shall serve for four-year terms with no restriction on re-election. This four-year term is proposed largely because of the advantages to be expected from the legislative experience and the capacity for teamwork which would result from working together in at least four annual sessions. It is also to be expected that a considerable number of the Representatives would be continued in office for more than one term. Through this combination of a fairly long term with eligibility for re-election, world leaders having the confidence of all the nations would naturally emerge, just as national leaders develop among those repeatedly elected to parliamentary bodies.

Concerning the *date for the convening* of the General Assembly, this has been fixed for the third Tuesday of September in order to conform with the present practice of the United Nations and because this should afford sufficient time to adopt the budgets of the United Nations for fiscal years beginning January 1 (see Annex V).

With regard to the *method of election* of the Representatives, it is proposed that a system of full popular elections shall be gradually introduced. This would be accomplished in three stages. During the first stage, covering the first three terms of the Assembly (twelve years), the choice of Representatives would be by the respective national legislatures of the member Nations, subject to the right of each legislature to prescribe popular election for all or part of the particular nation's quota of Representatives. During the second stage, again twelve years, it would be *required* that not less than half of the Representatives from each member Nation shall be elected by popular vote, the proportion, not less than half, so to be elected to be determined by each national legislature; and the remainder, if any, still to be chosen by the national legislature itself. It would be provided, however, that the first two stages could be extended, for not more than eight years in each case, by a special majority vote of the General Assembly. Finally after twenty-four years (unless the first two stages had been extended), the election by popular vote of *all* the Representatives would become mandatory. In all elections by "popular vote" it would be provided that those persons qualified to vote for the most numerous branch of the national legislature would be qualified to vote.

It will be noted that, as distinguished from the present method whereby delegates to the General Assembly are appointed by the executive branches of the respective governments, the Representatives would be chosen from the beginning either by the national legislature of each nation or by popular vote. Moreover, the plan would ensure a steadily increasing participation of the world's people in the selection of the Representatives, until at the end of the twenty-four years (or forty years in case of maximum postponement) the qualified voters themselves in every nation would elect *all* of their Representatives. These provisions are carefully framed to stress the desirability that the Representatives should receive their mandate directly from their peoples. In this way a genuinely popular control would gradually be established over the policies and administration of the strengthened United Nations.

It may be objected that certain member Nations may not possess anything that can properly be described as a "national legislature" at all. But since the case would be rare in which any nation would lack any sort of law-making body and since the phrase can be liberally construed, it seems unnecessary to provide any substitute method for the election of Representatives in the few cases in which national "legislatures" in the strict sense may be lacking. It may indeed be said that the prominent role given to the national legislatures in respect of the election of Representatives for many years after the revised Charter comes into force could be a strong inducement for any member Nation lacking a "national legislature" to provide something which would fairly meet that description.

The more important point can also be raised that even if nominally chosen by national legislatures the Representatives of certain nations would actually be appointees of the executive branches of their governments, and consequently would always vote in a bloc on important issues. For this reason it may be argued that it would be as well to retain indefinitely the present system whereby the "delegates" to the General Assembly are all avowedly the appointees of their governments. While, however, it is doubtless true that the Representatives of certain nations, however nominally chosen, would for a long time be mere executive appointees who would actually vote under governmental orders, it by no means follows that the consequence should be an abandonment of the whole idea of the ultimate selection of Representatives by popular vote. That purpose is too great and basic to be lightly given up. The deep divisions and rigid voting patterns in the present General Assembly are largely a consequence of the fears and tensions of an armed world. The adoption of the interrelated proposals of this book would go far to relieve those fears and tensions. Let complete national disarmament actually be carried out; let the proposed means for the peaceful settlement of all international disputes be actually used over a period of years; let the proposed World Development Authority function with adequate funds for even a decade,—and it can be expected that a new spirit would develop whereby it would be normal rather than exceptional for the Representatives in the General Assembly to vote in the common interest of all the people of the world rather than always to vote in the supposed interest of their particular nation as determined by its government of the day.

The development of this spirit would be nurtured and hastened by taking the choice of Representatives out of the hands of governments and entrusting it as soon as practicable to the peoples themselves. Recognizing, however, that so important a change should only be put into effect gradually, provision is made for a transition period in which the choice of all the Representatives by popular vote would proceed only step-by-step over a period of twenty-four years that could be extended to forty years. The essential point is that for the revised United Nations most effectively to fulfil its great purpose of maintaining peace, its controlling body—the General Assembly—should consist *as soon as possible* of Representatives directly chosen by the people whose security is involved. It should also be noted, however, that in the United States and some other nations, the selection of Representatives by popular vote or even by their legislative bodies might conflict with present constitutional provisions or practices, so that constitutional amendments would be necessary or at least desirable.

With respect to the political status of Representatives, it can be expected that the majority of Representatives of each nation would belong to the party or parties which are in harmony with the government for the time being of that nation. There might, it is true, be cases in which a national parliament, dominated by opposition parties, might elect Representatives who would be hostile to the policy of their own government. No provision, however, has been made to en-

33

sure the representation of all parties because in most democratic nations there should be no special difficulty about having members of all major parties included in the Representatives chosen. This is confirmed by the experience of the various Assemblies of European organizations in which, despite constantly shifting majorities in national parliaments, there has almost always been an equitable representation of the major parties.

Concerning the *selection of Representatives from the non-self-governing and trust territories,* provision is made for their choice "in such manner as the General Assembly shall determine", with the injunction to the Assembly, however, that the right of the people to participate directly should be recognized "to the maximum extent possible." In allocating Representatives among these non-self-governing and trust territories, the Assembly would also be required to "take into account their respective populations and the extent of their respective progress toward independent statehood." While some territories with large populations might be entitled to several Representatives, others would be entitled to only one. And, since there are many very small territories, the Assembly could combine some of them for electoral purposes into "groups of territories" to each of which groups a single Representative would be allocated.

The proposal for the *filling of vacancies* permits each member Nation to choose for itself what method shall be employed. This would enable each member Nation to use any of the optional methods prescribed for the election of Representatives, or any other method that the national legislature of the member Nation from which the original Representative was chosen may find desirable.

In respect of the *compensation* of Representatives, the purpose of the provision whereby "reasonable" compensation "shall" be paid by the United Nations is twofold: (a) to ensure that the Representatives shall not be financially dependent upon their governments, and (b) to emphasize that the Representatives in office are servants of the world community as well as of their respective nations. The provision is framed in broad terms so as to leave room for adequate expense, travel and retirement allowances.

The provisions of this revised Article 9 should be read in connection with the provision as to voting by the Representatives contained in revised Article 18. In that revised Article, it is provided that Representatives shall vote as individuals, and that they shall reach decisions on all important matters by a majority "of all the Representatives then in office, whether or not present or voting", rather than by a two-thirds majority of the member Nations as provided in the present Article 18. These new requirements would prevent decisions on important matters by any minority due to absences or abstentions, such as have occurred under the present Charter.

FUNCTIONS AND POWERS

Article 10

The General Assembly *may* discuss any questions or any matters

The General Assembly *shall have the power:*

within the scope of *the present* Charter *or relating to the powers and functions of any organs provided for in the present Charter,* and, except as provided in Article 12, *may* make recommendations to *the Members of the United Nations or to the Security Council or to both on any such questions or matters.*

a. to enact legislation binding upon member Nations and all the peoples thereof, within the definite fields and in accordance with the strictly limited authority hereinafter delegated;

b. to deal with disputes, situations, threats to the peace, breaches of the peace and acts of aggression, as hereinafter provided:

c. to make *nonbinding* recommendations to *the member Nations, as hereinafter provided;*

d. to elect the members of other organs of the United Nations, as hereinafter provided;

e. to discuss, and to direct and control the policies and actions of the other organs and agencies of the United Nations, with the exception of the International Court of Justice, the World Equity Tribunal and the World Conciliation Board; and

f. to discuss any questions or any matters within the scope of *this revised* Charter.

Comment. The present Article 10 merely empowers the General Assembly to *discuss* "any questions or any matters within the scope of the present Charter", or "relating to the powers and functions" of the organs of the Organization and to *make recommendations* on such subjects, with the exception (under present Article 12) that no recommendation is permitted as to any matters which are being dealt with by the Security Council.

In view of the proposed fundamental enlargement of the powers of the General Assembly, it is necessary to remodel this Article completely. The Assembly's broad authority to discuss all matters within the scope of the Charter is retained, together with its authority to recommend; but the authority to recommend has been strengthened by eliminating the above-mentioned restriction on recommendations. The present authority to discuss the operation of all the organs of the United Nations is also retained with the added authority to *direct and control* all the organs and agencies of the United Nations, except the International Court of Justice, the World Equity Tribunal and the World Conciliation Board, all of which should be independent of any political control whatever.

A more basic change is the grant to the General Assembly of new power to legislate within certain limits and new power to deal directly not only with disputes and situations but also with *threats to the peace, breaches of the peace and acts of aggression.*

It must be noted that this revised Article purports only to state the *general scope* of the General Assembly's authority, and that for various specific and detailed powers reference must be made to later Articles. For example, the enumeration of the limited legislative powers is in Article 11; the detailed provisions for dealing with disputes, situations, threats to the peace, breaches of the peace and acts of aggression are mainly in Chapters VI and VII; the specific authority to elect members of others organs is mainly conferred by Articles 23, 61 and 86; while the specific powers to recommend are mainly in Articles 12 to 14.

Article 11

1. The General Assembly *may consider the general principles of cooperation in* the maintenance of international peace and security, *including the principles governing* disarmament *and the regulation of armaments, and may make recommendations with regard to such principles to the Members or to the Security Council or to both.*

2. The General Assembly may discuss any questions relating to the maintenance of international peace and security brought before it by any *Member of the United Nations,* or by the *Security* Council, or by a *state* which is not a *Member* of the United Nations in accordance with Article 35, paragraph 2, and, *except as provided in Article 12,* may make recommendations with regard to any such questions to the *state* or *states* concerned or to the *Security* Council or to both. Any such question on which action is necessary *shall* be referred to the *Security* Council by the General Assembly either before or after discussion.

1. The General Assembly *shall have the primary responsibility for* the maintenance of international peace and security *and for ensuring compliance with this revised Charter and the laws and regulations enacted thereunder.*

2. *To this end the General Assembly shall have the following legislative powers:*

a. to enact such laws and regulations as are authorized by Annex I of this revised Charter relating to universal, enforceable and complete national disarmament, *including the control of nuclear energy and the use of outer space;*

b. to enact such laws and regulations as are authorized by Annex II of this revised Charter relating to the military forces necessary for the enforcement of universal and complete national disarmament, for the prevention and removal of threats to the peace, for the suppression of acts of aggression and other breaches of the peace, and for ensuring compliance with this revised Charter and the laws and regulations enacted thereunder;

c. to enact appropriate laws defining the conditions and establishing the general rules for the application of the measures provided for in Chapter VII;

d. to enact appropriate laws defining what acts or omissions of individuals or private organizations within the following categories shall be deemed offenses against the United Nations: (1) acts or omissions of government officials of any nation which either themselves constitute or directly cause a threat of force, or the actual use of force by one nation against any other nation, except that no use of force in self-defense under the circumstances defined in Article 51 of this revised Charter shall be made such an offense; (2) acts or omissions of any government official or any other individual or of any private organization which either themselves constitute or directly cause a serious violation of Annex I of this revised Charter or of any law or regulation enacted thereunder; (3) acts or omissions causing damage to the property of the United Nations or injuring any person in the service of the United Nations while engaged in the performance of official duties or on account of the performance of such duties; and (4) acts or omissions of any individual in the service of any organ or agency of the United Nations, including the United Nations Peace Force, which in the judgment of the General

Assembly are seriously detrimental to the purposes of the United Nations;

e. to enact appropriate laws: (1) prescribing the penalties for such offenses as are defined by the General Assembly pursuant to the foregoing subparagraph (d); (2) providing for the apprehension of individuals accused of offenses which the Assembly has defined as sufficiently serious to require apprehension, such apprehension to be by the United Nations civil police provided for in Annex III or by national authorities pursuant to arrangements with the United Nations or by the joint action of both; (3) establishing procedures for the trial of such individuals in the regional courts of the United Nations provided for in Annex III; and (4) providing adequate means for the enforcement of penalties.

3. The General Assembly may call the attention of the *Security* Council to situations which are likely to endanger international peace and security.

3. *No such law shall, however, relieve an individual from responsibility for any punishable offense by reason of the fact that such individual acted as head of state or as a member of a nation's government. Nor shall any such law relieve an individual from responsibility for any such offense on the ground that he has acted pursuant to an order of his government or of a superior, if, in the circumstances at the time, it was reasonably possible for him to refuse compliance with that order.*

4. *The powers of the General Assembly set forth in this Article shall not limit the general scope of*

4. *The member Nations agree to accept and carry out the laws and regulations enacted by the General*

Article 10.

Assembly under paragraph 2 of this Article, and the decisions of the Assembly made under this revised Charter including the Annexes; provided, however, that any member Nation shall have the right to contest the validity of any such law, regulation or decision by appeal to the International Court of Justice. Pending the judgment of the Court upon any such appeal, the contested law, regulation or decision shall nevertheless be carried out, unless the Assembly or the Court shall make an order permitting noncompliance, in whole or in part, during the Court's consideration of the appeal.

5. As soon as possible after the coming into force of this revised Charter, the Executive Council shall negotiate with any state which may not have become a member of the United Nations an agreement by which such state will agree to observe all the prohibitions and requirements of the disarmament plan contained in Annex I of this revised Charter, and to accept and carry out all the laws, regulations and decisions made thereunder, and by which the United Nations will recognize the right of any such state and of its citizens to all the protection and remedies guaranteed by this revised Charter to member Nations and their citizens with respect to the enforcement of Annex I and the laws, regulations and decisions made thereunder. If a state refuses to make such an agreement, the Executive Council shall inform the General Assembly which shall decide upon measures

39

to be taken to ensure the carrying out of the disarmament plan in the territory of such state.

Comment. This important Article deals with the proposed legislative powers of the General Assembly directly related to the enforcement of peace.

The present text of Article 11 merely empowers the General Assembly to "consider" the general principles of cooperation as to the maintenance of peace (including "the principles governing disarmament and the regulation of armaments"); to "discuss" any questions relating to the maintenance of peace; to make "recommendations" on these subjects; and to "call the attention" of the Security Council to situations likely to endanger peace.

By contrast, the proposed revision would empower the General Assembly to enact effective *laws* to implement universal and complete national disarmament. This authority would include power to enact legislation providing for the punishment of acts in violation of the disarmament plan and for the apprehension and fair trial of violators.

The purpose is to prevent war between any nations, however large or strong, by substituting the rule of law rather than force or the threat of it as the means of settling international disputes. The alternative means provided are: the enactment of clear law forbidding international violence, with definite penalties; complete disarmament of all the nations; an effective world police; judicial and other agencies with adequate powers to deal with disputes; and a well-financed program to mitigate the vast differences in the economic and social condition of the various peoples. These are measures corresponding to those long adopted for the maintenance of domestic order within local communities and nations, and they are no less necessary as between nations.

In furtherance of several of these objectives, it is proposed to delete all the provisions of the present Article 11, substituting therefor a wholly new text.

The present paragraph 1 is omitted as no longer appropriate. Its general language is replaced in the new text by a detailed grant of powers to enact certain kinds of *laws* as specifically defined. The present paragraph 4 is omitted because the reservation therein contained as to the powers of the General Assembly under Article 10 is no longer necessary in view of the proposed increase in the authority of the Assembly.

The present paragraphs 2 and 3 are also omitted because they have in substance been transferred to revised Article 12. This transfer is made in view of the fact that the subject matter of these paragraphs relates entirely to powers of discussion and recommendation; and it seems best to separate powers of that character from the new powers of legislation defined in the revised Article 11. In this way the General Assembly's main legislative powers would be concentrated in the new Article 11, while its main powers to discuss and recommend would be concentrated in the new Articles 12-14.

The proposed text of Article 11 embodies two fundamental changes: (1) the transfer of the "primary responsibility" for the maintenance of peace from the Security Council to the General Assembly; and (2) the grant to the Assembly of certain powers to make binding laws as distinguished from

40

mere recommendations. These new legislative powers are strictly limited, and yet would, it is believed, prove sufficient to enable the United Nations to fulfil its basic purpose of preventing war,—not merely minor wars, but any armed conflict between nations, small or great.

Disarmament. The first of the General Assembly's new powers (in (2) (a) of Article 11) would be to enact "such laws and regulations as are authorized by Annex I of this revised Charter relating to universal, enforceable and complete national disarmament, including the control of nuclear energy and the use of outer space." This power must, therefore, be read in relation to the proposed Annex I which contains a comprehensive and detailed disarmament plan. It should be read also in relation to the proposed Annex II which, by its provisions for a strong United Nations military force (the United Nations Peace Force), is designed to ensure the fulfillment of the disarmament plan and the supression of any attempted violation.

This comprehensive plan for complete national disarmament and its enforcement rests upon the premise that until the present system of national military forces is totally abolished, it will be impossible to achieve genuine peace. As the record of history shows, it has been repeatedly demonstrated that the existence of strong national military forces tends of itself to engender mutual fears which constitute a major influence toward ultimate conflict. The recent development of new and appalling weapons has intensified this tendency. The fears and tensions thus created make negotiation difficult and real progress toward peace almost impossible.

Moreover, the immense economic burden of armaments drains away human effort and natural resources to an extent that reduces standards of living in many countries, handicaps the effort to overcome poverty and ignorance, and thus tends to create unrest which may ultimately lead to war.

It seems essential that the *main features* of the disarmament plan shall be included in the Charter itself as "constitutional legislation". But since the necessary provisions covering even the main features involve considerable detail, it is deemed best to include them in an Annex rather than in the main body of the Charter. In this respect, the revision follows the precedent whereby the Statute of the International Court of Justice was included as an Annex to the present Charter.

Annex I, therefore, contains all the most important features of a comprehensive plan for the complete, although gradual, elimination of *all* national military forces and armaments and for confining internal police forces to such as are strictly necessary for the maintenance of internal order. Moreover, in view of the close relation between the use of nuclear energy and outer space for peaceful purposes and their use for military purposes, Annex I also includes provisions relative to the control of nuclear energy and the use of outer space.

Even though, however, all the main features of the disarmament plan are fully covered in Annex I, there will necessarily remain a considerable area requiring detailed regulation from year to year in order to supplement and make effective the basic provisions of that Annex. The purpose of the first legislative power (in (2) (a) of revised Article 11) is, therefore, to confer authority for the detailed implementation of Annex I. This is done by giving power to the General Assembly to adopt such "laws and regulations" as are "authorized by

41

Annex I". In this way, the disarmament plan can be enforced through the necessary detailed regulations and penalties while, at the same time, the Assembly's legislative power in this field would be strictly defined and limited.

Military Forces—the "United Nations Peace Force". The second legislative power (in (2) (b) of revised Article 11) enables the implementation of Annex II "relating to the military forces necessary for the enforcement of universal and complete national disarmament". The elaborate plan of Annex II for an effective "United Nations Peace Force" is based upon the premise that for a long time to come some effective military force in the hands of the United Nations will be essential to enable the United Nations to fulfil its basic purpose —"to maintain international peace and security" (Article 1).

The present Charter contains no *reliable* provision for the maintenance of a permanent international military force. After years of effort, it has proved impossible to make "special agreements" under the present Article 43 for making national contingents available to the United Nations on call; and even if the small United Nations Emergency Force organized in 1956 could be indefinitely maintained, it would clearly be inadequate to the need. Accordingly, the proposed Annex II contains a comprehensive plan for the creation of a permanent and substantial *international* police force, to be known as the "United Nations Peace Force" and to be organized over a period of years parallel with the step-by-step carrying out of the disarmament plan under Annex I.

As in the case, however, of Annex I, detailed laws and regulations will be necessary in order to implement the main features of this world police plan; and this second legislative power is designed to confer that authority, always within the strict limitations of Annex II itself.

Sanctions against nations. The third proposed legislative power would enable the General Assembly to implement the provisions of Chapter VII relating to measures which may be applied to nations failing to comply with the Charter or the laws enacted thereunder.

This provision in revised Article 11 (2) (c) must be read and interpreted together with revised Articles 39-50 which deal in greater detail with measures to be taken by the United Nations to maintain or restore peace or to ensure compliance with the Charter and the laws enacted by the General Assembly. These measures include provisional measures (Article 40), economic and diplomatic sanctions (Article 41), and the employment of the United Nations Peace Force (Article 42). The revised text of these three Articles would greatly strengthen the powers of the United Nations in this field and provide more effective procedures for the application of the various measures. In particular, the new text would make it mandatory on the United Nations to take these measures in the serious contingencies envisaged by Chapter VII. Under these circumstances the competent organs of the United Nations would be bound to take action; they would be *required* to decide upon the measures to be taken instead of merely having the option to adopt such measures.

The basic responsibility under the revised Chapter VII for enforcement measures against nations as such would be in the General Assembly, and the new Executive Council would act only as an arm of the Assembly and under

42

its direction and control. All the principal decisions would ordinarily be made by the Assembly and the Council's power to direct any enforcement action would be limited to temporary action in emergency cases.

While the *main provisions* on such enforcement measures are set forth in Chapter VII, it would still be necessary to enact appropriate laws "defining the conditions" under which the various measures provided for in Chapter VII may be applied. It would be the duty of the General Assembly to enact these laws. Thus the Assembly would determine the circumstances under which the various measures would be taken, so as to put the world on notice that the occurrence of certain events would bring about immediate action by the United Nations. Such approval in advance by the Assembly of general plans of action to be applied in various sets of circumstances would also allow a broader delegation of authority to the Executive Council, enabling it to proceed on defined lines without waiting for further action by the Assembly. Moreover, such preliminary decisions by the Assembly would obviate the necessity for prolonged discussions in time of emergency and would shorten the delay in directing the necessary measures.

In defining the various circumstances in which enforcement action could be taken, the General Assembly would necessarily take into account the broadened provisions of the revised Charter, whereby enforcement measures would be required not only in case of an imminent threat to the peace, serious breach of the peace or act of aggression, but also in the event of other serious failure to comply with the revised Charter and the laws and regulations enacted thereunder. Thus action might be necessary to remedy serious situations resulting from persistent refusal to permit inspections, from denial of access to bases or facilities leased by the United Nations, or from interference with the arrest of persons who have violated laws enacted by the United Nations.

By revised Article 11 (2) (c), the General Assembly would have power to enact appropriate laws "establishing the general rules" as to the application of enforcement measures. Under this provision, the Assembly could authorize plans for the coming into effect of economic sanctions, such as an embargo on exports to any nation violating the revised Charter. Such plans could also provide for proper coordination of the measures to be taken, for the prevention of evasion by nations or individuals, and for assistance to cooperating nations confronted with special economic problems arising from the carrying out of economic sanctions (see revised Article 50).

Under revised Article 11 (2) (c), the General Assembly could also define the circumstances under which the United Nations Peace Force could be employed for the enforcement of sanctions, including the conditions under which the Peace Force would be restricted to preliminary measures as distinguished from the stronger measures which might be called for in the most extreme case.

Sanctions against individuals. The fourth proposed legislative power of the General Assembly (in (2) (d) of revised Article 11) is to enact appropriate laws defining the "acts or omissions of individuals or private organizations" which "shall be deemed offenses against the United Nations". This power is based upon the premise that in certain cases of violation of the revised

43

Charter, or of the laws supplementary thereto, action should be taken not against nations but against individuals.

While it is true that in case of a large-scale defiance of the authority of the United Nations by the government of a nation sanctions against the nation itself might be necessary under revised Article 11 (2) (c) and under Chapter VII, such actions should be avoided whenever possible. Instead, direct steps should be taken, whenever possible, only against those individuals who have violated the revised Charter or the laws of the United Nations. For, as long as it is possible to prevent an armed conflict by prompt action against a few dangerous individuals, such action is certainly preferable to sanctions against an entire nation.

The power to act against individual offenders is appropriate not only if an individual unlawfully participates in military action, but also if an individual defies the regulations with respect to disarmament, as by building an arms factory or by manufacturing components of nuclear weapons, or if he obstructs proper activities of the United Nations Inspection Service or of the United Nations Peace Force.

There is no need, nor would it be practicable, to define all possible punishable offenses in the Charter itself; and it is consequently essential to confer legislative power on the General Assembly in this field. It is, however, advisable to limit the Assembly's power in this regard by defining the classes of acts or omissions which can be made punishable. This is done in the proposed subparagraph (2) (d) by limiting the authority to define "offenses against the United Nations" to four "categories" of cases where the act or omission would clearly constitute a serious defiance of the authority of the United Nations in the field of war prevention.

In connection with this power of the General Assembly to define offenses, the important provision of paragraph 3 of this revised Article, abolishing the defense of sovereign or official immunity, should be noted. In the past, proceedings against individuals guilty of offenses against the law of nations have been prevented or hampered by the defenses that heads of state enjoy sovereign immunity from prosecution, that certain of the highest officials are exempt from criminal responsibility for official acts and that subordinate officials are also exempt if they act pursuant to orders of their government or of a superior. If, however, there is to be an effective system of individual responsibility for violation of what amounts to world law against breaches of the peace and the maintenance of national armaments, it seems essential wholly to abolish all these exemptions so that no official, high or low, can escape individual prosecution for active participation in forbidden activities or for connivance in such acts. In evident accordance with this rationale, the Draft Code of Offenses against the Peace and Security of Mankind, adopted by the International Law Commission of the United Nations in 1954, proposes the abolition of all exemptions of this character. The provisions of paragraph 3 of revised Article 11 are modeled on Articles 3 and 4 of this Draft Code. Like the Draft Code, this paragraph removes without qualification the defenses of sovereign and official immunity. It also follows the Draft Code in respect of removing the defense of compliance with a superior's order, except that paragraph 3 permits such a defense if

44

the violator can show that it was not "reasonably" possible for him to refuse obedience to such an order.

It is not sufficient merely to empower the General Assembly to define offenses. In addition the Assembly must have authority to prescribe penalties and to provide methods for apprehending offenders and for their trial and for the enforcement of penalties against duly convicted persons. All these matters are covered in subparagraph (2) (e) of this revised Article 11.

With regard to penalties, the laws enacted by the General Assembly would presumably provide fines for minor offenses and imprisonment for major crimes. There should be no power to impose the death penalty and a provision to that effect would be included in the proposed Bill of Rights (Annex VII). Excessive bail and any cruel and unusual punishment, including excessive fines, would also be prohibited by the Bill of Rights.

The apprehension of alleged violators presents a difficult problem. For this purpose it will plainly be necessary for the strengthened United Nations to have *some* civil police force of its own. And yet it is advisable that such a force be relatively small. What is required, therefore, is a series of collaborative arrangements with all the nations whereby they would themselves arrest the alleged violator and turn him over to United Nations custody or would at least assist the United Nations civil police in arresting him. Subparagraph (2) (e) of this revised Article consequently calls not only for a United Nations civil police, but also for "arrangements" with national authorities. The numerical limit of this civil police force (10,000) and its specific functions are set forth in Part D of Annex III, which also establishes the procedures for making the proposed "arrangements" with national authorities.

The offenders would be tried before the regional tribunals of the United Nations, established under paragraph 3 of revised Article 93 and Part D of Annex III; and by this revised Article 11 (2) (e) the General Assembly is given the power to enact appropriate laws "establishing procedures for the trial of such individuals" before the regional tribunals. As provided in Annex III, decisions of these tribunals could be appealed to the International Court of Justice in cases of special importance.

Finally, it is necessary to make provision for the enforcement of judgments rendered by United Nations tribunals; and consequently revised Article 11 (2) (e) empowers the General Assembly to enact appropriate laws "providing adequate means for the enforcement of penalties". Machinery could thus be created for the collection of fines, and a United Nations court official could be appointed to sequester property under warrant whenever necessary. A few United Nations places of detention for serious offenders would also have to be provided.

Laws enacted pursuant to the authority thus conferred should provide sufficient means for the enforcement of an effective system of world law within the limited field of war prevention. On the other hand, it will be important to provide also against the possibility of abuse of power by the police and prosecuting authorities of the United Nations. To this end guarantees of fair trial, including the right to counsel, the right to be confronted with adverse witnesses, etc., are included in the proposed Bill of Rights (Annex VII).

Agreements to support United Nations laws and decisions. Paragraph 4 of revised Article 11 contains a pledge by member Nations "to accept and carry out the laws and regulations enacted by the General Assembly under paragraph 2 of this Article", and "the decisions of the Assembly made under this revised Charter including the Annexes". The present Charter contains a provision of this sort only with respect to decisions of the Security Council (Article 25), since only that Council can now make any binding decision.

As already noted, however, the primary responsibility for the maintenance of peace would, under the revised Charter, be transferred to the General Assembly, which would have power not only to make binding "decisions", but also, within strictly defined limits, to enact binding "laws and regulations" on the subject (paragraph 2 of revised Article 11). It is necessary, therefore, to broaden the obligation of the member Nations so as to include *both* the decisions made by the Assembly and those made by the Executive Council (under revised Article 25). In addition, it is proposed that this obligation shall extend to the laws and regulations enacted by the Assembly.

Both in paragraph 4 of revised Article 11 and in the new Article 25 (with respect to decisions of the Executive Council), provision has been made for a new right to test by appeal the validity of laws, regulations and decisions. It is fair and necessary to offset the increase in the obligations of member Nations by providing careful safeguards against an extension of these obligations into areas not contemplated in the Charter. Whenever, therefore, a member Nation believes that a law, regulation or decision is invalid, it would be entitled to bring the question before the International Court of Justice. But to make sure that such a challenge does not impede the orderly functioning of the United Nations, it is provided that "the contested law, regulation or decision shall nevertheless be carried out", unless the General Assembly or the Court shall permit a stay of execution during the Court's consideration of the appeal. In this way, both the interests of a complaining nation and of the United Nations would be properly safeguarded.

The above relates only to the obligation to carry out United Nations laws and decisions which would be assumed by every member Nation merely by virtue of its ratification of the revised Charter. However, as mentioned in the comments on revised Articles 2 and 3, it is also essential that any *nonmember nation*, although not obligated to carry out all United Nations laws and decisions, shall at least be bound to comply with the requirements of the disarmament plan and with the measures necessary to its enforcement. And since any nonmember nation would not be automatically bound in this respect, it would be advisable for the United Nations to have a special agreement with any such nonmember, whereby it would be bound to collaborate in the carrying out of the disarmament plan to the same extent as a member Nation. Accordingly, paragraph 5 of revised Article 11 directs the negotiation of agreements of this sort with every nonmember nation. It also provides for the remote contingency that a nonmember nation might refuse to make such an agreement, in which case the General Assembly would be required to decide

46

upon the necessary measures to enforce compliance with the disarmament plan even without an agreement.

Corresponding to the obligations to be accepted by nonmember nations under such agreements, paragraph 5 provides that the United Nations shall guarantee to them the same rights and remedies granted to member Nations and their citizens by the revised Charter with respect to the enforcement of the disarmament plan. This guarantee would include the right to contest the contitutional validity of any law, regulation or decision of the General Assembly or Executive Council, but would, of course, exclude the right to send Representatives to the Assembly.

Article 12

1. *While the Security Council is exercising in respect of any dispute or situation the functions assigned to it in the present Charter, the General Assembly shall not make any recommendation with regard to that dispute or situation unless the Security Council so requests.*

1. The General Assembly may discuss any questions relating to the maintenance of international peace and security brought before it by any *member Nation,* or by the *Executive* Council, or by a *nation* which is not a *member* of the United Nations in accordance with Article 35, paragraph 2, and may make recommendations with regard to any such questions to the *nation* or *nations* concerned or to the *Executive* Council or to both. Any such question on which action is necessary *may* be referred to the *Executive* Council by the General Assembly either before or after discussion.

2. *The Secretary-General, with the consent of the Security Council, shall notify the General Assembly at each session of any matters relative to the maintenance of international peace and security which are being dealt with by the Security Council and shall similarly notify the General Assembly, or the Members of the United Nations if the General Assembly is not in session, immediately the Security Council ceases to deal with such matters.*

2. The General Assembly may call the attention of the *Executive* Council to *disputes or* situations which are likely to endanger international peace and security.

Comment. As elsewhere noted, it is proposed (in revised Articles 23 and 24) to abolish the present Security Council and to replace it by a new organ to be called the Executive Council, which would be chosen by and act as an agent of the General Assembly; and under revised Article 11, the Assembly would take over the primary responsibility for the maintenance of peace, now entrusted to the Security Council. The new Executive Council, superseding the Security Council, would, therefore, function in this field not as an independent organ, but rather as an instrumentality of the Assembly. Consequently, the present Article 12, providing that the Assembly may not act on matters pending before the Security Council, becomes inapplicable and is wholly omitted.

This elimination permits the transfer to Article 12 of the powers of the General Assembly, now contained in paragraphs 2 and 3 of Article 11, to discuss any questions relating to the maintenance of peace and to make recommendations on that subject. By this rearrangement the Assembly's powers, on the one hand to legislate and on the other to discuss and recommend, are separated. The new Article 11 is confined to the Assembly's specific powers of legislation and the new Article 12 to its powers of discussion and recommendation.

At the same time, certain drafting changes are necessary. In view of the proposed substitution of the Executive Council for the present Security Council, four references to the "Security Council" in the former text have been changed to the "Executive Council".

A further change eliminates the phrase "except as provided in Article 12" from the provision authorizing the General Assembly to make recommendations as to the maintenance of peace. This restriction is no longer appropriate in view of the proposed transfer to the Assembly of the primary responsibility for the maintenance of peace.

Another result of this transfer of responsibility is the change from "shall" to "may" in the sentence relating to the reference by the General Assembly to the Executive Council of any question as to the maintenance of peace on which action is necessary. The former text made it obligatory for the Assembly to refer any such question to the Security Council. This was logical when the Security Council had the primary responsibility for the maintenance of peace. But with the proposed transfer of this function to the Assembly and the substitution of the Executive Council for the Security Council, the obligatory provision is plainly inapplicable. There is substituted the merely permissive phrase that the Assembly "may", if it wishes, refer the matter to its new agent, the Executive Council. In the usual case the Assembly would, under this provision, doubtless refer any situation *requiring action* for the maintenance of peace to the Executive Council. At the same time there is nothing in this provision to prevent the Assembly from dealing with the situation directly or from referring the matter to some organ other than the Executive Council or to a body specially constituted to deal with the particular problem.

Article 13

1. The General Assembly shall initiate studies and make recommendations for the purpose of:

a. promoting international cooperation in the political field and encouraging the progressive development of international law and its codification;

b. promoting international cooperation in the economic, social, cultural, educational, and health fields, and assisting in the realization of human rights and fundamental freedoms for all without distinction as to race, sex, language, or religion.

2. The further responsibilities, functions, and powers of the General Assembly with respect to matters mentioned in paragraph 1 (b) above are set forth in Chapters IX and X.

Comment. No changes are proposed in the above Article.

It should be noted, however, that the scope of the General Assembly's functions and influence under this Article would doubtless be greatly increased by the availability of the much larger funds which could be provided under the revenue plan set forth in Annex V. (See also revised Article 17 and the comment thereon.) Under the plan proposed in Annex V, there would be reliable means of raising revenue which would enable the Economic and Social Council and various specialized agencies to command funds far exceeding the meager budgets under which they have been obliged to operate in the absence of any adequate revenue system. This new revenue plan would enable not only the Economic and Social Council itself, but also such agencies as the Food and Agriculture Organization and the World Health Organization vastly to extend the scope and usefulness of their work. Similarly, more funds would be available for the codification of international law and the work of the International Law Commission might thus be speeded up.

Article 14

Subject to the provisions of Article 12, the General Assembly may recommend measures for the peaceful adjustment of any situation, regardless of origin, which it deems likely to impair the general welfare or friendly relations among nations, including situations resulting from a violation of the provisions of *the present* Charter setting forth the Purposes and Principles of the United Nations.

1. The General Assembly may recommend measures for the peaceful adjustment of any situation, regardless of origin, which it deems likely to impair the general welfare or friendly relations among nations, including situations resulting from a violation of the provisions of *this revised* Charter setting forth the Purposes and Principles of the United Nations.

2. Each member Nation undertakes to give prompt and due consideration to any recommendation addressed to such nation by the General Assembly under Articles

49

*12 and 13 and this Article, and to
report as soon as practicable what
action it has taken with reference
thereto, or, if no action has been
taken, its reasons therefor.*

Comment. The first change in this Article, namely, the omission of the introductory phrase, "Subject to the provisions of Article 12", is intended to broaden the power of the General Assembly to recommend measures for "peaceful change", i.e., for the peaceful adjustment of situations likely to impair the general welfare of the nations or friendly relations among them. In view of the proposed transfer to the Assembly of the primary responsibility for the maintenance of peace, it is no longer appropriate to prevent the Assembly from making such recommendations simply because another organ may also be dealing with the particular situation.

The purpose of the second change, embodied in the proposed new paragraph 2, is to provide a more adequate constitutional basis for the obligation of member Nations to give consideration to the General Assembly's recommendations. This is done in two ways. *First,* it is proposed to require the member Nations to undertake "to give prompt and due consideration to any recommendation addressed to such nation by the General Assembly under Articles 12 and 13 and this Article". *Second,* it is proposed to impose an explicit obligation "to report as soon as practicable" as to what action the nations concerned have taken with reference to the recommendation.

If a member Nation should find it inadvisable to take any action, it ought at least to report its reasons therefor. Its statement of reasons would then be subject to the scrutiny of the General Assembly and might lead to new recommendations taking into account the difficulties raised by such statement.

No sanctions are provided for failure merely to comply with recommendations made under Articles 12, 13 and 14. But it should be noted that if a refusal to comply with any such recommendation should result in a much more serious situation, i.e., one "likely to endanger the maintenance of international peace and security", the General Assembly could utilize its powers under Chapter VI, including its limited authority (under revised Articles 36 and 94) to refer the situation to the World Conciliation Board or to the International Court of Justice or to the World Equity Tribunal and, under careful safeguards, to enforce the decision of the Court or the recommendation of the Tribunal.

Article 15

1. The General Assembly shall receive and consider annual and special reports from the *Security* Council; these reports shall include an account of the measures that the *Security* Council has decided upon or taken to maintain international peace and security.

1. The General Assembly shall receive and consider annual and special reports from the *Executive* Council; these reports shall include an account of the measures that the *Executive* Council has decided upon or taken to maintain international peace and security.

2. The General Assembly shall receive and consider reports from the other organs of the United Nations.

2. The General Assembly shall receive and consider reports from the other organs of the United Nations.

Comment. The only changes in this Article are the substitution in two places of "Executive" for "Security" Council.

As already noted the status of the new Executive Council would be very different from that of the Security Council. Instead of being an independent body like the Security Council, the Executive Council would be in substance the agent of the General Assembly, since it would be chosen by the Assembly, would be subject to the Assembly's constant direction and even subject to discharge by the Assembly if it no longer commanded the Assembly's confidence.

The competence of the Executive Council would also be different from that of the Security Council. The competence of the new body would be broader in that it would include responsibility for "ensuring compliance with this revised Charter and the laws and regulations enacted thereunder" (see revised Article 24). It would be narrower in that its responsibility for the maintenance of peace would no longer be primary, since under the revised Charter that "primary" responsibility would be in the Assembly and the Executive Council's function in that regard would be as an instrument of the Assembly. Nevertheless, the *principal function* of the new Council would be the maintenance of peace. Consequently, it remains appropriate to continue the requirement that the Executive Council, like the Security Council, must include in its reports "an account of the measures" which it "has decided upon or taken to maintain international peace and security."

In this connection there should be noted the suggested changes in paragraph 3 of revised Article 24. One change would require the Executive Council to submit to the General Assembly such special reports as the Assembly may call for. This change would impose an obligation upon the Executive Council to submit such reports, in contrast to the present provision of Article 24, which leaves to the Security Council the option whether it shall report. The other change would require the Executive Council to report immediately to the Assembly on any emergency action taken by it under Chapter VII; and in such a case the Assembly, if not then in session, would be convened immediately.

As to paragraph 2 there is no reason to change the provision with respect to the receipt and consideration by the General Assembly of reports from other organs of the United Nations.

Article 16

The General Assembly shall perform such functions with respect to the international trusteeship system as are assigned to it under Chapters XII and XIII, including the approval of the trusteeship agreements *for areas not designated as strategic.*

The General Assembly shall perform such functions with respect to the international trusteeship system as are assigned to it under Chapters *XI,* XII and XIII, including the approval of the trusteeship agreements.

Comment. The first change in this Article is to eliminate the words "for areas not designated as strategic." This change is necessary in view of the proposed substitution of the Executive Council for the Security Council and the proposal to vest in the General Assembly the "primary responsibility" for the maintenance of peace. Under the present Charter (Article 83), the Security Council, by reason of this primary responsibility, has the function of approving trusteeship agreements for "strategic areas". But in consequence of the proposed transfer of this "primary responsibility" to the General Assembly, there is no longer any reason to distinguish between trusteeship agreements in general and such agreements relative to "strategic areas". It is proposed, therefore, to make the approval of both types of trusteeship agreements the function of the General Assembly (revised Articles 83 and 85).

The second proposed change is the addition of a reference to Chapter XI which deals with non-self-governing territories. The reason for this reference is that under revised Article 73 (and revised Article 87) important new functions have been conferred upon the General Assembly and its agent, the Trusteeship Council.

It should be noted also that certain important changes are proposed in Chapters XII and XIII with respect to the functions of the General Assembly in the trusteeship field.

Article 17

1. The General Assembly shall consider and approve the *budget* of the *Organization.*

2. *The expenses of the Organization shall be borne by the Members as apportioned by the General Assembly.*

3. The General Assembly shall consider and approve any financial and budgetary arrangements with specialized agencies referred to in Article 57 *and* shall examine the *administrative* budgets of such specialized agencies *with a view to making recommendations to the agencies concerned.*

1. The General Assembly shall consider and approve the *annual budgets* of the *United Nations.*

2. *The General Assembly shall have power to enact such laws and regulations as are authorized by Annex V of this revised Charter relating to the provision of sufficient and reliable revenues to meet the budgets of the United Nations through collaborative arrangements with the member Nations.*

3. *The General Assembly shall have power to enact such laws and regulations as are authorized by Annex V of this revised Charter relating to the borrowing of money on the credit of the United Nations.*

4. The General Assembly shall consider and approve any financial

52

and budgetary arrangements with specialized agencies referred to in Article 57, shall examine *and approve* the budgets of such specialized agencies, *and shall allocate to them in the annual budgets of the United Nations such funds as it deems necessary for their expenses.*

5. *All decisions of the General Assembly pursuant to this Article shall be made by a majority of all the Representatives then in office, whether or not present and voting, which majority shall in respect of votes on the adoption of the annual budgets of the United Nations include a majority of the Representatives then in office, whether or not present and voting, from the member Nations which would have the ten largest quotas of the budget then voted upon.*

Comment. The proposed Annex V embodies a carefully safeguarded plan for the raising of revenues to assure the fulfillment by the United Nations of its enlarged responsibilities, including the maintenance of such new organs or agencies as the United Nations Peace Force, the Inspection Service, the Nuclear Energy Authority, the Outer Space Agency and the World Development Authority. The maintenance of these new bodies, along with all the other organs and agencies, would necessarily require such large sums that it would be impracticable to depend upon the present system whereby the national authorities of every member Nation must annually make a new contribution. Instead, there is proposed a system of collaborative arrangements between the United Nations and the respective member Nations whereby specified national revenues would be assigned in advance for each nation's allotted portion of the annual budgets of the United Nations. Annex V contains an extended outline of this proposed plan which would be set forth in detailed text, just as Annex I provides in detail for the disarmament process and Annex II for the United Nations Peace Force.

Consequently this revised Article 17 is framed, like the corresponding legislative powers relating to disarmament and the Peace Force, so as broadly to empower the General Assembly to enact such laws and regulations "as are authorized by Annex V". The purpose in so doing is, on the one hand, to give the Assembly ample power to enact such legislation as is affirmatively necessary to carry out the revenue plan and, on the other hand, to incorporate by reference the constitutional limitations on that authority which are embodied in Annex V. For example, that Annex would provide that the budget of the United Nations in any year shall not exceed two per cent of the estimated gross world product in that year; and it would also provide a careful formula for the determination of the proportionate share of each annual budget to be contributed by the people of each member Nation.

Since the borrowing of money is usually regarded as a function separate from the raising of funds for current expenses, paragraph 3 of this revised Article confers explicit authority on the General Assembly to enact such laws and regulations "as are authorized by Annex V" with relation to the borrowing of funds. Here again the effect of the reference to Annex V is not only to confer the affirmative authority to borrow, but also to incorporate a constitutional limit on the total United Nations debt outstanding at the end of any year, i.e., an amount not exceeding, except in case of grave emergency, five per cent of the estimated world product for that year.

Paragraph 4 of this revised Article 17 would greatly broaden the control of the General Assembly over the activities of all the specialized agencies, not only by requiring that the separate budgets of these agencies be approved by the Assembly, but also by making the general budget of the United Nations the main source of their funds. At present these agencies are fairly independent with respect to both their policies and their finances; and, although the Assembly can examine their budgets, it can do no more than make recommendations to them concerning their finances. This power has proved to be insufficient to effect proper coordination of the activities of the specialized agencies, and a drastic change is necessary in order to forestall even greater difficulties in the future. This change would be accomplished through the proposed provision that the funds of these agencies shall no longer be separately collected by them from member Nations, but shall be provided by the United Nations itself out of its general budget. Under this new arrangement the specialized agencies would presumably receive far larger sums than they now have and could accomplish much more for the economic and social advancement of the world's people.

Paragraph 5 relates to the required voting majority on the financial questions arising under this Article. The proposal is that decisions on all such questions shall require a special majority of all the Representatives then in office whether or not present or voting; and that in respect of the adoption of the annual budgets of the United Nations, this special majority must include a majority of the Representatives from the ten member Nations which would be called upon to supply the largest revenue quotas for the budget which is being voted upon. This latter provision is proposed because it seems only fair that the nations which would furnish the largest amounts for a particular budget should have a major voice in determining the amount of that budget.

More detailed comment regarding this all-important revenue plan is contained in Annex V.

VOTING

Article 18

1. *Each member of the General Assembly* shall have one vote.

2. Decisions of the General Assembly on important questions shall be made by a *two-thirds* majority of *the members present and voting*. These questions shall include: *recommendations* with respect to the maintenance of international peace and security, the election of *non-permanent* members of the *Security* Council, the election of the members of the Economic and Social Council, the election of members of the Trusteeship Council in accordance with *paragraph 1 (c) of* Article 86, *the admission of new Members to the United Nations,* the suspension of the rights and privileges of membership, *the expulsion of Members, questions relating to the operation of the trusteeship system, and budgetary questions.*

1. *In the General Assembly the Representatives shall vote as individuals, and each Representative* shall have one vote.

2. Decisions of the General Assembly on important questions, *other than questions concerning which special majorities are specifically provided for in this revised Charter,* shall be made by a majority of *all the Representatives then in office, whether or not present or voting.* These questions shall include: *action* with respect to the *pacific settlement of disputes and the* maintenance of international peace and security, *in accordance with Articles 33 through 44, Articles 50 through 53 and Annexes I and II; the enactment of legislation, in accordance with Article 11;* the election of *the* members of the *Executive* Council *and their discharge by a vote of lack of confidence, in* accordance with Article 23; the election of the members of the Economic and Social Council *and their discharge by a vote of lack of confidence, in accordance with Article 61;* the election of members of the Trusteeship Council *and their discharge by a vote of lack of confidence,* in accordance with Article 86; *the taking of measures to give effect to judgments of the International Court of Justice and to recommendations of the World Equity Tribunal, in accordance with Article 94; and* the suspension *and restoration* of the rights and

privileges of membership, *in accordance with Article 5.*

3. Decisions on other questions, including the determination of additional categories of questions to be decided by *a two-thirds majority,* shall be made by a majority of the *members* present and voting.

3. Decisions on other questions, including the determination of additional categories of questions to be decided by *the special majority provided for in paragraph 2,* shall be made by a majority of the *Representatives* present and voting.

Comment. Radical changes in this Article 18 are necessary in order to give effect to the new conception of the United Nations embodied in other proposed changes. Under the present Charter, the United Nations is an organization of states based upon the principle of "sovereign equality"; and it was consistent with that conception to allot one vote to each member Nation irrespective of its population or power. Thus the Soviet Union with a population in 1960 of over 210,000,000 has no greater voice in the General Assembly than Albania with a population of less than 1,600,000; and the United States with a population more than one thousand times that of Iceland is entitled to cast only the same vote as the latter.

Under such a system of voting, it is natural, as already emphasized, that only powers of discussion and recommendation could be conferred on the General Assembly. For it would be unreasonable to expect large and powerful nations to be bound by decisions of a body in which they might be outvoted by a group of countries having only a small proportion of the world's population and power.

Under the proposed amendments, however, the structure and functions of the United Nations would be very different from those provided in the present Charter. While the additional powers of the new United Nations would be restricted and carefully safeguarded, the revised Charter would, nevertheless, embody definite limitations of national sovereignty in the interest of peace. Most of these limitations would be carefully spelled out by "constitutional legislation" in the text of the revised Charter itself (including the Annexes), so that the scope of the General Assembly's authority would be much less than might be imagined. Nevertheless, certain powers and responsibilities of considerable consequence would necessarily be entrusted to the Assembly. Besides the "primary responsibility" for peace these would include some definite legislative and financial powers (see revised Articles 11 and 17 and the comments thereon). It is essential therefore to have a new voting system in the Assembly, since the larger nations would certainly not consent to be bound by decisions, even within the Assembly's strictly limited field, if every nation had the same vote irrespective of population or any other factor.

As a solution for this problem, the new system of representation set forth in revised Article 9 is proposed, under which Representatives would be allotted by categories measured by population, with the proviso that every member Nation shall have at least one Representative and that no nation shall have more than thirty.

This leaves, however, several questions as to the mode of voting, the required quorum and the majorities necessary for decisions. The question of the required quorum is dealt with in revised Article 19; the others in the present Article.

As above noted (revised Article 9), it is proposed wholly to abolish the present system whereby each member state has a single vote, substituting therefor the system of apportionment of votes from one to thirty. In paragraph 1 of this revised Article 18 it is further proposed that the Representatives from each member Nation shall vote as individuals, each of them having a single vote. It is true that the Representatives of a particular nation would tend to vote together on issues of great importance to that nation; and it would be unwise to prohibit such a practice by constitutional provision. It can, however, be expected that there would develop in the course of time a spirit of representing the interests of the world as a whole rather than those of particular nations; and that the Representatives would more and more tend to vote in accordance with their individual judgment as to the best interests of all the people of the world, as in the case of national parliaments where the interests of the whole nation are usually regarded as of no less importance than the interests of a particular section or group.

Paragraphs 2 and 3 deal with the question of the required majority for Assembly decisions.

By revised paragraph 2, it is proposed in respect of "important" questions to substitute for the present requirement of a two-thirds majority of the member states present and voting the requirement of an absolute majority of the individual Representatives, i.e., "a majority of all the Representatives then in office, whether or not present or voting." The effect of this change would be to provide more adequate safeguards against possible decisions reflecting only a minority opinion of the world's people.

The present system of voting by member states, with no restriction on abstentions, permits the making of important decisions by even a minority of the member states, which minority in turn may represent only a very small proportion of the world's population. For example, some decisions of consequence have been made with less than one third of the member states taking a position, the remainder being recorded as abstaining. With the enlarged powers of the General Assembly under the proposed revision, it is essential to prevent any such possibility and to take precautions that important decisions shall reflect a clear majority opinion. This is done by the requirement of a majority of *all* the Representatives, since it would be virtually impossible to obtain such a vote in the Assembly which did not reflect a strong consensus of world opinion.

Concerning the definition of "important" questions, the principal changes are: (a) to include legislation and decisions relating to the pacific settlement of disputes and the maintenance of peace as authorized by revised Article 11, Articles 33 through 44, Articles 50 through 53 and Annexes I and II; (b) to include decisions under revised Article 94 relating to the enforcement of judgments of the International Court of Justice and of recommendations of the World Equity Tribunal which have been previously approved by the special majority provided for in revised Article 36; and (c) to exclude mere recommendations of any character. Other changes in the definition are con-

57

sequential upon proposed alterations elsewhere in the Charter, as for example the election of the members of the new Executive Council and their replacement, instead of the election of nonpermanent members of the present Security Council.

In addition to the special majority required on these "important" questions, the revised Charter elsewhere provides for some even larger special majorities; for example, the special majority under revised Article 36 relating to the approval of recommendations of the World Equity Tribunal, that called for by revised Article 108 with reference to amendments to the Charter and that required by Article 17 with respect to budgetary matters.

The revised paragraph 3, like the former paragraph 3, permits decisions of all questions, except those mentioned in paragraph 2 as "important" and those other questions on which even larger special majorities are provided for, by a simple majority of the Representatives "present and voting".

It could reasonably be expected that decisions of the General Assembly arrived at through this combination of the new system of representation, the method of individual voting by the Representatives and the requirements as to a quorum and as to special majorities, would reflect the clearly preponderant opinion of the world community.

Article 19

A Member of the United Nations which is in arrears in the payment of its financial contributions to the Organization shall have no vote in the General Assembly if the amount of its arrears equals or exceeds the amount of the contributions due from it for the preceding two full years. The General Assembly may, nevertheless, permit such a Member to vote if it is satisfied that the failure to pay is due to conditions beyond the control of the Member.

A majority of all the Representatives shall constitute a quorum to do business; but a smaller number may adjourn from day to day.

Comment. The present Article 19, dealing with the matter of arrears of member Nations, is wholly omitted in view of its inapplicability to the proposed new budgetary and revenue system. The space thus left open is utilized to cover the question of a quorum in the General Assembly.

Under the present Charter there is no provision whatever relating to a quorum in the General Assembly. As above noted, it has been thought wise, in view of the proposed new powers of the Assembly, to provide (in revised Article 18) that on important questions there shall be a vote of all the Representatives whether or not present or voting. For similar reasons it is deemed best to provide that no business of any sort except adjournment from day to day shall be transacted unless a majority of all the Representatives are actually present.

58

PROCEDURE

Article 20

The General Assembly shall meet in regular annual sessions and in such special sessions as occasion may require. Special sessions shall be convoked by the Secretary-General at the request of the *Security* Council or of a majority of the *Members of the United Nations.*

The General Assembly shall meet in regular annual sessions, *beginning on the third Tuesday of September,* and in such special sessions as occasion may require. Special sessions shall be convoked by the Secretary-General at the *written* request of the *Executive* Council, *or of the Standing Committee of the General Assembly on the Peace Enforcement Agencies,* or of a majority of the *member Nations, or of one third of all the Representatives in the General Assembly.*

Comment. The provision that the General Assembly shall meet annually and may have such special sessions as occasion may require is left intact, but with a further provision specifying the third Tuesday in September as the date on which the annual sessions shall begin.

The provision that special sessions may be convoked at the request of a majority of the member Nations (i.e., of their governments) is left intact; and, corresponding to the present provision that special sessions may be convoked at the request of the Security Council, provision is made for their convocation at the request of the new Executive Council. In addition, however, provision is made for the convoking of special sessions at the request of the proposed standing committee of the Assembly which would have the important function of watching over and reporting upon the peace enforcement agencies (see revised Article 22 and Annexes I and II); and at the request of one third of all the Representatives in the General Assembly.

These alternative methods would, it is believed, make ample provision for convoking a special session in the event of any real emergency.

Article 21

The General Assembly shall adopt its own rules of procedure. It shall elect its President for each session.

Comment. No change is proposed in this Article.

Article 22

The General Assembly may establish such subsidiary organs as it deems necessary for the performance of its functions.

1. The General Assembly may establish such subsidiary organs as it deems necessary for the performance of its functions.

59

2. In particular, the General Assembly shall establish a Standing Committee on the Peace Enforcement Agencies, with the functions set forth in Annexes I and II, and a Standing Committee on Budget and Finance, with the functions set forth in Annex V.

3. The Standing Committee on the Peace Enforcement Agencies shall consist of seventeen Representatives. They shall be elected by the General Assembly within thirty days from the beginning of the first regular session of each newly chosen Assembly, and shall serve during the four-year term of the Assembly by which they are elected and until their successors are elected by a new Assembly. In electing the members of the Committee, the Assembly shall apply the following formula and method: (a) eight of the members of this Committee shall be chosen from among the Representatives of those member Nations which, pursuant to Article 9, are entitled to fifteen or more Representatives in the Assembly; (b) the remaining nine members of the Committee shall be chosen from among the Representatives of those member Nations which, pursuant to Article 9, are entitled to less than fifteen Representatives in the Assembly and of the non-self-governing and trust territories; (c) no two members of the Committee shall be nationals of the same nation; (d) no member of the Committee shall be a national of any nation which has one of its nationals on the Military Staff Committee or the Inspection

Commission or the Nuclear Energy Commission or the Outer Space Commission; (e) subject to the foregoing limitations, the Committee shall be chosen with due regard to equitable geographical distribution.

4. The Standing Committee on Budget and Finance shall consist of seventeen Representatives. They shall be elected by the General Assembly within thirty days from the beginning of the first regular session of each newly chosen Assembly, and shall serve during the four-year term of the Assembly by which they are elected and until their successors are elected by a new Assembly. In electing the members of the Committee, the Assembly shall apply the following formula and method: (a) eight of the members of this Committee shall be chosen from among the Representatives of the member Nations which at the time the Committee is elected have the eight largest quotas for the budget of the United Nations, except that in choosing the first Committee the Assembly shall elect a Representative from each of the eight member Nations which in the judgment of the Assembly are likely to have the eight largest quotas for the first budget under this revised Charter; (b) the remaining nine members of the Committee shall be chosen from among the Representatives of all the other member Nations and the non-self-governing and trust territories; (c) no two members of the Committee shall be nationals of the same na-

tion; (d) subject to the foregoing limitations, the Committee shall be chosen with due regard to equitable geographical distribution.

5. Vacancies in the membership of these Standing Committees shall be filled by the General Assembly by the selection of a Representative from the same member Nation or non-self-governing or trust territory in the representation of which the vacancy has occurred.

6. The General Assembly may by a vote of lack of confidence discharge either of these Standing Committees as a whole, provided: (a) that the members of the Committee so discharged shall continue to serve until their successors are elected; (b) that the Assembly shall proceed forthwith to the election of a new Committee; (c) that the members of the new Committee shall be elected from among the Representatives of the same member Nations or non-self-governing or trust territories which were represented on the discharged Committee; except that if the Assembly desires to replace a member of the discharged Committee who is the only Representative from a member Nation or territory, the Assembly may elect a Representative from one of the other member Nations or territories entitled to either one or two Representatives in the Assembly and which would not otherwise be represented on the Committee; (d) that the members of the new Committee shall be elected by the same formula and method provided for in para-

graphs 3 or 4 of this Article as the case may be; and (e) that the new Committee shall serve, unless sooner discharged, until the regular quadrennial election of the Committee following the quadrennial election of the Assembly.

7. No member of either of these Standing Committees shall simultaneously be a member of the other Standing Committee, or a member of the Executive Council or the Economic and Social Council or the Trusteeship Council.

8. The members of these Standing Committees shall, during their period of service thereon, receive additional compensation to be fixed by the General Assembly.

Comment. No changes are proposed in this Article with respect to the general power of the General Assembly to establish subsidiary organs. Under this provision, the present Assembly has established many important committees and commissions to deal with special problems and to supervise the carrying out of its resolutions. For example, this provision formed the basis for the Commission on Korea (1948), the Atomic Energy Commission (1946) and the Disarmament Commission (1952). Under this provision also, the Assembly in 1947 established an Interim Committee (the "Little Assembly"), composed of representatives of all member Nations and empowered to function between sessions of the full Assembly. The present authority to establish "such subsidiary organs" as the Assembly "deems necessary" is, therefore, continued as paragraph 1 of the revised Article.

Apart from this general authority, however, it seems advisable to make mandatory the establishment of a standing "watchdog" committee of the General Assembly to aid the Assembly in its all-important function of supervising the carrying out and enforcement of the proposed plan for complete national disarmament. Moreover, the proposed United Nations revenue system makes advisable a second standing committee to aid in the preparation of the annual budgets of the United Nations and in the legislative supervision of the system. In order to make certain that these committees will be established and to give them constitutional status, it is proposed (in paragraph 2 of this revised Article) to make it obligatory on the Assembly to maintain these two standing committees. In view of their great importance, it is also deemed best to provide specifically for their composition, mode of appointment and term of service.

The proposal is that each committee shall have seventeen members chosen

63

by the General Assembly from among its own number, the committee members to be appointed by each new Assembly within thirty days after it convenes and to serve during the four-year term of that Assembly and until the appointment of their successors by the next Assembly. Definite provisions are also proposed in order to ensure well-balanced committees which would command the confidence of the Assembly itself and of the governments of the member Nations.

As to the Standing Committee on the Peace Enforcement Agencies, it is proposed (in paragraph 3) that there shall always be eight members from the large nations which, pursuant to revised Article 9, are entitled to fifteen or more Representatives; and that the other nine shall come from all the other member Nations and the non-self-governing territories. Furthermore, in order to provide the utmost assurance of the independence of this Committee, it would be provided that no member of the Committee could come from a nation which already has a national on the Military Staff Committee, the Inspection Commission, the Nuclear Energy Commission or the Outer Space Commission.

Concerning the Standing Committee on Budget and Finance, it seems fair to provide (in paragraph 4) that eight of its seventeen members shall be Representatives from the eight member Nations which are obligated to supply the largest amounts toward the budget of the United Nations, since the peoples of those nations would presumably supply considerably more than half the total annual revenue. The other nine members would be chosen from among the Representatives of the other member Nations and the non-self-governing territories.

As to both Standing Committees, it would be provided that, subject to the applicable limitations, their members shall be selected with "due regard to equitable geographical distribution"; and it would be made clear that no member Nation could have more than one of its Representatives on the same Committee at any one time.

The functions of the proposed Standing Committee on the Peace Enforcement Agencies are defined in the proposed Annexes I and II, which provide, respectively, for the disarmament plan (including the United Nations Inspection Service, the Nuclear Energy Authority and the Outer Space Agency) and for the military forces (the United Nations Peace Force) necessary to ensure compliance with the revised Charter. It is intended that this Committee shall keep a constant watch over the progress of the disarmament plan (including the operation of the inspection system) and over the organization, administration and activities of the Peace Force; and that it shall be responsible for keeping the General Assembly constantly informed on these subjects. Thus, one of this Committee's functions would be to inform the Assembly immediately of any danger of evasion, abuse or collusion in the fulfillment of the disarmament plan. It would also be empowered (by revised Article 20 and by Article 4 of Annex I and Article 3 of Annex II) to have the Assembly called into special session if an emergency arises which, in the Committee's judgment, requires prompt action by the Assembly itself.

The proposed Standing Committee on Budget and Finance is an essential part of the machinery under the proposed Annex V, which provides a careful procedure for the preparation and adoption of the annual budgets of the United Nations and for the allocation of the amounts to be supplied from the various member Nations. In these respects, Annex V would impose duties of the utmost importance on this Standing Committee, including the conduct of negotiations with each member Nation as to the national revenues to be assigned toward the payment of the particular nation's share of the budget of the United Nations from year to year.

In order to preserve the balanced composition of these two Standing Committees, special provision would be made (in paragraph 5) that in filling vacancies the General Assembly must select a Representative from the same member Nation (or non-self-governing or trust territory) whose Representative held the vacated membership.

As in the case of the Executive Council, the Economic and Social Council and the Trusteeship Council (revised Articles 23, 61 and 86), it is proposed (in paragraph 6) to empower the General Assembly to discharge either of the Standing Committees as a whole by a vote of lack of confidence, provided that a new Committee is immediately appointed and that its members are chosen from the same nations or territories and in the same manner as the discharged Committee.

In view of the nature of these Standing Committees, it is deemed essential that no member of either Committee shall simultaneously serve on the other Committee, or on any of the three Councils; and paragraph 7 so provides.

The delicate and important functions of these Standing Committees would doubtless require them to sit throughout the year; and, consequently, as in the case of the three Councils, provision is made (in paragraph 8) for additional compensation to the Representatives serving on the two Standing Committees.

CHAPTER V

THE *SECURITY* COUNCIL

THE *EXECUTIVE* COUNCIL

COMPOSITION

Article 23

1. The *Security* Council shall consist of *eleven Members of the United Nations. The Republic of China, France, the Union of Soviet Socialist Republics, the United Kingdom of Great Britain and Northern Ireland, and the United States of America shall be permanent members of the Security Council.* The General Assembly shall elect *six other Members of the United Nations to be non-permanent* members of the *Security* Council, *due regard being specially paid, in the first instance to the contribution of Members of the United Nations to the maintenance of international peace and security and to the other purposes of the Organization, and also to equitable geographical distribution.*

2. *The non-permanent members of the Security Council shall be elected for a term of two years. In the first election of the non-permanent members, however, three shall be chosen for a term of one year. A retiring member shall not be eligible for immediate re-election.*

1. The *Executive* Council shall consist of *seventeen Representatives. They shall be elected by the General Assembly within thirty days from the beginning of the first regular session of each newly chosen Assembly, and shall serve during the four-year term of the Assembly by which they are elected and until their successors are elected by a new Assembly.*

2. The General Assembly shall elect *the* members of the *Executive* Council *in accordance with the following formula and method:*

a. Each of the four member Nations which, pursuant to Article 9, are entitled to thirty Representatives in the Assembly shall have the right to have one of its Representatives elected to the Council at every quadrennial election of the Council.

b. Each of the eight member Nations which, pursuant to Article 9, are entitled to fifteen Representatives in the Assembly shall have the right to have one of its Representatives elected to the Council at every alternate quadrennial election of the Council. Prior to the first election, the Assembly shall designate the four member Nations in this category, two in Europe and two outside Europe, which shall be represented in the first Executive Council.

c. The member Nations other than the twelve mentioned in the foregoing subparagraphs (a) and (b) and the non-self-governing and trust territories under the administration of member Nations shall between them have the right to have nine of their Representatives elected to the Council at every quadrennial election of the Council. Prior to the first election and after each world census, the Assembly shall divide the member Nations and the non-self-governing and trust territories which together constitute this group into nine regional subgroups which shall be as nearly equal as possible in the number of member Nations in each subgroup. Prior to each election, the Assembly shall designate a member Nation or non-self-govern-

ing or trust territory in each subgroup which shall have the right to have one of its Representatives elected to the Council provided that: (1) in the case of a subgroup which does not include any non-self-governing or trust territory, no member Nation shall be redesignated until every other member Nation in that subgroup has been designated; and (2) that in the case of a subgroup which does include one or more non-self-governing or trust territories, no member Nation shall be redesignated until every other member Nation in that subgroup has been designated and also at least one of the non-self-governing or trust territories.

d. After the designations called for by the foregoing subparagraphs (b) and (c) have been made, the Representatives in the Assembly of the seventeen member Nations or the non-self-governing or trust territories which are entitled to have Representatives elected to the Council at the particular election, shall hold separate meetings which shall respectively nominate to the Assembly two of their own number deemed by the separate meetings best qualified to serve on the Council; provided that in the case of any such member Nation or non-self-governing or trust territory, which has only one or two Representatives, their names shall be deemed automatically nominated.

e. After the nominations called for by the foregoing subparagraph (d) have been made, the Assembly shall elect to serve on the Council one of the two nominees of each of the seventeen member Nations or non-self-governing or trust territories which are then entitled to have one of its Representatives on the Council, taking into account the personal qualifications of each nominee for service on the Council, except that if any of such seventeen member Nations or non-self-governing or trust territories has only one Representative in the Assembly, that Representative shall be deemed automatically elected.

3. Each member of the Security Council shall have one representative.

3. Vacancies in the membership of the Executive Council shall be filled in the following manner: The Representatives in the General Assembly of the member Nation or non-self-governing or trust territory in whose representation on the Council the vacancy has occurred shall nominate two of their own number, and thereupon the General Assembly shall elect one of the two nominees, taking into account the personal qualifications of each nominee for service on the Council; provided that in the case of any such member Nation or non-self-governing or trust territory which has only one or two Representatives their names shall be deemed automatically nominated, and in the case of any such member Nation or non-self-governing or trust territory which has only one Representative in the Assembly that Representative shall be deemed automatically elected.

4. The General Assembly may by a vote of lack of confidence discharge the Executive Council as a whole, provided: (a) that the members of the Council so discharged

69

shall continue to serve until their successors are elected; (b) that the Assembly shall proceed forthwith to the election of a new Council; (c) that the members of the new Council shall be elected from among the Representatives in the Assembly of the same member Nations or non-self-governing or trust territories which were represented on the discharged Council; except that if the Assembly desires to replace a member of the discharged Council who is the only Representative from a member Nation or territory, the Assembly may elect a Representative from one of the other member Nations or territories entitled to either one or two Representatives in the Assembly and which would not otherwise be represented on the Council; (d) that the members of the new Council shall be nominated and elected by the same formula and method as called for by paragraph 2 of this Article; and (e) that the new Council shall serve, unless sooner discharged, until the regular quadrennial election of the Council following the quadrennial election of the Assembly.

5. The members of the Executive Council shall retain their seats in the General Assembly.

6. The members of the Executive Council shall, during their period of service thereon, receive additional compensation to be fixed by the General Assembly.

Comment. The proposed revision requires important changes in Chapter V which deals with the present Security Council, since the revision proposes entirely to abolish the Security Council and to replace it with an Executive Council, differently composed and with different functions, powers and voting procedures.

Basic changes are needed in the present Articles 23-27 which deal with the "Composition", "Functions and Powers" and "Voting" of the Security Council; while minor changes are needed in the remaining Articles 28-32 of Chapter V. Detailed provisions for the composition and mode of selection of the new Executive Council are contained in this revised Article 23. The revised Articles 24-26 deal with the powers of the new Council; and revised Article 27 abolishes the present "veto" and provides for new voting procedures.

It will be recalled that by revised Article 11, paragraph 1, the *General Assembly* would have the "primary responsibility" for the maintenance of peace, so that the new Executive Council would not have the basic responsibility in this respect possessed by the Security Council under the present Article 24. Instead, the Executive Council would, by revised Article 24, function in this all-important field as "the agent of the General Assembly", subject at all times to the Assembly's supervision and direction.

Despite this different status, the proposed Executive Council would be an organ of great authority and importance. In particular, the new Council would have general *executive* responsibility for the carrying out and maintenance of the whole plan for complete national disarmament, including supervision over the proposed Inspection Commission, Nuclear Energy Commission and the Outer Space Commission (Annex I, Articles 4, 25 and 28). The new Council would also have general control of the United Nations Peace Force, and in an emergency not admitting of delay could even direct action by that Force to maintain or restore international peace (revised Article 42 and Annex II).

In view of these vitally important functions of the proposed Executive Council and its relationship to the General Assembly, it is clearly necessary to make most careful provisions for the composition of the Council and for the procedures whereby its members are chosen. Accordingly, this revised Article 23 embodies a necessarily elaborate plan for the selection of the Council, designed to create a carefully balanced body representative at all times of the whole membership of the United Nations.

In contrast to the present Security Council, composed as it is of delegates appointed by the governments of the member Nations, it is proposed that the Executive Council shall consist of seventeen Representatives in the General Assembly, *chosen by the Assembly itself from its own membership.* In this way no nation as such would be entitled to appoint any member of the new Council and the Council would consist solely of persons well known to the Assembly and enjoying its confidence.

The plan also provides that, while no member Nation would be entitled to "permanent" representation on the Council, the few very largest nations (comprising the first category under paragraph 2 of revised Article 9) would be entitled to representation at all times. It is also proposed that the nations comprising the second category under paragraph 2 of revised Article 9 shall be entitled to representation on the Council during *alternate* General Assemblies.

As of July 1965, the four member Nations in the first category (China,

71

India, the Soviet Union and the United States) would each be entitled to have one of its Representatives on the Executive Council at all times. Each of the next eight largest nations would be entitled to be represented in the Council for four years out of every eight years, under a provision whereby their representation would rotate within two geographical subgroups of four member Nations each. This second category of eight nations would initially be composed of four European nations (France, Germany, Italy and the United Kingdom) and four non-European nations (Brazil, Indonesia, Japan and Pakistan). It is, therefore, proposed that the four nations in this group which at any one time would be entitled to have Representatives on the Council shall be equally divided between the subgroups,—two from Europe and two from outside Europe.

The smaller member Nations (comprising the last four categories under paragraph 4 of revised Article 9), together with the non-self-governing and trust territories under the administration of member Nations, would as one group be entitled to nine seats on the Executive Council. In order to ensure equitable distribution of seats among the members of this large group, the smaller nations (assumed in revised Article 9 to number eighty-seven) and the territories would be divided into nine regional subgroups. These nine subgroups would be as nearly equal as possible in the number of nations in each subgroup; and each subgroup would have attached to it the non-self-governing and trust territories in its general area. While it is likely that each subgroup would itself *recommend* which nation (or non-self-governing or trust territory) in the subgroup should have one of its Representatives elected to the Council at a particular election, the final designation would be in the hands of the General Assembly itself. To ensure, however, that every one of these smaller nations shall in due course have one of its Representatives on the Council, it is proposed that no member of a subgroup shall be redesignated until every other member Nation in that subgroup has been designated. Provision is also made to ensure that in the subgroups which include one or more non-self-governing or trust territories (mostly in Africa and the Pacific), at least one such territory shall be designated before any member Nation can be redesignated.

In practice this plan for representation on the Executive Council would give a slight majority (nine to eight) to the group consisting of the smaller nations and the non-self-governing and trust territories. While on the basis of estimated populations as of July 1965 this group would contain only about 31 per cent of the world's population (an estimated 986 million out of 3172 million), the group would nevertheless include more than five sixths of the independent states of the world. The plan therefore represents a compromise between representation related to population and representation upon the basis of separate sovereignties. But it is a compromise which recognizes representation of the separate national states as the dominant factor, rather than relative populations as the dominant factor, just as the plan for representation in the General Assembly itself gives similar preponderant weight to the element of separate nationhood.

It may be argued that the eight middle-sized nations which would be entitled to fifteen Representatives each in the General Assembly should also have permanent seats on the Executive Council; and that the slight balance in favor of the many smaller nations (eighty-seven in 1965) could be maintained by allotting thirteen seats to them to make a Council of twenty-five. However, after weighing all factors, the authors have concluded that the proposed composition of the Council, whereby there would be permanent seats for the four largest nations, alternate seats for the eight nations with the next largest populations and nine seats for all the smaller nations and non-self-governing and trust territories together, is a sounder solution. For, while it is clearly necessary to have a considerable overrepresentation with relation to population of the smaller and middle-sized nations both in the General Assembly and the Executive Council, it will be wise in the long run not unduly to accentuate this.

Applying the above-estimated populations as of July 1, 1965 to the proposed formula for an Executive Council of seventeen, the four largest nations with permanent seats would have a combined population of 1602 million, while the eight nations in the second category, with a combined population of only 584 million, would likewise have four seats. Thus, as between the four largest and the eight next largest nations, the overrepresentation of these eight nations with relation to the four largest nations would, under the proposed formula, be in the ratio of nearly three to one; and this is believed to be sufficient recognition of the position of the eight middle-sized nations. Just as there is justification for the similar overrepresention of these eight middle-sized nations in the General Assembly where, with 120 Representatives, they would actually have the same representation as the four largest nations, despite the fact that the combined population of the four so greatly exceeds that of the eight, there is clearly no sound reason to accentuate this overrepresentation by giving more than four seats on the Executive Council to the eight middle-sized nations.

Moreover, an Executive Council of seventeen members would be at or near a maximum workable number for an effective body of this sort. Efficiency would almost certainly be impaired if the number were increased to twenty-five, which would be the minimum number required if all the twelve largest nations had permanent seats and the principle was preserved of giving a slight majority of seats to the much more numerous smaller nations. After receiving many criticisms and suggestions, the authors have found no better or fairer way to constitute the proposed Executive Council than by the suggested apportionment whereby, of the seventeen seats, four seats would go to the four largest nations, four seats to the eight next largest and nine to the eighty-seven smaller nations and non-self-governing and trust territories as a group.

The proposed method of choosing the *individual* members of the Executive Council from among the Representatives of the designated nations or territories embodies another careful balancing of the interests of particular nations and of the world community. Although it is proposed to vest in the General Assembly the *ultimate* power of choosing the individual members of the Council, the Assembly's choice would be restricted to Representatives *nominated* by the member Nations (or non-self-governing or trust territories) which are entitled to representation on the Council during a particular term of the Assembly. The Representatives of each member Nation (or territory) thus designated would be required to nominate two candidates for the seat allocated to that nation (or territory); and the Assembly would then select the one deemed to be the better qualified for service on the Council.

The proposed voting procedure in the Executive Council (revised Article

73

27), whereby a majority of twelve out of seventeen votes is required for all decisions rather than a bare majority of nine, is also designed to ensure that the Council's decisions shall reflect the opinion of a majority of the General Assembly and presumably of the world's people. In respect of important decisions, the further requirement is proposed that the majority of twelve shall include a majority of each of the two main groups of nations, i.e., the large nations entitled to fifteen or more Representatives and the much more numerous group of smaller nations.

The provisions concerning vacancies are also intended to ensure that the carefully planned balance in the composition of the Executive Council shall not be disturbed. For this reason, it is proposed that any vacancy must be filled by the election of a Representative from the same nation (or territory) from which the outgoing Council member came.

The close correlation between each General Assembly and the body which would serve as its executive is assured through the provisions whereby their periods of service would be almost identical. This results from the requirement that each new General Assembly shall elect a new Executive Council as soon as possible (within thirty days) after the beginning of the Assembly's first session; and from the further provision that the Council shall serve for the remainder of the full four-year term of the Assembly which elects it and for the short further period until the election of a new Council by the next Assembly.

This relationship would be further safeguarded by the proposed power of the General Assembly to declare that the Executive Council no longer has the confidence of the Assembly, with the consequence that an entirely new Council must be forthwith chosen. While provision is made only for the replacement of the Council as a whole and not of individual members, the Assembly might well re-elect some or most of the individuals composing the discharged Council, dropping out only those members whose continued service is no longer deemed desirable. Provision is also made that, as in the case of vacancies, the members of a new Council must come from among the Representatives of the same nations (or territories) which were represented on the discharged Council. This would not be possible, however, if the Assembly should desire to replace a Representative coming from a nation (or territory) which has only one Representative. In such a case, the Assembly would be permitted to depart slightly from the original distribution of seats on the Council and to elect a Representative from another small nation.

This provision with respect to the discharge of the Executive Council follows to some extent the usual parliamentary system. Similarly, the proposal that members of the Council shall retain their seats in the General Assembly and thus maintain close contact with the activities and trends of the Assembly reflects the usual parliamentary practice.

The provision for special compensation to the members of the Executive Council recognizes the justice of additional compensation in view of the fact that their duties would be far more arduous than those of the average Representative. It should here be recalled that similar extra compensation would be provided for those other members of the General Assembly who serve on the Standing Committee on the Peace Enforcement Agencies and the Standing Committee on Budget and Finance,—since the members of those committees would also have arduous duties and, like the members of the Executive Council, would doubtless need to be almost constantly available throughout the year (revised Article 22).

FUNCTIONS AND POWERS

Article 24

1. In order to ensure prompt and effective action by the United Nations, *its Members confer on* the *Security* Council *primary responsibility* for the maintenance of international peace and security, *and agree that in carrying out its duties under this responsibility the Security Council acts on their behalf.*

1. In order to ensure prompt and effective action by the United Nations, the *Executive* Council *shall act as the agent of the General Assembly in the fulfillment of the primary responsibility of the Assembly* for the maintenance of international peace and security *and for ensuring compliance with this revised Charter and the laws and regulations enacted thereunder. The General Assembly shall supervise the carrying out by the Executive Council of its duties, and the Assembly may from time to time issue such directions to the Council as the Assembly deems necessary.*

2. In discharging *these* duties the *Security* Council shall act in accordance with *the Purposes and Principles of the United Nations. The* specific powers granted to the *Security* Council for the discharge of these duties are laid down in Chapters VI, VII, VIII, and XII.

2. In discharging *its* duties the *Executive* Council shall act in accordance with *this revised Charter and the laws and regulations enacted by the General Assembly, and in accordance with the directions of the Assembly. Certain* specific powers granted to the Council for the discharge of these duties are laid down in Chapters VI, VII, VIII, and XII, *and in Annexes I and II.*

3. The *Security* Council shall submit annual and, *when necessary,* special reports to the General Assembly *for its consideration.*

3. The *Executive* Council shall submit annual reports to the General Assembly and *such* special reports *as the Council may deem necessary or as the Assembly may*

75

call for. If the Council decides to take emergency action under Chapter VII, it shall immediately submit a report thereon to the Assembly which, if not then in session, shall, in accordance with Article 39, be immediately convened to consider such report.

Comment. As already noted, the composition, status, functions and powers of the Executive Council would be very different from those of the present Security Council. The individuals composing the new Council, instead of being appointed by their respective governments, would be chosen by the General Assembly itself from among its own members. Moreover, instead of being, like the Security Council, an independent body, the Executive Council would, under paragraph 1 of this revised Article, act as the executive arm of the Assembly in respect of the maintenance of peace, being responsible to the Assembly and subject at all times to the Assembly's direction and control.

This relationship between the Executive Council and the General Assembly follows from the proposed transfer (by revised Article 11) of the "primary responsibility" for the maintenance of peace to the Assembly itself. In consequence the function of the new Council is defined in this revised Article as that of the "agent" of the Assembly "in the fulfillment" of the Assembly's basic responsibility to prevent war. The intention is that, while the new Council shall have vital functions in this field, its powers (in contrast to those of the present Security Council) would be exercised subject to the direction and control of the Assembly rather than independently of the Assembly.

In addition to the special function of the Executive Council as the General Assembly's agent for the maintenance of peace, revised paragraph 1 would vest in the Council the broad *executive* responsibility for "ensuring compliance with this revised Charter and the laws and regulations enacted thereunder." But in this respect also the new Council would at all times be subject to "such directions" of the Assembly "as the Assembly deems necessary."

It is not contemplated, however, that prior permission from the General Assembly would be required for all the acts of the Executive Council even in the field of sanctions against actual or threatened aggression. For since the Assembly would normally not be in session throughout the year, the Council should have sufficient authority to assure prompt action for the preservation of peace in case of pressing emergency; and express provisions to this effect are included in Chapter VII and Annexes I and II. Nevertheless, in order to preserve at all times the paramount authority of the General Assembly, the new text of paragraph 3 would require the Executive Council, if it takes emergency action, immediately to convoke a session of the Assembly, if the Assembly is not then in session, and to submit a report to the Assembly which could then exercise the power (under paragraph 1) to issue "such directions to the Council as the Assembly deems necessary."

The powers of the Executive Council would be further limited and governed by the express requirement in paragraph 2 of this revised Article that it must discharge all its duties in accordance with the Charter, and the laws, regulations and directions of the General Assembly. Thus the obligation of the present Security Council to "act in accordance with the Purposes and Principles of the United Nations" has been made more precise.

The new Executive Council would have the same obligation as the present Security Council to submit both annual and special reports to the General Assembly. The new text, however, clarifies a possible ambiguity in the present text by specifying that special reports shall be presented not only when the Executive Council deems them necessary, but also when the Assembly calls for such reports. This provision has its parallel in revised Article 15 under which the Assembly "shall receive and consider annual and special reports from the Executive Council", which reports "shall include an account of the measures that the Executive Council has decided upon or taken to maintain international peace and security." On the basis of such reports, the General Assembly could issue further directives to the Executive Council, or, in case of complete dissatisfaction, could (revised Article 23, paragraph 4) replace it by a new Council.

The provisions of this revised Article 24 relate only to the general character of the functions of the Executive Council. Its specific functions are defined in other parts of the revised Charter, especially in Chapters VI, VII, VIII, and XII and in the proposed Annexes I and II. Under Chapter VI, the new Council could be authorized by the General Assembly to exercise important functions with regard to the pacific settlement of international disputes. Under Chapter VII it would be authorized to take temporary emergency measures to maintain or restore international peace in case of a threat to or breach of the peace. It would supervise regional arrangements in accordance with Chapter VIII; and under Chapter XII would administer territories under the direct trusteeship of the United Nations itself. The duties of the new Council with relation to the disarmament plan and the United Nations Peace Force are set forth in Annexes I and II.

As compared with the functions of the present Security Council, it will be seen that the responsibilities of the proposed Executive Council would in one respect be less, i.e., in that, instead of being charged with the *primary* responsibility for the maintenance of peace, the new Council would act in this regard only as the arm or agent of the General Assembly. On the other hand, as compared with the Security Council, the Executive Council would have a larger responsibility under the provision which broadly charges the Council with the duty of "ensuring compliance" with the revised Charter and all the laws and regulations enacted by the Assembly. The new Council would also have much greater day-to-day executive responsibilities by reason of its highly important duties under Annexes I and II to direct the carrying out of the whole plan of national disarmament and to supervise the United Nations Peace Force. Moreover, for the fulfillment of these various executive responsibilities, the new Council would (under revised Article 23) be a far more representative body than the present Security Council and would, of course, be freed from the crippling "veto" which has so often

77

frustrated action by the Security Council. All in all, therefore, the new Executive Council would doubtless prove to be not only more important, but also much more effective than the Security Council.

Article 25

The *Members of the United Nations* agree to accept and carry out the decisions of the *Security* Council *in accordance with the present Charter*.

The *member Nations* agree to accept and carry out the decisions of the *Executive* Council, *subject only to the right to contest the validity of any such decisions by appeal to the International Court of Justice. Pending the judgment of the Court upon any such appeal, the contesting member Nation shall nevertheless carry out the decision of the Council, unless the Council or the Court shall make an order permitting noncompliance, in whole or in part, during the Court's consideration of the appeal.*

Comment. Corresponding to the present Article 25, which requires the member Nations to comply with the decisions of the Security Council, this revised Article obligates them to comply with the decisions of the new Executive Council. The revised Article, however, makes this obligation subject to the right to test the validity of a decision of the Executive Council by appeal to the International Court of Justice.

This new feature is, in part, a consequence of the fact that, while under the revised Charter the authority of the United Nations would be largely increased, it would, nevertheless, be constitutionally restricted to functions directly related to the prevention of war. Member Nations should, therefore, have the right to challenge the constitutional validity of the orders of any organ or agency of the United Nations. Under revised Article 11, paragraph 4, such a right would be accorded with relation to laws, regulations or decisions of the General Assembly itself; and it is equally important to provide that the Executive Council shall not be immune from a challenge on the ground of unconstitutionality. In addition, there might be legitimate claims of invalidity for reasons which could not strictly be called constitutional reasons as, for example, that the Assembly had not authorized the Council to make a particular decision, although the Assembly could constitutionally have done so; and it should be possible to question the validity of a Council decision on grounds of this kind.

An appeal to the International Court of Justice is therefore made available to a member Nation claiming that a decision of the Executive Council is invalid for any reason,—as being, for example, not in accordance with the revised Charter itself, or in conflict with a law or regulation properly enacted by the General Assembly, or as being inconsistent with a prior direction of the Assembly.

Provision has been made, however, that decisions of the Executive Council must be carried out despite such an appeal, unless the Council itself or the International Court shall allow a stay of execution pending the judgment of the Court. This provision seems essential because the decisions of the Council under Chapter VII (in case of a breach of the peace) or under Annex I (in case of a violation of the disarmament plan) would usually be of so urgent a character that they should be carried out notwithstanding a challenge of their validity unless in special circumstances a stay of compliance, in whole or in part, should be granted .

Similar provisions for appeal are unnecessary in the case of action by the Economic and Social Council or the Trusteeship Council, since even under the proposed revision these organs would be empowered only to make recommendations, as distinguished from binding orders.

Article 26

In order to promote the establishment and maintenance of international peace and security *with the least diversion for armaments of the world's human and economic resources,* the *Security* Council shall *be responsible for formulating, with the assistance of the Military Staff Committee referred to in Article 47, plans to be submitted to the Members of the United Nations for the establishment of a system for the regulation of armaments.*

In order to promote the establishment and maintenance of international peace and security, the *Executive* Council shall, *subject to the supervision of the General Assembly, see to it that the provisions of this revised Charter with respect to disarmament are carried out.*

Comment. In contrast to the present Article 26, which merely provides for the preparation of disarmament plans to be submitted to the respective member Nations, a basic concept of the proposed revision is that detailed provisions for total national disarmament (Annex I) should be included *in the Charter itself,* so that, upon acceptance of the revised Charter, each member Nation would be automatically bound to carry out the disarmament plan. Accordingly, what is required is an effective agency charged with the executive responsibility for ensuring that the constitutionally established plan of disarmament shall be duly fulfilled. Under this revised Article 26, that result would be accomplished by imposing upon the Executive Council the duty to "see to it that the provisions of this revised Charter with respect to disarmament are carried out."

Pursuant to revised Article 24, the Executive Council would have the broad responsibility for ensuring compliance with the Charter in general, so that it seems fitting in this Article 26 to emphasize the Council's duty to ensure compliance with the disarmament plan in particular. Annex I contains detailed provisions covering the functions of the Executive Council in this regard. Under that Annex the Council would have "general supervision" over the United Nations Inspection Service with authority to issue all necessary instructions to the Service. Moreover, although responsibility for imposing sanctions in case of serious violation of the disarmament plan would *ordinarily* be that of the General Assembly, the Council would have certain interim and emergency powers in this respect. Thus if the Assembly were not in session and a serious violation of the disarmament plan should occur, the Council would not be helpless but could, in case of an emergency requiring "immediate action" (revised Article 39, paragraph 2, of the Charter itself), declare such an emergency and could resort to interim measures under Chapter VII, including action by the United Nations Peace Force (revised Articles 40 and 42). In such case, however, the Council would be required to report at once to the General Assembly if in session (revised Article 24, paragraph 3) or, if the Assembly were not then in session, to have it convoked as soon as possible and in any case within a week (revised Article 39, paragraph 2). The Assembly would then (revised Article 39, paragraph 2) make the final decisions with respect to further action or the cancellation or modification of the Council's interim measures. (See also Article 34 of Annex I.)

VOTING

Article 27

1. *Each member* of the *Security* Council shall have one vote.

1. *The members* of the *Executive* Council *shall vote as individuals, and each of them* shall have one vote.

2. Decisions of the *Security* Council on *procedural* matters shall be made by an affirmative vote of *seven* members.

2. Decisions of the *Executive* Council on *important* matters shall be made by an affirmative vote of *twelve* members, *which majority shall include a majority of the members of the Council elected from among the Representatives in the General Assembly from the member Nations entitled to fifteen or more Representatives in the Assembly and also a majority of the members of the Council elected from among the Representatives in the General Assembly from the member Nations entitled to less than fifteen Representatives in the Assembly and from*

80

the non-self-governing or trust territories. Important matters shall include: action with respect to the pacific settlement of international disputes and the maintenance of international peace and security in accordance with Articles 33 through 53 and Annexes I and II; and any other matters which the General Assembly may from time to time define as important.

3. Decisions of the *Security* Council on all other matters shall be made by an affirmative vote of *seven* members *including the concurring votes of the permanent members; provided that, in decisions under Chapter VI, and under paragraph 3 of Article 52, a party to a dispute shall abstain from voting.*

3. Decisions of the *Executive* Council on all other matters shall be made by an affirmative vote of *any twelve* members.

Comment. As noted in the comments on revised Articles 23-26, the proposed Executive Council would be a body of the highest importance. In fact, the greatly increased scope and authority of the United Nations under the revised Charter would make the Executive Council of greater importance than the present Security Council, even though the new Council would mainly function as an agent of the General Assembly rather than as an independent body. It is by reason of the vital functions of this new Executive Council that the elaborate procedures for its selection are proposed in revised Article 23,—in order, by ensuring a careful balance in its composition, to promote a high degree of confidence in the Council. The voting procedures in this revised Article 27 are also intended to promote maximum confidence in the decisions of the new Council.

No provision is made corresponding to the "veto" power of any one of the "Big Five" contained in the present Charter, since it is clear that in the new Executive Council no decision, great or small, should be blocked by any single vote. On the other hand, it would be best to require that all decisions of the Council shall be by a substantial majority of its members; and it is of the utmost consequence that every *important* decision shall command a clear majority of members from both the main groups of nations, i.e., from the group comprising the largest and medium-sized nations and also from the more numerous group of smaller nations. It is believed that the proposed requirement of a minimum majority of twelve of the seventeen Council members for any decision (paragraph 3), together with the requirement that on "important matters" this majority shall include a majority of Council members from the nations entitled to fifteen or more Representatives in the General Assembly and also a majority of the members from the smaller nations (paragraph 2), meets these tests.

The proposed voting procedure would eliminate the distinction between procedural and substantive matters under paragraphs 2 and 3 of the present Article 27. This distinction does not exist in the other two Councils of the United Nations (the Economic and Social Council and the Trusteeship Council). Neither does it exist in the International Court of Justice, nor in most parliamentary and executive bodies. The difficulties arising from that distinction have often been demonstrated by the experience of the present Security Council; and there seems to be no good reason for the continuance of this complication. The revised Article, therefore, merely distinguishes between "important" matters and other matters; and as to what matters shall be deemed "important" it specifies that they shall include all decisions with regard to the pacific settlement of international disputes and the maintenance of peace, and "any other matters" which the General Assembly may choose to define as important.

It may be noted that the proposed requirement for a stricter voting procedure in respect of "important" questions is analogous to the special provision in revised Article 18 with regard to decisions of the General Assembly itself, whereby decisions of the Assembly on "important" matters would require a majority of all the Representatives whereas decisions on other matters would require no more than a majority of the Representatives present and voting.

Another and fundamental difference from the present Article 27 is proposed by the provision of revised paragraph 1 that the members of the Executive Council "shall vote as individuals". This corresponds to a similar provision in revised Article 18 in respect of voting by Representatives in the General Assembly.

Both provisions embody the conception that the revised United Nations would be something very different from and more than a league of sovereign states represented by delegates selected by governments; and that its governing bodies should be more directly representative of and responsible to the *peoples* of the world. It is a reasonable expectation that through these provisions there would develop a spirit of world citizenship whereby the Representatives in the General Assembly, and especially those Representatives chosen to serve on the Executive Council, would come to think of themselves as representing not only their own nations but also the entire world community. For just as in a parliamentary government the members of the national legislature commonly regard themselves as responsible for the interests of the entire people even though they may properly pay special attention to the interests of their constituencies, so in the revised General Assembly and new Executive Council a corresponding sense of responsibility for the interests of the whole world may be expected to develop.

The provision in revised Article 23, whereby the General Assembly could discharge the Executive Council by a vote of lack of confidence, might well operate to aid the development of such a sense of world responsibility. For, if it seemed to the Assembly that too many members of the Council were adopting excessively nationalistic or narrow views, the Assembly could at any time discharge the Council and omit those particular Representatives upon the appointment of the new Council.

It should be emphasized that the provisions of revised Article 23 relating to the Executive Council's composition, of revised Articles 24-26 relating to its powers and of this revised Article 27 relating to its voting procedures are closely interrelated and should be read together. Taken together, it is believed that they would produce a well-balanced executive body which could not only function effectively but also command world confidence.

PROCEDURE

Article 28

1. The *Security* Council shall be so organized as to be able to function continuously. *Each member of the Security Council shall for this purpose be represented at all times at the seat of the Organization.*

1. The *Executive* Council shall be so organized as to be able to function continuously, *and it shall hold regular meetings at least twice in each month.*

2. *The Security Council shall hold periodic meetings at which each of its members may, if it so desires, be represented by a member of the government or by some other specially designated representative.*

2. *The members of the Executive Council shall hold themselves at the disposal of the Council at all times, unless on leave or prevented from attending by illness or other serious reason.*

In case of the temporary absence of any member, due to illness or other cause, the Executive Council may appoint as substitute a Representative from the same member Nation as that of the absent member, to serve during such absence but for not more than four months. An absence of more than four months shall be deemed to create a vacancy to be filled in accordance with paragraph 3 of Article 23.

3. The *Security* Council may hold meetings at such places other than the seat of the *Organization* as in its judgment will best facilitate its work.

3. The *Executive* Council may hold meetings at such places other than the seat of the *United Nations* as in its judgment will best facilitate its work.

Comment. While the General Assembly would not normally be in session throughout the whole of each year, it is important that the body which acts as its executive agent shall be constantly available. It is therefore proposed (paragraph 1) that, as in the case of the present Security Council, the new Executive Council "shall be so organized as to be able to function continuously". It is further proposed that the new Council shall be required to hold regular meetings at least twice a month,—on the ground that, in view of the Council's vital responsibilities, it should not fail to meet frequently and regularly throughout the year.

The second sentence of the present paragraph 1 is no longer applicable, since the members of the Executive Council would not be appointed by governments but would be elected by the General Assembly itself from among the Representatives (revised Article 23). Nor is the present paragraph 2 applicable, since it also contemplates meetings of *governmental* delegates.

The new paragraph 2 would impose an obligation on the members of the Executive Council to hold themselves personally "at the disposal of the Council at all times", except when on leave or in case of illness or "other serious reason." The purpose is to emphasize the important and continuous character of the Council's duties, and the language is modeled on Article 23 of the present Statute of the International Court of Justice.

In view of the importance of the Executive Council, it is desirable that, to the extent possible, the Council shall have its full membership of seventeen at all times. It is to meet this situation that provision is made in the second part of the new paragraph 2 that substitutes may be appointed to act in place of regular members during even temporary absences. The provision that the substitute must be a Representative from the same member Nation ensures that the plan of distribution of the members of the Council shall not be disturbed even by temporary absence. The time limit of four months for the service of a substitute is designed to emphasize the temporary character of the appointment of substitutes by the Executive Council itself. A longer absence would automatically create a vacancy, requiring the General Assembly to exercise its power under revised Article 23 to elect a new member.

Paragraph 3 of the present Article remains unchanged in substance.

Article 29

The *Security* Council may establish such subsidiary organs as it deems necessary for the performance of its functions.

The *Executive* Council may establish such subsidiary organs as it deems necessary for the performance of its functions.

Comment. Although no change is proposed in the power to appoint subsidiary organs, it should be noted that the exercise of this power by the new Executive Council would be subject, under revised Article 24, to the supervision and direction of the General Assembly.

The difficulties encountered by the present Security Council in the exercise of this power have been mainly due to the question as to whether the unanimity ("veto") rule applies to the appointment of investigative commissions. A remedy for this situation is provided by the new voting procedures in revised Article 27, whereby the "veto" is eliminated.

Article 30

The *Security* Council shall adopt its own rules of procedure, including the method of selecting its President.

The *Executive* Council shall adopt its own rules of procedure, including the method of selecting its President.

Comment. The power of the new Executive Council to adopt its own rules of procedure is left untrammeled. It is to be hoped, however, that the practice of the present Security Council which calls for monthly changes in the presidency would be abandoned. The tenure of the President of the Executive Council should ordinarily last from one election of the Council's members by the General Assembly to the next election. Such a tenure should enhance the President's status and influence and should contribute to the effective performance of the functions of the new Council.

Article 31

Any Member of the United Nations which is not a member of the *Security* Council may participate, without vote, in the discussion of any question brought before *the Security Council whenever the latter* considers that the interests of *that Member* are specially affected.

1. If the Executive Council considers that in the discussion of any question brought before *it*, the interests of *a member Nation* are specially affected, *and if no Representative from such member Nation is then* a member of the *Executive* Council, *the Council shall invite the Representatives in the General Assembly from that member Nation to designate one of their number to* participate, without vote, in the discussion; *or if such member Nation has only one Representative, that Representative shall be invited to participate.*

2. If the Executive Council considers that in the discussion of any question brought before it, the interests of a non-self-governing or trust territory are specially affected, and if no Representative from such territory is then a member of the Council and if there is a Representative from such territory in the General Assembly, the Council shall invite that Representative to participate, without vote,

85

in the discussion. If, however, there is then no Representative from such territory in the Assembly, the Council shall appoint a properly qualified person resident in such territory to represent the interests of such territory and to participate, without vote, on its behalf in the discussion.

Comment. The purpose of the present Article is to permit a member Nation not represented on the Security Council to participate in its discussions, although without vote, if the interests of that nation are specially involved.

The revised Article retains this general purpose but makes some changes in the method. Instead of having an advocate appointed by the government of the member Nation concerned, provision is made for the designation by the Representatives from that nation of one of their own number to represent that nation in the Executive Council's discussion, if the Council finds that the interests of that particular nation are "specially affected".

The reason for this change is that, since the Executive Council would be composed of Representatives chosen by the General Assembly itself instead of persons appointed by governments (revised Article 23), it is more appropriate that a member Nation should be represented before the Council by one of its Representatives then in the Assembly.

Moreover, in order to be fair to any non-self-governing or trust territory whose interests might be "specially affected", provision is made that the Representative, if any, from such territory shall be invited to take part on the same basis as a Representative from a member Nation. As an additional safeguard, it is further provided that if there is then no Representative from such territory, the Executive Council shall appoint a properly qualified person to represent the interests of such territory and to participate, without vote, on its behalf in the discussions of the Council.

Article 32

Any Member of the United Nations which is not a member of the Security Council or any state which is not a Member of the United Nations, if it is a party to a dispute under consideration by the Security Council, shall be invited to participate, without vote, in the discussion relating to the dispute. The Security Council shall lay down such conditions as it deems

1. If *any member Nation* is a party to a dispute under consideration by the *Executive* Council, *and if no Representative from such member Nation is then a member of the Executive Council, the Council shall invite the Representatives from that member Nation to designate one of their number* to participate, without vote, in the discussion relating to the dis-

86

just for the participation of a state which is not a Member of the United Nations.

pute; *or if such member Nation has only one Representative, that Representative shall be invited to participate.*

2. If any state which is not a *member* of the United Nations is a party to a dispute under consideration by the *Executive* Council, *the Council shall invite its government to appoint a delegate* to participate, without vote, in the discussion relating to the dispute. The *Executive* Council shall lay down such conditions as it deems just for the participation of *such* a state.

Comment. The present Article 31 applies only to participation in the discussion of *questions* by the Security Council and only when that Council considers that the interests of a member Nation are "specially affected". On the other hand, the present Article 32 applies to any *dispute* between member Nations and does so automatically whenever such dispute is under consideration by the Security Council without the necessity for any decision by the Council that the member Nation's interests are "specially affected". The present Article 32 also applies if a *nonmember* nation is "a party" to the "dispute" before the Security Council.

The proposed revision of Article 32 in no way changes the automatic right to be heard of any "party to a dispute", but merely affects the method of a nation's participation in the "discussion" before the Executive Council.

It should be observed that while this revised Article 32 makes no provision for participation in the discussions of the Executive Council by non-self-governing or trust territories, since they obviously cannot be "parties" to "disputes" between *nations,* provision is made under revised Article 31 for their participation in the discussion of "any question" in which their interests are deemed by the Council to be "specially affected".

In the event of a dispute to which a member Nation not represented on the Executive Council is a party, the Council would be required to invite the Representatives in the General Assembly from that member Nation to designate one of their own number to participate in the discussion; and care is taken to provide that any such member Nation with only one Representative could likewise participate. The reason for this change is the same as the reason for the corresponding change in Article 31,—namely, that since the Executive Council would be composed of members of the General Assembly itself (instead of governmental delegates as in the case of the present Security Council), it is more fitting that a member Nation should be represented before the Council by a fellow Representative in the Assembly.

In the case, however, of nonmember nations (if there are any such), the present practice would be followed whereby the government of the nonmember nation concerned would be invited to appoint a delegate. And in so doing, the Executive Council would be empowered (as the Security Council is now) to prescribe such conditions "as it deems just" with regard to the participation of the invited nonmember nation.

CHAPTER VI

PACIFIC SETTLEMENT OF DISPUTES

General Comment. The nations of the world can be expected to renounce force or the threat of force as a means of dealing with international disputes only if *adequate alternative means* are provided for the peaceful settlement of these controversies. This is the age-old experience as to disputes between individuals and communities within a nation. It is no less true of international disputes.

Since the very fact that the nations possess dangerous armaments engenders fears and suspicions which render peaceful settlements difficult, it follows that complete national disarmament is itself an essential element in any plan for "pacific settlement".

But even when all the nations are totally disarmed, pressures and tensions could easily be built up which might lead to violent encounters between them, if only with improvised weapons; and while this violence could be suppressed by a world police force, it is important that violence or the threat of it shall not be used at all.

In this connection it is especially necessary to take into account the recurring and inevitable dissatisfactions of various nations and peoples with the *status quo*. As conditions change these dissatisfactions are normal; and it is almost certain that some of them will be so acute as to lead to violence unless alternative methods are provided to deal with them upon principles of justice and under procedures giving assurance of a fair hearing for all concerned.

Accordingly, the United Nations must not be limited to the suppression of attempts to change existing conditions by force *after* the violence has occurred or is imminent. On the contrary, it should be clearly understood that all violent efforts to change the existing order can be prevented in the long run only by providing adequate and flexible means for peaceful change such as negotiation, mediation, arbitration, conciliation and adjudication, or such a combination of these as may be most suitable to the particular case. To this end it is plain that carefully organized world institutions are essential.

Another important consideration is that the means provided should include suitable procedures to deal with potential threats to the peace *before* they become really dangerous,—as distinguished from waiting until the threat is imminent and serious. For the peace and welfare of the world community such preventive measures are no less necessary than is preventive medicine for the health of the individual.

For all these reasons it is clear that, for the maintenance of peace, national disarmament alone is not sufficient, no matter how complete and efficiently supervised and even when supplemented by an effective world police. It is also essential to equip the United Nations with more comprehensive and improved machinery to deal at an early stage with all important international controversies.

This vital objective of equipping the United Nations with adequate means to forestall, rather than merely to suppress international violence, can be achieved only through a complete revision of Chapter VI. The changes relate not only to the settlement of an actual "dispute", but also to the adjustment of any dangerous or potentially dangerous "situation". The changes concern the jurisdiction and powers of the organs established for these purposes and the procedures to be employed in order to achieve just and satisfactory settlements.

A main concept governing the changes is that the new powers granted to the United Nations in this field of pacific settlement should be exercised or controlled by the organ in which *all* member Nations are represented, i.e., by the General Assembly. It is proposed, therefore, to vest in the Assembly itself the specific and primary responsibility for "pacific settlement",—a change which is in harmony with revised Article 11 whereby the Assembly would have general and "primary" responsibility for the "maintenance of international peace and security".

The General Assembly would, therefore, be expressly empowered: *first*, to call upon the nations concerned to seek a solution of any "dispute", or any "situation" which "might lead to international friction or give rise to a dispute", by "peaceful means of their own choice" (revised Article 33); and *second*, to determine what other procedures should be followed if the nations concerned fail to agree on their own "peaceful means" or if, having sought an agreed settlement, their efforts to reach a settlement have failed (revised Article 36).

It is to be anticipated, however, that, by reason of its size and many responsibilities, the General Assembly might find it necessary to delegate in advance some of its powers in respect of pacific settlement (as, e.g., concerning disputes or situations likely to become serious when the Assembly is not in session); or the Assembly might wish to delegate its authority as to a particular dispute or situation. Accordingly, the revised text of several Articles of this Chapter VI permits such a delegation to the Executive Council by empowering the Council to deal with disputes and situations "if authorized by the Assembly", or "when acting in the matter pursuant to authority from the Assembly" (revised Articles 33, 34, 36 and 37).

The action to be taken by the General Assembly (or by the Executive Council, if authorized by the Assembly) would naturally depend upon the gravity of the particular dispute or situation. In a minor dispute or in a situation likely to give rise to no more than minor difficulty, the Assembly (or the Council) would no doubt merely call upon the nations concerned to settle the dispute or adjust the situation by the above-mentioned "peaceful means of their own choice" (revised Article 33).

If, however, what was originally a minor dispute or situation should later become dangerous, or if a dispute or situation were from the very beginning considered by the General Assembly (or by the Executive Council) to be one "likely" to endanger peace, further action could be directed. Thus if legal questions should be involved, the Assembly (or Council) could direct the nations concerned to submit these questions to the International Court of Justice for a binding decision under revised Article 36. Paragraph 3 of that Article definitely establishes the principle of compulsory jurisdiction as to legal questions involving world peace. And, if the nations concerned were unwilling to comply with the direction of the Assembly (or Council), an advisory opinion could readily be obtained, pursuant to revised Article 96, at the request of the Assembly or Council.

On the other hand, if the issues were of a sort which could not be satisfactorily resolved on the basis of applicable legal principles, the General Assembly (or the Executive Council) could refer the issues, as might be most suitable, either to the new World Conciliation Board or the new World Equity Tribunal. The powers of the Conciliation Board would be limited to mediation directed toward bringing the nations concerned to a mutually agreed solution; while the Equity Tribunal would be authorized to recommend its own solution which, in certain circumstances, could be made binding upon all the nations concerned. (See revised Article 36, paragraphs 4-10.)

With these changes made, the United Nations would no longer lack adequate means for settling or adjusting *any* dangerous international "dispute" or "situation", and for achieving peaceful change. Recourse to force would no longer be necessary to obtain an equitable solution; and one of the principal excuses for resort to international violence would no longer exist.

The text of the six revised Articles of this Chapter and the detailed comments thereon will more fully explain the much stronger and more comprehensive system for "pacific settlement" contemplated by the proposals.

Article 33

1. *The* parties to any dispute, *the continuance of which is likely to endanger the maintenance of international peace and security,* shall, first of all, seek a solution by negotiation, enquiry, mediation, conciliation, arbitration, judicial settlement, resort to regional agencies or arrangements, or other peaceful means of their own choice.

1. *Nations which are* parties to any dispute *or are involved in any situation which might lead to international friction or give rise to a dispute* shall, first of all, seek a solution by negotiation, enquiry, mediation, conciliation, arbitration, judicial settlement, resort to regional agencies or arrangements, or other peaceful means of their own choice.

2. The *Security* Council shall, when *it deems* necessary, call upon the *parties* to settle *their* dispute by such means.

2. The *General Assembly, or the Executive* Council *if authorized by the Assembly,* shall, when *deemed* necessary, call upon the

91

nations concerned to settle *the* dispute *or adjust the situation* by such means.

Comment. The present Article 33 limits the obligation to settle any dispute by pacific means to a dispute "the continuance of which is likely to endanger the maintenance of international peace and security".

This restriction, whereby the obligation to settle disputes peacefully applies only to disputes obviously dangerous to peace, seems inconsistent with revised Article 2, paragraph 3, which imposes on all nations the obligation to settle by peaceful means "their international disputes", without any qualification as to how serious the dispute must be in order for this obligation to apply. The restriction also seems inconsistent with a fundamental principle of the United Nations whereby the use of force or the threat of it by one nation against another is forbidden under *all* circumstances, save in self-defense against attack (Preamble; Article 2, paragraph 4; and Article 51).

Another objection to the present limitation on the duty of the nations to settle their disputes by peaceful means is that, in practice, there may be many disputes which, although not yet "likely" to endanger peace, are yet serious enough to warrant the attention of the United Nations. It is not desirable that disputes of this sort should simmer for a long time, poisoning friendly relations between nations; and the nations concerned should be obligated to attempt their solution by means at their own disposal, whether or not the controversy has yet reached a dangerous stage.

For these several reasons it is proposed in this revised Article 33 to enlarge the obligation to seek settlements by negotiation or other peaceful means chosen by the parties, so that there can be no question of the duty of *all* nations in this regard as to *all* international controversies. Consistently with this principle the actual means employed would naturally be in proportion to the seriousness of the issues, so that, if the questions involved were of minor importance, it might not be necessary to employ the carefully provided machinery for mediation, conciliation or judicial settlement.

It will be further noted that the revised Article is intended to assure that nations shall deal peacefully not only with actual "disputes" but also with any "situation" which "might lead" to international trouble. The situations to be dealt with are defined in paragraph 1 as situations "which might lead to international friction or give rise to a dispute", a phrase which is taken from the present text of Article 34 and adequately describes the type of situations which should be of concern to the United Nations. There seems to be no valid reason for dealing with a "situation" of that sort in later Articles of this Chapter and neglecting to do so in this Article 33.

A change in paragraph 2 is also proposed in order to confer on the General Assembly (rather than on the Security Council, as at present) the responsibility for calling upon the nations concerned to deal with "any dispute" or troublesome "situation" by peaceful means. This is one of the consequences of the transfer to the Assembly of the general responsibility for the maintenance of peace (revised Articles 11 and 24). The proposed change

92

contemplates, however, the possible delegation by the Assembly to the new Executive Council of this power to require nations involved in a controversy to seek a peaceful settlement. To this end, that Council would be empowered to deal with a dispute or situation "if authorized" by the Assembly. This authority might, for example, be conferred for periods when the Assembly is not in session or might be restricted to certain kinds of disputes or situations, or to a particular one.

Finally, it should be noted that the beginning clause of revised paragraph 1 makes it clear that the general obligation to settle international controversies by peaceful means would apply to *all* nations, whether or not they are members of the United Nations. Since the plan for complete national disarmament and the prohibition against the use of force would apply equally to member and nonmember nations, it seems appropriate to impose the supplementary obligation to settle all international controversies by peaceful means not only on the member Nations, but also on those few nations which might choose not to become members under the revised Charter.

Article 34

The *Security* Council may investigate any dispute, or any situation which might lead to international friction or give rise to a dispute, *in order to determine whether the continuance of the dispute or situation is likely to endanger the maintenance of international peace and security.*

The *General Assembly, or the Executive* Council *if authorized by the Assembly*, may investigate any dispute or any situation which might lead to international friction or give rise to a dispute.

Comment. The principal change in this Article is in harmony with previous changes which confer on the General Assembly the primary responsibility for the maintenance of peace. In accord with that concept the revised text vests in the Assembly itself the primary authority to investigate any "dispute" or troublesome "situation". The power of the Executive Council to make investigations of this sort would be limited to those disputes or situations as to which the Assembly has delegated authority to the Council.

The other change omits the present restriction that the purpose of the investigation must be limited to determining "whether the continuance of the dispute or situation is likely to endanger the maintenance of international peace and security." The reasons for this omission are similar to those mentioned in the comment on revised Article 33. For, just as the General Assembly (or the Executive Council when authorized by the Assembly) should have power to "call upon" the nations to seek a peaceful solution of *any* dispute or situation which might cause trouble, the Assembly (or Council) should be empowered itself to look into any such dispute or situation.

The purpose of this revised Article 34, as of the present Article, is to give express authority for investigations by the General Assembly (or the Executive Council) *upon its own initiative* as distinguished from authority to investigate when the dispute or situation is brought to the Assembly (or Council) by a nation under revised Article 35. The rules of the Assembly (or Council) would presumably provide for the procedure and conditions under which investigations of this sort would be initiated and conducted.

Article 35

1. Any *Member of the United Nations* may bring any dispute, or any situation of the nature referred to in Article 34, to the attention of the *Security* Council or of the General Assembly.

1. Any *member Nation* may bring any dispute, or any situation of the nature referred to in Article 34, to the attention of the General Assembly or, *if such dispute or situation is one with which the Executive Council has been authorized by the Assembly to deal,* to the attention of *that* Council.

2. A state which is not a *Member* of the United Nations may bring to the attention of *the Security* Council or of the General Assembly any dispute *to which it is a party* if *it* accepts in advance, for the purposes of the dispute, the obligations of pacific settlement provided in the *present* Charter.

2. A state which is not a *member* of the United Nations may bring any *such* dispute *or situation* to the attention of the General Assembly or, *if such dispute or situation is one with which the Executive Council has been authorized to deal, to the attention* of *that* Council, if *such state* accepts in advance, for the purposes of the dispute *or situation,* the obligations of pacific settlement provided in *this revised* Charter.

3. *The proceedings of the General Assembly in respect of matters brought to its attention under this Article will be subject to the provisions of Articles 11 and 12.*

Comment. While the general purpose of this revised Article is in accord with the present Article, i.e., to enable any troublesome international problem to be brought to the attention of the United Nations, the proposed changes would somewhat broaden the scope of the Article. Moreover, in view of previous provisions conferring on the General Assembly the primary responsibility for peace, the revised Article provides that recourse must be to the Assembly

94

itself, unless the Assembly shall have delegated authority in this respect to the Executive Council.

Another change is proposed, in paragraph 2, to enable a nonmember nation to bring to the United Nations not only a "dispute" but also a "situation" of the kind described in Article 34, i.e., a situation "which might lead to international friction or give rise to a dispute." It is proposed also to remove the present limitation that a nonmember nation, as distinguished from a member Nation, shall be entitled to bring before the United Nations only a dispute "to which it is a party". This change is in harmony with a basic principle of the revision, namely, that in the field of maintaining peace the rights and duties of nonmember nations should so far as possible be the same as those of member Nations.

Paragraph 3 of the present Article is omitted because the proposed changes in Articles 11 and 12 remove the restriction, contained in the present Article 12, whereby the General Assembly is forbidden to make "any recommendation" with regard to a dispute or situation under consideration by the Security Council "unless the Security Council so requests." Since, therefore, the Assembly would have full authority to deal with disputes or situations at any stage, the restriction imposed by the present paragraph 3 is obviously inappropriate and should be removed.

Article 36

1. The *Security* Council may, at any stage of a dispute of the nature referred to in Article 33 *or of a situation of like nature*, recommend appropriate procedures or methods of adjustment.

1. The *General Assembly, or the Executive* Council *if authorized by the Assembly*, may, at any stage of a dispute, *or of a situation* of the nature referred to in Article 33, recommend appropriate procedures or methods of adjustment.

2. The *Security* Council should take into consideration any procedures for the settlement of the dispute which have already been adopted by the *parties*.

2. The *General Assembly, or the Executive* Council *when acting in the matter pursuant to authority from the Assembly*, should take into consideration any procedures for the settlement of the dispute *or adjustment of the situation* which have already been adopted by the *nations concerned*.

3. *In making recommendations under this Article, the Security Council should also take into consideration that legal disputes*

3. *In case the General Assembly, or the Executive Council when acting in the matter pursuant to authority from the Assembly, decides*

95

should as a general rule be referred by the parties to the International Court of Justice in accordance with the provisions of the Statute of the Court.

that the continuance of any dispute or situation is likely to endanger the maintenance of international peace and security and that the dispute or situation involves questions which can be satisfactorily decided upon the basis of applicable legal principles, the Assembly or Council may direct that these legal questions be submitted to the International Court of Justice for final determination. If the nations which are parties to the dispute or are involved in the situation fail, within two months after the direction by the Assembly or the Council, to agree on the submission to the Court of such legal questions, any nation which is a party to the dispute or is involved in the situation may bring the questions before the Court by written application. The Court shall have authority to pronounce final judgment in accordance with the provisions of the Statute of the Court on the legal questions submitted to it under this paragraph. If any nation fails to comply with a judgment of the Court, the provisions of Article 94 concerning the enforcement of judgments of the Court shall apply.

4. In case the General Assembly, or the Executive Council when acting in the matter pursuant to authority from the Assembly, decides that the continuance of any dispute or situation is likely to endanger the maintenance of international peace and security and that the dispute or situation involves questions which cannot be satisfactorily decided upon the basis of applicable legal principles, the Assembly or the Council may refer such nonlegal questions to the World Conciliation Board. The Board shall thereupon, in accordance with the provisions of its Statute contained in Part C of Annex III, conduct such investigations as it may deem necessary and shall endeavor to bring the nations concerned to an agreement.

5. If no agreement is reached within six months from the date on which such nonlegal questions were referred to the World Conciliation Board pursuant to the foregoing paragraph 4, or within such extension of that period as the nations concerned assent to, the Board shall notify the General Assembly of this fact.

6. Thereupon the General Assembly may, by a three-fifths majority vote of all the Representatives then in office, whether or not present or voting, refer such nonlegal questions to the World Equity Tribunal; provided that if any important legal questions involved in the dispute or situation have been referred to the International Court of Justice, the nonlegal questions shall not be referred to the Tribunal until the legal questions have been decided by the Court.

7. Alternatively the General Assembly may, by a three-fifths majority vote of all the Representatives then in office, whether or not present or voting, refer such nonlegal questions directly to the

97

*World Equity Tribunal without
first referring them to the World
Conciliation Board; provided that
if any important legal questions involved in the dispute or situation
have been referred to the International Court of Justice, the nonlegal questions shall not be referred
to the Tribunal until the legal questions have been decided by the
Court.*

8. *When questions have been
referred to the World Equity Tribunal under either paragraph 6 or
paragraph 7 of this Article, the Tribunal shall, in accordance with its
Statute contained in Part B of
Annex III, conduct public hearings
and make such investigations as it
may deem necessary, and shall
submit to the General Assembly
such recommendations as the Tribunal may deem reasonable, just
and fair for the solution of the
questions referred to it.*

9. *The General Assembly shall
promptly consider any such recommendations of the World Equity
Tribunal and shall vote upon them
in their entirety. If the Assembly,
by a three-fourths majority vote of
all the Representatives then in office, including a two-thirds majority
of the Representatives then in office
from the member Nations entitled
to fifteen or more Representatives
in the Assembly, approves the
recommendations of the Tribunal
in their entirety and decides that
the dispute or situation is likely to
continue unless the recommendations are carried out and that such*

continuance will constitute a serious danger to peace, the Assembly shall call upon the nations concerned to comply with the recommendations so approved. If any nation fails to comply with any recommendation of the Tribunal so approved by the Assembly, the provisions of Article 94 concerning the enforcement of approved recommendations of the Tribunal shall apply.

10. If the recommendations of the World Equity Tribunal are not approved in their entirety by the General Assembly by the special majority required by the preceding paragraph, the Assembly may refer the questions involved back to the Tribunal for further consideration; or the Assembly may itself make such recommendations in the light of the recommendations of the Tribunal as it shall consider appropriate; or the Assembly may propose to the nations concerned some other procedure for the settlement of the dispute or adjustment of the situation.

Comment. As already noted in the General Comment on this Chapter VI, it is fundamental to domestic order that individuals shall be required to use some means other than violence for the settlement of all their disputes. And since the time has come when the world can no longer neglect the application of this simple principle to international controversies, the purpose of Chapter VI, as revised, is to create a comprehensive and flexible system for "pacific settlement" in order to provide fully adequate *alternative means* to deal fairly and peacefully with *any* international controversy.

In harmony with this purpose, revised Article 33 would bind *all* the nations (including any nonmember nations) to seek the settlement of *all* controversies "which might lead to international friction or give rise to a dispute" by "peaceful means of their own choice". Revised Article 33 would also authorize the General Assembly (or the Executive Council "when authorized by the Assembly") to "call upon" the nations concerned to employ "such means". Revised Article 34 would empower the Assembly (or the Executive Council) to in-

99

vestigate any "dispute", or troublesome "situation", while revised Article 35 would authorize any nation to bring any "dispute" or any such "situation" to the attention of the Assembly (or of the Council).

The function of this revised Article 36 is to supplement these obligations to seek solutions through means chosen by the nations themselves by providing procedures whereby in serious controversies which are "likely to endanger" peace, the nations concerned, if unable to agree upon peaceful methods "of their own choice", can be *required* to settle their controversies without violence.

This is done: (a) by requiring all nations to submit to the International Court of Justice for final decision all *legal* issues involved in dangerous disputes or situations; and (b) by authorizing the General Assembly (or the Executive Council under authority of the Assembly) to refer any dangerous *nonlegal* dispute or situation to either or both of the two proposed new organs for "pacific settlement", namely, the World Conciliation Board and the World Equity Tribunal.

By reason of these new *compulsory* procedures, revised Article 36 is of prime importance; and the circumstances in which these procedures would apply require careful explanation.

As above indicated, revised Article 36 takes into account that international controversies fall into two main categories which should be dealt with in different ways, namely: (a) controversies wholly or partly dependent upon legal questions, i.e., questions which are susceptible of decision upon accepted legal principles; and (b) controversies which are wholly or largely dependent upon nonlegal considerations.

The first category includes controversies which depend *solely* upon legal questions and also controversies which, while not wholly dependent upon legal questions, involve one or more legal questions the final adjudication of which would facilitate the settlement of the controversy. For example, there may be an international dispute which depends entirely upon the interpretation of a treaty and involves nothing more than a strictly legal issue. Or there may be a controversy in which, although the authoritative interpretation of a treaty would not settle the whole dispute, such interpretation would narrow the issues and open the way to a settlement. (The legal questions, still unsettled early in 1960, as to rights of access to the Gulf of Aqaba furnish a good example; and one may also note that, in the dispute between France and the United Kingdom concerning the nationality decrees in Tunis and Morocco in 1923, an agreed settlement was reached following an advisory opinion by the Permanent Court of International Justice on a jurisdictional legal issue.)

Even if the adjudication of the legal questions in a particular "dispute" or "situation" did not settle the entire controversy, a final decision of these questions might well lead to a full settlement by negotiation; and that settlement might be all-important to the maintenance of peace. Accordingly, paragraph 3 of this revised Article provides that where in any international "dispute" or "situation" questions capable of determination on legal principles are involved, the General Assembly (or the Executive Council when so authorized by the Assembly) may "direct" that such legal questions "be submitted" to the International Court of Justice "for final determination", provided that in the opinion of the Assembly (or the Council) "the continuance" of the dispute or situation is "likely to endanger" the maintenance of peace.

It is sometimes forgotten that, under the present Charter and Statute of the International Court of Justice, there is no compulsory jurisdiction whatever. Accordingly, no matter how clearly a dispute endangers the peace of the world and no matter how plainly it is susceptible of decision upon purely legal principles, no provision of the present Charter or Statute of the International Court *obliges* the parties to submit to a judicial determination. In so far as such jurisdiction exists, it is solely by virtue of declarations made under the so-called "optional clause" of the Statute of the International Court or by special treaties. And although as of January 1960 about forty nations had accepted compulsory jurisdiction under the optional clause, these acceptances were often subject to such weakening reservations that there is in practice no assurance that even the most dangerous international legal dispute between these nations can in fact be judicially determined.

It should be emphasized, therefore, that the proposed power to "direct" the judicial determination of "legal questions" in cases where, in the opinion of the General Assembly (or the Executive Council), the dispute endangers the peace of the world, would constitute a new departure in that *all* nations would be *obligated* to submit such legal questions without reservation to *final and binding* decision by the International Court of Justice.

In respect of the enforcement of judgments of the International Court of Justice, the last sentence of paragraph 3 prescribes that Article 94 shall apply. This means not only that diplomatic and economic sanctions would be available (under revised Article 41) but also, in the last resort, military sanctions through the United Nations Peace Force (under revised Article 42).

It is obvious that the proposed authority to *direct* the submission of legal questions for final adjudication by the International Court of Justice, together with the provisions for the enforcement of the Court's judgments, would definitely establish the principle of compulsory jurisdiction in respect of all legal issues substantially affecting international peace, and would constitute a great step forward in the acceptance of the rule of law between nations.

It may be noted that this authority to direct the submission of legal questions to the International Court of Justice is supplemented by the further authority of the General Assembly (or the Executive Council), pursuant to Article 96, to refer the legal questions involved in a dispute or situation to the Court for an advisory opinion whenever the disputing nations refuse to submit their case directly to the Court.

Of at least equal importance with the proposals for the enlarged jurisdiction of the International Court of Justice are the new paragraphs 4-10 of revised Article 36, providing for the reference to the World Conciliation Board or the World Equity Tribunal, or to both, of dangerous international disputes or situations which are primarily *not* of a legal nature.

The proposed methods, under paragraphs 4-10, for dealing with these non-legal disputes and situations take account of the fact that they vary greatly in character and need to be handled in diverse ways. With regard to these paragraphs, it should be stressed that the procedures therein provided for are in no way intended as a substitute for diplomacy and the voluntary settlement of nonlegal controversies, but only as alternative methods in case the nations concerned cannot agree upon some procedure to achieve a settlement or, having agreed upon a procedure, nevertheless fail to reach a settlement.

Thus revised Article 33 envisages various voluntary methods which might be agreed upon by the disputants themselves among which are "negotiation", "enquiry", "mediation", "conciliation", "arbitration", "judicial settlement", and "resort to regional agencies or arrangements". Moreover, the General Assembly (or the Executive Council) would continue to have ample power to "recommend" such methods and to "call upon" the nations concerned to use any or all of them (revised Article 33, paragraph 2, and revised Article 36, paragraphs 1 and 2). Accordingly, the proposed power under paragraphs 4-10, whereby disputes or situations "likely to endanger" peace could be referred to the World Conciliation Board or the World Equity Tribunal without regard to the consent of the parties is not to be understood as discouraging the use of voluntary methods. Rather, this power is an all-important alternative in cases where the nations concerned either fail to employ any agreed upon procedure at all, or where such a procedure has been tried but has failed to produce a solution.

In respect of nonlegal questions endangering world peace, it is of no less vital consequence than in respect of legal questions which endanger peace that the United Nations shall not be helpless to require their final settlement. And to this end there must be well-defined peaceful procedures which the nations concerned can be *required* to employ just as under paragraph 3 they can be required to submit legal questions of the same consequence to the International Court of Justice.

With these considerations in mind, paragraph 4 would authorize the General Assembly (or the Executive Council) to refer to the World Conciliation Board any dispute or situation, even over the opposition of the nations concerned, provided that the Assembly (or the Council) had first determined: (a) that the continuance of that particular dispute or situation "is likely to endanger the maintenance of international peace and security"; and (b) that the dispute or situation "involves questions which cannot be satisfactorily decided upon the basis of applicable legal principles".

The World Conciliation Board would then be required to make "such investigations as it may deem necessary" and to "endeavor to bring the nations concerned to an agreement." If those nations should reach a mutually acceptable solution, the Board would inform the General Assembly (or the Executive Council) of its terms and declare the matter closed. If, however, the Board should not succeed in bringing about an agreement within six months, the Board would so notify the Assembly. The Assembly might then decide that no further action need be taken,—for example if the controversy had in the meantime lost its dangerous character. But if the "dispute" or "situation" continued, in the opinion of the Assembly, to be "likely to endanger peace", the Assembly could and presumably would refer the controversy to the World Equity Tribunal by the three-fifths vote required by paragraph 6.

In contrast to the World Conciliation Board, which would be strictly confined to efforts to bring the parties to a voluntary agreement, the World Equity Tribunal would have authority itself to recommend a solution; and if the General Assembly, by the preponderant majority required by paragraph 9, approves the recommended solution in its entirety and further decides that the dangerous dispute or situation is likely to continue unless the solution thus approved is carried out and that such continuance will seriously endanger peace, the approved solution would become enforceable under revised Article 94 through precisely the same diplomatic, economic and military sanctions available for the enforcement of judgments of the International Court.

The proposal should here be noted (paragraphs 6 and 7) that, in order to avoid conflicts of jurisdiction between the World Equity Tribunal and the International Court of Justice, the Tribunal would be empowered to deal with the nonlegal questions involved in any dispute or situation referred to it only after the legal questions therein involved had been decided by the Court. In this way simultaneous consideration by the Court and the Tribunal of the same dispute or situation would be carefully avoided.

On the other hand, there seems to be no objection to the simultaneous consideration of different aspects of a dispute or situation by the International Court and the World Conciliation Board, since a settlement or adjustment by agreement arrived at with the assistance of the Board would make it unnecessary for the Court to render a judgment in the case. As between private litigants, there is no reason why negotiation and mediation should not proceed simultaneously with the trial of the case; and if an agreed settlement is reached before the Court decides the issues, it is often to the best interests of all concerned. Similar considerations apply to international controversies, and would make it unwise to forbid mediation or conciliation merely because the Court has the case under consideration.

The practical application of the alternative procedures provided for in paragraphs 4-10 can best be envisaged in relation to some of the more urgent international problems which actually threatened world peace in 1959 or may do so unless taken in hand.

A list of such problems, made early in 1960 and by no means complete, would include: the division of Korea and of Viet-Nam, where large opposing armies stand on guard; the problem of Formosa (Taiwan) and of Quemoy and Matsu; the Kashmir problem; the question of assured access to the oil of the Middle East; the problem of international control of vital passages between seas and oceans, such as the Turkish Straits, Suez and Panama; the problem of fair apportionment of the waters of various international rivers; the questions of a less controversial regime for Berlin, and the division of Germany; the problem of the repression in certain parts of Africa of nonwhite majorities by white minorities; and the acute Israeli-Arab hostility.

It may well be that a peaceful solution of some of these problems can only be expected when the disarmament plan, which is so vital a feature of these proposals, is completed or is well under way. For example, it is hardly to be supposed that any Soviet government would think it safe *while the arms race continues* to relinquish its position in East Germany, Poland, Czechoslovakia, Romania and Bulgaria. And until national armaments are well on their way to abolition, it is hard to see how Korea or Viet-Nam can be reunited, or how Communist China and Nationalist China can be reconciled.

On the other hand, certain other problems could be adequately dealt with under revised Article 36 soon after the adoption of the revised Charter and without waiting for disarmament. One of these would be the Israeli-Arab problem; and it will illustrate the application of revised Article 36, especially the procedure for referring a complex and hard controversy to the World Equity Tribunal, to consider how a nonviolent and permanent settlement of that long-standing problem could be achieved.

Let us assume that the revised Charter has been in force for several years and that while disarmament is by no means complete, the new institutions which would function under revised Articles 9, 23 and 36 are well established, i.e., the General Assembly on its new basis, the new Executive Council, the strengthened International Court of Justice, the World Conciliation Board and the World Equity Tribunal. Let us also assume that the United Nations Peace Force has been organized to the point that it has sufficient strength to police all the borders between Israel and its neighbors.

Let us further assume that the hostility between Israel and certain Arab states continues to be so acute that it would be futile to urge direct negotiations between them, and even futile to invoke the good offices of the World Conciliation Board.

In these circumstances, the normal remedy would be to refer the entire "situation" to the World Equity Tribunal by the three-fifths vote of the General Assembly required by paragraph 7. This vote would be upon the ground that the continuance of the situation would be "likely to endanger" international peace, as would certainly be the case. Simultaneously the Assembly might well order the United Nations Peace Force to patrol all the borders between the hostile nations pending the recommendations of the Tribunal and action of the Assembly thereon.

The World Equity Tribunal, acting under paragraph 8, would then hold hearings, conduct its own investigation and review all aspects of the situation, —subject to the proviso that if any legal questions had been referred to the International Court of Justice, the Tribunal would suspend its proceedings until the Court's decision was rendered.

The World Equity Tribunal's function would be, after full inquiry and fair hearing of all sides, to recommend a comprehensive solution on the basis of what is "reasonable, just and fair" to all the nations concerned. Accordingly, the Tribunal could and would consider the problem of the resettlement of the Arab refugees, the problem of the use of Jordan River water, the problem of access to the Gulf of Aqaba and of Israel's rights of transit through the Suez Canal in the light of any decision by the International Court, and the whole question of workable boundaries as between Israel and all its neighbors.

The World Equity Tribunal would then present to the General Assembly a comprehensive set of recommendations for a "solution" on the basis of what is "reasonable, just and fair".

At this point, all the nations concerned would have the opportunity to accept the recommended solution, in which event the matter would be deemed closed. Failing such acceptance, however, the General Assembly would consider the World Equity Tribunal's report and could act on that report in several ways: (1) The Assembly could vote a nonacceptance of the report, in which case the situation could, at the Assembly's option, be returned to the Tribunal for further consideration (paragraph 10). (2) The Assembly could accept the report, in whole or with modifications, but by no more than the normal majority required on important questions (i.e., by a majority of all the Representatives), in which case the proposed solution, as so approved by the Assembly, would go to the nations concerned as a recommendation only, although necessarily a powerful one (paragraph 10). (3) Or finally, the Assembly could approve the solution recommended by the Tribunal "in its entirety" by the preponderant majority of three fourths of all the Representatives, including two thirds of the Representatives from the twelve largest nations, in which event that solution would become enforceable by all the available sanctions (paragraph 9).

If, as could normally be expected, the General Assembly did approve the World Equity Tribunal's report even by no more than the ordinary majority of all the Representatives, it could be expected that the moral effect would be such as to bring about voluntary acceptance. And in case the approval were by the very large preponderant majority which would automatically authorize the use of sanctions against any noncomplying nation, the pressure for voluntary acceptance would be almost irresistible.

While, therefore, it would be important to have the possibility of sanctions in reserve, it is reasonable to expect that all the nations concerned would voluntarily comply with the World Equity Tribunal's proposed solution either at the point when the Tribunal's report was made, or at the later stage of its approval by the General Assembly.

In this way, there is every reasonable prospect that even so complex and embittered a situation as the Israeli-Arab problem could and would be peacefully adjusted,—through the use of machinery which is lacking under the present Charter.

What applies to the Israeli-Arab problem applies also to various other disputes and situations in the world "likely to endanger" peace. Some of them would be easier of solution than the Israeli-Arab conflict because less bitter and prolonged; while some might be still more difficult of solution and could, indeed, yield to the procedures of revised Article 36 only when national disarmament has been completed and the fears and tensions engendered by the arms race have subsided.

In the supposed Israeli-Arab case, it is assumed that no "domestic jurisdiction" question would be involved. But in several other of the existing dangerous situations, matters would certainly be involved in which, under the present Charter (Article 2, paragraph 7), the United Nations would not be clearly authorized to intervene, no matter how serious they may become. For example, in the problem of racial repression in South Africa, it would probably be a valid objection *under the present Charter* that this situation is of no concern to the United Nations, no matter what world-wide emotions may be stirred or how much world peace may be actually endangered, so long as the actual events causing the disturbance are confined to the territory of the Union of South Africa.

It is to meet this difficulty that the amendment of Article 2, paragraph 7, is proposed whereby it is expressly provided that the principle of nonintervention by the United Nations in matters of "domestic jurisdiction" shall not prejudice the employment of the procedures for pacific settlement under revised Article 36 when the General Assembly has decided that the situation, even though *ordinarily* "domestic", has so developed that it has become a serious danger to world peace.

Thus, the impotence of the United Nations in such "domestic jurisdiction" matters would be abolished, although only in exceptional circumstances and subject to the most careful safeguards. Through the modification of Article 2, paragraph 7, together with revised Article 36, it would be established, in effect, that a situation, which would otherwise be "domestic" ceases to be such when its effect is actually to create serious danger of international violence.

In summary: The new system provided by this revised Article 36 for the pacific settlement of disputes and situations which are "likely to endanger" peace embodies three main concepts: *First,* there should be such comprehensive and flexible world machinery for peaceful settlements on the basis of fair hearing, law and equity that no nation could any longer have even a plausible reason to plead the lack of such machinery as an excuse for violence; and this machinery should include mediation, the compulsory adjudication of legal issues and authoritative recommendations on nonlegal questions. *Second,* when a particular international controversy has been judged dangerous to peace by a vote of the world's representative body (the revised General Assembly), there should be workable *practical means* (through the enforcement of judgments of the International Court of Justice and of solutions proposed by the World Equity Tribunal, when overwhelmingly approved by the Assembly) to deal effectively with threatening situations *before* they erupt into international violence. *Third,* while the United Nations should have no power to deal with troubles within a nation, no matter how hideous, unless those troubles clearly endanger world peace, there should be no "domestic jurisdiction" dogma so rigid as to prevent United Nations intervention as a last resort if and when the peace of the world is plainly involved.

The rationale of these proposals is that the world can no longer afford to be without adequate institutions not only to suppress international violence *after* it occurs, but also, so far as reasonably possible, to *prevent* it from occurring. The provisions of this revised Article 36 (together with interrelated provisions of other Articles and Annexes) have this sole purpose in view. They would, it is believed, be effective to achieve that purpose.

Article 37

1. *Should the parties to a dispute of the nature referred to in Article 33 fail to settle it by the*

1. *In case the General Assembly, or the Executive Council when acting in the matter pursuant to*

106

means indicated in that Article, they shall refer it to the Security Council.

authority from the Assembly, determines, in accordance with paragraph 3, 4 or 7 of Article 36, that the continuance of any dispute or situation is likely to endanger the maintenance of international peace and security, it shall prescribe provisional measures to be adopted by the nations concerned. The Assembly, or the Council when authorized by the Assembly, may from time to time modify any such provisional measures, taking into account any recommendations which may be made by the International Court of Justice, the World Conciliation Board or the World Equity Tribunal.

2. If the Security Council deems that the continuance of the dispute is in fact likely to endanger the maintenance of international peace and security, it shall decide whether to take action under Article 36 or to recommend such terms of settlement as it may consider appropriate.

2. The nations concerned shall be bound to observe such provisional measures and to abstain from any sort of action which might aggravate the dispute or situation.

3. In order to ensure that the nations concerned will observe such provisional measures, the General Assembly, or the Executive Council when authorized by the Assembly, may direct that units of the United Nations Peace Force be stationed temporarily in the territory of the nations concerned, whether or not with their consent; and in such a case the nations concerned shall furnish to the Peace Force such assistance and facilities as may be required for the purpose of maintaining peace in the area.

Comment. The subject matter of the present text of this Article 37 is covered by the revised text of Article 36, which provides various alternative methods for dealing with disputes or situations the continuance of which is likely to endanger the maintenance of peace. The present text of Article 37 has, therefore, been deleted and a new text dealing with a different subject matter has been substituted in its place.

The purpose of the proposed new text is to close an important gap in the provisions of the present Charter relating to the pacific settlement of any threatening "dispute" or "situation", i.e., the lack of any *requirement* that the General Assembly (or the Executive Council) shall prescribe provisional measures when peace is endangered and while the problems involved are being investigated, mediated, arbitrated or adjudicated by the World Conciliation Board, the World Equity Tribunal or the International Court of Justice, as the case may be.

Even before any steps are taken relative to the merits of a dispute or situation, it may be of vital importance to prevent any *further aggravation* of the dispute or situation. Accordingly, this revised Article not only confers the necessary authority on the General Assembly (or the Executive Council) to order provisional measures, but also imposes a duty upon the Assembly (or the Council) to direct such measures whenever the Assembly (or the Council) determines that a dispute or situation is likely to endanger peace. Broad power would be conferred on the Assembly (or the Council) to modify the initial provisional measures; and if the dispute or situation were referred to the World Conciliation Board, the World Equity Tribunal or the International Court, any one of these organs could recommend such further provisional measures as it deemed necessary. On the basis of these recommendations, as well as on its own initiative, the Assembly (or the Council) could modify the original provisional measures from time to time.

This revised Article also provides (paragraph 2) that the nations concerned shall be bound to take all the steps necessary to ensure compliance with the prescribed provisional measures. They might be required, for instance, to suspend the enforcement of a national law or the execution of a national decision, the validity of which had been challenged before the International Court of Justice.

Still further (by paragraph 2), all the nations concerned would be required, even before any provisional measures were prescribed, to "abstain from any sort of action which might aggravate the dispute or situation."

Finally this revised Article provides (paragraph 3) that the General Assembly (or the Executive Council when authorized by the Assembly) may order the temporary stationing of units of the United Nations Peace Force in the territory of any nation to the extent necessary to ensure compliance with the provisional measures; and it is made clear that this may be done irrespective of the consent of any nation concerned.

These provisions should be effective to ensure that a serious danger to peace would become no worse during the possibly long period that might be needed to work out a solution through the organs and procedures provided for in the preceding revised Articles of this Chapter VI.

Without prejudice to the provisions of Articles 33 to 37, the *Security* Council may, if all the parties to any dispute so request, make recommendations to the *parties* with a view to a pacific settlement of the dispute.

Without prejudice to the provisions of Articles 33 to 37, *the General Assembly or* the *Executive* Council may, if all the *nations which are* parties to any dispute *or are involved in any situation* so request, make recommendations to the *nations concerned* with a view to a pacific settlement of the dispute *or adjustment of the situation; or if so requested the Assembly or Council may decide the dispute or define the terms upon which the situation shall be adjusted, the decision in either case to be binding on all the nations concerned.*

Comment. This Article relates to the contingency that all the nations involved in any dispute or situation, even if not sufficiently serious to endanger peace, decide that they wish to have the General Assembly or Executive Council deal with the problem. They may wish to have the Assembly or Council do no more than make recommendations or they may go further and wish to have a final decision made. The present text partially provides for such a contingency in permitting mere "recommendations" regarding any dispute. There seems every reason, however, for enlarging the scope of this voluntary procedure. The revised Article does so by providing: (a) that the nations concerned may, by unanimous agreement, designate either the General Assembly or the Executive Council to deal with the matter; (b) that the Assembly or Council, as the case may be, may be asked to deal with a "situation" as well as with a "dispute"; and (c) that the nations concerned may not only request the making of "recommendations" but, alternatively may ask the Assembly or Council, as the case may be, to render a binding decision.

It should be noted that this proposed provision for the unanimous reference of any "dispute" or "situation" to the General Assembly or Executive Council is in no way inconsistent with the various alternative procedures provided under the preceding revised Articles of Chapter VI.

It may sometimes, or even often, occur that all the nations concerned in a difficult "dispute" or "situation" would prefer to have the General Assembly itself, or its agent, the Executive Council, deal directly with the subject matter rather than contest the issues before the International Court of Justice or the World Equity Tribunal or invoke the aid of the World Conciliation Board or resort to any other process. When such is the unanimous wish of the nations concerned, the Assembly or Council (whichever may have been requested to deal with the matter) should have clear authority to comply with the request. And this authority should be not only to make "recommendations", but actually to make a final and binding decision, if so requested.

While the latter procedure might be seldom invoked, it might well provide the best solution when the nations concerned unite on this method. A precedent is found in the final settlement of the fate of the former Italian colonies under the 1947 Peace Treaty with Italy, which contained a provision authorizing the General Assembly to make recommendations on that subject. The parties to the Treaty all agreed to accept as binding the recommendations subsequently made by the Assembly; and the final result was a solution reasonably satisfactory to all concerned.

CHAPTER VII

ACTION WITH RESPECT TO THREATS TO THE PEACE, BREACHES OF THE PEACE, AND ACTS OF AGGRESSION

Article 39

The *Security* Council shall determine the existence of any threat to the peace, breach of the peace, *or* act of aggression and shall *make recommendations, or* decide what measures shall be taken in accordance with Articles 41 *and* 42, to maintain or restore international peace and security.

1. The General Assembly, or the Executive Council to the extent authorized by paragraph 2 of this Article, shall determine the existence of any *imminent* threat to the peace, *serious* breach of the peace, act of aggression, *or serious refusal to comply with this revised Charter or the laws and regulations enacted thereunder,* and shall decide what measures shall be taken, in accordance with Articles 40, 41, 42 *and* 43, to maintain or restore international peace and security *or to ensure compliance with this revised Charter and the laws and regulations enacted thereunder.*

2. When the General Assembly is not in session and an emergency arises which the Executive Council considers to require immediate action, the Council shall declare such emergency and shall take such interim measures of the kind referred to in Articles 40 and 42 as it may deem necessary, provided that the Council shall simultaneously request the Secretary-General to convoke a special session of the Assembly to meet as soon as possible and in any case within a week from such declaration. At such special session the Assembly shall approve, modify or revoke the declaration and interim measures of the Council; and the Assembly may direct such other measures as it deems necessary. The authority of the Council to take interim measures shall cease as soon as the Assembly convenes.

Comment. The broad purpose of this revised Article is similar to that of the present Article, i.e., to confer authority: (1) to declare the existence of actual or imminent breaches of international peace or of serious violations of the Charter; and (2) to decide upon and apply effective measures to prevent violence, restore order or vindicate the authority of the Charter. In several important respects, however, the revised Article modifies and strengthens the powers granted by the present Article.

The proposed grant of authority to the General Assembly (paragraph 1) to determine the existence of actual aggression or serious threats to the peace or serious refusals to comply with the Charter and the laws of the United Nations, and of authority to decide what measures shall be taken, is a further consequence of the previous proposal that the Assembly itself shall have the general and "primary" responsibility for the maintenance of peace (revised Articles 11 and 24). The new Executive Council would, in this regard, have authority only when the Assembly is not in session and when the Council decides that an emergency exists which requires "immediate action"; and even then the Council's action would be subject to prompt review by a special session of the Assembly to be convoked within a week after the Council's action (paragraph 2).

The proposed inclusion in the General Assembly's authority of power to determine the existence not only of any direct danger to peace but also of any "serious refusal" to comply with the Charter or with "the laws and regulations enacted thereunder" is a consequence of the proposed enlargement of the general scope of the Assembly's power and in particular of the grant of authority to legislate within certain strict limits. Since to be effective it is essential that the Assembly's legislation be properly enforced, it is clearly necessary to grant adequate authority to the Assembly (within the limits of revised Articles 40, 41, 42 and 43) to see to it that the duly enacted and valid laws and regulations of the Assembly are obeyed. At the same time it is appropriate to include express authority to ensure compliance with the Charter itself.

It is important to have in mind the difference between: (a) the authority and procedures covered by this revised Article 39 and the other revised Articles of this Chapter VII; and (b) the authority and procedures covered by revised Articles 33-38 of the preceding Chapter VI. The latter provide a variety of methods for the peaceful settlement of "disputes" or the adjustment of "situations" at the stage when they are "likely" to "endanger" peace, but *before* any such dispute or situation has reached the stage of an actual aggression or breach of the peace or imminent threat to the peace. In other words, all the elaborate provisions of Chapter VI relate to the *pacific* settlement of disputes or situations which, while dangerous, have not yet become imminent threats to or actual breaches of the peace. By contrast, the provisions of Chapter VII relate to the treatment of actual or imminent breaches of the peace by means which are *not* pacific, i.e., through diplomatic and economic sanctions (revised Article 41) and, if necessary, through military action by the United Nations Peace Force (revised Articles 42 and 43).

The employment of means of this sort (except on an interim basis during acute emergency) should be a function of the General Assembly itself; and the use of these enforcement measures, when necessary, should be not only the right but also the duty of the Assembly.

Consequently, the provision of the present Article permitting mere "recommendations" in these serious contingencies has been eliminated. The new wording makes it clear that when a formal finding has been made by the General Assembly that the authority of the United Nations has been flouted, the Assembly shall be bound to *order* direct measures rather than merely to recommend them,—although the Assembly may, of course, vary the strength of such measures depending upon the circumstances of each case.

It will be noted that two important obstacles to effective enforcement action would be removed by the proposed changes in this Article. *First,* the obstacle of the veto in the present Security Council would be abolished, and either the General Assembly would be able to take action by the majority provided for in revised Article 18, or the new Executive Council could take emergency interim action by the majority provided for in revised Article 27. *Second,* the ability of the United Nations to take effective enforcement measures would be greatly increased by the availability of the United Nations Peace Force which the General Assembly (or the Executive Council in an emergency when the Assembly was not in session) could order into action without delay.

Article 40

In order to prevent an aggravation of the situation, the *Security* Council may, before *making the recommendations or* deciding upon the measures provided for in Article 39, call upon the parties concerned to comply with such provisional measures as it deems necessary *or desirable*. Such provisional measures shall be without prejudice to the rights, claims, or

In order to prevent an aggravation of the situation, *the General Assembly, or* the *Executive* Council *in the circumstances defined in paragraph 2 of Article 39*, may, before deciding upon the measures provided for in Article 39, call upon the parties concerned to comply with such provisional measures as it deems necessary. Such provisional measures shall be without position of the parties concerned. *The Security Council shall duly take account of failure to comply with such provisional measures.*

prejudice to the rights, claims, or position of the parties concerned. *In case of noncompliance with such provisional measures, the General Assembly, or the Executive Council in the circumstances defined in paragraph 2 of Article 39, shall decide what measures shall be taken in accordance with Articles 41, 42 and 43 to enforce compliance therewith; and such measures may, in accordance with paragraph 3 of Article 37, include the stationing of the United Nations Peace Force in the territory of the nations concerned.*

Comment. The proposed grant of authority to the General Assembly to direct compliance with "provisional measures" is one more recognition of the "primary responsibility" of the Assembly for the maintenance of peace (revised Articles 11 and 24). In view of the proposed general responsibility of the Assembly in this regard, it should likewise have authority to prescribe "provisional measures" designed to "prevent an aggravation of the situation". The authority given to the Executive Council in this respect is limited to "the circumstances defined in paragraph 2 of Article 39", i.e., when the General Assembly is not in session and the Council declares an emergency requiring "immediate action".

The new last sentence confers more direct and decisive authority than does the present Article for the enforcement of provisional measures. The present clause, providing only that due "account" shall be taken of a failure to comply with provisional measures, seems to imply that a nation has no real obligation to comply with a provisional measure, and that there is nothing that the United Nations could do at this stage to require compliance. It is proposed to substitute a clear-cut mandate to the General Assembly (or the Executive Council to the limited extent permitted in an emergency) to decide upon the measures to be taken in order to ensure compliance. These measures would be subject to the limitations of revised Articles 41, 42 and 43; but it is specifically provided that such measures may include the use of the United Nations Peace Force under the provisions of revised Article 37. As in the case of the powers conferred by revised Article 39, the increased powers under this revised Article 40 would be in harmony with the greatly strengthened authority to enforce peace which the United Nations would possess under the whole revision.

In the event that any interim provisional measures were prescribed by the Executive Council, all such measures would be subject to approval, modifica-

114

tion or revocation by the General Assembly at its special session to be forthwith convoked (paragraph 2 of revised Article 39).

Article 41

The *Security Council may* decide what measures not involving the use of armed force are to be employed to give effect to its decisions, *and it may call upon the Members of the United Nations to apply such measures.* These may include complete or partial interruption of economic relations and of rail, sea, air, postal, telegraphic, radio, and other means of communication, and the severance of diplomatic relations.

1. The *General Assembly shall* decide what measures not involving the use of armed force are to be employed to give effect to its decisions. These may include complete or partial interruption of economic relations and of rail, sea, air, postal, telegraphic, radio, and other means of communication, and the severance of diplomatic relations.

2. The General Assembly shall direct the member Nations to apply the measures decided upon, and shall invite any state which is not a member of the United Nations to do likewise.

Comment. Although it is proposed by the creation of a United Nations Peace Force (revised Articles 11 and 42 and Annex II) to equip the United Nations itself with effective *military* means to enforce peace, it is eminently desirable to retain and strengthen the present powers to impose diplomatic and economic sanctions so as to obviate, if possible, the use of military force.

The proposal to empower the General Assembly itself to order diplomatic and economic sanctions is in harmony with corresponding changes in other Articles whereby the Assembly, in view of its "primary responsibility" for the maintenance of peace, is granted specific powers to fulfil that responsibility. In contrast with revised Articles 39, 40 and 42 which contemplate measures requiring the utmost speed in order to be effective, this revised Article 41 deals only with diplomatic and economic measures as to which it is almost inconceivable that interim action by the Executive Council (reviewable by the Assembly within a week) would be essential. Consequently, this revised Article confers no such interim emergency authority on the Council as is conferred by revised Articles 39, 40 and 42.

By paragraph 2 of this revised Article, the General Assembly would be required to "direct" all the member Nations to apply the economic sanctions and the severance of diplomatic relations decided upon and to "invite" any state which might not be a member of the United Nations to do likewise.

115

The changes from "may decide" to "shall decide" and from "may call upon" to "shall direct" are proposed in order to clarify and strengthen both the responsibility and the power of the United Nations to maintain peace. Again this is a recognition of the fact that the proposed revision creates, within the limited sphere of preventing war, a world authority equipped with genuine and effective power not only to make decisions, but also to enforce them.

This revised Article 41 should be read in connection with revised Article 48 whereby the member Nations *obligate* themselves to carry out all enforcement measures required of them by the General Assembly,—including the nonmilitary sanctions covered by this revised Article.

Article 42

Should the *Security* Council consider that measures provided for in Article 41 would be inadequate or have proved to be inadequate, it *may take* such action by air, sea, or land *forces* as may be necessary to maintain or restore international peace and security. Such action may include demonstrations, blockade, and other operations *by air, sea, or land forces of Members of the United Nations.*

1. Should *the General Assembly, or* the *Executive* Council *in the circumstances defined in paragraph 2 of Article 39,* consider that measures provided for in Article 41 would be inadequate or have proved to be inadequate, it *shall direct* such action by air, sea, or land *elements of the United Nations Peace Force* as may be necessary to maintain or restore international peace and security *or to ensure compliance with this revised Charter and the laws and regulations enacted thereunder.* Such action may include demonstrations, blockade, and other operations; *but any such action shall be taken pursuant to the procedures and subject to the limitations contained in Annex II.*

2. In case the United Nations has directed action by the United Nations Peace Force, all the member Nations shall, within the limitations and pursuant to the procedures contained in Annex II, make available to the United Nations such assistance and facilities, including rights of passage, as the United Nations may call for.

116

Comment. The changes proposed in this Article are obviously of extreme importance. As already noted, the United Nations under the proposed revision would no longer have to depend on the willingness of member Nations to contribute military forces, but would have its own "United Nations Peace Force" ready to act on a moment's notice (revised Article 11 and Annex II). The purpose of this revised Article 42 is to define the circumstances in which and the procedures by which the Peace Force can be utilized to maintain or restore international peace.

In harmony with other proposals whereby the General Assembly (fully representative as it would be of all or nearly all the world's people) would have the "primary responsibility" for maintaining peace, all the critical decisions for that purpose should be made by that body. It follows, therefore, that the authorization of so important a step as the use of military sanctions ought to be solely the function of the Assembly,—save only that (as provided in revised Article 39) the Executive Council should have some *interim* authority to direct such sanctions in case of an emergency requiring "immediate action".

This revised Article 42 embodies that conception. By paragraph 1 the General Assembly is given authority to order the United Nations Peace Force into action if the Assembly considers that nonmilitary sanctions under revised Article 41 "would be inadequate or have proved to be inadequate". As already noted, the authority of the Executive Council in this regard would be much more limited. For that Council could order action by the Peace Force only: (a) if the Assembly is not in session and (b) if the Council determines that there is an emergency requiring "immediate action". Even then, the Council's action would be of no more than an interim character, since it would be subject to review and change within not more than one week by the special session of the Assembly which would have to be convoked immediately (revised Article 39).

In the first sentence of paragraph 1 of this revised Article, it is proposed to change "may take" to "shall direct", in order to clarify and strengthen the obligation and authority of the General Assembly (and, in an emergency, of the Executive Council) in this field of military sanctions. The conception is that, if the Assembly (or the Council) has reached a decision that measures short of armed force are or would be inadequate, it should be *required* to employ the United Nations Peace Force, since otherwise the United Nations would have to confess impotence to maintain peace.

The omission in the second sentence of revised paragraph 1 of the phrase "by air, sea, or land forces of Members of the United Nations" is obviously necessary, since military action under this revised Article would be exclusively by the United Nations Peace Force (including any Peace Force reservists called into service of the United Nations under revised Article 43) and not by any national forces.

Paragraph 1 also provides that "any such action" (i.e., military sanctions) must be taken "within the limitations and pursuant to the procedures contained in Annex II." Hence it follows that this revised Article must be read in connection with the detailed provisions of Annex II. On this subject Article 4, paragraph 5, of Annex II provides that "any action by the United Nations Peace Force pursuant to Articles 37, 40, 42 or 43 of this revised Charter shall be limited to such operations as are strictly necessary to maintain or restore international peace or to ensure compliance with this revised Charter and the laws and regulations enacted thereunder." And Article 4 of Annex II goes on to provide more definite safeguards to ensure that the use of military force shall be limited to that which is absolutely essential to deter or suppress violence.

The new paragraph 2 of this revised Article 42 contains the requirement that "all the member Nations" must give all necessary assistance to the United Nations (within the limits of Annex II) if the United Nations Peace Force has been called into action.

Article 43

1. *All Members of the United Nations, in order to contribute to the maintenance of international peace and security, undertake to make available to the Security Council, on its call and in accordance with a special agreement or agreements, armed forces, assistance, and facilities, including rights of passage, necessary for the purpose of maintaining international peace and security.*

1. *If the standing component of the United Nations Peace Force has been called into action pursuant to Article 42, but the General Assembly determines that the situation is of so serious a character that it cannot be dealt with by the then existing strength of such standing component, the Assembly shall declare the existence of a grave emergency and shall call to active duty as many members of the Peace Force Reserve as the Assembly may deem necessary. Any such call shall be made pursuant to the procedures and subject to the limitations contained in Annex II.*

2. *Such agreement or agreements shall govern the numbers and types of forces, their degree of readiness and general location, and the nature of the facilities and assistance to be provided.*

2. *If the General Assembly determines that the strength of the United Nations Peace Force would be insufficient to deal adequately with the situation, even when the authorized strength of its standing component and of the Peace Force Reserve has been increased to the maximum limits provided for in Annex II and even when all the*

118

members of the Peace Force Reserve have been called to active duty, the Assembly shall declare the existence of an extreme emergency and shall direct that for the period of such emergency only the strength of the Peace Force shall be increased beyond the maximum limits provided for in Annex II to such number as the Assembly deems necessary and that the member Nations shall cooperate with the United Nations in obtaining additional recruits; provided that such increase shall be made pursuant to the procedures and subject to the limitations contained in Annex II.

3. The agreement or agreements shall be negotiated as soon as possible on the initiative of the Security Council. They shall be concluded between the Security Council and Members or between the Security Council and groups of Members and shall be subject to ratification by the signatory states in accordance with their respective constitutional processes.

Comment. Hard experience in the 1946-1959 period has demonstrated the inadequacy of the present Article 43. It relies entirely on voluntary agreements between nations to supply military forces to the United Nations; and despite years of negotiation it has proved impossible to conclude such agreements. In consequence, when the Korean emergency arose in 1950 and the attacks on Egypt by Israel, France and the United Kingdom occurred in 1956, the United Nations neither had any military forces of its own nor any forces which it was entitled to call for as a matter of right. In consequence, although a number of nations voluntarily supplied contingents, the burden fell unequally upon the various members of the United Nations.

To remedy this situation it is proposed completely to remodel this Article in order that the United Nations shall have adequate means, even in the most extreme contingency, to maintain or restore peace and to enforce compliance with the revised Charter and the laws of the United Nations.

The situation envisaged is not only that diplomatic and economic sanctions

119

under revised Article 41 have proved insufficient, but also that the situation is so serious that, in the General Assembly's opinion, it cannot be dealt with by the then existing strength of the United Nations Peace Force. Such a contingency would, indeed, be extremely remote, since after universal and complete national disarmament has been accomplished, a strong United Nations military force should be able to deal readily with any possible threat to peace. Nevertheless, the importance of maintaining the authority of the United Nations in all circumstances is so vital that every precaution should be taken to see that the United Nations shall have reserve power which would be unquestionably sufficient to suppress any conceivable defiance of its authority.

This would be in part accomplished by revised paragraph 1 whereby the United Nations Peace Force Reserve (to be established pursuant to Annex II and to be composed of a large number of individual reservists with basic training) would be subject to call for active service if the General Assembly decided that the then existing strength of the standing component of the Peace Force was inadequate. This provision would be supplemented by the further authority, under revised paragraph 2, greatly to strengthen the Peace Force in case of extreme emergency by obtaining new recruits to whatever number may be required, but for the period of the emergency only. To this end revised paragraph 2 authorizes the General Assembly to require the member Nations to aid (within the limits of Annex II) in the recruitment of the additional personnel.

It should be noted that the authority to summon into service the members of the Peace Force Reserve and to call on the member Nations for cooperation in the still further increase of the Peace Force would be granted to the General Assembly alone. Since the Assembly could be quickly convoked in special session and since there could hardly be any situation in which a few days difference in the summoning of the Peace Force reservists would be important, it seems unnecessary to give interim emergency power to the Executive Council in this regard.

Article 44

When the Security Council has decided to use force it shall, before calling upon a Member not represented on it to provide armed forces in fulfillment of the obligations assumed under Article 43, invite that Member, if the Member so desires, to participate in the decisions of the Security Council concerning the employment of contingents of that Member's armed forces.

The General Assembly shall enact in advance such general regulations as the Assembly may deem necessary in order to enable the member Nations to comply promptly and effectively with any call or direction by the Assembly under Articles 41, 42 and 43.

Comment. The present text of this Article is no longer applicable, since under the revised Charter the United Nations would have its own military forces in the shape of the United Nations Peace Force.

The purpose of the entirely new text is to require the General Assembly to adopt "advance" general regulations with regard to: (1) the carrying out by the member Nations of diplomatic and economic sanctions under revised Article 41; and (2) the facilities to be supplied and the assistance to be rendered by member Nations under revised Articles 42 and 43 if military sanctions are being imposed. It would obviously facilitate the carrying out of the obligations of the member Nations with regard to all these sanctions if careful provision were made in advance as to what would be expected of them.

Article 45

In order to enable the United Nations to take urgent military measures, Members shall hold immediately available national air-force contingents for combined international enforcement action. The strength and degree of readiness of these contingents and plans for their combined action shall be determined, within the limits laid down in the special agreement or agreements referred to in Article 43, by the Security Council with the assistance of the Military Staff Committee.

The member Nations shall adopt such internal legislation and administrative measures as may be necessary to assure prompt and effective compliance with such general regulations as are enacted by the General Assembly under Article 44 and under Annex II.

Comment. The present text of this Article is no longer applicable: (1) because under the revised Charter the United Nations would have its own military forces available for any military sanctions which might be necessary (namely, the standing United Nations Peace Force supplemented, if necessary, by the calling up of Peace Force reservists); and (2) because, under the disarmament plan (Annex I), the member Nations would have no "air-force contingents" since they would be permitted to have only such strictly limited and lightly armed forces as would be necessary for the maintenance of internal order.

The new text of this Article supplements the previous revised Articles of Chapter VII so that, taken together, they constitute a complete scheme for the application of diplomatic, economic and military sanctions as required.

Revised Article 41 provides for diplomatic and economic sanctions; revised Articles 42 and 43 for military sanctions; while the purpose of revised Article 44 is to ensure the enactment by the United Nations of advance regulations to facilitate the carrying out by the member Nations of their duty to collaborate in the application of sanctions, if and when they are called upon to act. Finally, this revised Article 45 completes the plan by obligating every member Nation to adopt such stand-by *internal* measures as may be necessary to effectuate the "general regulations" adopted by the Assembly under revised Article 44. In this way there would be maximum assurance that all the measures directed by the United Nations would be taken without undue delay.

Article 46

Plans for *the application of armed force* shall be made by the *Security* Council with the assistance of the Military Staff Committee.

Plans for *possible action by the United Nations Peace Force to maintain or restore international peace and security or to ensure compliance with this revised Charter and the laws and regulations enacted thereunder, pursuant to Article 42 and Annex II*, shall be made *in advance* by the *Executive* Council with the assistance of the Military Staff Committee.

Comment. The general purpose of the revised text is the same as that of the present text. The changes are intended only to make clear that the plans for the use of armed force by the United Nations shall be made "in advance". This planning activity would, of course, cover not only potential action by the regular standing United Nations Peace Force but also by the Peace Force as it might be enlarged by the calling out of reservists and, in extreme circumstances, by additional recruits obtained with the aid of member Nations pursuant to revised Article 43.

Article 47

1. There shall be established a Military Staff Committee to advise and assist the *Security* Council on all questions relating to the *Security Council's* military requirements for the maintenance of international peace and security, *the employment and command of forces placed at its disposal, the regulation of armaments, and possible disarmament.*

1. There shall be established a Military Staff Committee to advise and assist *the General Assembly and* the *Executive* Council on all questions relating to the military requirements *of the United Nations* for the maintenance of international peace and security *and for ensuring compliance with the revised Charter of the United Nations and the laws and regulations enacted thereunder. The functions of the Military Staff Committee*

122

*shall include advice and assistance
concerning the organization, administration, recruitment, discipline, training, equipment, compensation and disposition of the
United Nations Peace Force, including the reservists enrolled in
the Peace Force Reserve.*

2. The Military Staff Committee
shall consist of *the Chiefs of Staff
of the permanent members of the
Security Council or their representatives. Any Member of the United
Nations not permanently represented on the Committee shall be
invited by the Committee to be
associated with it when the efficient discharge of the Committee's
responsibilities requires the participation of that Member in its
work.*

2. The Military Staff Committee
shall consist of *five persons, none
of whom shall be a national of
any of the member Nations then
having fifteen or more Representatives in the General Assembly, and
no two of whom shall be nationals
of the same member Nation. They
shall be appointed by the Executive Council for terms not exceeding five years, subject to confirmation by the General Assembly.
The Executive Council shall have
authority to remove any member
of the Military Staff Committee,
whenever the Council deems it
necessary.*

3. The Military Staff Committee
shall be responsible under the *Security* Council for the *strategic direction* of *any armed forces placed
at the disposal of the Security
Council. Questions relating to the
command of such forces shall be
worked out subsequently.*

3. *When action by the United
Nations Peace Force has been directed pursuant to Articles 42 and
43, the Executive Council, with
the assistance of the Military Staff
Committee, shall be responsible
for the general strategic direction
of that Force.* The Military Staff
Committee shall be responsible,
under *the direction and control of*
the Council, for the *actual operations of the Peace Force. When any
such action by the Peace Force has
been directed, the Council may
with the advice of the Committee,
appoint the principal commanders
of the Peace Force. No such ap-*

123

pointment shall in any case, however, extend beyond the period of actual operations; and the Council shall have authority to remove any such commander whenever the Council deems it necessary.

4. *The Military Staff Committee with the authorization of the Security Council and after consultation with appropriate regional agencies, may establish regional subcommittees.*

Comment. The purposes of this revised Article 47 are: (a) to provide for a carefully selected professional group to advise the General Assembly and the Executive Council with respect to military matters; and (b) to provide for the professional direction of any actual military operations by the United Nations Peace Force. It should, however, be stressed that the final authority would at all times remain in civilian hands, i.e., in the General Assembly and the Executive Council. This principle is implemented by the terms of revised Articles 46 and 47 and of Annex II which between them clearly provide: (1) that the Council (subject to general laws and regulations adopted by the Assembly) would have general control over the organization, discipline, training, equipment and disposition of the Peace Force; (2) that the Council would also be responsible, with the advice of the Military Staff Committee, for the preparation of advance plans and for the general strategic direction of the Peace Force; and (3) that the Council would also have ultimate direction and control even of actual operations.

Subject to this ultimate responsibility of the Executive Council and its powers of control, the strictly military command of the Peace Force would be left in the hands of military men. It is deemed advisable, however, to assign this power of command not to a single individual but to a committee of five, to be known as the Military Staff Committee.

This Military Staff Committee would be appointed by the Executive Council, subject to confirmation by the General Assembly. Safeguards against the domination of the Peace Force by any nation or by the military command are contained in the requirements that: (1) no two members of the Military Staff Committee shall be nationals of the same member Nation; (2) all members of the Committee must come from the smaller nations, i.e., from nations other than those nations having fifteen or more Representatives in the Assembly; (3) their terms of appointment shall not exceed five years; (4) the members of the Committee shall be subject to dismissal at the discretion of the Executive Council; and (5) the terms of appointment of principal commanders in the field shall be limited to the period of actual operations of the Peace Force in a particular situation, and all such commanders shall be removable at will

124

by the Council. These safeguards are further supplemented by various provisions of Annex II with respect to the composition, distribution and equipment of the Peace Force.

These careful and interrelated safeguards embody, it is believed, every reasonable precaution against abuse of power by the armed forces of the United Nations, and should provide strong assurance that the world police force would be "tyranny-proof".

Article 48

1. *The* action *required to carry out the decisions of the Security Council* for the maintenance of international peace and security shall be taken by all the *Members of the United Nations* or by some of them, as the *Security* Council may determine.

1. *To the extent that member Nations are directed by the General Assembly, or by the Executive Council in the circumstances defined in paragraph 2 of Article 39, to take* action for the maintenance of international peace and security *or for ensuring compliance with this revised Charter and the laws and regulations enacted thereunder, such action* shall be taken by all the *member Nations* or by some of them, as *the Assembly, or* the Council *in the circumstances defined in paragraph 2 of Article 39,* may determine.

2. *Such decisions* shall be *carried out* by the *Members of the United Nations* directly and through *their action in* the appropriate international agencies of which they are members.

2. *Any such required action* shall be *taken* by the *member Nations* directly and through the appropriate international agencies of which they are members.

Comment. The broad purpose of the revised Article is the same as that of the present Article, namely to obligate all the member Nations loyally to carry out such measures to maintain peace and to ensure compliance with the Charter as have been determined upon by the appropriate organs of the United Nations. The changes merely recognize the proposed "primary responsibility" of the General Assembly for the maintenance of peace and for ensuring compliance with the Charter (revised Article 11) and the substitution of the proposed Executive Council for the present Security Council (revised Articles 23 and 24).

Article 49

The *Members of the United Na-*

The *member Nations* shall join

tions shall join in affording mutual assistance in carrying out the measures decided upon by the *Security* Council.

in affording mutual assistance in carrying out the measures decided upon *by the General Assembly, or* by the *Executive* Council *in the circumstances defined in paragraph 2 of Article 39.*

Comment. The purpose of the revised Article is the same as that of the present Article. The reference to the General Assembly and the change from the "Security Council" to the "Executive Council" are made for the same reasons as the corresponding changes in revised Article 48.

Article 50

If preventive or enforcement measures against any state are taken by the *Security* Council, any other state, whether a *Member* of the United Nations or not, which finds itself confronted with special economic problems arising from the carrying out of those measures shall have the right to *consult the Security Council with regard to a solution of those problems.*

If preventive or enforcement measures against any state are taken *by the General Assembly, or* by the *Executive* Council *in the circumstances defined in paragraph 2 of Article 39,* any other state, whether a *member* of the United Nations or not, which finds itself confronted with special economic problems arising from the carrying out of those measures shall have the right to *obtain relief from the General Assembly.*

Comment. This revised Article is directed toward the same end as the present one, i.e., to provide for assistance to any nation (even a nonmember nation) which is confronted with special economic difficulties as a result of its participation in the application of sanctions directed by the United Nations. The changes take into account the fact that the proposed revision would set up a really effective system of diplomatic, economic and military sanctions, and that the possible consequences of the required collaboration might be more serious to a particular nation than under the present Charter. Fairness requires that the right to special relief of any nation which suffers disproportionate economic loss by reason of its participation in enforcement measures shall be correspondingly broadened.

The present right "to consult . . . with regard to a solution of those problems" seems inadequate, and it is proposed to substitute the right to "obtain relief from the General Assembly" in such circumstances. Such relief would ordinarily take the form of a temporary exemption for a particular member Nation from participation in certain economic sanctions, or of an arrangement to substitute trade with other nations for trade with the nation against which the sanctions are directed. In exceptional circumstances, however, the relief could take the form of actual money grants from the general funds of the United Nations available under the revenue system established by revised Article 17 and Annex V.

Under this revised Article 50, for example, Korea would have had the *right* to United Nations relief for the damage suffered during the conflict on Korean soil in 1950-1953; and instead of taking up a voluntary subscription among the nations for a relief fund, the United Nations itself would have had authority to appropriate funds for the purpose of helping to repair the damage.

In this way, relief for exceptional economic damage suffered by a particular nation would be recognized as a matter of right rather than charity. Moreover, the burden of the relief, instead of falling unevenly upon particular nations by reason of their voluntary contributions, would be distributed equitably among the peoples of the member Nations through their payments for the budget of the United Nations pursuant to Annex V.

Other changes in this Article result from the enlargement of the responsibility of the General Assembly for the maintenance of peace (revised Article 11) and from the substitution of the Executive Council for the Security Council (revised Article 23).

It may also be noted that there is no need to provide for interim relief by the Executive Council, since if the General Assembly were not in session it would be convoked in special session within a week after the decision to apply sanctions (revised Article 39), and would thus be able promptly to adopt such measures of relief as might be needed.

Article 51

Nothing in *the present* Charter shall impair the inherent right of individual or collective self-defense if an armed attack occurs against *a Member of the United Nations,* until the *Security* Council has taken the measures necessary to maintain international peace and security. Measures taken by *Members* in the exercise of this right of self-defense shall be immediately reported to the *Security* Council and shall not in any way affect the authority and responsibility of the *Security* Council under the *present* Charter to take at any time such action as it deems necessary in order to maintain or restore international peace and security.

Nothing in *this revised* Charter shall impair the inherent right of individual or collective self-defense if an armed attack occurs against *any nation,* until *the General Assembly, or* the *Executive* Council *in the circumstances defined in paragraph 2 of Article 39,* has taken the measures necessary to maintain international peace and security. Measures taken by *any nation* in the exercise of this right of self-defense shall be immediately reported to *the General Assembly and* the *Executive* Council and shall not in any way affect the authority and responsibility *of the Assembly, or* of the Council *in the circumstances defined in paragraph 2 of Article 39,* under the *revised* Charter to take at any time such action as it deems necessary in order to maintain or restore international peace and security.

Comment. The combined plan for universal, complete and enforceable disarmament (revised Article 11 and Annex I), for the United Nations Peace Force (revised Articles 11 and 42 and Annex II) and for the strengthened International Court of Justice and the new World Conciliation Board and World Equity Tribunal (revised Article 36 and Annex III) would provide interrelated world institutions affording solid assurance for the prevention of war and the pacific settlement of all international disputes. Assuming the development and successful operation of these institutions, the nations in a disarmed and better-ordered world would have no motive to maintain leagues of self-defense. Such arrangements would almost automatically fall into disuse; they would be no more necessary than self-defense arrangements in well-ordered and well-policed local communities. Since, however, it would take time for the new world institutions to develop and prove themselves, it now seems best to recognize not only the right of self-defense by a single nation, but also the right of groups to maintain collective arrangements for this purpose.

Even in a "disarmed" world it is conceivable that excited groups, although equipped only with rifles and other small arms, might invade a neighboring nation necessitating temporary measures of self-defense until a contingent of the United Nations Peace Force can arrive at the scene. Such defense would be justified for the same reason that peaceful citizens may defend themselves against a riot even in the best-ordered city pending the arrival of the local police.

It is because of such possibilities that it seems proper to retain the recognition of the "inherent right" of "individual or collective self-defense" notwithstanding the assumed total abolition of all national armaments.

Several drafting changes in this Article are designed merely to recognize the broadened responsibility of the General Assembly for the maintenance of peace (revised Article 11) and the substitution of the Executive Council for the Security Council (revised Article 23). It may also be noted that, in view of the various duties imposed upon nonmember nations by the revised Charter, it is proposed to recognize explicitly that "any nation", and not merely member Nations, shall be entitled to exercise the right of self-defense.

CHAPTER VIII

REGIONAL ARRANGEMENTS

Article 52

1. Nothing in *the present* Charter precludes the existence of regional arrangements or agencies for dealing with such matters relating to the maintenance of international peace and security as are appropriate for regional action, provided that such arrangements or agencies and their activities are consistent with the Purposes and Principles of the United Nations.

2. The *Members of the United Nations* entering into such arrangements or constituting such agencies shall make every effort to achieve pacific settlement of local disputes through such regional arrangements or by such regional agencies before referring them to the *Security* Council.

3. The *Security* Council shall encourage the development of pacific settlement of local disputes through such regional arrangements or by such regional agencies either on the initiative of the states concerned or by reference from the *Security* Council.

4. This Article in no way impairs the application of Articles 34 and 35.

1. Nothing in *this revised* Charter precludes the existence of regional arrangements or agencies for dealing with such matters relating to the maintenance of international peace and security as are appropriate for regional action, provided that such arrangements or agencies and their activities are consistent with the Purposes and Principles of the United Nations.

2. The *nations* entering into such arrangements or constituting such agencies shall make every effort to achieve pacific settlement of local disputes through such regional arrangements or by such regional agencies before referring them *to the General Assembly, or* to the *Executive* Council *if the Council has been authorized by the Assembly to deal with such disputes.*

3. The *General Assembly and the Executive* Council shall encourage the development of pacific settlement of local disputes through such regional arrangements or by such regional agencies either on the initiative of the states concerned or by reference from the *Assembly or* Council.

4. This Article in no way impairs the application of Articles 34 and 35.

Comment. As in the case of collective self-defense under Article 51, it seems best to leave undisturbed the right to have regional arrangements or agencies in relation to the pacific settlement of disputes. Nor is there any reason to change the proviso that any such "arrangements" or "agencies" must be consistent with the "Purposes and Principles" of the United Nations. If it should develop that any such arrangement or agency is in fact functioning in a manner contrary to the basic purposes of the United Nations, there is an implied power to require its dissolution.

The drafting changes in paragraphs 2 and 3 take into account the enlarged responsibility of the General Assembly for the maintenance of peace (revised Article 11); the substitution of the Executive Council for the Security Council (revised Article 23); and the extension of the duty to seek pacific settlement of disputes to all nations, whether member Nations or not (revised Article 2, paragraph 3, and revised Article 33).

Article 53

1. The *Security* Council shall, where appropriate, utilize such regional arrangements or agencies for enforcement action under its authority. But no enforcement action shall be taken under regional arrangements or by regional agencies without the authorization of the *Security* Council, *with the exception of measures against any enemy state, as defined in paragraph 2 of this Article, provided for pursuant to Article 107 or in regional arrangements directed against renewal of aggressive policy on the part of any such state, until such time as the Organization may, on request of the Governments concerned, be charged with the responsibility for preventing further aggression by such a state.*

2. *The term enemy state as used in paragraph 1 of this Article applies to any state which during the Second World War has been an enemy of any signatory of the present Charter.*

The *General Assembly, or the Executive* Council *in the circumstances defined in paragraph 2 of Article 39,* shall, where appropriate, utilize such regional arrangements or agencies for enforcement action under its authority. But no enforcement action shall be taken under regional arrangements or by regional agencies without the authorization *of the Assembly, or* of the Council *in the circumstances defined in paragraph 2 of Article* 39.

Comment. This revised Article retains the conception that regional arrangements or agencies may be utilized for enforcement action, but that no such action shall be taken unless duly approved by the appropriate authority of the United Nations. As such authority the revised text merely substitutes the General Assembly (or the Executive Council to the limited extent permitted in a pressing emergency) for the Security Council.

The other change wholly eliminates the reservation that action against enemy states in World War II (Germany, Italy, Japan, etc.) may be taken without authorization by the United Nations. This change and the corresponding one in revised Article 107 are made partly because the situation giving rise to this reservation has become obsolete; and also because the revised Charter would establish an effective system for dealing with aggression by any nation, whether or not a former enemy state. It would be inconsistent with this system of effective world law in the limited field of war prevention to permit enforcement action by any nation or group of nations except pursuant to express prior authorization or special request of the United Nations.

Article 54

The *Security* Council shall at all times be kept fully informed of activities undertaken or in contemplation under regional arrangements or by regional agencies for the maintenance of international peace and security.

The *General Assembly and the Executive* Council shall at all times be kept fully informed of activities undertaken or in contemplation under regional arrangements or by regional agencies for the maintenance of international peace and security.

Comment. The only change in this Article substitutes the General Assembly and the Executive Council for the Security Council, for the same reasons that a similar change has been made in various other Articles.

It should be noted that this revised Article, requiring notice to the General Assembly and the Executive Council of any "activities" undertaken or contemplated by regional agencies, applies both to activities relating to peaceful settlement of disputes (revised Article 52) and to "enforcement action" authorized or requested by the Assembly or Council (revised Article 53). As to the latter, it should be remembered that revised Article 53 contains an unqualified prohibition against any regional enforcement action whatever without specific authority from the General Assembly or Executive Council.

CHAPTER IX

INTERNATIONAL ECO-   WORLD ECONOMIC AND
NOMIC AND SOCIAL   SOCIAL *ADVANCEMENT*
COOPERATION

General Comment. It seems very desirable to continue the existing provisions for the promotion of economic and social advancement by means of recommendations and by the coordination of specialized agencies; and the only basic change in this Chapter is the proposed establishment of the World Development Authority (revised Articles 7 and 59).

In this connection it should be emphasized that the proposed changes in other parts of the Charter would have a tremendous effect in enlarging the ability of the United Nations to accomplish results in the economic and social field.

It should be noted, for instance, that the proposed changes in the domestic jurisdiction clause (paragraph 7 of revised Article 2) would remove the present restrictions on "nonbinding recommendations". In other words, the "domestic jurisdiction" restriction would no longer apply at all to mere recommendations on any subject within the broad purposes of the revised Charter, including any matter of an economic, social, cultural or humanitarian character.

It is also to be remembered that by the Preamble it will remain one of the basic purposes of the United Nations to promote the "economic and social advancement of all peoples"; and that the capacity of the United Nations to accomplish this end would be vastly increased through the new power to raise funds for such purposes under the proposed revenue system (revised Article 17 and Annex V). These provisions would provide a reliable means for raising very large funds for the work of the Economic and Social Council, including the World Development Authority, and the specialized agencies. The new World Development Authority in particular would greatly add to the capacity of the United Nations to improve world economic and social conditions,—especially through grants-in-aid and interest-free loans to governments.

Technical and financial assistance to economically underdeveloped countries would thus be put on a much more adequate basis, and long-term plans could be put into effect without fear that member Nations would suddenly cease their voluntary contributions. It could be confidently expected that the enlarged activities of the United Nations in this field would greatly accelerate world economic development, and that, through steady increases in the world's gross product, constantly increasing funds for further improvement would be provided in the budgets of the United Nations. Moreover, with the growth of new centers of economic strength throughout the world, the financial burden which would mainly fall at first on only a few nations would become better distributed.

By these means the "conditions of stability and well-being" mentioned in Article 55 could actually be established in every part of the world instead of being only a remote objective as they must be under the present wholly inadequate machinery.

Article 55

With a view to the creation of conditions of stability and well-being which are necessary for peaceful and friendly relations among nations based on respect for the principle of equal rights and self-determination of peoples, the United Nations shall promote:

a. higher standards of living, full employment, and conditions of economic and social progress and development;

b. solutions of international economic, social, health, and related problems; and international cultural and educational cooperation; and

c. universal respect for, and observance of, human rights and fundamental freedoms for all without distinction as to race, sex, language, or religion.

Comment. No changes are proposed in this Article. But it should be noted, as explained in the General Comment on this Chapter IX, that the proposed revision would vastly increase the capacity of the United Nations to achieve the great objectives stated in this Article.

Article 56

All *Members* pledge themselves to take joint and separate action in cooperation with the *Organization* for the achievement of the purposes set forth in Article 55.

All *member Nations* pledge themselves to take joint and separate action in cooperation with the *United Nations* for the achievement of the purposes set forth in Article 55, *and to submit such reports as may be required by the Economic and Social Council under Article 64.*

Comment. The only important change in this Article is the added requirement that all member Nations shall submit reports to the Economic and Social Council. This change and the change in revised Article 64 which requires the Council to obtain reports are proposed in order to facilitate the work of the Council.

Pursuant to paragraph 3 of Article 63 and Annex V, the Economic and Social Council would be responsible for scrutinizing the budgets covering all activities in the economic and social field, not only of the organs of the United Nations proper, but also of all the specialized agencies; and would also be responsible for submitting all these budgets to the General Assembly. For this purpose, the Council would need to have all the necessary data, which it could best obtain through reports from member Nations. The Council should, therefore, have the necessary power to prescribe the form of these reports and the information to be furnished; and the member Nations should be bound to submit the information requested.

Article 57

1. The various specialized agencies, established by intergovernmental agreement and having wide international responsibilities, as defined in their basic instruments, in economic, social, cultural, educational, health, and related fields, shall be brought into relationship with the United Nations in accordance with the provisions of Article 63.

2. Such agencies thus brought into relationship with the United Nations are hereinafter referred to as specialized agencies.

1. The various specialized agencies, established by intergovernmental agreement and having wide international responsibilities, as defined in their basic instruments, in economic, social, cultural, educational, health, and related fields, shall be brought into relationship with the United Nations in accordance with the provisions of Article 63.

2. Such agencies thus brought into relationship with the United Nations are hereinafter referred to as specialized agencies.

3. The *United Nations* shall, where appropriate, *establish such* new specialized agencies *as may be* required for the accomplishment of the purposes set forth in Article 55. *The constitutions of such agencies shall be prepared by the Economic and Social Council and shall be approved by the General Assembly. They shall come into force upon the deposit of ratifications by a majority of the member Nations but shall bind only those nations which have then ratified them or thereafter accede to them.*

Comment. This Article authorizes the United Nations to establish close relations with other international organizations which are "established by intergovernmental agreements" and have "wide international responsibilities". Twelve such organizations have already been brought into relationship with

134

the United Nations and have thus become the "specialized agencies" referred to in the Article. As of early 1960 these agencies were: The Food and Agriculture Organization of the United Nations (FAO), the World Health Organization (WHO), the United Nations Educational, Scientific and Cultural Organization (UNESCO), the International Labor Organization (ILO), the International Bank for Reconstruction and Development (IBRD), the International Monetary Fund (IMF), the International Finance Corporation (IFC), the International Civil Aviation Organization (ICAO), the International Consultative Maritime Organization (ICMO), the Universal Postal Union (UPU), the International Telecommunication Union (ITU), and the World Meteorological Organization (WMO). New organizations coming into existence in the future would be brought into a similar relationship with the United Nations.

While no changes are proposed in the first two paragraphs of this Article, it should again be noted that the proposed changes in other Articles would have an important effect on the future development and effectiveness of the various specialized agencies. Through the authority of the General Assembly to pass upon their budgets and to provide the funds for the expenses (new paragraph 4 of revised Article 17), the General Assembly would be able to exercise closer control than at present over the policies of all these specialized agencies.

The new paragraph 3 embodies the substance of present Article 59. It is proposed, however, to strengthen the powers of the United Nations concerning the creation of new specialized agencies. This would be done by removing the requirement of intergovernmental negotiations and by authorizing the United Nations (i.e., the General Assembly with the assistance of the Economic and Social Council) to establish such agencies by its own action.

Article 58

The *Organization* shall make recommendations for the coordination of the policies and activities of the specialized agencies.

The *United Nations* shall make recommendations for the coordination of the policies and activities of the specialized agencies.

Comment. Only a small drafting change is proposed in this Article. But see revised Articles 17 and 63 with regard to the strengthened control of the United Nations over the specialized agencies.

Article 59

The *Organization* shall, where appropriate, *initiate negotiations among the states concerned for the creation of any* new specialized agencies required for the accomplishment of the purposes set forth in Article 55.

The World Development Authority, established by Article 7 of this revised Charter, shall promote the economic and social advancement of all peoples. It shall function in accordance with the annexed Statute which forms an integral part of this revised Charter as Annex IV.

135

Comment. It is proposed to delete the present text of Article 59 because its contents have been transferred, with important changes, to the new paragraph 3 of Article 57.

The new text of this Article defines the general purpose of the World Development Authority (established by paragraph 2 of revised Article 7) and provides that it shall function under the proposed Annex IV. It is intended that this new Authority shall be of utmost consequence as the most important medium for the realization by the United Nations of its great purpose to advance "social progress and better standards of life in larger freedom" through "international machinery for the promotion of the economic and social advancement of all peoples" (see Preamble).

This new World Development Authority would function as the principal executive arm of the Economic and Social Council, the members of which would constitute in effect the Board of Directors of the Authority. If the governments and peoples of the world desire to do so, they would have available through the new revenue system (revised Article 17 and Annex V) the machinery for supplying this new Authority with ample funds to deal with the vast problem of mitigating the differences in economic status between various regions of the world. A more detailed explanation of the structure, procedures, financing and functions of this proposed Authority is contained in Annex IV.

Article 60

Responsibility for the discharge of the functions of the *Organization* set forth in this Chapter shall be vested in the General Assembly and, under authority of the General Assembly, in the Economic and Social Council, which shall have for this purpose the powers set forth in Chapter X.

Responsibility for the discharge of the functions of the *United Nations* set forth in this Chapter shall be vested in the General Assembly and, under authority of the General Assembly, in the Economic and Social Council, which shall have for this purpose the powers set forth in Chapter X.

Comment. No change, except the formal change from "Organization" to "United Nations", is proposed in this Article, since the present text provides sufficiently for the control and supervision of the Economic and Social Council by the General Assembly.

CHAPTER X

THE ECONOMIC AND SOCIAL COUNCIL

COMPOSITION

Article 61

1. The Economic and Social Council shall consist of *eighteen Members of the United Nations* elected by the General Assembly.

2. *Subject to the provisions of paragraph 3, six members of the Economic and Social Council shall be elected each year for a term of three years. A retiring member shall be eligible for immediate re-election.*

1. The Economic and Social Council shall consist of *twenty-four Representatives, none of whom shall simultaneously be a member of the Executive Council. They shall be elected by the General Assembly within thirty days from the beginning of the first regular session of each newly chosen Assembly, and shall serve during the four-year term of the Assembly by which they are elected and until their successors are elected by a new Assembly.*

2. *The General Assembly shall elect the members of the Economic and Social Council in accordance with the following formula and method:*

a. Each of the twelve member Nations with the highest adjusted national product, as defined in Annex V and as estimated by the Standing Committee on Budget and Finance for the year in which the quadrennial election of the Council occurs, shall have the right to have one of its Representatives elected to the Council at every quadrennial election.

b. The member Nations other than the twelve mentioned in the foregoing subparagraph and the non-self-governing and trust territories under the administration of member Nations shall between them have the right to have twelve of their Representatives elected to the Council at every quadrennial election of the Council. Prior to each election, the Assembly shall designate the twelve member Nations or non-self-governing or trust territories each of which shall have the right to have one of its Representatives elected to the Council, due regard being specially paid to equitable geographical distribution.

c. After the designations called for by the foregoing subparagraph have been made, the Representatives in the Assembly of the twenty-four member Nations or non-self-governing or trust territories which are entitled to have Representatives elected to the Council at the particular election, shall hold separate meetings which shall respectively nominate to the Assembly two of their own number deemed by the separate meetings best qualified to serve on the Council; provided that in the case of any such member Nation or non-self-governing or trust territory, which has only one or two Representatives, their names shall be deemed automatically nominated.

d. After the nominations called for by the foregoing subparagraph (c) have been made, the Assembly shall elect to serve on the Council one of the two nominees of each of the twenty-four member Nations or non-self-governing or trust territories then entitled to have

138

one of its Representatives on the Council, taking into account the personal qualifications of each nominee for service on the Council, except that if any of such twenty-four member Nations or non-self-governing or trust territories has only one Representative in the Assembly, that Representative shall be deemed automatically elected.

3. At the first election, eighteen members of the Economic and Social Council shall be chosen. The term of office of six members so chosen shall expire at the end of one year, and of six other members at the end of two years, in accordance with arrangements made by the General Assembly.

3. Vacancies in the membership of the Economic and Social Council shall be filled in the following manner: The Representatives in the Assembly of the member Nation or non-self-governing or trust territory in whose representation on the Council the vacancy has occurred shall nominate two of their own number, and thereupon the General Assembly shall elect one of the two nominees, taking into account the personal qualifications of each nominee for service on the Council; provided that in the case of any such member Nation or non-self-governing or trust territory which has only one or two Representatives their names shall be deemed automatically nominated, and in the case of any such member Nation or non-self-governing or trust territory which has only one Representative in the Assembly that Representative shall be deemed automatically elected.

4. Each member of the Economic and Social Council shall have one representative.

4. The General Assembly may by a vote of lack of confidence discharge the Economic and Social Council as a whole, provided: (a) that the members of the Coun-

cil so discharged shall continue to serve until their successors are elected; (b) that the Assembly shall proceed forthwith to the election of a new Council; (c) that the members of the new Council shall be elected from among the Representatives in the Assembly of the same member Nations or non-self-governing or trust territories which were represented on the discharged Council; except that if the Assembly desires to replace a member of the discharged Council who is the only Representative from a member Nation or territory, the Assembly may elect a Representative from one of the other member Nations or territories entitled to either one or two Representatives in the Assembly and which would not otherwise be represented on the Council; (d) that the members of the new Council shall be nominated and elected by the same formula and method as called for by paragraph 2 of this Article; and (e) that the new Council shall serve, unless sooner discharged, until the regular quadrennial election of the Council following the quadrennial election of the Assembly.

5. The members of the Economic and Social Council shall retain their seats in the General Assembly.

6. The members of the Economic and Social Council shall, during their period of service thereon, receive additional compensation to be fixed by the General Assembly.

Comment. Certain changes in this Article are parallel to those in the Articles relating to the composition of the other two councils of the United Nations, namely the Executive Council and the Trusteeship Council (revised Articles 23 and 86). Thus no member Nation would be entitled to appoint its own representative on the Economic and Social Council; and, in lieu of that method of appointment, the individuals comprising this Council would be chosen by the General Assembly from among its own membership.

The increase in the number of members of the Economic and Social Council from eighteen to twenty-four is intended to assure proper representation for member Nations from all regions of the world and belonging to different forms of economic and social development. In this connection it should be noted that the number of member Nations has steadily increased and that the ultimate number may well exceed one hundred, as compared with the original fifty-one member Nations in 1945.

The formula and method for the selection of the twenty-four members of the Economic and Social Council follow in principle the formula and method proposed for the selection of the Executive Council (revised Article 23), the purpose being to ensure a fair and broad distribution of the membership among all the member Nations. In view of the special functions of the Economic and Social Council, however, the formula for the eligibility of nations to have members on the Council is somewhat different from that proposed for the Executive Council. For since a primary function of the Economic and Social Council would be to supervise the administration of the World Development Authority with its potentially large funds for the advancement of the social and economic welfare of the world's peoples, it seems right that those nations which would contribute most to those funds should be ensured of representation on the Council. To this end, it is proposed that the twelve member Nations having the largest adjusted national products (as defined in Annex V and as estimated by the Standing Committee on Budget and Finance) shall be entitled to seats on the Council at all times. It should be noted that these nations are not the twelve with the highest per capita incomes, but the twelve nations whose national products, as adjusted for the purpose of the apportionment of annual budgets of the United Nations, are the highest. The other twelve member Nations entitled to representation from time to time would be selected by the Assembly, with due regard for equitable geographical distribution.

Through these careful provisions it is believed that the Economic and Social Council would at all times comprise so representative a cross section of the nations of the world that it would command a high degree of confidence.

As in the case of the Executive Council and Trusteeship Council (revised Articles 23 and 86), it is proposed to give the General Assembly full authority to discharge the Economic and Social Council as a whole by a vote of lack of confidence, provided that a new Council is forthwith appointed and that its members are chosen to the utmost practicable extent from the same nations and in the same manner as the discharged Council.

Article 62

1. The Economic and Social Council may make or initiate studies and reports with respect to international economic, social, cultural, educational, health, and related matters and may make recommendations with respect to any such matters to the General Assembly, to the *Members of the United Nations,* and to the specialized agencies concerned.

2. It may make recommendations for the purpose of promoting respect for, and observance of, human rights and fundamental freedoms for all.

3. It may prepare draft conventions for submission to the General Assembly, with respect to matters falling within its competence.

4. It may call, in accordance with the rules prescribed by the United Nations, international conferences on matters falling within its competence.

1. The Economic and Social Council may make or initiate studies and reports with respect to international economic, social, cultural, educational, health, and related matters and may make recommendations with respect to any such matters to the General Assembly, to the *member Nations,* and to the specialized agencies concerned.

2. It may make recommendations for the purpose of promoting *economic and social advancement and* respect for, and observance of, human rights and fundamental freedoms for all.

3. It may prepare draft conventions for submission to the General Assembly, with respect to matters falling within its competence.

4. It may call, in accordance with the rules prescribed by the United Nations, international conferences on matters falling within its competence.

Comment. The only material change proposed in this Article is the addition in paragraph 2 of a reference to "economic and social advancement". The purpose of this addition is to make it perfectly clear that the Economic and Social Council would be empowered to promote the objective of "higher standards of living, full employment, and conditions of economic and social progress and development" as set forth in subparagraph (a) of Article 55.

While this change is not important, since the power thus stated probably already exists by implication, it should again be noted that, under the revised Charter, the scope of the Economic and Social Council would in practice be much enlarged by reason of its responsibility for allocating the greatly increased funds for economic and social advancement which would presumably be available under the proposed new revenue system. (For further explanation, see the General Comment on Chapter IX, the comment on revised Article 59 and Annexes IV and V.)

Article 63

1. The Economic and Social Council *may* enter into agreements with *any of* the agencies referred to in Article 57, defining the terms on which the *agency* concerned shall be brought into relationship with the United Nations. Such agreements shall be subject to approval by the General Assembly.

2. It *may* coordinate the activities of the specialized agencies through consultation with and recommendations to such agencies and through recommendations to the General Assembly and to the *Members of the United Nations.*

1. The Economic and Social Council *shall* enter into agreements with *all* the agencies referred to in Article 57, defining the terms on which the *agencies* concerned shall be brought into relationship with the United Nations. Such agreements shall be subject to approval by the General Assembly.

2. It *shall* coordinate the activities of the specialized agencies through consultation with and recommendations to such agencies and through recommendations to the General Assembly and to the *member Nations.*

3. It shall scrutinize the budgets of the specialized agencies and shall submit these budgets with its recommendations to the General Assembly.

Comment. The changes in this Article are intended to make it clear that the Economic and Social Council shall be bound to make agreements with all the specialized agencies defining their relations with the United Nations; and that it shall also be obliged to coordinate their activities. The optional character of the present provisions is inconsistent with the proposed enlarged scope and responsibilities of this Council.

The new paragraph 3 would also make it the duty of the Economic and Social Council to examine the budgets of all the specialized agencies and to submit these budgets with its recommendations to the General Assembly. Thereupon the budgets would be referred to the Standing Committee on Budget and Finance of the Assembly which would further scrutinize them and report thereon to the Assembly. The Assembly as a whole would then

143

have the final responsibility for the approval of the budgets and the appropriation of the necessary funds (see revised Articles 17 and 22 and Annex V).

Article 64

1. The Economic and Social Council *may* take appropriate steps to obtain regular reports from the specialized agencies. *It may make arrangements with the Members of the United Nations* and *with* the specialized agencies to obtain reports on the steps taken to give effect to its own recommendations and to recommendations on matters falling within its competence made by the General Assembly.

1. The Economic and Social Council *shall* take appropriate steps to obtain regular reports from the specialized agencies. *The Council shall also take appropriate steps* to obtain reports *from the member Nations* and the specialized agencies on the steps taken to give effect to its own recommendations and to recommendations on matters falling within its competence made by the General Assembly.

2. It *may* communicate its observations on these reports to the General Assembly.

2. It *shall* communicate its observations on these reports to the General Assembly.

Comment. The purpose of the main change in this Article from "may" to "shall" and of the corresponding change in Article 56 is to make it more certain that the Economic and Social Council would be supplied with full information concerning the activities of the specialized agencies and of the member Nations in the economic and social field.

Mandatory power to obtain full information both from the specialized agencies and from the member Nations seems essential in view of the large appropriations for economic and social purposes which would presumably be made by the United Nations from the revenues made available by the proposed new revenue system (Annex V).

Article 65

The Economic and Social Council may furnish information to the *Security* Council *and shall assist the Security Council* upon *its* request.

The Economic and Social Council *shall furnish such information and assistance to the General Assembly as the Assembly may request; and the Council* may furnish information *and assistance* to the *Executive* Council *and other organs of the United Nations* upon *their* request.

144

Comment. In view of the new responsibilities and paramount position of the General Assembly under the revised Charter, it seems proper that the Assembly shall have the *right* to receive assistance and information from the Economic and Social Council. It also seems proper to include "other organs" with the Executive Council in the provision permitting the Economic and Social Council to furnish information and assistance.

Article 66

1. The Economic and Social Council shall perform such functions as fall within its competence in connection with the carrying out of the recommendations of the General Assembly.

2. It may, with the approval of the General Assembly, perform services at the request of *Members of the United Nations* and at the request of specialized agencies.

3. It shall perform such other functions as are specified elsewhere in *the present* Charter or as may be assigned to it by the General Assembly.

1. The Economic and Social Council shall perform such functions as fall within its competence in connection with the carrying out of the *directions and* recommendations of the General Assembly.

2. It may, with the approval of the General Assembly, perform services at the request of *member Nations* and at the request of specialized agencies.

3. It shall perform such other functions as are specified elsewhere in *this revised* Charter or as may be assigned to it by the General Assembly.

Comment. The only substantial change in this Article is in paragraph 1, where it seems logical and necessary to make it clear that the Economic and Social Council is subject to "directions" as well as "recommendations" of the General Assembly.

VOTING

Article 67

1. Each member of the Economic and Social Council shall have one vote.

1. Each member of the Economic and Social Council shall have one vote.

145

2. Decisions of the Economic and Social Council shall be made by *a majority of the members present and voting.*

2. Decisions of the Economic and Social Council *on important questions* shall be made by *an affirmative vote of eighteen* members. *These questions shall include: recommendations on budgetary matters in accordance with Article 63 and Annex V; decisions under Annex IV concerning the World Development Authority; and any other questions which the General Assembly may from time to time define as important.*

3. *Decisions of the Economic and Social Council on all other questions shall be made by an affirmative vote of thirteen members.*

Comment. As above noted, revised Article 61 provides that in lieu of the present provision whereby the General Assembly chooses eighteen member Nations to be represented on the Economic and Social Council whose governments respectively name their delegates, the Council shall be composed of twenty-four Representatives chosen individually by the Assembly itself from among its own number. This important proposal, however, calls for no change in the text of paragraph 1 of this Article 67, since the term "member" of the Council applies equally to the individual Representatives serving on the Council, each of whom would have an equal vote.

On the other hand, an important change is proposed in paragraph 2, namely that decisions of the Economic and Social Council on certain important questions shall require the vote of eighteen of its twenty-four members, and on other questions the vote of thirteen members,—instead of a mere majority of the members present and voting as provided in the present text. In view of the greatly enlarged scope and authority of the Council under the proposed revision, it seems wise to require a majority vote of the whole membership of the Council on any question; and a special majority of three fourths of all the members in respect of recommendations concerning the presumably very large budgets on which the Council would be required to report to the General Assembly; and also in respect of decisions under Annex IV relating to the World Development Authority. The required eighteen out of twenty-four votes would give assurance that these important recommendations and decisions represent the considered opinion of preponderant majorities and are acceptable to at least one half of each of the two groups of nations represented on the Council. The same three-fourths majority would be required on other questions which the Assembly might designate as "important".

146

Article 68

The Economic and Social Council shall set up commissions in economic and social fields and for the promotion of human rights, and such other commissions as may be required for the performance of its functions.

Comment. No change is proposed in this Article.

Article 69

The Economic and Social Council shall invite any Member of the United Nations to participate, without vote, in its deliberations on any matter of particular concern to that Member.

1. If the Economic and Social Council considers that any matter brought before it is of particular concern to any member Nation, and if no Representative from such member Nation is then a member of the Council, the Council shall invite the Representatives in the General Assembly from that member Nation to designate one of their number to participate, without vote, in the deliberations of the Council; or if such member Nation has only one Representative, that Representative shall be invited to participate.

2. If the Economic and Social Council considers that any matter brought before it is of particular concern to any state which is not a member of the United Nations, the Council shall invite its government to appoint a delegate to participate, without vote, in the deliberations of the Council. The Council shall lay down such conditions as it deems just for the participation of such a state.

3. If the Economic and Social Council considers that any matter brought before it is of particular

147

concern to any non-self-governing or trust territory, and if no Representative from such territory is then a member of the Council and if there is a Representative from such territory in the General Assembly, the Council shall invite that Representative to participate, without vote, in the deliberations of the Council. If, however, there is then no Representative from such territory in the Assembly, the Council shall appoint a properly qualified person resident in such territory to represent the interests of such territory and to participate, without vote, on its behalf in the deliberations of the Council.

Comment. The purpose of the proposed new text is similar to that of the present Article, namely, to give opportunity to any nation (or non-self-governing or trust territory) which is especially concerned with any matter under consideration by the Economic and Social Council to participate, but without vote, in the Council's deliberations.

The first change, in paragraph 1, whereby the Economic and Social Council itself is empowered to decide whether a particular matter is of special concern to a member Nation, is advisable in order to remove the ambiguity in the present text as to how this preliminary question is to be decided. The second change establishes a definite procedure for the representation of the interests of a member Nation thus especially concerned. The proposal is that, unless the affected nation happens already to have one of its Representatives on the Council, the Representatives of that nation in the General Assembly shall be asked to designate one of their number to participate in the Council's discussion. This procedure is in harmony with the proposed change (revised Article 61) whereby the members of the Economic and Social Council, instead of being appointed by member Nations selected by the General Assembly as entitled to representation on the Council, shall be directly selected by the Assembly itself from among its own membership.

The new paragraph 2 gives to possible nonmember states especially concerned in a matter before the Economic and Social Council the same right to be represented in the Council's deliberations as is accorded to nonmember states before the Executive Council under similar circumstances (revised Article 32). As previously mentioned, there would probably be few, if any, nonmember nations,—in view of the ratification provisions whereby the revised Charter could come into effect only with the assent of a preponderant majority of the nations and in view of the provision against withdrawal (revised Articles

110 and 6). And yet the mere possibility that membership might not be universal makes it advisable to provide that any nonmember state shall have a right to be heard before the Council.

The new paragraph 3 makes it possible for any non-self-governing or trust territory especially concerned in a matter brought before the Economic and Social Council to participate in the discussion on the same basis as a non-member nation under similar circumstances. The procedure established for this purpose is analogous to the procedure for the participation of such territories in the discussions of the Executive Council (revised Article 31).

Article 70

The Economic and Social Council may make arrangements for representatives of the specialized agencies to participate, without vote, in its deliberations and in those of the commissions established by it, and for its representatives to participate in the deliberations of the specialized agencies.

Comment. No change is proposed in this Article.

Article 71

The Economic and Social Council may make suitable arrangements for consultation with nongovernmental organizations which are concerned with matters within its competence. Such arrangements may be made with international organizations and, where appropriate, with national organizations after consultation with the *Member of the United Nations* concerned.

The Economic and Social Council may make suitable arrangements for consultation with nongovernmental organizations which are concerned with matters within its competence. Such arrangements may be made with international organizations and, where appropriate, with national organizations after consultation with the *member Nation* concerned.

Comment. The only change in this Article is consequential on the use of "member Nation" instead of "Member of the United Nations" throughout the revision.

Article 72

1. The Economic and Social Council shall adopt its own rules of procedure, including the method of selecting its President.

2. The Economic and Social Council shall meet as required in accordance with its rules, which shall include provision for the convening of meetings on the request of a majority of its members.

Comment. No change is proposed in this Article.

CHAPTER XI

DECLARATION REGARDING NON-SELF-GOVERNING TERRITORIES

General Comment on Chapters XI-XIII. Chapter XI and the following two Chapters deal with two categories of non-self-governing territories: (a) possessions acquired by colonial Powers prior to World War I; and (b) the colonial territories which were transferred from the defeated Powers to the victors as a result of World War I.

The territories in the second group were placed under an international mandate to be exercised by the mandatory Powers "on behalf of" the League of Nations (Article 22 of the Covenant of the League of Nations). These territories were to a certain extent under the supervision of the Council of the League, and a special commission was established to examine annual reports of the Mandatories.

Some of the territories under mandate achieved independence prior to the establishment of the United Nations in 1945 (Iraq, Syria, Lebanon) and the mandate for Palestine was terminated by the creation of the states of Israel and Jordan in 1948. All other mandated territories in this group, i.e., those in Africa and the Pacific, were placed under the trusteeship system of the United Nations in accordance with Chapter XII of the Charter. Only the Union of South Africa refused to place the mandated territory of South-West Africa under trusteeship, and the special status of that territory—i.e., limited supervision by the United Nations in place of the League, but in accordance with the terms of the mandate and not of the trusteeship provisions of the Charter— was determined by an advisory opinion of the International Court of Justice in 1950.

Most of the trust territories were placed by the United Nations under the administration of the former mandatory powers: the Cameroons (France and the United Kingdom), Nauru (Australia), New Guinea (Australia), Ruanda-Urundi (Belgium), Tanganyika (United Kingdom), Togoland (France and the United Kingdom) and Western Samoa (New Zealand). The Japanese mandate over the Marianas, Marshalls and Carolinas became the Trust Territory of the Pacific, a strategic area under the administration of the United States. A new trusteeship was created for the Italian colony of Somaliland; Italy became the administering authority, but only for a period of ten years ending in 1960, at which time Somaliland will become the independent state of Somalia. (Other Italian colonies were not placed under trusteeship: Libya became independent and Eritrea was joined to Ethiopia in a federal union.) On March 6, 1957, the trusteeship agreement for British Togoland was terminated; and that territory was joined to the new state of Ghana (formerly the Gold Coast) which attained independent status on the same day. By a vote of the General Assembly, French Togoland and the French

150

Cameroons will become independent in 1960; and the British Cameroons may also become independent in 1960.

Many other colonial territories attained independence since 1945 without going through the intermediary stage of mandate or trusteeship. This group includes, besides Ghana, the new states of Burma, Cambodia, Ceylon, Guinea, India, Indonesia, Laos, Malaya, Morocco, Pakistan, the Philippines, Sudan, Tunisia, North Viet-Nam and South Viet-Nam; and all of these, except North and South Viet-Nam, are early in 1960 members of the United Nations.

Other former colonial territories (e.g., Puerto Rico and Singapore) had prior to 1960 become self-governing, although not fully independent; or had obtained a special constitutional status within the framework of a larger union (e.g., several French possessions and the Dutch territories of Curaçao and Surinam). There still remain, however, about sixty colonial possessions which are clearly non-self-governing and thus fall within the scope of the special declaration contained in Chapter XI rather than under the trusteeship provisions of Chapters XII and XIII.

In summary, there are, apart from those territories which had achieved independence or full self-government by early in 1960 or will soon do so, some seventy territories, with a population of about 95,000,000, which still require the assistance of the United Nations in their progress toward self-government or full independence. Ten of these territories, with a population of about 20,000,000, fall under the Trusteeship provisions of Chapters XII and XIII. The remainder, about sixty in number and having a population of around 75,000,000, fall under the less stringent general provisions of Chapter XI.

It should be noted, however, that these non-self-governing and trust territories are at various stages of development, and that some of them are fast approaching the stage of full self-government or complete independence. It follows that when any territory achieves either full self-government or independence, it will cease to be subject to the provisions of Chapters XI, XII and XIII. In consequence, it is to be expected that the number of people for whom the Trusteeship Council would have responsibility will quite rapidly diminish. When a territory considers that it has reached the stage of full self-government or complete independence, it would so notify the United Nations; and if the General Assembly agrees, the duties of the administering authority and of the Trusteeship Council with respect to that territory would cease. On the other hand, if the Assembly should not agree, it would presumably request the International Court of Justice for an advisory opinion on the subject and be guided thereby.

Since the creation of the United Nations, many disputes have arisen as to the meaning of Chapter XI. But it is clear that in this Chapter the colonial Powers accepted very broad general obligations to promote the well-being and political advancement of the non-self-governing territories under their administration. The present Charter, however, leaves indefinite the specific means whereby these general obligations should be carried out, and also leaves indefinite the functions of the United Nations in respect of the fulfillment by member Nations of their obligations. It is therefore proposed: (a) to amend Article 73 in order to clarify the obligations accepted by member Nations as to non-self-governing territories under their administration; and (b) completely to revise Article 87 so as to broaden the responsibility and authority of the General Assembly and the Trusteeship Council in respect of the many non-self-governing territories other than "trust" territories.

The purpose of these changes is to enable the United Nations more effectively to achieve its stated objectives in the field of advancing the economic and social well-being and political development of *all* the non-self-governing territories.

Article 73

Members of the United Nations which have or assume responsibilities for the administration of territories whose peoples have not yet attained a full measure of self-government recognize the principle that the interests of the inhabitants of these territories are paramount, and accept as a sacred trust the obligation to promote to the utmost, within the system of international peace and security established by *the present* Charter, the well-being of the inhabitants of these territories, and, to this end:

a. to ensure, with due respect for the culture of the peoples concerned, their political, economic, social, and educational advancement, their just treatment, and their protection against abuses;

b. to develop self-government, to take due account of the political aspirations of the peoples, and to assist them in the progressive development of their free political institutions, according to the particular circumstances of each territory and its peoples and their varying stages of advancement;

c. to further international peace and security;

d. to promote constructive measures of development, to encourage research, and to cooperate

Member Nations which have or assume responsibilities for the administration of territories whose peoples have not yet attained a full measure of self-government recognize the principle that the interests of the inhabitants of these territories are paramount, and accept as a sacred trust the obligation to promote to the utmost, within the system of international peace and security established by *this revised* Charter, the well-being of the inhabitants of these territories, and, to this end:

a. to ensure, with due respect for the culture of the peoples concerned, their political, economic, social, and educational advancement, their just treatment, and their protection against abuses;

b. to develop self-government, to take due account of the political aspirations of the peoples, and to assist them in the progressive development of their free political institutions, according to the particular circumstances of each territory and its peoples and their varying stages of advancement;

c. to further international peace and security;

d. to promote constructive measures of development, to encourage research, and to cooperate with one another and, when and where appropriate, with specialized international bodies with a view to the practical achievement of the social, economic, and scientific purposes set forth in this Article; and

e. to transmit regularly to the *Secretary-General for information purposes, subject to such limitation as security and constitutional considerations may require,* statistical and other information *of a technical nature* relating to economic, social, and educational conditions in the territories for which they are respectively responsible *other than those territories to which Chapters XII and XIII apply.*

with one another and, when and where appropriate, with specialized international bodies with a view to the practical achievement of the social, economic, and scientific purposes set forth in this Article;

e. to transmit regularly to the *Trusteeship Council* statistical and other information relating to *political,* economic, social, and educational conditions in the territories for which they are respectively responsible; and

f. to cooperate with the General Assembly and the Trusteeship Council in the discharge of all their functions as defined in Articles 87 and 88.

Comment. The changes made in the introductory paragraph of this Article—from "Members of the United Nations" to "Member Nations" and from "the present" Charter to "this revised" Charter—are consequential on the use of "this revised" Charter and "member Nations" throughout the revision.

The changes in subparagraph (e) are intended to remove an ambiguity in the present text due to an inconsistency between this subparagraph and the preceding subparagraphs. On the one hand, subparagraphs (a) and (b) deal with the obligation of the nations administering non-self-governing territories to ensure the "political" advancement of the peoples concerned, to develop self-government, to take due account of the "political" aspirations of the peoples, and to assist them in the progressive development of their free "political" institutions. On the other hand, the present subparagraph (e) obligates the administering nations to transmit to the United Nations only "statistical and other information of a technical nature relating to economic, social, and educational conditions" in non-self-governing territories other than those under trusteeship, without mentioning "political" information. Even under the present Charter strong contentions have been made that political information should be transmitted to the proper authorities of the United Nations in order to enable them to appraise the fulfillment by the administering nations of their "sacred trust" to develop the political institutions of the peoples under their administration. Accordingly, it seems right to make explicit the obligation of the administering nations to submit to the United Nations information on "political" as well as on economic, social and educational matters.

It is also necessary to remove from subparagraph (e) some phrases which could be construed as nullifying the obligation to submit any information. Thus it seems inappropriate to limit that obligation to information "of a technical nature", since information on social and political conditions is often nontechnical in nature. It would also seem contradictory to allow an administering authority to withhold legitimate and reasonable information as to the political advancement of a territory on the ground of "security and constitutional considerations", since many political developments have constitutional implications.

It is further proposed to omit the phrase "for information purposes" in subparagraph (e), which at present limits the purposes for which the information may be utilized. This phrase has in the past provided some basis for the contention that the information submitted may not even be discussed by the United Nations. The omission of the phrase should remove any possible ambiguity with respect to the power of the General Assembly to discuss all information submitted under this revised Article 73, and would harmonize the Assembly's authority under this Article with its general authority under revised Article 10 to discuss any "questions or matters" within the scope of the Charter.

It is also proposed that information shall be submitted not to the Secretary-General but directly to the Trusteeship Council which, under revised Articles 87 and 88, would be responsible for the examination of the information submitted under this revised Article 73.

Finally it is proposed to add a new subparagraph (f) requiring all member Nations which are administering non-self-governing territories "to cooperate with the General Assembly and the Trusteeship Council" in the execution of their new functions under revised Articles 87 and 88.

Article 74

Members of the United Nations also agree that their policy in respect of the territories to which this Chapter applies, no less than in respect of their metropolitan areas, must be based on the general principle of good-neighborliness, due account being taken of the interests and well-being of the rest of the world, in social, economic, and commercial matters.

Member Nations also agree that their policy in respect of the territories to which this Chapter applies, no less than in respect of their metropolitan areas, must be based on the general principle of good-neighborliness, due account being taken of the interests and well-being of the rest of the world, in social, economic, and commercial matters.

Comment. The only change in this Article is consequential on the use of "member Nations" instead of "Members" throughout the revision.

CHAPTER XII

INTERNATIONAL TRUSTEESHIP SYSTEM

Article 75

The United Nations shall establish under its authority an international trusteeship system for the administration and supervision of such territories as may be placed thereunder by subsequent individual agreements. These territories are hereinafter referred to as trust territories.

Comment. No change is proposed in this Article.

Article 76

The basic objectives of the trusteeship system, in accordance with the Purposes of the United Nations laid down in Article 1 of *the present* Charter, shall be:

a. to further international peace and security;

b. to promote the political, economic, social, and educational advancement of the inhabitants of the trust territories, and their progressive development towards self-government or independence as may be appropriate to the particular circumstances of each territory and its peoples and the freely expressed wishes of the peoples concerned, and as may be provided by the terms of each trusteeship agreement;

c. to encourage respect for human rights and for fundamental freedoms for all without distinction as to race, sex, language, or religion, and to encourage recogni-

The basic objectives of the trusteeship system, in accordance with the Purposes of the United Nations laid down in Article 1 of *this revised* Charter, shall be:

a. to further international peace and security;

b. to promote the political, economic, social, and educational advancement of the inhabitants of the trust territories, and their progressive development towards self-government or independence as may be appropriate to the particular circumstances of each territory and its peoples and the freely expressed wishes of the peoples concerned, and as may be provided by the terms of each trusteeship agreement;

c. to encourage respect for human rights and for fundamental freedoms for all without distinction as to race, sex, language, or religion, and to encourage recognition of the interdependence of the peoples of the world; and

d. to ensure equal treatment in social, economic, and commercial matters for all *Members of the United Nations* and their nationals, and also equal treatment for the latter in the administration of justice, without prejudice to the attainment of the foregoing objectives and subject to the provisions of Article 80.

tion of the interdependence of the peoples of the world; and

d. to ensure equal treatment in social, economic, and commercial matters for all *member Nations* and their nationals, and also equal treatment for the latter in the administration of justice, without prejudice to the attainment of the foregoing objectives and subject to the provisions of Article 80.

Comment. Only two changes are proposed in this Article, i.e., from "the present" to "this revised" Charter and from "Members of the United Nations" to "member Nations". These changes are merely consequential on the use of "this revised" Charter and "member Nations" throughout the revision.

Article 77

1. The trusteeship system shall apply to such territories in the following categories as may be placed thereunder by means of trusteeship agreements:

a. territories now held under mandate;

b. territories which may be detached from enemy states as a result of the Second World War; and

c. territories voluntarily placed under the system by states responsible for their administration.

2. It will be a matter for subsequent agreement as to which territories in the foregoing categories will be brought under the trusteeship system and upon what terms.

Comment. No change is proposed in this Article.

Article 78

The trusteeship system shall not apply to territories which have become *Members of the United Nations, relationship among which shall be based on respect for the principle of sovereign equality.*

The trusteeship system shall not apply to territories which have become *member Nations.*

156

Comment: The first change in this Article, i.e., from "Members of the United Nations" to "member Nations" is merely consequential on the use of "member Nations" instead of "Members" throughout the revision.

The second change would delete the reference to the principle of "sovereign equality" for the reasons stated in the comment on revised Article 2.

Article 79

The terms of trusteeship for each territory to be placed under the trusteeship system, including any alteration or amendment, shall be agreed upon by the states directly concerned, including the mandatory power in the case of territories held under mandate by a *Member of the United Nations,* and shall be approved as provided for in Articles 83 and 85.

The terms of trusteeship for each territory to be placed under the trusteeship system, including any alteration or amendment, shall be agreed upon by the states directly concerned, including the mandatory power in the case of territories held under mandate by a *member Nation,* and shall be approved as provided for in Articles 83 and 85.

Comment. The only change in this Article is consequential on the use of "member Nation" instead of "Member of the United Nations" throughout the revision.

Article 80

1. Except as may be agreed upon in individual trusteeship agreements, made under Articles 77, 79, and 81, placing each territory under the trusteeship system, and until such agreements have been concluded, nothing in this Chapter shall be construed in or of itself to alter in any manner the rights whatsoever of any states or any peoples or the terms of existing international instruments to which *Members of the United Nations* may respectively be parties.

1. Except as may be agreed upon in individual trusteeship agreements, made under Articles 77, 79, and 81, placing each territory under the trusteeship system, and until such agreements have been concluded, nothing in this Chapter shall be construed in or of itself to alter in any manner the rights whatsoever of any states or any peoples or the terms of existing international instruments to which *member Nations* may respectively be parties.

2. Paragraph 1 of this Article shall not be interpreted as giving grounds for delay or postponement

2. Paragraph 1 of this Article shall not be interpreted as giving grounds for delay or postponement

of the negotiation and conclusion of agreements for placing mandated and other territories under the trusteeship system as provided for in Article 77.

of the negotiation and conclusion of agreements for placing mandated and other territories under the trusteeship system as provided for in Article 77.

Comment. No change is proposed in this Article, except that "member Nations" is substituted for "Members of the United Nations", consequential on the use of "member Nations" instead of "Members" throughout the revision.

Article 81

The trusteeship agreement shall in each case include the terms under which the trust territory will be administered and designate the authority which will exercise the administration of the trust territory. Such authority, hereinafter called the administering authority, may be one or more states or the *Organization* itself.

The trusteeship agreement shall in each case include the terms under which the trust territory will be administered and designate the authority which will exercise the administration of the trust territory. Such authority, hereinafter called the administering authority, may be one or more states or the *United Nations* itself.

Comment. The only change proposed in this Article is from "Organization" to "United Nations" in the second sentence, consequential on the substitution throughout the revision of the term "United Nations" for "Organization".

It should be emphasized, however, that this Article may become of great importance. It would, for example, permit the direct administration by the "United Nations itself" of important straits and canals between seas and oceans which are now administered by particular nations. If the United Nations should in the future be designated as the administering authority for such passages and adjoining zones for the benefit of all nations, acceptable solutions might well be found for serious conflicts concerning these vital waterways. Similar arrangements might be made for the administration by the United Nations of the high seas and of certain important rivers, the waters of which are of vital concern to two or more nations.

This power to designate the United Nations itself as administering authority might also apply to the temporary administration of disputed areas pending their final assignment to or division between contending nations.

Article 82

There may be designated, in any trusteeship agreement, *a strategic* area or areas which may include part or all of the trust territory to

There may be designated, in any trusteeship agreement, *an* area or areas *for the use of the United Nations* which may include part or all which the agreement applies, *with-out prejudice to any special agreement or agreements made under Article 43.*

of the trust territory to which the agreement applies.

Comment. The elimination of the last clause of this Article is proposed because of the important changes in revised Articles 42 and 43. The present Articles 42 and 43 call for United Nations military measures to be taken by national forces made available under special agreements between the Security Council and the governments of the member states comprising the United Nations. The proposed revision of Articles 42 and 43 would, however, eliminate the necessity for any such special agreements, since the United Nations would possess its own military forces (the United Nations Peace Force) in accordance with Annex II. The reference to agreements under Article 43 is, therefore, no longer relevant.

In view also of the comprehensive disarmament plan called for by the proposed Annex I, which would completely abolish all national military forces, it is obvious that when the disarmament process is completed no "strategic areas" would be needed for any national forces. This Article 82 and Article 83 may, however, be usefully adapted to provide for the designation in trust territories of certain areas which the United Nations Peace Force might need for the stationing of its units and for the production and storage of military equipment. Various areas throughout the world would be needed by the United Nations for these purposes, and several trusteeship areas might be very suitable.

Article 83

1. *All* functions of the United Nations *relating to strategic* areas, including the approval of the terms of the trusteeship agreements and of their alteration or amendment, shall be exercised by the *Security* Council.

1. *The* functions of the United Nations *with regard to trusteeship agreements for trust territories which may be administered by the United Nations itself under Article 81 and for* areas *which may be designated for the use of the United Nations under Article 82,* including the approval of the terms of the trusteeship agreements and of their alteration or amendment, shall be exercised by *the General Assembly with the assistance of* the *Executive* Council.

2. The basic objectives set forth in Article 76 shall be applicable to

2. The basic objectives set forth in Article 76 shall be applicable to

the people of each *strategic* area.

the people of each *such territory or* area.

3. The *Security* Council shall, subject to the provisions of the trusteeship agreements and without prejudice to security considerations, avail *itself* of the assistance of the Trusteeship Council to perform those functions of the United Nations under the trusteeship system relating to political, economic, social, and educational *matters in* the *strategic* areas.

3. *The General Assembly may authorize the Executive Council to perform on its behalf, and subject to its supervision and direction, such functions with respect to the administrative arrangements for the territories and areas referred to in paragraph 1, the appointment of the administrative staffs for such territories and areas, and the general control over their administration, as the Assembly may deem appropriate.*

4. The *General Assembly and the Executive* Council shall, subject to the provisions of the trusteeship agreements and without prejudice to security considerations, avail *themselves* of the assistance of the Trusteeship Council to perform those functions of the United Nations under the trusteeship system relating to *the* political, economic, social, and educational *development of the peoples of* the *territories and* areas *referred to in paragraph 1.*

Comment. As noted in the comment on revised Article 82, no national "strategic areas" whatever would exist upon the completion of the process of national disarmament pursuant to Annex I; and Articles 82 and 83 have therefore been remodeled to enable the setting aside of areas for the use of the United Nations Peace Force.

In view of the transfer to the General Assembly of the primary responsibility for the maintenance of peace (revised Article 11), it is suitable that the general responsibility for areas set aside for the use of the United Nations Peace Force should likewise be in the Assembly; and this is provided for in revised paragraph 1 of this Article 83.

It is also suitable that the General Assembly should have over-all responsibility for any areas which may be placed under the direct trusteeship of the United Nations itself (such as important straits and canals between seas and

160

oceans or areas in dispute between two or more nations pending settlement as to their disposition); and this responsibility is therefore provided for in paragraph 1.

As to the actual administration of the areas in both of these categories, the most appropriate organ to be entrusted with such administration is the Executive Council. This is so in the case of the areas set aside for the use of the United Nations Peace Force because these would constitute facilities actually in use by the United Nations itself for the maintenance of peace. Similar considerations apply to the administration of disputed areas temporarily administered by the United Nations. The problem of how best to administer vital international waterways (such as the Suez and Panama Canals and the Turkish Straits) and other places of common interest which may in the future be placed under United Nations trusteeship presents a different question. But, on the whole, it seems that the Executive Council would in this instance also be the most suitable administrative agent.

In the case of any and all of these areas, it is proposed, however, that the aid of the Trusteeship Council shall be availed of in so far as the administration relates to political, economic, social, and educational development in those areas.

Article 84

It shall be the duty of the administering authority to ensure that the trust territory shall play its part in the maintenance of international peace and security. To this end the administering authority *may make use of volunteer forces,* facilities, and assistance from the trust territory in carrying out the obligations toward the *Security Council* undertaken in this regard by the administering authority, *as well as for local defense and the maintenance of law and order within the trust territory.*

1. *The trust territories shall be subject to the disarmament provisions of Annex I of this revised Charter and to the limitations of that Annex relative to internal police forces for the maintenance of law and order within the trust territory, to the same extent as the metropolitan areas of all the nations.*

2. It shall be the duty of the administering authority to ensure that the trust territory shall play its part in the maintenance of international peace and security. To this end the administering authority *shall aid recruitment in the*

161

trust territory for the standing component of the United Nations Peace Force and the United Nations Peace Force Reserve, and shall provide facilities in and assistance from the trust territory in carrying out the obligations toward the *United Nations* undertaken in this regard by the administering authority *under Annex II of this revised Charter.*

Comment. The purpose of the first change in this Article (new paragraph 1) is to make it perfectly clear that the trust territories are subject to the disarmament provisions of the proposed Annex I and to the limitations on the maintenance of internal police forces therein contained, to the same extent as all the independent states. Subject to those limitations, however, the administering authority would be permitted to recruit such voluntary forces as it might need for the maintenance of law and order within the trust territory.

The purpose of the second change (in paragraph 2) is to confirm, in modified form, the equal duty of the trust territories to do their part, on the same basis as all the member Nations, in the maintenance of peace,—by helping to recruit for the standing component of the United Nations Peace Force and the Peace Force Reserve, by providing facilities to the United Nations, etc.

Article 85

1. The functions of the United Nations with regard to trusteeship agreements for all areas *not designated as strategic,* including the approval of the terms of the trusteeship agreements and of their alteration or amendment, shall be exercised by the General Assembly.

1. The functions of the United Nations with regard to trusteeship agreements for all areas *other than trust territories administered by the United Nations itself under Article 81 and areas designated for the use of the United Nations under Article 82,* including the approval of the terms of the trusteeship agreements and of their alteration or amendment, shall be exercised by the General Assembly *with the assistance of the Trusteeship Council.*

2. *The Trusteeship Council, operating under the authority of the*

2. *The General Assembly may authorize the Trusteeship Council*

162

General Assembly, shall assist the
General Assembly in carrying out
these functions.

to perform on its behalf, and sub-
ject to its supervision and direc-
tion, such functions with respect to
the trust territories referred to in
paragraph 1 as the Assembly may
deem appropriate.

Comment. The purpose of the changes in this Article is to harmonize its provisions with those of revised Article 83.

Since as already noted there would, under the revised Charter, no longer be any "strategic areas", the areas covered by this Article 83 are described as those which are not designated under revised Articles 81 and 82 either as direct United Nations trusteeships or as set aside for the use of the United Nations Peace Force. In other words, the areas covered by this revised Article would be those which are under trusteeships administered by member Nations as distinguished from the United Nations itself. As to these areas, the general responsibility would be left, as under the present Article, with the General Assembly. Moreover, the actual supervision of the carrying out of their responsibilities by the administering nations would remain, as now, with the Trusteeship Council. But certain changes in the language have been made in order to broaden and clarify the functions of the Trusteeship Council as agent for the General Assembly in this regard.

163

CHAPTER XIII

THE TRUSTEESHIP COUNCIL

COMPOSITION

Article 86

1. The Trusteeship Council shall consist of *the following Members of the United Nations:*

1. The Trusteeship Council shall consist of *Representatives elected by the General Assembly within thirty days from the beginning of the first regular session of each newly chosen Assembly. They shall serve during the four-year term of the Assembly by which they are elected and until their successors are elected by a new Assembly. The Assembly shall elect the members of the Council in accordance with the following formula and method:*

a. *those Members* administering trust territories;

a. *Each of the member Nations administering trust territories or other non-self-governing territories shall have the right to have one of its Representatives elected to the Council at every quadrennial election of the Council.*

b. *such of those Members mentioned by name in Article 23 as are not administering trust territories; and*

b. *The member Nations which have achieved independence since 1939 and the non-self-governing and trust territories under the administration of member Nations shall between them have the right to have as many of their Representatives elected to the Council as are equal in number to those elected*

c. *as many other Members elected for three-year terms by the General Assembly as may be necessary to ensure that the total number of members of the Trusteeship Council is equally divided between those Members of the United Nations which administer trust territories and those which do not.*

under subparagraph (a) of this paragraph.

c. *The member Nations other than those mentioned in the foregoing subparagraphs (a) and (b) shall between them have the right to have as many of their Representatives elected to the Council as are equal in number to those elected under subparagraph (a) of this paragraph.*

d. *Prior to each quadrennial election, the Assembly shall designate those of the member Nations or non-self-governing or trust territories in the groups mentioned in subparagraphs (b) and (c) of this paragraph each of which shall have the right to have one of its Representatives elected to the Council, due regard being specially paid to equitable geographical distribution.*

e. *After the designations called for by the foregoing subparagraph (d) have been made, the Representatives in the Assembly from all the member Nations or non-self-governing territories which are entitled to have Representatives elected to the Council at the particular election shall hold separate meetings which shall respectively nominate to the Assembly two of their own number deemed by the separate meetings best qualified to serve on the Council; provided that in the case of any such member Nation or non-self-governing or trust territory which has only one or two Representatives, their names shall be deemed automatically nominated.*

f. *After the nominations called*

for by the foregoing subparagraph (e) have been made, the Assembly shall elect to serve on the Council one of the two nominees of each of the member Nations or non-self-governing or trust territories then entitled to have one of its Representatives on the Council, taking into account the personal qualifications of each nominee for service on the Council, except that in the case of any such member Nation or non-self-governing or trust territory which has only one Representative in the Assembly, that Representative shall be deemed automatically elected.

2. Each member of the Trusteeship Council shall designate one specially qualified person to represent it therein.

2. Vacancies in the membership of the Trusteeship Council shall be filled in the following manner: The Representatives in the Assembly of the member Nation or non-self-governing or trust territory in whose representation on the Council the vacancy has occurred shall nominate two of their own number, and thereupon the General Assembly shall elect one of the two nominees taking into account the personal qualifications of each nominee for service on the Council; provided that in the case of any such member Nation or non-self-governing or trust territory which has only one or two Representatives their names shall be deemed automatically nominated, and in the case of any such member Nation or non-self-governing or trust territory which has only one Representative in the Assembly that Representative shall be deemed automatically elected.

3. *The General Assembly may by a vote of lack of confidence discharge the Trusteeship Council as a whole, provided: (a) that the members of the Council so discharged shall continue to serve until their successors are elected; (b) that the Assembly shall proceed forthwith to the election of a new Council; (c) that the members of the new Council shall be elected from among the Representatives in the Assembly of the same member Nations or non-self-governing or trust territories which were represented on the discharged Council; except that if the Assembly desires to replace a member of the discharged Council who is the only Representative from a member Nation or territory, the Assembly may elect a Representative from one of the other member Nations or territories entitled to either one or two Representatives in the Assembly and which would not otherwise be represented on the Council; (d) that the members of the new Council shall be nominated and elected by the same formula and method as called for by paragraph 1 of this Article; and (e) that the new Council shall serve, unless sooner discharged, until the regular quadrennial election of the Council following the quadrennial election of the Assembly.*

4. *No member of the Trusteeship Council shall simultaneously be a member of the Executive Council or of the Economic and Social Council.*

5. *The members of the Trustee-*

ship Council shall retain their seats in the General Assembly.

6. The members of the Trusteeship Council shall, during their period of service thereon, receive additional compensation to be fixed by the General Assembly.

Comment. In harmony with the method proposed for the selection of the new Executive Council (revised Article 23) and the enlarged Economic and Social Council (revised Article 61), it is proposed that the Trusteeship Council shall be chosen by the General Assembly from among its own number, instead of having its members appointed by national governments. As in the case of the Executive Council and the Economic and Social Council, the purpose is to make the Trusteeship Council more responsive to the policies and control of the Assembly itself, which (revised Articles 16, 85 and 87) would have general supervising responsibility for the trusteeship system. To the same end, the Assembly would have authority (paragraph 3), as in the case of the two other Councils, to discharge the Trusteeship Council by a vote of lack of confidence, provided that a new Council is appointed forthwith.

The other major change here proposed is an increase in the number of members of the Trusteeship Council to be chosen from nations other than the nations which are administering trust territories. Under the present Charter there were (as of January 1960) seven member Nations which under the present subparagraph (1) (a) were entitled to representation on the Council by reason of being administrators of trust territories; two member Nations represented under subparagraph (1) (b) by virtue of permanent membership on the Security Council; and five member Nations elected by the General Assembly under subparagraph (1) (c). In practice, this has resulted in a more or less continuous deadlock between the seven administering nations and a combination of the nations represented under the two other categories. As a result of the many seven to seven votes, the work of the Council has been seriously hampered.

With this situation in view and also because it is proposed to enlarge the functions of the Trusteeship Council to include the supervision of the administration by member Nations not only of trust territories, but also of all other non-self-governing territories (revised Articles 73 and 87), an entirely new plan for the composition of the Council is proposed. The practical result of this change would be to increase the Council's responsibility so that, instead of covering only the 20,000,000 inhabitants of the trust territories proper, it would embrace some 75,000,000 others living in non-self-governing territories other than the territories administered under trust agreements with the United Nations. It seems advisable, therefore, that the Council should have a larger and more broadly representative membership.

To this end, the proposal is that the Trusteeship Council shall consist of three groups of equal number: (a) a group of Representatives from the member Nations which are actually administering either trust territories or other non-self-governing territories; (b) a group of Representatives from the member Nations which have achieved independence since 1939; and (c) a group of Representatives from all the other member Nations, i.e., from all the member Nations not covered by the two preceding categories.

As above mentioned, the three groups would be equal in number so that the number in each of the two latter groups would be dependent upon the number from time to time in the first group of administering member Nations. As of January 1960, the nine nations indisputably in this first group were Australia, Belgium, France, Italy, the Netherlands, New Zealand, the Union of South Africa, the United Kingdom and the United States. In addition, Spain and Portugal may be considered as belonging to this group dependent upon whether their non-European possessions are deemed to be "provinces" or "non-self-governing territories". Consequently, assuming either nine or eleven as the number of the first group, the Council would consist of twenty-seven or thirty-three Representatives.

It seems clear that the group of nations which are actually administering trust or other non-self-governing territories should all be represented on the Trusteeship Council. It also seems advisable that those nations which have recently emerged from a dependent status should, in view of their experience, have an equal representation; and finally, as a balancing force, it seems advisable that all the other member Nations taken together should have similar representation.

It is believed that under this plan the Trusteeship Council would be so widely representative and so well-balanced as to command world confidence.

FUNCTIONS AND POWERS

Article 87

The General Assembly and, under its authority, the Trusteeship Council, *in carrying out their functions, may:*

a. consider reports submitted by the *administering authority;*

b. accept petitions and examine them in consultation with the *administering* authority;

1. **The General Assembly and,** under its authority, the Trusteeship Council *shall have the following functions:*

a. *to supervise the system for the administration of trust territories, established pursuant to Chapter XII; and*

b. *to examine the administration of all other non-self-governing territories with relation to the fulfillment of the obligations accepted by member Nations in Article 73.*

169

c. provide for periodic visits to the respective trust territories at times agreed upon with the *administering authority; and*

d. take these and other actions in conformity with the terms of the trusteeship agreements.

2. *In carrying out these functions, the Trusteeship Council, subject to the authority of the General Assembly, shall:*

a. consider reports *and information* submitted by the *respective authorities responsible for the trust territories and the other non-self-governing territories;*

b. accept petitions and examine them in consultation with the authority *responsible for the trust or non-self-governing territory from which the petition has come;*

c. provide for periodic visits to the respective trust *and other non-self-governing* territories at times agreed upon with the *authorities responsible for them;*

d. make recommendations to the authorities responsible for the trust territories and the other non-self-governing territories concerning the fulfillment by them of their obligations under trusteeship agreements or under Article 73, as the case may be;

e. make reports to the Assembly concerning the fulfillment by the respective authorities responsible for the trust territories and the other non-self-governing territories of their obligations under trusteeship agreements or under Article 73, as the case may be, together with recommendations as

> *to measures to be taken in any*
> *case of nonfulfillment; and*
> *f.* take these and other actions,
> *in so far as they relate to trust*
> *territories,* in conformity with the
> terms of the trusteeship agree-
> ments.

Comment. Together with revised Article 73 this revised Article so enlarges the responsibility of the Trusteeship Council (under the authority of the General Assembly) that it would extend to some sixty more areas and some 75,000,000 more people than the Council is responsible for as of January 1960.

Revised Article 73 contains the acceptance by all member Nations responsible for the administration of non-self-governing territories of "a sacred trust" to promote the well-being of the inhabitants of those territories and to "develop self-government" through assisting the "progressive development of their free political institutions" in accordance with their particular circumstances.

Supplementing that revised Article 73, this revised Article 87 sets forth in some detail the specific functions of the General Assembly and the Trusteeship Council in respect of the fulfillment of this "sacred trust". As to territories administered under trust agreements, the revised Article confirms the functions of the Council under the present Charter making more explicit, however (in subparagraphs (d) and (e) of paragraph 2), some functions which have been performed in practice under the present Charter but are not explicitly mentioned in the present Article 87. Beyond this, the revised Article extends all these functions to the larger field of non-self-governing territories which are not subject to trust agreements.

It is believed that this revised Article 87, read with revised Article 73, would make clear not only the broad responsibility of the United Nations for *all* the non-self-governing territories in charge of member Nations, but would also provide adequate procedures for the effective fulfillment of this responsibility.

Article 88

The Trusteeship Council shall formulate a questionnaire on the political, economic, social, and educational advancement of the inhabitants of each trust territory, and the administering authority for each *trust* territory *within the competence of the General Assembly* shall make an annual report to the *General Assembly* upon the basis of such questionnaire.

The Trusteeship Council shall formulate a questionnaire on the political, economic, social, and educational advancement of the inhabitants of each trust territory *and of each non-self-governing territory other than trust territories,* and the administering authority for each *such* territory shall make an annual report to the *Trusteeship Council* upon the basis of such questionnaire.

171

Comment. The changes in this Article are necessary in order to coordinate its terms with revised Articles 73 and 87. Since by those revised Articles the obligations of the United Nations in respect of non-self-governing territories of every kind and the corresponding duties of the Trusteeship Council in that regard would be greatly increased, it follows that the Council should be supplied with full information by the administering authorities of all these non-self-governing territories. Therefore, the language of this Article has been modified to state broadly that every administering authority must make an annual report upon the basis of the Trusteeship Council's questionnaire. In this way the language would harmonize with the obligation, assumed by member Nations under subparagraph (e) of revised Article 73, to furnish this information.

VOTING

Article 89

1. Each member of the Trusteeship Council shall have one vote.

2. Decisions of the Trusteeship Council shall be made by a majority of *the members present and voting*.

1. Each member of the Trusteeship Council shall have one vote.

2. Decisions of the Trusteeship Council *on important questions* shall be made by a *two-thirds* majority *vote* of *all its* members *whether or not* present *or* voting, *including a majority of all the Representatives then on the Council from the member Nations administering trust territories or other non-self-governing territories. These questions shall include: recommendations in accordance with Article 87 to the authorities responsible for the trust territories and other non-self-governing territories concerning the fulfillment by them of their obligations under trusteeship agreements or under Article 73, as the case may be; recommendations to the General Assembly in accordance with Article 87 in cases of nonfulfillment of these obligations; and any other questions which the Assembly may from time to time define as important.*

172

3. Decisions of the Trusteeship Council *on all other questions* shall be made by a majority of *all its* members, *whether or not* present *or* voting.

Comment. As called for in revised Article 86, the individual members of the Trusteeship Council would be chosen by the General Assembly itself from among its own number, instead of being appointed by the national governments of the member Nations represented on the Council. That change, however, calls for no alteration in the language of paragraph 1 of Article 89, since the present language is entirely appropriate to confer an equal vote on each individual person serving on the Council.

Moreover, under revised Article 86 the composition of the Trusteeship Council would be carefully balanced by having three equal groups of members (i.e., Representatives) from: (a) each of the member Nations actually administering non-self-governing or trust territories; (b) the member Nations which have achieved independence since 1939; and (c) all the other member Nations.

With this composition of the Trusteeship Council in mind, the proposed voting procedure calls for a special majority on "important questions" of two thirds of all the Council's members, with the proviso that such two-thirds majority shall include a majority of that one third of the Council's members who come from member Nations administering non-self-governing or trust territories. It is proposed that the "important questions" to which this special majority would apply shall include direct recommendations to member Nations, pursuant to revised Article 87, relative to the fulfillment of their obligations to the peoples under their charge; and recommendations to the General Assembly, in accordance with revised Article 87, concerning steps to be taken in case of the nonfulfillment of such obligations. If the Assembly considers that other questions should be designated as "important" so as to require this special majority vote in the Council, the Assembly would have authority to designate those questions.

The reason for the requirement that the proposed special majority shall include a majority of the Representatives on the Trusteeship Council from administering nations, is that in view of the greatly increased scope and authority of the Council and the fact that two thirds of its members would come from nations which are not themselves administering any non-self-governing territory, it seems desirable to have a safeguard against possible unreasonable demands upon the administering nations. Under the proposed formula, the administering nations would have some measure of protection against demands which a majority of them considered impracticable in the requirement that at least a majority of their Representatives on the Council would need to assent to the recommendations.

On all questions not classified as "important", an ordinary majority of all the members of the Trusteeship Council is proposed.

PROCEDURE

Article 90

1. The Trusteeship Council shall adopt its own rules of procedure, including the method of selecting its President.

2. The Trusteeship Council shall meet as required in accordance with its rules, which shall include provision for the convening of meetings on the request of a majority of its members.

Comment. No change is proposed in this Article.

Article 91

The Trusteeship Council shall, when appropriate, avail itself of the assistance of the Economic and Social Council and of the specialized agencies in regard to matters with which they are respectively concerned.

Comment. It is not necessary to make any changes in this Article.

174

CHAPTER XIV

THE *INTERNATIONAL* COURT OF JUSTICE

THE *JUDICIAL AND CON- CILIATION SYSTEM OF THE UNITED NATIONS*

General Comment. The title of this Chapter has been changed from "The International Court of Justice" to "The Judicial and Conciliation System of the United Nations". This is partly in view of the proposals for a World Equity Tribunal and a World Conciliation Board empowered to deal with questions of a nonlegal character which would not fall within the jurisdiction of the International Court of Justice (revised Article 93, paragraphs 1 and 2). It also takes into account the new tribunals inferior to the International Court of Justice which the General Assembly would be empowered to establish for the trial of offenses by individuals against the Charter or the laws and regulations enacted thereunder and for safeguarding the rights of individuals and nations against abuse of power by the organs and officials of the United Nations (revised Article 93, paragraph 3).

The general purpose of the changes in this Chapter is to bring its provisions into harmony with various other provisions of the revised Charter, including the Annexes, which provide for: (1) the continuance of the International Court of Justice with new authority to interpret the Charter and with extensive compulsory jurisdiction over legal disputes between all nations; (2) the establishment of the new World Equity Tribunal, with broad authority to deal with disputes between nations of a nonlegal nature; (3) the establishment of the World Conciliation Board to assist the nations in finding agreed solutions for their disputes; and (4) the establishment of a system of inferior tribunals empowered to try individual offenders against the Charter and the limited class of laws for the prevention of war which could be enacted by the General Assembly and to pass upon the validity of various acts of United Nations organs and officials.

Article 92

The International Court of Justice shall be the principal judicial organ of the United Nations. It shall function in accordance with the annexed Statute, which is based upon the Statute of the Permanent Court of International Justice and forms an integral part of *the present* Charter.

1. The International Court of Justice shall be the principal judicial organ of the United Nations. It shall function in accordance with the annexed Statute, which is based upon the Statute of the Permanent Court of International Justice and forms an integral part of *this revised* Charter *as Part A of Annex III.*

2. All *member Nations* are *ipso facto* parties to the Statute of the International Court of Justice.

3. A state which is not a *member* of the United Nations may become a party to the Statute of the International Court of Justice on conditions to be *set forth in general regulations to be adopted* by the General Assembly.

Comment. Paragraph 1 of this revised Article continues the International Court of Justice as "the principal judicial organ" of the United Nations. The only change is the reference to the Statute of the International Court as Part A of the proposed Annex III instead of referring to it as the only Annex to the Charter. It is to be noted, however, that the jurisdiction and importance of the Court would be greatly increased by the proposals that compulsory jurisdiction be granted to the Court in respect of several categories of cases. Pursuant to the new paragraph 3 of revised Article 96 and Part A of Annex III, this compulsory jurisdiction would include: (a) dangerous legal disputes between nations referred to the Court under revised Article 36; (b) disputes involving the interpretation or application of the Charter or the interpretation, application or constitutional validity of laws and regulations enacted thereunder; and (c) certain other important disputes mentioned in Part A of Annex III.

To the new paragraph 2 has been transferred the subject matter of paragraph 1 of the present Article 93. This is to the effect that all member Nations by joining the United Nations automatically become parties to the Statute of the International Court of Justice.

To the new paragraph 3 has been transferred the subject matter of paragraph 2 of the present Article 93 which relates to the conditions under which a nonmember nation may become a party to the Statute of the International Court of Justice. The new paragraph, however, requires the General Assembly to prescribe these conditions in general regulations rather than to stipulate the conditions "in each case" as under the present provision.

It should here be noted that nonmember nations would not, unless they voluntarily become parties to the Statute of the International Court of Justice, be bound to submit to its jurisdiction except in the contingencies provided for in revised Article 36, i.e., when the General Assembly has referred a dispute or situation to the Court on the ground that its continuance is "likely to endanger" peace.

Article 93

1. All *Members of the United Nations* are *ipso facto* parties to

1. *The World Equity Tribunal, established by Article 7 of this re-*

the Statute of the International Court of Justice.

2. A state which is not a *Member* of the United Nations may become a party to the Statute of the International Court of Justice on conditions to be *determined in each case* by the General Assembly *upon the recommendation of the Security Council.*

vised Charter, shall function in accordance with the annexed Statute which forms an integral part of this revised Charter as Part B of Annex III.

2. The World Conciliation Board, established by Article 7 of this revised Charter, shall function in accordance with the annexed Statute which forms an integral part of this revised Charter as Part C of Annex III.

3. The regional courts of the United Nations, established by Part D of Annex III, shall function in accordance with the provisions thereof. Subject to these provisions, the General Assembly shall determine from time to time the organization, jurisdiction and procedure of the regional courts.

Comment. Both of the two paragraphs of the present Article have been eliminated, their subject matter having been transferred to revised Article 92, as noted above in the comment on that Article.

This elimination permits the inclusion under Article 93 of new subject matter, i.e., of provisions relative to the World Equity Tribunal, the World Conciliation Board and the regional courts of the United Nations.

As to the World Equity Tribunal which is established by revised Article 7, provision is made that it shall function pursuant to Part B of Annex III. Similarly as to the World Conciliation Board, also established by revised Article 7, it is provided that this organ shall function in accordance with Part C of Annex III. As to nonlegal "disputes" and "situations" between nations which are "likely to endanger" peace, these two new organs, as explained in the comment on revised Article 36, should provide effective means for the pacific settlement of dangerous international difficulties. The purpose and mode of functioning of these two organs are described elsewhere. The effect of this revised Article 93 would be to make explicit constitutional provision for their status.

Finally, as to the regional courts system, established by Part D of Annex III, it is provided that these courts shall function in accordance therewith, subject to laws to be enacted by the General Assembly regulating their organization,

177

jurisdiction and procedure. Concerning the jurisdiction of these regional courts, it should be noted that their main functions would be: the trial of violators of the revised Charter and of laws and regulations enacted thereunder, especially in respect of the enforcement of the disarmament plan (Annex I); and the hearing of complaints against organs and officials of the United Nations.

Article 94

1. Each *Member of the United Nations* undertakes to comply with the decision of the International Court of Justice in any case to which it is a party.

2. If any party to a case fails to perform the obligations incumbent upon it under a judgment rendered by the Court, the other party may have recourse to the *Security Council,* which *may, if it deems necessary, make recommendations or* decide upon measures to be taken to give effect to the judgment.

1. Each *member Nation* undertakes to comply with the decision of the International Court of Justice in any case to which it is a party.

2. If any party to a case fails to perform the obligations incumbent upon it under a judgment rendered by the Court, the other party may have recourse to the *General Assembly* which *shall* decide upon measures to be taken to give effect to the judgment, *including measures under Articles 41 and 42.*

3. *If any nation fails to comply with any recommendation of the World Equity Tribunal which has been approved by the General Assembly in accordance with paragraph 9 of Article 36, the Assembly shall decide upon measures to be taken to give effect to the recommendation, including measures under Articles 41 and 42.*

Comment. Revised paragraph 1 merely reaffirms the provision whereby every member Nation promises to comply with any decision of the International Court of Justice in any case to which it is a party.

Revised paragraph 2 strengthens the procedure for the enforcement of judgments of the Court by providing: (a) that if any nation, party to a case before the Court, fails to comply with the Court's judgment the other party may resort "to the General Assembly"; and (b) that in such event the Assembly "shall" determine the measures to be taken for the enforcement of the judgment.

178

Under the present Charter a party aggrieved by noncompliance with a judgment of the International Court of Justice has recourse only to the Security Council. The new provision, allowing recourse to the General Assembly, is proposed because of the great importance which due compliance with a solemn judgment of the Court might have in upholding the authority of the strengthened United Nations; and it takes into account that under the revised Charter the primary responsibility for the maintenance of peace would rest with the Assembly. Thus, any defiance of a judgment of the Court would have to be dealt with in the first place by the Assembly itself which, however, might employ the Executive Council or other organs for the actual carrying out of such enforcement measures as the Assembly might have decided upon.

The other important change in paragraph 2 is the substitution of an obligation to see to the enforcement of a judgment of the Court for the merely discretionary authority in that respect provided for in the present Article 94. This is done by the substitution of the word "shall" for the phrase "may, if it deems necessary" and by requiring the Assembly to "decide upon" measures of enforcement rather than giving it the option merely to "make recommendations" in that regard.

The new paragraph 3 deals with the measures to be taken in case of noncompliance with recommendations of the World Equity Tribunal if and when such recommendations become enforceable pursuant to revised Article 36. Under the terms of paragraph 9 of that revised Article and Part B of Annex III, the recommendations of the Tribunal would become binding only when the following conditions have been fulfilled: (a) the Tribunal has adopted the recommendations by a two-thirds vote; (b) the General Assembly has approved the recommendations by a three-fourths majority vote of all the Representatives then in office, including a two-thirds majority of the Representatives from the nations having fifteen or more Representatives in the Assembly; and (c) the Assembly has declared by the same special majority that the dispute or situation is likely to continue unless the recommendations are carried out and that such continuance will constitute a serious danger to peace. When, however, these stringent requirements are fulfilled, the Assembly would be bound to "decide upon measures" to enforce the recommendations of the Tribunal as approved by the Assembly in exactly the same way as it would be required to enforce the judgments of the International Court of Justice.

It is to be noted that pursuant to revised Article 18 the "taking of measures" to enforce either a judgment of the International Court of Justice or of approved recommendations of the World Equity Tribunal would be "important questions" requiring the approval of a majority of all the Representatives then in office, whether or not present or voting.

Since the recommendations of the World Equity Tribunal would relate to nonlegal questions, as distinguished from legal questions adjudicated by the International Court of Justice, it may be argued that the recommendations of the Tribunal should not be enforceable at all or that, at least, the measures for the enforcement of the Tribunal's recommendations should go no further than diplomatic and economic sanctions. On the other hand, it might well be that the recommendations of the Tribunal concerning a dangerous situation would be of greater real importance for the maintenance of international peace than any judgment of the Court, so that the carrying out of those recommendations, when approved by the General Assembly, would, as a practical matter, be no less important for the authority of the United Nations than the enforcement of any possible judgment of the Court. Moreover, it must be remembered that no recommendations of the Tribunal would become enforceable at all unless they had received the overwhelming approval of the Assembly under the above-mentioned severe requirements of paragraph 9 of revised Artice 36. In other words, as distinguished from judgments of the International Court, the recommendations of the Tribunal could be enforced only after they had been declared essential for the maintenance of peace by a greatly preponderant vote of the world's representative body. Having passed that test, there would seem to be no sound reason to provide any different procedure or means for the enforcement of approved recommendations of the Tribunal than for the enforcement of judgments of the Court.

Article 95

Nothing in *the present* Charter shall prevent *Members of the United Nations* from entrusting the solution of their differences to other tribunals by virtue of agreements already in existence or which may be concluded in the future.

Nothing in *this revised* Charter shall prevent *member Nations* from entrusting the solution of their differences to other tribunals by virtue of agreements already in existence or which may be concluded in the future.

Comment. No change is proposed in this Article except the consequential changes whereby "this revised" is substituted for "the present" Charter and "member Nations" for "Members of the United Nations".

Article 96

1. The General Assembly or the *Security* Council may request the International Court of Justice to give an advisory opinion on any legal question.

1. The General Assembly, the *Executive* Council, *the Economic and Social Council, the Trusteeship Council* or *the World Equity Tribunal* may request the International Court of Justice to give an advisory opinion on any legal question.

2. Other organs of the United Nations and specialized agencies, which may at any time be so authorized by the General Assembly,

2. Other organs of the United Nations, specialized agencies and *regional organizations,* which may at any time be so authorized by

180

may also request advisory opinions of the Court on legal questions arising within the scope of their activities.

the General Assembly, may also request advisory opinions of the Court on legal questions arising within the scope of their activities.

3. Any dispute relating to the interpretation or application of this revised Charter, or the constitutionality, interpretation or application of any law or regulation enacted thereunder, may be submitted for decision to the Court by any member Nation or any other state, either on its own behalf or on behalf of any of its citizens.

Comment. Paragraphs 1 and 2 relate to strictly advisory opinions by the International Court of Justice. Under the present paragraph 1 only the General Assembly or Security Council has the right to request such an opinion. By the proposed change this right would be given to the new Executive Council and would be extended to the Economic and Social Council, the Trusteeship Council and the new World Equity Tribunal. Under the present paragraph 2 the Assembly has given the Economic and Social Council and Trusteeship Council permission to ask advisory opinions; but in view of the importance of these two councils, it seems proper to make this a matter of right rather than a privilege dependent upon the Assembly's discretion. The change would also extend this right to the World Equity Tribunal, which might find it of great importance to obtain a prompt legal opinion on some question relating to the problem referred to it.

Present paragraph 2 empowers the General Assembly to authorize "other organs" and "specialized agencies" to obtain advisory opinions of the Court. In view of the increasingly important role being played, especially in the economic field, by various regional organizations, such as the Organization of American States and the European Coal and Steel Community, it is proposed to extend the right to request advisory opinions to these organizations, subject to a prior authorization by the Assembly.

The new paragraph 3 proposes the most important change in this Article. This is the provision whereby "any member Nation or any other state" shall have the right to submit "for decision" by the International Court of Justice "any dispute relating to the interpretation or application of this revised Charter, or the constitutionality, interpretation or application of any law or regulation enacted thereunder".

The direct right thus given to every nation in the world to ask for a "decision" by the International Court concerning the interpretation and application of the revised Charter itself and concerning the constitutionality, interpretation and application of a law or regulation enacted thereunder, would be entirely independent of the above-mentioned privilege of organs of the United Nations to seek advisory opinions. In view of the enlarged powers of the United Nations under the revised Charter, this independent right seems a necessary and proper safeguard. It should extend not only to all member Nations but also to any nonmember nations which in certain important respects, such as the obligation to disarm, would be bound equally with the member Nations.

It seems only right that machinery be provided whereby any nation, "either on its own behalf or on behalf of any of its citizens" would be enabled to ascertain from the highest world judicial authority how any provision of the revised Charter, or of any law or regulation enacted thereunder, should be interpreted or applied, and to test the constitutional validity under the revised Charter of any particular law or regulation. To this end, it is proposed that any nation, including any nonmember state, shall be entitled to bring before the International Court any "dispute", either with another nation or with the United Nations itself, with respect to any of these questions.

CHAPTER XV

THE SECRETARIAT

Article 97

The Secretariat shall comprise a Secretary-General and such staff as the *Organization* may require. The Secretary-General shall be appointed by the General Assembly upon the recommendation of the *Security* Council. He shall be the chief administrative officer of the *Organization*.

The Secretariat shall comprise a Secretary-General and such staff as the *United Nations* may require. The Secretary-General shall be appointed by the General Assembly upon the recommendation of the *Executive* Council. *He shall serve for a term of six years and until his successor has been appointed; and shall be eligible for reappointment but for no more than one term. The Assembly shall have authority to remove him, by a vote of two thirds of all the Representatives then in office, whether or not present or voting, whenever the Assembly deems it necessary.* He shall be the chief administrative officer of the *United Nations*.

Comment. The principal changes in this Article relate to the term of the Secretary-General and to his removal from office. The present text contains no provision on these subjects. In view, however, of the greatly increased scope of the United Nations under the revised Charter, and the consequent increase in the importance of the Secretary-General, it is desirable to specify the length of his term and to provide for his possible dismissal if by a large majority the General Assembly should deem it essential.

The other changes in this Article are consequential on the use of the term "United Nations" instead of "Organization", and on the substitution of the new "Executive Council" for the "Security Council". As to the latter it is to be remembered that since there would be no veto in the Executive Council (revised Article 27), it is unlikely that any prolonged deadlock would occur as to the recommendation by the Council of a new Secretary-General.

Article 98

The Secretary-General shall act in that capacity in all meetings of

The Secretary-General shall act in that capacity in all meetings of

183

the General Assembly, of the *Security* Council, of the Economic and Social Council, and of the Trusteeship Council, and shall perform such other functions as are entrusted to him by these organs. The Secretary-General shall make an annual report to the General Assembly on the work of the *Organization*.

the General Assembly, of the *Executive* Council, of the Economic and Social Council, and of the Trusteeship Council, and shall perform such other functions as are entrusted to him by these organs. The Secretary-General shall make an annual report to the General Assembly on the work of the *United Nations*.

Comment. The only changes in this Article are consequential on the substitution of the "Executive Council" for the "Security Council" and of the "United Nations" for the "Organization".

Article 99

The Secretary-General *may* bring to the attention of the *Security* Council any matter which in his opinion may threaten the maintenance of international peace and security.

The Secretary-General *shall* bring *to the attention of the General Assembly or, if the Assembly is not in session,* to the attention of the *Executive* Council any matter which in his opinion may threaten the maintenance of international peace and security, *and any refusal to comply with this revised Charter or the laws and regulations enacted thereunder which in his opinion is of an especially serious character.*

Comment. The three proposed changes of substance in this Article are: (a) the substitution of "shall" for "may" in connection with the Secretary-General's function of giving warning of threats to the peace; (b) the extension of his duty to give warning to any serious "refusal to comply with this revised Charter or the laws and regulations enacted thereunder"; and (c) the requirement that the General Assembly shall receive any such warning if in session; and otherwise the Executive Council as its agent.

As to the first, there seems no reason why the Secretary-General should have discretion as to warning the organs directly responsible for the maintenance of peace. If in his judgment a threat to the peace actually exists, it should be his *constitutional duty* to give warning of so serious a state of affairs.

As to the second, it seems desirable to impose on the Secretary-General the duty to warn the organs of the United Nations responsible for maintaining the authority of the United Nations of any serious violation of the Charter (or of the laws or regulations enacted thereunder).

As to naming the General Assembly as entitled to receive the warning, this requirement follows from the proposal that the Assembly shall have the "primary responsibility" for the maintenance of peace (revised Article 11); while the requirement that the Executive Council be notified if the Assembly is not in session is merely to make certain that the other organ directly responsible for maintaining peace shall receive the warning when the Assembly is not able immediately to deal with the matter. In that event it would be the duty of the Executive Council to take emergency measures if the situation were so serious as to demand immediate action, and to request the Secretary-General immediately to convoke a special session of the Assembly (revised Article 39).

Article 100

1. In the performance of their duties the Secretary-General and the staff shall not seek or receive instructions from any government or from any other authority external to the *Organization*. They shall refrain from any action which might reflect on their position as international officials responsible only to the *Organization*.

2. Each *Member of the United Nations* undertakes to respect the exclusively international character of the responsibilities of the Secretary-General and the staff and not to seek to influence them in the discharge of their responsibilities.

1. In the performance of their duties the Secretary-General and the staff shall not seek or receive instructions from any government or from any other authority external to the *United Nations*. They shall refrain from any action which might reflect on their position as international officials responsible only to the *United Nations*.

2. Each *member Nation* undertakes to respect the exclusively international character of the responsibilities of the Secretary-General and the staff and not to seek to influence them in the discharge of their responsibilities.

Comment. The only suggested changes in this Article are consequential on the use throughout the revision of "United Nations" instead of "Organization" and of "member Nation" instead of "Member of the United Nations".

Article 101

1. The staff shall be appointed by the Secretary-General under regulations established by the General Assembly.

1. The staff shall be appointed by the Secretary-General under regulations established by the General Assembly.

2. Appropriate staffs shall be permanently assigned to the Economic and Social Council, the Trusteeship Council, and, as required, to other organs of the United Nations. These staffs shall form a part of the Secretariat.

2. Appropriate staffs shall be permanently assigned to *the General Assembly, the Executive Council*, the Economic and Social Council, the Trusteeship Council, and, as required, to other organs of the United Nations. These staffs shall form a part of the Secretariat.

3. The paramount consideration in the employment of the staff and in the determination of the conditions of service shall be the necessity of securing the highest standards of efficiency, competence, and integrity. Due regard shall be paid to the importance of recruiting the staff on as wide a geographical basis as possible.

3. The paramount consideration in the employment of the staff and in the determination of the conditions of service shall be the necessity of securing the highest standards of efficiency, competence, and integrity. Due regard shall be paid to the importance of recruiting the staff on as wide a geographical basis as possible.

Comment. The only change in this Article is the addition of the General Assembly and the Executive Council in the mention of the organs to which "appropriate staffs" shall be "permanently assigned". While authority to supply the General Assembly and the new Executive Council with appropriate staffs would presumably be implied, it seems best to list them specifically among the organs to be thus equipped.

CHAPTER XVI

MISCELLANEOUS PROVISIONS

Article 102

1. Every treaty and every international agreement entered into by any *Member of the United Nations* after the *present* Charter comes into force shall as soon as possible be registered with the Secretariat and published by it.

1. Every treaty and every international agreement entered into by any *member Nation* after the *original* Charter *came* into force *in 1945, including every such treaty or agreement entered into by any member Nation after this revised Charter comes into force,* shall as soon as possible be registered with the Secretariat and published by it.

2. No party to any such treaty or international agreement which has not been registered in accordance with the provisions of paragraph 1 of this Article may invoke that treaty or agreement before any organ of the United Nations.

2. No party to any such treaty or international agreement which has not been registered in accordance with the provisions of paragraph 1 of this Article may invoke that treaty or agreement before any organ of the United Nations.

Comment. The first change in paragraph 1 is consequential on the use throughout the revision of "member Nation" instead of "Member of the United Nations". The other change is to make it perfectly clear that the treaties and international agreements required to be registered shall include not only the treaties and agreements made during the period between the adoption of the 1945 Charter and the adoption of the revised Charter, but also all future treaties and agreements made after the revised Charter comes into force.

Article 103

In the event of a conflict between the obligations of the *Members of the United Nations* under *the present* Charter and their obligations under any other international agreement, their obligations

1. In the event of a conflict between the obligations of the *member Nations* under *this revised* Charter *or the laws and regulations enacted thereunder* and their obligations under any other inter-

under *the present* Charter shall prevail.

national agreement, their obligations under *this revised* Charter *or such laws and regulations* shall prevail.

2. This revised Charter and the laws and regulations of the United Nations which shall be made in pursuance thereof shall be the supreme law of the United Nations, and all authorities of the member Nations shall be bound thereby, anything in the constitution or laws of any member Nation to the contrary notwithstanding.

Comment. Apart from consequential changes it is proposed to revise paragraph 1 by providing that not only the revised Charter itself shall prevail over any other international obligation, but also any laws and regulations enacted under the revised Charter. This change is made necessary by the new, although carefully limited, legislative powers conferred upon the General Assembly by the proposed revision (revised Article 11).

The new paragraph 2 makes explicit the superiority of the revised Charter and the laws and regulations enacted thereunder over the constitutions and laws of the member Nations. It seems wise to make perfectly clear that although the strengthened United Nations would have only limited powers strictly confined to the maintenance of peace, its authority in that field shall be superior to any other authority whatever. This is necessary because on no other terms could the United Nations fulfil its main function of maintaining peace. In harmony with this conception, paragraph 2 makes definite the obligation of "all authorities" of the member Nations to be bound by the revised Charter and the laws and regulations enacted thereunder. It follows that when necessary the constitutions of member Nations would need to be revised so as to accord with this provision.

Article 104

The *Organization* shall enjoy in the territory of each *of its Members* such legal capacity as may be necessary for the exercise of its functions and the fulfillment of its purposes.

1. The *United Nations* shall enjoy in the territory of each *member Nation* such legal capacity as may be necessary for the exercise of its functions and the fulfillment of its purposes.

2. The United Nations shall have the right to acquire buildings and

188

such other property as it may need for its offices. Such properties shall be acquired from or with the assistance of member Nations, by agreement if possible and otherwise by condemnation with just compensation. In case of a dispute as to whether the compensation paid or offered by the United Nations is just, the private owner of the property in question, or the nation which owns such property or within which such property is situated acting on its own behalf or on behalf of the private owner of such property as the case may be, may submit the dispute for decision to the United Nations regional court within the jurisdiction of which such property is situated. If either the United Nations or the private owner of the property in question or the nation which owns such property or in the territory of which such property is situated is dissatisfied with the decision of the regional court, any of them shall have the right to appeal to the International Court of Justice; except that in the case of a private owner, such right shall be subject to any legislation which may be enacted by the General Assembly pursuant to Part D of Annex III. In the case of such an appeal to the International Court of Justice, the decision of that Court shall be final.

Comment. Apart from consequential changes in this Article, it is proposed to add a new paragraph dealing with the right of the United Nations to acquire such properties as it may need for its offices. Ordinarily the United Nations would acquire such properties with the assistance of the nation in the territory of which the property is situated. If, however, a particular na-

189

tion should not be willing to cooperate, the United Nations would have authority to institute condemnation proceedings and to acquire the properties in question by paying just compensation. Should there be any dispute concerning the fairness of the compensation, such dispute would be submitted in the first instance to a United Nations regional court, from which an appeal could be taken to the International Court of Justice.

Article 105

1. The *Organization* shall enjoy in the territory of each *of its Members* such privileges and immunities as are necessary for the fulfillment of its purposes.

1. The *United Nations* shall enjoy in the territory of each *member Nation* such privileges and immunities as are necessary for the fulfillment of its purposes.

2. Representatives *of the Members of the United Nations* and officials of the *Organization* shall similarly enjoy such privileges and immunities as are necessary for the independent exercise of their functions in connection with the *Organization*.

2. Representatives *in the General Assembly, members of the other organs of the United Nations, members of the United Nations Peace Force,* and officials *and employees* of the *United Nations, including officials and employees of its various authorities and agencies,* shall similarly enjoy such privileges and immunities as are necessary for the independent exercise of their functions in connection with the *United Nations.*

3. The General Assembly *may make recommendations with a view to determining the details of the application of paragraphs 1 and 2 of this Article or may propose conventions to the Members of the United Nations for this purpose.*

3. The General Assembly *shall have the power to implement the provisions of Annex VI of this revised Charter relating to the principles which shall govern the privileges and immunities mentioned in paragraphs 1 and 2 of this Article.*

Comment. Only consequential changes are made in paragraph 1.

In paragraph 2, however, substantial changes are proposed in the definition of the individuals entitled to privileges and immunities. The proposal is that these shall be enjoyed: (a) by the Representatives in the General Assembly; (b) by those who are serving as members of the various other organs of the United Nations; (c) by those serving in the United Nations Peace Force; and (d) by "officials and employees" of the staff of the United Nations and of its various authorities and agencies.

For the effective functioning of a greatly strengthened United Nations it is clearly necessary that all within these categories shall have well-understood and carefully defined privileges and immunities.

The question of what those privileges and immunities ought to be presents a problem that has already caused great difficulties; and several nations (including the United States) have refused to ratify a convention on the subject proposed by the General Assembly. It is very necessary that the basic principles governing these privileges and immunities be clearly defined in order to enable the strengthened United Nations properly to fulfil its purposes; and the matter is of such great importance that it is believed wise to make such definition constitutional. It is therefore proposed to set forth the principles covering privileges and immunities in a special Annex (the proposed Annex VI). In this way the basic rules to be followed in defining such privileges and immunities would be made constitutional in the same way as, for example, the principles of the proposed disarmament plan and of the revenue system would be defined in Annexes I and V. Within the framework of the principles thus constitutionally laid down in Annex VI, the General Assembly would have authority to make the necessary detailed regulations to implement those principles.

CHAPTER XVII

TRANSITIONAL SECURITY ARRANGEMENTS

Article 106

Pending *the coming into force of such special agreements referred to in Article 43 as* in the opinion of the *Security Council* enable *it to begin the exercise of* its responsibilities under Article 42, the parties to the Four-Nation Declaration, signed at Moscow, October 30, 1943, and France, shall, in accordance with the provisions of paragraph 5 of that Declaration, consult with one another and as occasion requires with other *Members of the United Nations* with a view to such joint action on behalf of the *Organization* as may be necessary for the purpose of maintaining international peace and security.

Pending *the organization of the United Nations Peace Force under Annex II of this revised Charter to an extent which,* in the opinion of the *General Assembly, will* enable *the United Nations to exercise* its responsibilities under Article 42, the parties to the Four-Nation Declaration, signed at Moscow, October 30, 1943, and France *and India,* shall in accordance with the provisions of paragraph 5 of that Declaration, consult with one another and as occasion requires with other *member Nations* with a view to such joint action on behalf of the *United Nations* as may be necessary for the purpose of maintaining international peace and security.

Comment. Besides the obvious consequential changes, two changes of substance are proposed in this Article. One is a change in the interim period during which certain Powers are obliged to consult as to joint action for the maintenance of peace. This period would now be defined as the period prior to "the organization of the United Nations Peace Force under Annex II of this revised Charter to an extent which, in the opinion of the General Assembly, will enable the United Nations to exercise its responsibilities under Article 42" instead of the period until the coming into force of adequate special agreements under the present Article 43. The reason for this change is that the revised Article 42 would abolish the present plan for the negotiation of special agreements under Article 43 through which national forces would be made available for military sanctions, the plan for a United Nations Peace Force being substituted therefor.

The other change is the addition of India to the group of Powers which would be obligated to consult during the interim period. The group would then consist of the following six nations: China, France, India, the U.S.S.R., the United Kingdom and the U.S.A. This addition of India is proposed because, under the revision, India would be one of the four largest nations which, with China, the U.S.S.R. and the U.S.A., would be entitled to thirty Representatives each in the General Assembly; and also because its inclusion would more nearly balance the Western and Eastern nations in the consulting group, i.e., France, the United Kingdom and the U.S.A. in the West, with China and India in the East and the U.S.S.R. in both.

Article 107

Nothing in *the present* Charter shall invalidate or preclude action, in relation to any state which during the Second World War *has been* an enemy of any signatory to the *present* Charter, taken or authorized as a result of that war by the Governments having responsibility for such action.

Pending the organization of the United Nations Peace Force under Annex II of this revised Charter to an extent which, in the opinion of the General Assembly, will enable the United Nations to exercise its responsibilities under Article 42, nothing in *this revised* Charter shall invalidate or preclude action, in relation to any state which during the Second World War *was* an enemy of any *original* signatory to the Charter, taken or authorized as a result of that war by the Governments having responsibility for such action.

Comment. Besides the necessary consequential changes, a substantial change is proposed through a limitation on the period during which the reserved right to take action against "enemy" states in the Second World War may be exercised.

Under the present Article the period during which the right is reserved to act against former enemy states appears to be unlimited. In view, however, of the plan whereby the United Nations would have its own adequate and independent military force—the United Nations Peace Force—there is no reason why the reserved right to act against enemies of the Western Alliance in World War II should exist in perpetuity. It is therefore proposed that this period be limited to the period prior to "the organization of the United Nations Peace Force under Annex II of this revised Charter to an extent which, in the opinion of the General Assembly, will enable the United Nations to exercise its responsibilities under Article 42".

The plan for the organization of the United Nations Peace Force (Annex II) provides for building up that Force concurrently with the carrying out of the progressive disarmament plan. This would normally require a period of thirteen years from the ratification of the revised Charter, but might be shortened to ten years (Article 10 of Annex I). Accordingly, if that disarmament plan is

193

adopted and fulfilled, the maximum period during which action could be taken against former "enemy" states would not exceed thirteen years after the ratification of the revised Charter, and might be considerably shorter if before that time the General Assembly should determine that the Peace Force has become strong enough adequately to safeguard the peace of the world.

CHAPTER XVIII

AMENDMENTS

Article 108

Amendments *to the present* Charter shall come into force for all *Members of the United Nations* when they have been adopted by a vote of two thirds of *the members of* the General Assembly and ratified in accordance with their respective constitutional processes by *two thirds* of the *Members of the United Nations, including all the permanent members of the Security Council.*

After the adoption of this revised Charter, amendments *thereto* shall come into force for all *member Nations* when they have been adopted by a vote of two thirds of *all the Representatives in* the General Assembly *then in office, whether or not present or voting,* and ratified in accordance with their respective constitutional processes by *four fifths* of the *member Nations and provided that the ratifying member Nations shall include three fourths of the member Nations entitled under Article 9 to fifteen or more Representatives in the Assembly.*

Comment. Alternative methods for the proposal of amendments are provided by the two Articles of Chapter XVIII. One is the method provided in Article 108, i.e., the proposal of amendments by the General Assembly itself. The other is the method provided in Article 109, i.e., the proposal of amendments through a General Conference called for the special purpose of reviewing the Charter.

Under revised Article 108 important changes are envisaged in the procedures both for the proposal and the ratification of amendments, that is to say of amendments subsequent to the coming into force of the revised Charter. The present Article provides for the *submission* of such future amendments for ratification when they have been adopted by a vote of two thirds of the member states through their delegates in the General Assembly. The revised Article would, however, provide for the submission of future amendments when adopted, not by any vote of member Nations as such, but by a vote of two thirds of all the Representatives in the General Assembly whether or not present or voting, i.e., by a two-thirds vote of all the individuals serving in the Assembly.

In respect of the *ratification* of future amendments, other important changes are proposed. The present Article 108 calls for ratification by "two thirds of the

195

Members of the United Nations, including all the permanent members of the Security Council." Instead of this provision, it is proposed: (a) that ratification by "four fifths" of the member Nations be required; and (b) that "the ratifying member Nations shall include three fourths of the member Nations entitled under Article 9 to fifteen or more Representatives in the Assembly."

In one respect, these proposed requirements for ratification are stricter than the present formula in providing for ratification by "four fifths", instead of "two thirds", of the member Nations. On the other hand, the new requirements would be less rigid, in that no single nation of the "Big Five" or of any other group would have a "veto" power over any amendment. In place of the present "veto" on amendments there would be substituted the provision that if the required four fifths of the member Nations includes three fourths of the largest nations which are in the two top categories for the purpose of representation in the General Assembly, the proposed amendment would come into force. As of January 1960, this would require the assent of nine of the following twelve nations: Brazil, China, France, West Germany, India, Indonesia, Italy, Japan, Pakistan, the United Kingdom, the United States and the U. S. S. R.

This revised Article 108 and revised Article 109 should be read in relation to revised Article 110; and the distinction should be noted that whereas revised Article 110 deals with the ratification of the revised Charter itself, Articles 108 and 109 deal with the proposal and ratification of amendments to the revised Charter *after* its adoption.

In respect of the ratification of the revised Charter itself, the proposal (revised Article 110) is that ratification shall require not only the assent of five sixths of the member Nations which shall contain at least five sixths of the world's population, but also that the ratifying nations shall include *all* the twelve nations having the largest populations. By contrast, the corresponding provisions of revised Articles 108 and 109 (relating not to the ratification of the revised Charter but to its future amendment) would require the assent of only three fourths of those twelve largest nations. The reason for this difference is that in order to ensure the necessary overwhelming support for the revised Charter in its initial stage, it is considered essential to have the prior assent of literally all the world's largest nations,—defined as the twelve nations with the largest populations. On the other hand, in the case of future amendments *after* the strengthened United Nations is functioning under the revised Charter, it seems unduly severe to require absolutely unanimous approval by the twelve largest nations. Instead, it seems sufficient to require the assent of no more than three fourths of those nations. In practice, this formula for the approval of future amendments would mean that an amendment to the revised Charter could come into force even if three of those twelve nations did not ratify it.

On the one hand, these requirements for the ratification of amendments after the adoption of the revised Charter would make their ratification so difficult as to ensure that the revised Charter could be altered only with the overwhelming approval of the nations and peoples. On the other hand, the requirements would not be so rigid as virtually to preclude any amendment whatever, notwithstanding its approval by a great preponderance of the member Nations.

Article 109

1. A General Conference of the Members of the United Nations for the purpose of reviewing the *present* Charter may be held at a date and place to be fixed by a two thirds vote of *the members of the General Assembly and by a vote of any seven members of the Security Council. Each Member of the United Nations* shall have one vote *in the conference.*

1. After the adoption of this revised Charter, General Conferences for the purpose of reviewing the *revised* Charter or considering a particular amendment or amendments thereto may be held pursuant to the following provisions:

a. Such a General Conference shall be held at a date and place to be fixed by a two thirds vote of all the Representatives in the General Assembly then in office, whether or not present or voting.

b. On application of two thirds of the member Nations, the Assembly shall call such a General Conference, and shall fix the place and date for the convening thereof, which shall not be more than one year after the receipt of such application.

c. The number of delegates which the member Nations and the non-self-governing and trust territories shall be entitled to send to a General Conference shall be the same as the number of Representatives which the member Nations and the non-self-governing and trust territories are respectively entitled to have in the Assembly at the time of the conference. The delegates shall be chosen in each member Nation and in the non-self-governing and trust territories in the same manner as that provided in Article 9 for the choice of Representatives in the Assembly.

d. Delegates shall vote as individuals and each delegate shall have one vote.

2. Any alteration of *the present* Charter recommended by a two-thirds vote of *the conference* shall take effect when ratified *in accordance with their respective constitutional processes by two-thirds of the Members of the United Nations including all the permanent members of the Security Council.*

2. Any alteration of *this revised* Charter recommended by a two-thirds vote of *all the delegates in the General Conference, whether or not present or voting,* shall take effect when ratified *by the same method and subject to the same conditions as are provided in Article 108 in respect of amendments proposed by the General Assembly.*

3. If such a conference has not been held before the tenth annual session of the General Assembly following the coming into force of *the present* Charter, the proposal to call such a conference shall be placed on the agenda of that session of the *General* Assembly, and the conference shall be held if so decided by a majority *vote of the members of the General Assembly and by a vote of any seven members of the Security Council.*

3. If such a conference has not been held before the tenth annual session of the General Assembly following the coming into force of *this revised* Charter, the proposal to call such a conference shall be placed on the agenda of that session of the Assembly, and the conference shall be held if so decided by *a vote of* a majority *of all the Representatives in the Assembly then in office, whether or not present or voting; and if in each ensuing ten-year period such a conference has not been held, the same procedure shall apply.*

Comment. As in the case of revised Article 108, this revised Article 109 relates only to the submission and ratification of amendments *after* the adoption of the revised Charter.

In respect of such future amendments, paragraph 1 provides that in addition to the submission of amendments by the General Assembly itself under revised Article 108, such amendments may be submitted for ratification through a General Conference. Such a conference, under revised paragraph 1, could be called either to review the revised Charter as a whole or for the purpose of "considering a particular amendment or amendments".

By paragraph 1 of the present Article a General Conference for either of these purposes may be called by a vote in the General Assembly of two thirds of the member states with the assent of any seven members of the Security Council. In lieu of this single method for the convening of a General Conference, subparagraphs (a) and (b) of revised paragraph 1 provide two alternative methods for convening such a conference. The first of these would be action of the General Assembly upon its own initiative through a two-thirds vote of all the Representatives. The other would be through action by the Assembly upon the application of two thirds of the member Nations, in which case it would be mandatory for the Assembly to convoke the General Conference within a year from the receipt of the application. The second alternative is proposed in order to ensure that if a large majority of the governments of the member Nations themselves believe that a General Conference should be called (either for a review of the whole Charter or for the consideration of specific amendments) such a conference would be convened whether or not the Assembly happens to be sympathetic.

Subparagraph (c) of revised paragraph 1 covers the composition of a General Conference and the selection of delegates thereto. As to the composition of a General Conference, the proposal is that it shall consist of a number of delegates precisely equal to the number of Representatives in the General Assembly to which the member Nations and the non-self-governing and trust territories are then respectively entitled. As to the mode of selection of the delegates, it is proposed that they be chosen by the same method in each member Nation and in the non-self-governing and trust territories as is used by that nation or territory for the selection of its Representatives in the Assembly (revised Article 9).

As to voting in a General Conference, subparagraph (d) of revised paragraph 1 provides that each delegate shall have one vote and shall vote as an individual.

Revised paragraph 2 provides for the taking effect of any amendments submitted by a General Conference through precisely the same ratification requirements as are provided for by revised Article 108 in respect of amendments submitted directly by the General Assembly; and precisely the same considerations apply as are stated in the comment on revised Article 108.

Revised paragraph 3 adopts and extends the basic idea of the present paragraph 3 in recognizing the advisability of periodical consideration of the question of Charter review. But whereas the present paragraph 3 provides for the mandatory consideration of this question by the General Assembly only on one occasion, i.e., in its tenth session after the coming into force of the 1945 Charter, the revised paragraph 3 provides that the Assembly shall consider the advisability of a review conference at the end of every ten-year period after the adoption of the revised Charter, if during that period no such conference has been held. It will be observed that this provision does not make a review conference mandatory during each ten-year period, but only makes it mandatory for the Assembly to consider the question of whether it is advisable to hold such a conference. On the other hand, it is proposed that, when the question of a General Conference under this provision comes up in the Assembly, no more than a majority vote of all the Representatives shall be required for a decision to convoke the conference.

CHAPTER XIX

RATIFICATION AND SIGNATURE

Article 110

1. *The present* Charter shall be *ratified by the signatory states* in accordance with *their respective* constitutional processes.

1. *This revised* Charter shall be *submitted for ratification to all the independent nations of the world, namely those listed in Article 9. Ratification by each nation shall be* in accordance with *its* constitutional processes.

2. The ratifications shall be deposited with the *Government of the United States of America, which* shall notify all the *signatory states* of each deposit *as well as the Secretary-General of the Organization when he has been appointed.*

2. The ratifications shall be deposited with the *Secretary-General of the United Nations, who* shall notify all the *nations* of each deposit.

3. *The present* Charter shall come into force upon the deposit of ratifications by *the Republic of China, France, the Union of Soviet Socialist Republics, the United Kingdom of Great Britain and Northern Ireland, and the United States of America, and by a majority of the other signatory states. A protocol of the ratifications deposited shall thereupon be drawn up by the Government of the United States of America which shall communicate copies thereof to all the signatory states.*

3. *This revised* Charter shall come into force upon the deposit of ratifications by *five sixths of all the nations of the world as listed in Article 9; provided that the population of the ratifying nations as estimated by the Secretary-General of the United Nations shall be at least five sixths of the population of the world as estimated by the Secretary-General, and that the ratifying nations shall include all the twelve nations having the largest populations as estimated by the Secretary-General, such estimates to be as of the date when this revised Charter is submitted for ratification; and further provided that this revised Charter shall come into force only if the required ratifica-*

tions are deposited with the Secretary-General within ten years from the date of its submission for ratification. Upon the deposit of the required ratifications with the Secretary-General within the ten-year period, he shall forthwith notify all the nations of the world of the coming into force of this revised Charter and the date thereof.

4. *The states signatory to the present Charter which ratify it after it has come into force will become original Members of the United Nations on the date of the deposit of their respective ratifications.*

4. *After the coming into force of this revised Charter and until the new or modified organs and authorities called for by the revised Charter are ready to assume their functions, the then existing organs of the United Nations shall continue in operation with the functions and powers possessed by them under the Charter of 1945.*

5. *The period of one year from the date on which this revised Charter comes into force shall be known as the transition period.*

6. *During the transition period:*
a. The General Assembly, constituted in pursuance of this revised Charter, shall be chosen as soon as practicable and shall be convoked by the Secretary-General to meet within seven months after the date upon which the revised Charter comes into force.
b. The Executive Council shall be elected by the General Assembly within one month from the date on which the Assembly meets.
c. Such other steps shall be taken by the General Assembly as may be necessary for the establishment

201

and organization of the new or modified organs, authorities and agencies provided for in the revised Charter.

Comment. It is assumed that the procedure governing the *submission* for ratification of the proposals contained in this book would be in accordance with either the present Article 108 or the present Article 109, i.e., either through adoption of the proposals by a two-thirds vote of the member states in the General Assembly pursuant to Article 108, or by a similar vote in a General Conference called pursuant to Article 109 for the purpose of reviewing the present Charter. Accordingly in so far as the procedure for the adoption and recommendation of the proposed revision is concerned, there is no occasion for changing the present provisions of Articles 108 and 109. On the other hand, in so far as *ratification* is concerned, this revised Article 110 provides for much stricter conditions for ratification than those provided for the ratification of the 1945 Charter under paragraph 3 of the present Article 110 or for the ratification of amendments thereto pursuant to the present Articles 108 and 109.

The proposal is that the revised Charter shall come into force only upon the following conditions: (1) Ratification shall be by at least five sixths of all the nations of the world as listed in revised Article 9. As of July 1965 when it is assumed that a comprehensive revision of the Charter of the sort proposed in this book will be under serious consideration throughout the world, this would require ratification by at least eighty-three of the ninety-nine nations which will probably be then recognized as independent states. (2) The estimated population of the ratifying nations shall be at least five sixths of the total world population, these estimates to be made by the Secretary-General as of the date when the revised Charter is submitted for ratification. (3) The ratifying nations shall include, without exception, all the twelve nations then having the largest populations as similarly estimated by the Secretary-General. As of July 1, 1965, this would probably require ratification by twelve such nations. (4) The required ratifications, adopted in accordance with the constitutional processes of each nation, shall be notified to the Secretary-General within ten years from the submission of the revised Charter for ratification.

At first impression these requirements may seem unduly severe. It is believed, however, that it would be unwise to initiate the far-reaching changes in the political system of the world called for by the revision, unless the plan has advance assurance of overwhelming support in world opinion; and the proposed requirements are intended to ensure that prior support.

Concerning the changes called for by the revised Charter, it is necessary to recognize their far-reaching character, notwithstanding the many careful safeguards by which the changes would be balanced and limited. These safeguards include the required majorities in the General Assembly; the elaborate provisions for the selection and control of the Executive Council, the Economic and Social Council and the Trusteeship Council; the close controls over the United Nations Peace Force; the precisely defined functions of the International Court of Justice, the World Equity Tribunal and the World

Conciliation Board; the limitations on the proposed revenue system and on the functions of the World Development Authority; the reservations and guarantees of the proposed Bill of Rights; and so on. Nevertheless, it should be clearly recognized that, with all these safeguards, the net result of the revision would be a vast change from the present regime of virtually "sovereign" states under which the nations can arm without restriction and there are no reliable means to settle international disputes without violence.

In lieu of this age-old system, the revised Charter would provide for nothing less than complete national disarmament and the absolute renunciation of war as a means of dealing with international disputes. Nor would these provisions be without sufficient backing, since the revised Charter would actually create world institutions with fully adequate power to enforce peace in all circumstances. There would be universal and complete national disarmament under strict inspection. There would be a powerful world police force. There would be alternative procedures and tribunals for the peaceful settlement of all kinds of international disputes. There would be a revenue system whereby the member Nations would be required to contribute in proportion to their ability to pay for the expenses of the United Nations, including its Peace Force and the World Development Authority. In short, the United Nations, instead of being, as now, a league of independent states retaining their "sovereign equality", would become a world authority equipped with adequate rights and powers of its own in the field of preventing war. While these rights and powers would be carefully limited to the field of war prevention, the member Nations would, within that field, accept definite and unprecedented limitations on their traditional freedom of action; and moreover, there would be no right of withdrawal by the ratifying nations once the revised Charter had come into effect.

In these circumstances, it seems clear that there should be a method of ratification for the revised Charter different from and stricter than that which was provided (under the present Article 110) for the ratification of the 1945 Charter and even stricter than the method for the ratification of amendments provided in the present Articles 108 and 109.

The formula for the ratification of the 1945 Charter called for unanimous approval by the "Big Five" (China, France, the U.S.S.R., the United Kingdom and the U.S.A.) and by a majority of the other nations which signed the Charter at San Francisco, while the present formula for the ratification of amendments calls for approval by two thirds of all the member Nations, including all of the "permanent members of the Security Council", namely the same "Big Five". Although this present formula for the approval of amendments requires unanimous approval by the "Big Five", it would, nevertheless, permit ratification of even the most extensive changes without the assent of one third of the member Nations.

In relation to the revised Charter this possibility should be out of the question in view of the great changes which the revision would bring about. Because of these changes whereby vastly greater authority would be granted to the United Nations, it is believed that ratification of the revised Charter should require the virtually unanimous approval of all the people of the world.

In practical effect, the proposed conditions would meet this requirement. For these conditions would mean not merely that five sixths of all the nations had accepted the new world system, but that every single one of the twelve nations having the largest populations had pledged its support. With the Charter in force under these circumstances, it is hardly to be supposed that many of the small minority of nations which might not have ratified the revised Charter when it came into force would wish to remain outside,—especially since the total population of any such minority would necessarily be less than one sixth of the world's population. In actual practice, therefore, the effect would be to ensure that the revised Charter, when ratified under the required conditions, would have the virtually unanimous approval of all the world's people.

It is proposed that the new formula for ratification embodied in this revised Article 110 shall form part of the revision itself,—just as the Constitution of the United States when adopted in 1787 contained the formula for its own ratification. Although it would be possible to raise the technical point that any alterations of the present Charter should be ratified under the existing formula pursuant to the present Articles 108 and 109, it seems unlikely that any such objection would be pressed in view of the fact that the new ratification provisions: (a) would require the assent of all the twelve nations having the largest populations in the world, without exception; and (b) would require the assent of a far larger number of all the nations and a far larger proportion of the world's population than does the present formula.

It is reasonably to be hoped that, in view of the vast tangible and intangible advantages to be expected from the revised Charter, its ratification, even under the proposed severe requirements, would follow quite promptly after its submission. The provision in paragraph 3 that the revised Charter must be ratified within ten years from its submission is, however, included upon the theory that if within ten years the requirements for its acceptance have not been met, the way should be cleared for a new start in view of possible changed conditions and of objections which might have been raised. This ten-year period seems appropriate because the restrictions and obligations of the revised Charter should certainly not be undertaken inadvisedly or lightly and because certain nations, including the United States, would almost certainly find it necessary or advisable to amend their respective constitutions in order clearly to authorize their acceptance of the revised Charter. On the other hand, ten years should be ample for the required deliberations in the respective nations in view of the extensive debates which would necessarily have occurred before the revised Charter was even submitted for ratification.

Concerning the probable necessity that certain nations would in all probability find it advisable or necessary to amend their own constitutions in order validly to ratify the revised Charter, it should be pointed out that the requirement whereby each nation shall ratify the revised Charter "in accordance with its constitutional processes" is to be interpreted in a broad sense. In many nations there would doubtless be no question as to the authority of their governments to ratify the revised Charter by the same procedures as are applicable to the ratification of ordinary treaties. If, however, because of the greatly enlarged powers which the United Nations would have under the revised Charter, its acceptance would or might conflict with the constitution of a particular nation (as in the case of the United States), the term "constitutional processes" should be interpreted as including any changes in a nation's own constitution as might be necessary or advisable to clear up any doubts as to the capacity of that nation to accept the revised Charter.

The purpose of the provisions (in the new paragraphs 4, 5 and 6) for a "transition period" of one year after the revised Charter comes into effect and for the continued functioning of the existing organs until the machinery under the revised Charter is organized, is to ensure continuity and an orderly transfer of authority.

Article 111

The present Charter, of which the Chinese, French, Russian, English, and Spanish texts are equally authentic, shall remain deposited in the archives of the *Government of the United States of America.* Duly certified copies thereof shall be transmitted by *that Government* to the Governments of *the other signatory states.*

This revised Charter, of which the Chinese, French, Russian, English, and Spanish texts are equally authentic, shall remain deposited in the archives of the *United Nations.* Duly certified copies thereof shall be transmitted by *the Secretary-General of the United Nations* to the Governments of *all the independent nations of the world as listed in Article 9.*

IN FAITH WHEREOF the representatives of the *Governments* of the United Nations have signed *the present* Charter.

IN FAITH WHEREOF the representatives of the *peoples* of the United Nations have signed *this revised* Charter.

DONE at *the city of San Francisco* the *twenty-sixth* day of *June,* one thousand nine hundred and *forty-five.*

DONE at ....
the .... day of ....., one thousand nine hundred and ......

Comment. Apart from consequential changes, the only change proposed in this Article is that the "peoples" of the United Nations instead of "Governments" shall through their representatives sign the Charter. So changed, this final clause would conform to the Preamble of the revised Charter where it is said that "We the peoples of the United Nations" have decided to continue the United Nations with the amended "structure, functions and powers" set forth in the revised 111 Articles and the Annexes.

ANNEX I

DISARMAMENT

General Comment. The disarmament plan contained in this Annex is based on the assumption that genuine peace can be effectively maintained only in a world in which *all* the nations have been *completely* disarmed.

Under modern conditions it seems clear that any effort to prevent war through mere "deterrents" and a "balance of terror" can afford no solid assurance of peace.

Experience teaches that long-continued arms races have usually ended in violent conflict, since the fears and tensions engendered by the competition create an atmosphere in which war may break out almost by accident and without a fixed design for war on either side. Moreover, while it is often said that the appalling power of modern weapons provides a guarantee against serious war, the situation is so unprecedented that there is no clear experience to support this conclusion. For while the terrific destruction which could be wrought is a strong deterrent, that very fact might tempt an ambitious or desperate nation under reckless leadership.

In short, life under a long "balance of terror" would at best be precarious, wasteful of talent, energy and material resources; and consequently less satisfactory than it ought to be and could be for almost everyone in the world.

While, therefore, competition in armaments may provide time to seek a solution, it is of itself no solution at all. The true and permanent solution lies elsewhere. It lies in recognizing without reserve that there can in truth be "no peace without law", and that for world order disarmament is indispensable.

Nor can the mere "reduction" or "limitation" of armaments provide a solution.

One reason is that mere reduction would be ineffective to eliminate the mutual fears and suspicions which poison the world's atmosphere. If we assume that in 1960 the West has 20,000 nuclear bombs and the East 10,000, would it greatly help to reduce these even by nine tenths to 2000 and 1000, if each of the remaining bombs could raze a city and destroy a million people? Or would it materially lessen world tension if all arms industries were reduced by half, or even more, having in mind that, under modern conditions, they could be readily expanded at any time? The fact is that so long as *any* national forces are permitted (together with the arms production and military research which would accompany them), they would remain formidable; and much of the suspicion and fear that might lead to new wars would still remain.

Another reason for complete disarmament is that mere reduction, unless it amounted to the virtual elimination of all national forces and armaments, would make it impracticable to maintain a world police force of sufficient strength to deter or suppress any conceivable attempt at international violence. It is of the essence of domestic law and order that the internal police shall be sufficiently strong to put down any potential defiance of law; and this is correspondingly true as to world order and the world police. It would, however, be unwise and impracticable for financial and other reasons to attempt the maintenance of a world police of sufficient strength to dominate any considerable national military forces which might combine to resist the world authority. And since an *effective* and *respected* world police is an indispensable element of world order, it follows that for this reason alone national states should not be permitted to maintain any military forces whatever, and should be confined to such police forces as are essential for internal order only.

What the matter comes to, therefore, is that if the peoples of the world really want to prevent war, they must be willing to pay the price in the shape of disarmament which is not only universal and enforceable, but also *complete*.

If the Western nations want to see the communist bloc disarmed, they must recognize the fact that the communist bloc has an equal desire and interest to see a disarmed West. And if the communist nations cannot feel safe until the West is disarmed, they must accept the proposition that their own freedom from fear cannot be achieved until they also disarm at the same time and to the same extent. In short, they must *both* realize that disarmament can be achieved only by the *simultaneous* and *reciprocal* abolition of *all* their military forces and implements of war.

The purpose of this Annex I is, therefore, to provide a *detailed plan* for achieving universal and complete national disarmament, and for the effective supervision and enforcement not only of the disarmament process itself, but also of the state of complete disarmament once it is achieved. It is proposed to accomplish this aim by carefully supervised stages, and in a simultaneous and proportionate manner.

After the completion of the process of disarmament, *all* national military forces would be abolished. The only *military* force in the world would then be the world police force, to be established under Annex II and consisting of the standing "United Nations Peace Force" supplemented by the "United Nations Peace Force Reserve". It would, of course, be necessary to permit the nations to maintain some strictly limited and lightly armed *police* forces needed for the maintenance of internal order; but even these nonmilitary forces would be under constant United Nations supervision in order to ensure that none of them could become the nucleus of an effective military force.

It cannot be expected that the nations of the world will agree to eliminate all their military forces except by gradual stages. They will lack sufficient confidence in each other to discard their armaments except through a carefully verified stage-by-stage process. On the one hand, these stages must be long enough to ensure thorough verification. On the other hand, they must be short enough to demonstrate adequate progress, and thus to maintain the pressure of public opinion which would be a main guarantee that the governments would not abandon the plan before its completion. Accordingly, two main stages are proposed: a preparatory stage of two years and an actual disarmament stage of ten years.

The two-year preparatory stage would begin at the end of a transition period of twelve months following the coming into force of the revised Charter, during which transition period the main organs of the revised and strengthened United Nations would be constituted. It is proposed that the first eight months of the preparatory stage shall be devoted to the creation of a new instrument—the United Nations Inspection Service—and to the taking by the Inspection Service of an arms census. At the end of the eighth month an arms truce would come into effect, and thereafter no nation would be entitled to enlarge its military forces, armaments or facilities for the production of armaments beyond those then possessed by it and reported in its reply to an arms-census questionnaire. During the following ten months, the Inspection Service would verify: (a) the accuracy and completeness of the information furnished by each nation, and (b) the observance by each nation of the arms truce. The remaining six months of the preparatory stage would be utilized for the scrutiny by the Executive Council and the General Assembly of the reports of the Inspection Service as to the over-all results of the verification. If everything were found satisfactory, the preparatory stage would terminate on schedule, and the actual disarmament stage would begin immediately; otherwise a postponement could be ordered by the General Assembly for a period not longer than six months. Further postponements, in no case exceeding six months, could be ordered by the General Assembly if necessary. It should be emphasized, however, that in ordinary course the preparatory stage would end two years after the one-year transition period, i.e., three years from the date on which the revised Charter comes into force.

During the normal ten-year period of actual disarmament, every nation in the world (including any nonmember nations) would be obliged to reduce *all* its military strength by ten per cent annually; while if the General Assembly decided to shorten the normal period, the reductions after the first four years would be correspondingly larger. It would be required that all the reductions be distributed proportionally among the personnel of the major military services and among their major components; and proportionally also among the various categories of the armaments of the various services and components; and likewise among the various facilities for armament production. Annual reduction plans would be subject to approval and supervision by the Inspection Service, and a serious violation could result in the postponement of further annual reductions, for periods of not more than six months at a time, until the violation was remedied.

After the end of the actual disarmament stage, no nation would possess any *military* establishment whatever; various prohibitions or limitations as to military training, the production of armaments and the production and use of nuclear materials would come into effect; and all potentially dangerous activities would become subject to license by the United Nations Inspection Service.

The Inspection Service would be directly and primarily responsible for supervising the execution of the disarmament plan and the observance of the various prohibitions and licensing requirements necessary to guarantee the maintenance of complete disarmament. It is proposed that the Inspection

Service shall be under the administrative direction of an Inspector-General and under the general direction of an Inspection Commission, composed of five nationals of smaller nations. Careful safeguards are also proposed to ensure the impartiality of the Inspection Service and to eliminate the possibility of its domination by any nation or group of nations. It is provided, for example, that among the Inspectors of the Service the nationals of no nation shall exceed four per cent of the total number of Inspectors.

The proposed powers of the Inspection Service are carefully defined in this Annex I itself, and the General Assembly would be empowered to adopt further regulations to ensure, on the one hand, the efficacy of the inspection system and, on the other hand, to protect nations and individuals against possible abuses of power. While Inspectors would be given unlimited access to establishments with especially dangerous potentials, periodic inspections of less dangerous activities would be restricted to a reasonable number per year. Additional inspection of activities subject only to periodic inspection and of places not ordinarily subject to inspection could be conducted only on the basis of a special authorization issued by a United Nations regional court (to be established under Part D of Annex III). Such an authorization could be granted only upon a showing to the court of reasonable cause to believe or suspect that a prohibited activity was being conducted in the place sought to be inspected. Regular aerial surveys would be provided for, subject to the limitation that no more than three regular surveys of any particular territory could be conducted in any year. Special aerial surveys could also be made, but only upon court authorization and a showing to the court of reasonable cause.

In contrast to the official United States proposals presented to the United Nations in 1946, the proposals of this Annex do not envisage United Nations *ownership* of the potentially dangerous facilities which produce or utilize nuclear materials. In view of the tremendous development in both these types of facilities, it no longer seems feasible to place their actual ownership and management in the hands of an international monopoly. Instead, it is proposed that special methods of *supervision* be established for these facilities. For example, United Nations guards would be stationed at crucial production points, and especially qualified persons would be appointed by the Inspection Service or by the United Nations Nuclear Energy Authority (mentioned in the next paragraph) to take part in the actual operation of dangerous facilities on all levels (as directors, accountants, engineers, research scientists, etc.). Such a distribution of international officials among the staffs of all these potentially dangerous facilities would supplement the regular processes of inspection, so that the combination should provide effective safeguards against the diversion of nuclear materials from these facilities.

While it is proposed that the Inspection Service shall exercise its inspection powers both in relation to nuclear weapons and "conventional" weapons, certain additional safeguards in respect of nuclear (atomic) energy would be provided through a new and separate world agency—the United Nations Nuclear Energy Authority. By this assignment various functions relative to ensuring the use of nuclear energy for peaceful purposes only would be placed in the hands of the Nuclear Energy Authority, and a double-check would be provided against the diversion of nuclear materials for military use.

It is proposed that the Nuclear Energy Authority shall take over by purchase at a fair price all the stocks of "special nuclear materials"* which the nations would be required to discard during the period of actual disarmament and keep them in temporary custody until they can be properly allocated to industrial or other nonmilitary purposes. The Nuclear Energy Authority would also assist the General Assembly in determining annual maximum quotas for the total world production of "special nuclear materials" and of any raw materials from which these materials are processed. The Authority would also fix maximum quotas for the production within each nation of such "special nuclear materials" and raw materials. All such quotas would be based upon the estimated need of such materials for various peaceful purposes.

In order to prevent a potentially dangerous accumulation of stocks of nuclear materials in any region of the world, the Nuclear Energy Authority would also be required to arrange for the proportionate distribution of all such materials in its custody and of all facilities for their production and utilization, among at least eleven and not more than twenty regions of the world to be delineated by the General Assembly. It is proposed that not less than five per cent or more than ten per cent of the total of these materials and facilities shall be situated in any one of these regions.

The Nuclear Energy Authority would also be given broad powers to promote the peaceful use of nuclear (atomic) energy. To this end it could engage directly in research, stimulate national and private research, build and operate its own laboratories and experimental facilities, and assist in the building and operation of national and private laboratories and facilities. With the consent of the nation concerned, the Authority could also build and operate plants for the practical utilization of nuclear energy; but its operation of such plants would be temporary only and could in no case exceed ten years.

Moreover, the plan provides that the Nuclear Energy Authority shall have important responsibilities as to the possible use of nuclear energy for military purposes. In this regard the plan contemplates (as provided in Annex II) that the United Nations Peace Force may be authorized by the General Assembly to employ nuclear weapons, in case of dire need and to the extent absolutely necessary, in the unlikely but conceivable contingency of a serious actual aggression in which clandestine nuclear weapons are actually used or in which their use is imminently threatened. And however unlikely this contingency may be, some limited stocks of nuclear weapons would be needed for the sole use of the Peace Force, if and when authorized by the Assembly.

In order to ensure that these nuclear weapons would not even get into the possession of the Peace Force unless the General Assembly had author-

* Pursuant to the definition in Article 5 of this Annex of the term "special nuclear materials", that term, as used in this Annex and elsewhere throughout these proposals, applies to materials which may be capable of employment in nuclear weapons, whether fissionable or fusionable. Such materials would doubtless include uranium 235, plutonium and uranium 233, as well as such other materials as are capable of releasing substantial quantities of atomic energy through nuclear fission or fusion or other nuclear reaction of the material; and the General Assembly would be empowered by Article 23 of Annex I from time to time to define what materials shall be deemed to be included within this technical term.

ized such possession under the above-mentioned extreme conditions, this Annex I would further provide that the custody of such limited stocks of nuclear weapons as the Assembly might authorize shall be in the hands of the Nuclear Energy Authority. The limited stocks so authorized would at the outset consist of nuclear weapons discarded from national stockpiles during the period of actual disarmament. The Authority would, however, be authorized to conduct such research as might be needed to offset any possible clandestine production of new types of nuclear weapons, and itself to produce new types to the extent permitted by the Assembly. Any such new types as well as the nuclear weapons originally placed in the Authority's custody could be handed over by the Authority to the Peace Force solely upon the basis of the above-mentioned special authorization of the Assembly.

Controls similar to those proposed for the field of nuclear energy need to be inaugurated also relative to the exploration and exploitation of outer space. It is therefore proposed to establish for this purpose a United Nations Outer Space Agency with broad powers to supervise the activities of nations, organizations and individuals in this rapidly growing field.

A careful balance would be required between activities to be undertaken by the Outer Space Agency itself and those which should be left to national and private initiative, and the General Assembly must have the authority to draw the line between the activities to be reserved to the Agency and those which it would merely supervise. The basic criterion would be whether a particular activity is an exclusively "peaceful" one or one having military implications. Consequently, the Outer Space Agency would have several distinct functions: (a) the direct operation of certain dangerous space activities with definite military implications; (b) participation by the staff of the Agency in the operation of potentially dangerous facilities and instruments for space exploration; and (c) the licensing by the Agency of all other space activities. Under such a system some rockets, satellites and spacecraft would be reserved for the direct operation by the Agency, others would be launched and operated by nations and private persons, but under close observation by the Agency, while still others would be merely subject to licensing by the Agency.

It is proposed to empower the General Assembly to enact regulations governing all navigation in space. Such regulations would also authorize the United Nations to exercise for the benefit of all mankind such control as may be advisable and possible over the moon and any other planet or body within the solar system which may be reached by spacecraft from earth. Under such regulations the Outer Space Agency would also be given the necessary means to police outer space.

The plan provides for the payment by the United Nations of just compensation for all arms, weapons, ammunition and equipment transferred to the United Nations Peace Force; for all nuclear materials transferred to the Nuclear Energy Authority, including any nuclear weapons, whether finished or partly finished, which might be transferred by the various nations during the disarmament process to the custody of the Authority for the possible use of the Peace Force; and for all the rockets, satellites and spacecraft transferred to the Outer Space Agency. The United Nations would, therefore, need to be provided with sufficient funds for the prompt payment of such compensation. And while in the period following the completion of the actual disarmament process such payments might readily be made out of the current revenues of the United Nations (including revenues received from the sale or lease of nuclear materials by the Authority), the very large sums which would need to be paid as compensation during the actual disarmament stage would doubtless require the use of borrowed funds. Accordingly, this Annex I authorizes the United Nations to issue its bonds for this purpose, within the limitation on the total borrowing power of the United Nations contained in Annex V.

Finally, this Annex makes provision for enforcement measures against individuals, organizations and nations who may commit violations of the Annex or of any law or regulation enacted thereunder. With respect to individuals and private organizations, it is impracticable to define the punishable offenses, the penalties therefor and the procedures to be followed for the punishment of offenders in the constitutional document itself; and consequently it is obvious that the General Assembly must be authorized to legislate upon these matters. The laws enacted for that purpose should also include specific guarantees against any abuses of power, in addition to the general safeguards embodied in the proposed United Nations Bill of Rights (Annex VII). All penal proceedings against individuals and private organizations would be brought by a new legal official—the United Nations Attorney-General—to be appointed pursuant to Part D of Annex III; and the cases would be tried before the regional courts of the United Nations to be established under Part D of Annex III. This Annex makes provision for all these matters.

It seems reasonable to assume that in most instances action against individuals or private organizations, either by warning or legal proceedings, would suffice to prevent or remedy a violation. But procedures must also be provided for dealing with violations for which a nation's government is directly or indirectly responsible, and with respect to which action against an individual would not suffice. Accordingly this Annex covers the procedures applicable to such cases. While the Inspection Commission would be given authority to deal with such violations in the first place and to conduct special investigations to establish the facts of each case, a nation disagreeing with the findings of the Commission would have a right of appeal to the Executive Council, and further to the International Court of Justice. If a violation of this sort were not promptly remedied, the Executive Council could either itself take appropriate measures, short of sanctions of any sort, to obtain compliance; or, if in the Council's opinion sanctions were required, could refer the question to the General Assembly. The Assembly, if not then in session, would be called into special session for the purpose of considering sanctions. Except in a most unusual situation, the imposition of diplomatic and economic sanctions would be sufficient to obtain compliance by the nation concerned. But in extreme circumstances military sanctions through the use of the United Nations Peace Force would be available.

A variety of procedures would, therefore, be available to the authorities

212

of the United Nations for dealing with possible violations of the disarmament plan; and the various measures thus provided for should effectively deter any serious attempt at violation.

* * *

The above is a description of only the main features of Annex I. To understand fully the proposed detailed powers and safeguards requires careful study of the text of the thirty-four Articles and of the comment on each Article.

No apology is made for the elaborate character of the proposed disarmament plan. While it is now generally recognized that the world can no longer tolerate the arms race and the risk of modern war, it is an illusion to suppose that war can be abolished except under a highly developed system which will provide the detailed supervision and the confidence which are indispensable to the acceptance by all the nations of complete national disarmament and of the obligation to settle all international disputes by peaceful means only.

CHAPTER I

BASIC PRINCIPLE

Article 1

1. Since universal and complete disarmament, effectively supervised and enforced, is essential for world peace, all national military forces, armaments and facilities for the production of armaments shall be abolished. This abolition shall be accomplished by stages and in a simultaneous and proportionate manner, as provided in this Annex.

2. The abolition of all national military forces shall not prevent the maintenance of such strictly limited and lightly armed internal police forces as are permitted by this Annex.

Comment. The reasons for the basic principle of this Article have been explained in the Introduction and in the General Comment on this Annex. Other provisions of this Annex should be interpreted in the spirit of this principle, namely, that the *abolition* of all national military forces, armaments and armament facilities is essential for world peace.

CHAPTER II

DISARMAMENT PLAN AND PROCEDURE

Article 2

The abolition of all national military forces, armaments and facilities for the production of armaments called for by Article 1 of this Annex shall be carried out in accordance with a plan consisting of two main stages, namely, a first stage to be known as the preparatory stage covering the first two years after the transition period of one year provided for in Article 110 of this revised Charter, and a second stage to be known as the actual disarmament stage covering the ten subsequent years; except that the preparatory stage may be lengthened and that the actual disarmament stage may be either shortened or lengthened as hereinafter provided.

Comment. By this Article the disarmament plan envisaged by this Annex would be divided into two main stages: a preparatory stage of two years and an actual disarmament stage of ten years, the former being subject to lengthening under Articles 5 and 7 of this Annex and the latter being subject to shortening or lengthening under Articles 10 and 12 of this Annex.

This two-stage plan should, however, be read in connection with those provisions of Article 110 of the revised Charter which call for a transition period of one year during which several important preliminary steps would be taken. That transition period would commence on the day of the coming into force of the revised Charter, i.e., when five sixths of all the nations of the world (having at least five sixths of the world's population and including each of the twelve nations having the largest populations) have deposited their ratifications with the Secretary-General of the United Nations (revised Article 110, paragraph 3). The new General Assembly organized under the revised Charter would be required: (a) to meet for its first session not later than the seventh month of the transition period; (b) to elect the members of the first Executive Council within a month after the Assembly's first meeting; and (c) to take such other steps as are necessary to establish the new or modified organs provided for in the revised Charter (revised Article 110, paragraph 6).

In addition, under Article 4 of this Annex, the first Inspection Commission would be appointed within two months after the election of the first Executive Council and the first Inspector-General would be appointed within two months after the appointment of the Inspection Commission itself.

In this way the basic measures preparatory to the organization of the system required for the carrying out of the disarmament plan would be taken within the one-year transition period after the revised Charter comes into force.

215

Article 3

During the preparatory stage, a United Nations Inspection Service shall be organized; an arms census shall be taken and verified; an arms truce shall be inaugurated, verified and maintained; the types, arms and training of the internal police forces which each nation shall be allowed to maintain shall be determined; all as hereinafter provided for.

Comment. It is proposed that the following steps be taken during the two-year preparatory stage: (a) the organization of the Inspection Service, as provided for by Article 4 of this Annex; (b) the taking of an arms census pursuant to Article 5 of this Annex; (c) the inauguration of an arms truce, to be maintained pursuant to Article 6 of this Annex; (d) the verification of the arms census and of the arms truce, as provided for in Article 7 of this Annex; and (e) the determination of the types, arms and training of the internal police forces which each nation shall be allowed to maintain, as provided for in Article 8 of this Annex. Only when all these steps have been satisfactorily completed will the actual disarmament stage become operative.

While it is desirable to start diminishing the burden and danger of armaments at the earliest possible moment, every one of these preliminary steps is absolutely necessary in order to provide confidence and to ensure success; and adequate time is required for the satisfactory completion of each step. Although some of the preliminary steps may be taken simultaneously, the beginning of several of these steps must be preceded by the building of the necessary machinery for their verification; in particular, the arms truce cannot start prior to the completion of the organization of the Inspection Service. On the other hand, each step should begin as soon as possible, and it is therefore proposed that the arms truce shall commence after the end of the eighth month of the preparatory stage (Article 6 of this Annex). In this way, the armaments race would be stopped at the end of twenty months after the coming into force of the revised Charter, and sixteen months in advance of the inauguration of the actual disarmament stage.

Article 4

As provided by Article 3 of this Annex, the United Nations Inspection Service shall be organized during the preparatory stage. Its direction and composition shall be as follows:

1. A United Nations Inspection Commission shall have the direction and control of the United Nations Inspection Service. The Inspection Commission shall consist of five persons, none of whom shall be a national of any of the nations then having fifteen or more Representatives in the General Assembly, and no two of whom shall be nationals of the same nation. The members of the Inspection Commission

shall be appointed by the Executive Council, subject to confirmation by the General Assembly. The first members of the Inspection Commission shall be appointed by the first Executive Council within two months after the election of the Council by the General Assembly pursuant to Article 110 of this revised Charter. The terms of office of the first members of the Commission shall begin on the same date and shall expire, as designated by the Council at the time of their appointment, one at the end of one year, one at the end of two years, one at the end of three years, one at the end of four years and one at the end of five years from that date; later appointments shall be for terms of five years. The Executive Council shall have general supervision over the Inspection Commission and may from time to time issue such instructions to it as the Council deems necessary. The Executive Council shall also have authority to remove any member of the Inspection Commission whenever the Council deems it necessary.

The General Assembly, through its Standing Committee on the Peace Enforcement Agencies provided for in Article 22 of this revised Charter, shall watch over the carrying out by the Inspection Commission and the Executive Council of their responsibilities under this Chapter and other provisions of this Annex. The Standing Committee shall be entitled to obtain from the Commission and the Council all relevant information and shall make such investigations as it may deem necessary or as the Assembly may request it to make. If in the judgment of the Standing Committee a situation exists which requires the convoking of a special session of the Assembly, it shall be entitled in accordance with Article 20 of this revised Charter to request the Secretary-General to convoke such special session.

2. An Inspector-General shall be the administrative head of the United Nations Inspection Service, subject to the direction and control of the United Nations Inspection Commission. The Inspector-General shall not be a member of the Inspection Commission, nor a national of any nation which at the time of his appointment has one of its nationals on the Inspection Commission, nor a national of any of the nations then having fifteen or more Representatives in the General Assembly. The Inspector-General shall be appointed by the Inspection Commission for a term of six years, subject to confirmation by the Executive Council. The first Inspector-General shall be appointed by the first Inspection Commission, subject to confirmation by the first Executive Council, within two months after the appointment of the first Inspection Commission. The Inspection Commission shall have authority to remove the Inspector-General whenever the Commission deems it necessary.

3. During the first eight months of the preparatory stage, the Inspector-General shall complete to the extent possible the recruitment and

217

training of the Inspectors and other personnel of the United Nations Inspection Service, subject to regulations concerning qualifications, tenure, compensation and other conditions of service to be adopted by the General Assembly after receiving proposals therefor from the Inspection Commission and the recommendations of the Executive Council as to such proposals. Such regulations shall include provisions for the following:

a. That all members of the Inspection Service shall be selected on the basis of their competence, integrity and devotion to the purposes of the United Nations.

b. That they shall make a solemn declaration that they will perform their functions impartially and conscientiously.

c. That they shall not seek or receive instructions from any government or other authority external to the United Nations.

d. That they shall refrain from any conduct which might reflect on their position as international officials.

e. That they shall receive fully adequate pay and allowances, together with fully adequate retirement pensions after loyal and reasonably long service, all such compensation and pensions to be free from all taxation.

f. That they shall be recruited on as wide a geographical basis as possible.

g. That with respect to those members of the Inspection Service who are to perform duties of actual inspection, the number of nationals of any nation shall be limited to not more than four per cent of the total number of such Inspectors.

Comment. The whole disarmament plan depends on a *combination* of: (1) effective supervision and enforcement through an adequate system of inspection; and (2) an effective world police—the proposed United Nations Peace Force—and to be organized pursuant to Annex II.

It is clear that the very first step should be the organization of an efficient inspection service in order to verify and supervise from the outset the various successive steps of the disarmament process. Accordingly it is proposed that the first Inspection Commission and the first Inspector-General shall be appointed during the one-year transition period, i.e., the first Inspection Commission by the first Executive Council within the first two months after its election by the General Assembly, and the first Inspector-General by the first Inspection Commission within the first two months after its appointment by the Council. In this way the basic steps for the organization of the Inspection Service would be taken even before the beginning of the preparatory stage.

Other provisions covering the organization of the Inspection Service are designed to provide careful safeguards against the domination of the Service by any nation or group of nations, and against abuse of power by the persons in control of the Service. To this end it is proposed that the general direction and control of the Service shall be vested, not in the hands of a single individual, but in a group of five persons (the Inspection Commission), no two of whom shall be nationals of the same nation. Moreover, in order to prevent the large nations from exerting too much influence on the Inspection Service and to avoid undue competition between them for the limited number of seats on the Inspection Commission, it is desirable to exclude from the Commission nationals of the twelve largest nations, i.e., those which would be entitled to fifteen or more Representatives in the General Assembly and which by virtue of that fact would be assured adequate representation on the Executive Council (see Articles 9 and 23 of the revised Charter). Similarly, provision is made that the Inspector-General shall come from one of the smaller nations, i.e., those having less than fifteen Representatives in the General Assembly. Even in the lower ranks of the Inspection Service the large nations should not be represented to an undue extent; and it is therefore proposed that the number of Inspectors from any nation shall not exceed four per cent of the total number of Inspectors. Finally, in order to prevent the undue influence of any nation, large or small, in the administration of the Inspection Service, it is proposed that the Inspector-General shall not come from any nation already having one of its nationals on the Inspection Commission.

To provide a proper balance between the need for change in the membership of the Inspection Commission and the desirability of adequate continuity, it is proposed that one member of the Commission be elected each year and that their terms be for five years. The Inspector-General, for administrative reasons, ought to have a slightly longer term than the members of the Commission, and for him a six-year term is suggested.

In respect of administrative matters, it is proposed to confer authority upon the Inspector-General and the Inspection Commission, while in respect of general supervision and ultimate control the Executive Council and General Assembly would have the responsibility.

The Inspector-General would be the administrative head, responsible for the day-to-day operations of the Inspection Service, for the recruitment, training and assignment of Inspectors, for the coordination of the various inspection activities, and for the preparation of reports to the Inspection Commission on the verification of the successive steps of the disarmament plan. On the other hand the Inspection Commission would have the general direction and control of the Inspection Service, would have authority to remove the Inspector-General, would prepare proposed regulations governing the conditions of service for submission to the General Assembly through the Executive Council, and would submit progress reports to the Council on the verification of the successive steps of the disarmament process. In turn, general supervision over the activities of the Inspection Commission would be in the hands of the Executive Council, which would have authority to issue instructions, to pass upon regulations, to remove any member of the Inspection Commission and to take action on the reports of the Commission. In its turn, the Council would submit to the Assembly reports on the progress of the disarmament program, and would be finally responsible to the Assembly and subject to its directions. The Assembly would have the power to approve the main regulations governing the conditions of service of the Inspectors and other personnel of the Inspection Service, to approve the appointments of the members of the Inspection Commission and to vote the budget of the Inspection Service. The Assembly would also be empowered to take all such measures authorized by the revised Charter, including this Annex, as it might deem necessary in case of a serious violation; and in general would have the ultimate responsibility for the due execution of the disarmament plan.

A continuing relationship between the General Assembly and the necessarily elaborate machinery for inspection and enforcement is provided for through the Assembly's Standing Committee on the Peace Enforcement Agencies to be appointed pursuant to Article 22 of the revised Charter. This Standing Committee would be empowered to call for the fullest information from the Inspection Commission and the Executive Council with regard to the operation and enforcement of every step of the disarmament process, and to conduct such investigations as the Assembly or the Standing Committee might deem necessary.

All possible measures need to be adopted to ensure the highest standards of competence and integrity among the personnel of the Inspection Service. Well-qualified persons must receive proper compensation for their services. Their salaries must be high enough to provide reasonable assurance of financial independence during service and they should have adequate pensions upon retirement. They must be free from all taxation by any nation or any political subdivision thereof and by the United Nations. They must neither seek nor receive instructions from national governments.

The vital process of effective inspection should be participated in by all nations. It is, therefore, proposed that the Inspectors shall be recruited on as wide a geographical basis as possible; and in order to prevent the domination of the inspection process by any nation, it is proposed that the nationals of no nation shall exceed four per cent of the total number of Inspectors.

The proposed duties and powers of the Inspection Service during the execution of the disarmament plan are defined in succeeding Articles of this Chapter II. Its duties and powers with respect to the maintenance of complete disarmament after the completion of the disarmament process are defined in Chapter III of this Annex, especially in Article 17. Finally, Chapter IV describes the actual inspection process, further defines the powers of the Inspection Service and establishes safeguards against abuse of these powers.

Article 5

As provided by Article 3 of this Annex, an arms census shall be taken during the preparatory stage as follows:

1. Not later than the end of the second month of the preparatory stage, the Inspector-General shall send to every nation a questionnaire approved by the Inspection Commission. This questionnaire shall require from each nation full information concerning:

a. The location and description of all its military installations.

b. The manpower strength, organization, composition and disposition of all its active and reserve military forces and of all its internal police forces, as determined by the General Assembly pursuant to Article 8 of this Annex.

c. The location, kind and quantity of all finished and unfinished arms and weapons (including nuclear, biological, chemical and other weapons of mass destruction), ammunition and military equipment, possessed by or at the disposal of these forces.

d. The location, description and rate of current output of all facilities within its territory which are engaged in the production of arms, weapons, ammunition, explosives, or military equipment of any kind, or of tools for such production; and the location and description of all facilities within its territory which, although not currently engaged in the production of any such arms, weapons, ammunition, explosives, equipment or tools, have been engaged therein at any time during the five years preceding the coming into force of this revised Charter, together with the record of output of all such facilities for the last year in which they were engaged in the production of any such arms, weapons, ammunition, explosives, equipment or tools.

e. The location, description and rate of current output of all heavy industry plants within its territory (including all plants of the tool-manufacturing industry), which are capable of easy adaptation to the production of armaments of any description (including arms, weapons, ammunition, explosives, and military equipment of any kind) or of tools for such production.

f. The location and description of all laboratories or other facilities within its territory which are engaged in any work relating to the development of new weapons of any kind.

g. The location, type, amount and stage of processing of all raw materials within its territory which might enter into the production of special nuclear materials and which have been removed from their place of deposit in nature; of all special nuclear materials; and of all materials which have been made radioactive by artificial means. By "special nuclear materials" is meant materials capable of employment in nuclear weapons, whether fissionable or fusionable, and defined as such by the General Assembly pursuant to Article 23 of this Annex.

h. The location, description and rate of past and current output of all mines within its territory which are engaged in the mining of raw materials which might enter into the production of special nuclear materials.

i. The location, description and rate of past and current output of all facilities of any kind within its territory which are engaged: in the processing of raw materials which might enter into the production of special nuclear materials; or in the processing of special nuclear ma-

221

terials themselves; or in the production of auxiliary materials which might be employed in the making of special nuclear materials or nuclear weapons, such as graphite, heavy water, beryllium, lithium and cobalt; or in the production of radioactive materials in substantial quantity.

j. The location and description of all laboratories or other facilities within its territory which are concerned with the study of nuclear energy.

k. The location and description of all facilities within its territory which are utilizing special nuclear materials or substantial quantities of radioactive materials for research, industrial, commercial or other nonmilitary purposes.

l. The number, kind, location, and stage of completion of all rockets, satellites or spacecraft within its territory or which are owned or operated by it or its nationals.

m. The location, description and rate of current output of all facilities within its territory which are engaged in the production of rockets, satellites or spacecraft, or of tools for such production; and the location and description of all facilities within its territory which are equipped for the launching of rockets, satellites or spacecraft.

The questionnaire may require such other information as the Inspector-General, with the approval of the Inspection Commission, shall deem necessary or advisable in order to obtain from every nation complete information as to its armed forces and armaments, as to all special nuclear materials within its territory and as to all means and facilities for the production of such armaments or materials within its territory.

2. Every nation shall duly complete the questionnaire and return it to the Inspector-General not later than the end of the eighth month of the preparatory stage.

3. During the first two weeks of the ninth month of the preparatory stage, the Inspector-General shall make a report to the Inspection Commission as to whether or not all the nations have returned questionnaires which appear to be duly completed in accordance with the requirements of paragraphs 1 and 2 of this Article. If the Inspector-General reports any case or cases of noncompliance, the Commission shall consider what measures shall be taken. If the Commission determines that any noncompliance is serious, it shall immediately present a special report to the Executive Council to that effect, stating whether or not in the Commission's judgment the noncompliance is so serious as to prejudice the execution of the entire disarmament plan. If the Council accepts the conclusion of the Commission that any such noncompliance is so serious as to prejudice the execution of the entire disarmament plan, it shall so state and shall recommend that further execution of the disarmament plan ought to be suspended. The General Assembly shall consider such a recommendation of the Council as soon as possible,

and if the Assembly is not then in session, a special session thereof shall be convoked immediately. If the Assembly approves the recommendation of the Council, the Assembly shall by resolution determine the duration of the suspension, which suspension shall in no case exceed six months. If the noncompliance which led to the suspension has not been remedied before the end of the period of suspension, the Commission shall report this fact to the Council, which shall present to the Assembly its recommendations on the subject. In the light of these recommendations, the Assembly shall decide whether another suspension, not exceeding six months, is necessary. In case more than one suspension is necessary, a similar procedure shall be followed in each instance, but the period of suspension shall in no case exceed six months.

Comment. In any system of disarmament based on periodic reductions by a predetermined percentage, it is clearly necessary to establish in advance the starting point for such reductions. The size and quantities of the military forces, armaments and facilities for the production of armaments possessed by each nation at the beginning of the disarmament process should, therefore, be determined as early as possible in the disarmament process through a complete arms census. Accordingly it is proposed that the gathering of information for such a census shall take place during the same first eight months of the preparatory stage during which the Inspection Service is being organized pursuant to Article 4, paragraph 3, of this Annex. One of the first tasks of the Inspection Service when sufficiently organized would be to verify the accuracy and completeness of the data thus obtained.

In furtherance of this plan, it is proposed that the Inspector-General (appointed during the one-year transition period preceding the preparatory stage pursuant to paragraph 2 of Article 4 of this Annex), shall send a detailed questionnaire to all the nations before the end of the second month of the preparatory stage. Every nation (including any nonmember nations) would be required to complete the questionnaire and return it to the Inspector-General not later than the end of the eighth month of the preparatory stage, i.e., at the very moment when the Inspection Service would be ready for action.

The information to be furnished by every nation pursuant to the questionnaire must give a complete picture of that nation's military strength and of its capacity to produce armaments. This information must include complete data with respect to "special nuclear materials" (i.e., materials which might enter into the production of nuclear weapons) and with respect to facilities engaged in the production of such materials.

Compliance with the obligation to furnish all this information would constitute the first test of the willingness of all the nations to fulfil their obligations as to disarmament. Soon after the end of the period set for the completion and return of the questionnaires, the Inspector-General would have a clear picture as to how completely the various nations have furnished the required information; and it is proposed that he shall make a report to the Inspection Commission on that subject during the first two weeks of the ninth month of the preparatory stage. The Commission would then consider what measures should be taken in case of noncompliance by one or more nations. In ordinary circumstances no strong action would be required. For example, if the noncompliance were due to negligence of an official or if the nation were a small one, an admonition should suffice to bring about compliance; while if the noncompliance were due to extraordinary circumstances, e.g., an earthquake, flood or revolution, an extension of the time limit would naturally be granted to the nation in question. If, however, the Commission were confronted with a case of noncompliance by an important nation of so serious a character that in the Commission's opinion a continued noncompliance would "prejudice the execution of the entire disarmament plan", the Commission would be required to refer the matter immediately to the Executive Council. The Council might either disagree with the finding of the Commission and allow the next step of the disarmament plan to start on time, or it might agree with the judgment of the Commission as to the seriousness of the noncompliance. In the latter case the Council would be obliged to recommend to the General Assembly that further execution of the disarmament plan be suspended until the elimination of the noncompliance. If the Assembly were not then in session, a special session would have to be convoked to deal speedily with the matter.

At this point the General Assembly might disagree with the Inspection Commission and the Executive Council as to the seriousness of the noncompliance in question and decide to adhere to the original disarmament schedule. But if the Assembly should agree that the noncompliance was serious enough to justify the suspension of the whole disarmament plan, it would be required to determine the duration of the suspension, which in no case could exceed six months. If the noncompliance were eliminated before the end of the period of suspension, the next steps of the disarmament plan would come into effect at the end of that period. If, however, an important nation (or a group of nations) should persist in noncompliance of so serious a sort as to prejudice the further execution of the disarmament plan, an additional period or periods of suspension would doubtless be ordered by the Assembly, none of which could, however, exceed six months.

Careful safeguards would thus be provided to ensure that complying nations shall not be required to go forward with the disarmament plan if there has been any important default by other nations in the fulfillment of their obligation under this Article to furnish timely and complete information. At the same time, the relatively short suspensions which could be authorized —not more than six months at a time—would sustain the pressure on any recalcitrant nation to supply all the required information and thus to permit the resumption of the disarmament process.

Article 6

1. The arms truce, to be inaugurated during the preparatory stage as called for by Article 3 of this Annex, shall commence on the first day of the ninth month of the preparatory stage, or on the first day after the end of such period or periods of suspension as may be determined by the

General Assembly pursuant to paragraph 3 of Article 5 of this Annex. Beginning with that date the following limitations and prohibitions shall apply during the remainder of the preparatory stage:

a. No nation shall possess any military forces, armaments or facilities for the production of armaments in excess of those possessed by it on the date when the arms truce takes effect and reported in its questionnaire returned to the Inspector-General pursuant to Article 5 of this Annex.

b. No nation shall make any increase in the forces, armaments and facilities so possessed and reported, provided, however, that replacement of personnel by new recruits and of discarded or used-up weapons, equipment and supplies by new weapons, equipment and supplies of no greater military value shall not be construed as an increase.

c. No nation shall produce or allow the production of any arms, weapons or military equipment whatever, or of tools for such production, except: (1) to provide the replacements which are permitted under subparagraph b of this paragraph; (2) to supply the light arms, ammunition and equipment which its internal police forces are allowed to have; (3) for the sale to other nations of permissible light arms, ammunition or equipment needed by internal police forces in their territories; and (4) such small arms as are required to meet the reasonable needs of duly licensed hunters or of duly licensed individuals for personal protection, either in the nation where such arms are produced or elsewhere.

d. No nation shall permit any research directed toward the invention of new military weapons or the improvement of existing military weapons, including the use for military purposes of any nuclear materials; and no nation shall make or permit the making of tests of nuclear weapons or ballistic missiles.

e. No nation shall construct or allow the construction of any ship or airplane containing any feature which would facilitate the adaptation of such ship or airplane to military purposes.

f. No nation shall prepare or allow the preparation of its heavy industry (including its tool-manufacturing industry) for the production of armaments of any description (including arms, weapons, ammunition, explosives and military equipment of any kind) or of tools for such production.

g. No nation shall prepare or allow the preparation of any plant within its territory for the production of chemical or biological weapons.

h. No nation shall produce or allow the production of any special nuclear materials, except to the extent that the General Assembly may authorize such production for research, industrial, commercial, or other nonmilitary purposes.

i. No nation shall produce or allow the production of any rockets, satellites or spacecraft, or of tools for such production, except to the extent that the General Assembly may authorize such production for research, industrial, commercial, or other nonmilitary purposes.

2. The General Assembly, after receiving proposals therefor from the Inspection Commission and the recommendations of the Executive Council as to such proposals, shall adopt regulations prescribing the conditions and limitations which shall apply: (a) to the production of weapons, equipment and supplies for the replacements referred to in paragraph 1 (b) of this Article, and (b) to the production of light arms for the internal police forces and of small arms for the use of licensed hunters and licensed individuals for personal protection referred to in paragraph 1 (c) of this Article.

Comment. Once the revised Charter, including the disarmament plan, has come into force, it is important to stop the armaments race at the earliest possible moment. For it would not augur well for the whole disarmament plan if any nation were permitted to utilize the entire preparatory stage for a last-minute attempt to gain a competitive advantage over other nations before the disarmament process actually begins.

On the other hand, an arms truce should not be established until means are available to ensure that every nation is properly maintaining it, i.e., until an adequate inspection service is available.

Accordingly, the earliest possible moment for starting an arms truce is deemed to be the beginning of the ninth month of the preparatory stage by which time the new General Assembly would have met in its first session, the Executive Council and the Inspection Commission would have been chosen, the Inspector-General would have been appointed and the organization of the Inspection Service would have begun. Since it would then be possible to enforce a set of prohibitions to prevent violations of the arms truce, it is appropriate that such prohibitions should go into effect at this point. If, however, the General Assembly should suspend the execution of the disarmament plan because of a serious noncompliance with the obligations under Article 5 of this Annex with respect to the arms census, the start of the arms truce would have to be postponed until the end of the period or periods of suspension. Apart from this contingency, the arms truce would start on the first day of the ninth month of the preparatory stage.

Subparagraphs (1) (a) and (1) (b) of this Article 6 specifically require that from the moment when the arms truce begins (i.e., ordinarily on the first day of the ninth month of the preparatory stage) no nation shall be permitted to increase its military forces, armaments and facilities for the production of armaments beyond those then possessed by it and reported in its return to the arms-census questionnaire. Since, however, the military forces of many nations consist of short-term recruits, those nations should be permitted to replace one group of recruits with another. Similarly, it should be permissible to replace worn-out equipment and used-up munition stocks by new arms and equipment, provided that the new material is of no greater military value than the old. To ensure against abuse of this authority to make replacements, the General Assembly would be empowered (paragraph 2) to issue upon the basis of proposals by the Inspection Commission and of the recommendations of the Executive Council as to such proposals, detailed regulations governing such replacements, and in particular to prescribe the amounts of military material which any nation would be permitted to produce for replacement purposes. The broad authority to adopt such regulations would include power to prescribe methods for assessing the military value of such replacements.

By subparagraph (1) (c) of this Article, no nation in the world would be permitted from the moment that the arms truce goes into effect to produce any military equipment and supplies or arms of any sort whatever save only: (a) such replacements as would be permitted under the General Assembly's regulations; and (b) such limited amounts of light arms as would be permitted for internal police forces pursuant to Article 14 of this Annex, and for the use of licensed hunters and licensed individuals for personal protection pursuant to subparagraph (1) (c) of this Article.

Subparagraph (1) (d) prohibits any research by any nation for the invention or improvement of military weapons from the moment that the arms truce takes effect. This prohibition is in accord with the above proposition that when the preliminary steps have been taken to enable supervision of the arms truce, it would be inconsistent with the disarmament plan to permit any further national military activity except the bare minimum required to maintain the then existing national forces.

In harmony with this purpose, subparagraphs (1) (e)–(g) prohibit various activities which might directly or indirectly sustain the military potential of any nation. These provisions would forbid the inclusion in ships or airplanes of features which would facilitate their adaptation to military use and the preparation of industrial plants for any military production.

Subparagraph (1) (h) limits the production of "special nuclear materials" to amounts authorized by the General Assembly for nonmilitary purposes.

Subparagraph (1) (i) allows the production of rockets, satellites and spacecraft only to the extent authorized by the General Assembly for nonmilitary purposes.

It will be noted that the provisions of this Article would cover only the period of the arms truce which, unless postponed or extended by the General Assembly, would be the period of sixteen months from the beginning of the ninth month of the preparatory stage to the beginning of the actual disarmament stage. A similar set of prohibitions would be in effect, pursuant to paragraph 6 of Article 11 of this Annex, covering the period of the actual disarmament stage, during which all national armaments would be eliminated. Finally, under Article 14 of this Annex, there would be a set of prohibitions for the permanent enforcement of universal and complete disarmament.

Article 7

As provided by Article 3 of this Annex, the arms census and the arms truce shall be verified during the preparatory stage as follows:

1. During the ten months following the eighth month of the prepara-

tory stage, or in case of suspension under paragraph 3 of Article 5 of this Annex during the ten months after the beginning of the arms truce, the United Nations Inspection Service shall verify the accuracy and completeness of the information furnished by the respective nations pursuant to Article 5 of this Annex, and shall also verify the observance of the arms truce inaugurated under Article 6 of this Annex. This verification shall be accomplished by Inspectors of the Inspection Service acting with the authority and subject to the limitations provided for in Articles 18 to 24 of this Annex.

2. If the Inspection Service reports any case or cases of noncompliance, the Inspection Commission shall consider what measures shall be taken and if it determines that there has been a serious deficiency in the information furnished by any nation or a serious nonobservance of the arms truce or that any nation has placed any serious obstacle in the way of verification by the Inspection Service, it shall immediately present a special report on the subject to the Executive Council stating whether or not in the Commission's judgment the deficiency, nonobservance or obstacle is so serious as to prejudice the execution of the entire disarmament plan.

3. In addition to such special reports, if any, the Inspection Commission shall during the nineteenth month of the preparatory stage, or in case of suspension under paragraph 3 of Article 5 of this Annex during the eleventh month after the beginning of the arms truce, make a general report to the Executive Council concerning the adequacy of the information furnished by all the nations and concerning the observance of the arms truce and the over-all results of the verification.

4. The Executive Council shall forthwith consider all reports of the Inspection Commission; and if the Commission has determined that there has been a serious deficiency in the information furnished by any nation, or a serious nonobservance of the arms truce or that any nation has placed any serious obstacle in the way of verification by the Inspection Service, the Council shall consider what measures shall be taken. If the Council accepts the conclusion of the Inspection Commission that any such deficiency, nonobservance or obstacle is so serious as to prejudice the execution of the entire disarmament plan, the Council shall take such interim action as it is authorized to take pursuant to Article 34 of this Annex and shall immediately present a special report on the subject to the General Assembly for possible action by it under that Article.

In addition to such special reports, if any, the Executive Council shall during the twentieth month of the preparatory stage, or in case of suspension under paragraph 3 of Article 5 of this Annex during the twelfth month after the beginning of the arms truce, make a general report to the General Assembly, which report shall include the conclusions of the

Council as to the completeness of the information furnished by all the nations, as to the observance of the arms truce and as to the adequacy of the verification of such information and such observance.

If the Executive Council concludes that such information, observance or verification is so unsatisfactory as to prejudice the execution of the entire disarmament plan, it shall so state and shall immediately present a special report to the General Assembly recommending that the coming into operation of the actual disarmament stage ought to be postponed, but the period of such postponement shall in no case exceed six months. If, however, the Council concludes that such information, observance and verification are reasonably satisfactory, it shall so state; and the Council shall then decide and announce that the first or preparatory stage of the disarmament plan shall terminate on schedule at the end of the two-year period provided for in Article 2 of this Annex, and that the second or actual disarmament stage of the plan shall then begin, subject only to a resolution of the General Assembly under paragraph 5 of this Article disagreeing with such decision of the Council.

5. If the Executive Council has presented a special report to the General Assembly informing it that there has been a serious deficiency in the information furnished by any nation or a serious nonobservance of the arms truce or that any nation has placed a serious obstacle in the way of verification by the Inspection Service, the Assembly shall deal with the matter as soon as possible, and shall have authority to take such action under Article 34 of this Annex as it may deem necessary. If the Assembly is not then in session, a special session thereof shall be convoked immediately.

In any event, the General Assembly shall consider the general report of the Executive Council within one month after its submission; and, if necessary, a special session shall be convoked for the purpose.

If the Executive Council has decided that the actual disarmament stage shall come into operation on schedule at the end of the preparatory stage, that decision shall be deemed final unless the General Assembly before that date shall disagree with the decision of the Council and by resolution specifying its objections postpone the operation of the actual disarmament stage, which postponement shall in no case exceed six months.

If, however, the Executive Council has recommended that the coming into operation of the actual disarmament stage ought to be postponed, the General Assembly shall by resolution approve or disapprove that recommendation. If the recommendation of the Council for a postponement is approved, the Assembly shall in its resolution determine the duration of the postponement, which postponement shall in no case exceed six months. If the recommendation of the Council for a postponement is disapproved, the Assembly shall in its resolution direct that the actual disarmament stage shall come into operation on schedule at the end of the two-year period of the preparatory stage.

6. In the event of any postponement of the coming into operation of the actual disarmament stage, the question whether that stage shall come into operation at the end of the period of postponement shall be considered by the General Assembly in advance of the date on which the period of postponement is to end. The Executive Council shall report to the Assembly whether the conditions which led to the postponement have been remedied and the Assembly in the light of such report shall decide whether the actual disarmament stage shall come into operation at the end of the period of postponement or whether another postponement, not exceeding six months, is necessary. In case more than one postponement is necessary, a similar procedure shall be followed in each instance, but the period of postponement shall in no case exceed six months.

Comment. Under the plan proposed in this Article the central period of the preparatory stage (ordinarily the ninth through the eighteenth month) would be devoted to the verification of both the arms census and the arms truce. It cannot be expected that this task could be accomplished in less than ten months, since the Inspection Service would be obliged not only to check the accuracy of the information supplied by each nation, but also its completeness. It would have to verify not only the amount of arms and weapons existing at depots mentioned in the returns of the arms-census questionnaire, but also, to the extent possible, whether any weapons have been secreted in other localities. Similar enquiries would have to be made with respect to the other items of the questionnaire: military installations, manpower strength of the military forces, facilities for the production of armaments, materials which might enter into the production of nuclear weapons, etc. A determined effort on the part of the Inspection Service would be required to finish this tremendous task in only ten months; and yet it should be possible within that period.

In conducting their inspections, the United Nations Inspectors would be guided by regulations on the subject, to be adopted by the General Assembly under Chapter IV of this Annex. These regulations would determine not only the powers of the Inspectors but also the limitations necessary to protect nations and individuals against any possible abuses by the Inspectors of their powers. The regulations would embody and supplement the basic principles enunciated in Chapter IV of this Annex. They would provide, for instance, that certain facilities and establishments can be inspected at any time; that other facilities and establishments may be entered only after an advance notice or on the basis of a special authorization by an appropriate United Nations judicial authority; that Inspectors shall observe all rights of personal privacy and private property to the fullest extent consistent with the effective discharge of their duties; and that the Inspectors shall not disclose any confidential information or commercial secrets acquired incidentally in the course of inspection.

It is proposed that if an Inspector discovers that information furnished by a nation is incomplete or inaccurate or that a nation is not observing the arms truce, he shall report immediately to the Inspector-General who, under Chapter VIII of this Annex, could either call on the nation concerned to remedy the violation or refer the matter to the Inspection Commission. If the nation concerned did not make amends and the Inspection Commission then determined that the action of that nation constituted a serious violation, the Commission would forthwith present a report on the subject to the Executive Council, which could either take appropriate action itself or refer the matter to the General Assembly. Any action in respect of a violation of this Annex would be taken in accordance with the provisions of Chapter VIII of this Annex, which permit in the last resort the taking of enforcement measures under Chapter VII of the revised Charter.

If no difficulties had arisen, or if they had been satisfactorily met, the Inspection Commission would, in the nineteenth month of the preparatory stage, make a general report to the Executive Council concerning the adequacy of the information furnished, the observance of the arms truce and the over-all results of the verification. During the following month, the Council would make a similar report to the General Assembly. If the Council was satisfied with the progress of events, it would then make an official announcement that the preparatory stage of the disarmament plan would end at the end of the two-year period, and that the actual disarmament stage would, therefore, begin on schedule.

The General Assembly, to be convened during the twenty-first month of the preparatory stage, would consider the report of the Executive Council and, if it disagreed with the Council's estimate of the situation, could postpone for no longer than six months the beginning of the actual disarmament stage. If, however, the Assembly made no such decision before the end of the preparatory stage, the decision of the Council would stand and the actual disarmament stage would begin on schedule.

On the other hand, it is possible that the Executive Council might itself decide that the actual disarmament stage should be temporarily postponed, in which case, however, its recommendation to that effect would require explicit approval by the General Assembly. If the Assembly should approve the Council's recommendation, it would be required to determine the duration of the postponement, which in no case could exceed six months. If the Assembly should disapprove such a recommendation for postponement, it would itself announce the commencement on schedule of the actual disarmament stage.

A similar procedure would apply at the end of the postponement period, and a further postponement could be ordered by the General Assembly if the conditions which led to the original postponement had not been remedied, provided always that no postponement could exceed six months.

The general purpose of these careful safeguards is to ensure that no nation faithfully complying with the requirements shall be placed at a disadvantage, and thus to create that atmosphere of confidence which is indispensable to the working out of the plan.

The limitation of six months upon any single postponement is intended to force renewed attention of the General Assembly at frequent intervals to any cause for postponement. The effect of frequent Assembly debates on possible postponements would also be to center the attention of all the peoples of the world on the reasons for and against any proposed postponement; and the result should be to discourage any delay in starting the process of actual disarmament unless such a delay were clearly essential.

Article 8

1. During the first two months of the preparatory stage, the General Assembly shall, after receiving proposals on the subject from the Inspection Commission and the recommendations of the Executive Council as to such proposals, determine by regulations uniformly applicable to all nations:

a. What types of forces shall be deemed to be internal police forces, provided that in making such determination, the General Assembly shall be guided by the principle that all national, provincial, state and local police, border guards, and other public and private police, whether uniformed or not, shall be deemed to be internal police forces.

b. What types of arms and equipment internal police forces shall be entitled to possess, provided that in making such determination, the General Assembly shall be guided by the principles that such arms shall be limited to light arms, such as revolvers, rifles and automatic rifles, and that all equipment shall be limited to such as is appropriate for internal police duties.

c. What kind of training of internal police forces shall be permissible, provided that in making such determination, the General Assembly shall be guided by the principle that such forces shall receive only such training as is necessary to enable them properly to perform internal police duties only.

2. The General Assembly may from time to time and after receiving proposals on the subject from the Inspection Commission and the recommendations of the Executive Council as to such proposals make such changes in the determinations made under paragraph 1 of this Article as it may deem necessary.

Comment. The plan for *complete* disarmament contained in this Annex is based upon the premise that during the actual disarmament stage all national *military* forces will be reduced to zero. On the other hand, each nation would be permitted to retain certain internal police forces, but only within such limits as to numbers, training and equipment as are strictly necessary for the maintenance of internal order.

During the actual disarmament stage each nation would, therefore, be obliged not only to eliminate all its military forces but also to reduce its internal police forces to the strength plainly necessary for the maintenance of internal order, for which purpose they would alone be permitted. To this end it is proposed in Article 14 of this Annex that the strength of the internal police force of any nation shall not exceed two for each 1000 of its population nor in any case 500,000; and also that all such internal police forces shall be limited to light arms suitable for police duties and that their training and equipment shall be limited to such as are appropriate to police duties only.

In order to carry out this plan, it is essential as a preliminary step to define with precision the meaning of "internal police forces" and the exact scope of the limitations as to their training and equipment. Accordingly, this Article 8 authorizes the General Assembly, with advice from the Inspection Commission and the Executive Council, to make these definitions, subject in each case to the principles stated in the text.

The initial definitions are required to be made within the first two months of the preparatory stage in order to enable the nations to separate under a common standard their internal police forces from their military forces for the purpose of returning their arms-census questionnaires pursuant to Article 5 of this Annex. But since these initial definitions may later need to be changed, paragraph 2 of this Article 8 authorizes the General Assembly to make changes therein from time to time.

THE ACTUAL DISARMAMENT STAGE

Article 9

1. On the first day of the actual disarmament stage, the Executive Council shall announce the beginning of the period of actual disarmament.

2. Within two weeks thereafter, the Executive Council shall publish a schedule listing as of the beginning of the actual disarmament stage all the military forces of every nation in the world, together with all the armaments and facilities for the production of armaments of each nation. The Council shall at the same time publish a second schedule listing as of the beginning of the actual disarmament stage the existing strength of the internal police forces of every nation in the world, together with all their arms and equipment; and also setting forth an estimate by the Council of the maximum strength of the internal police forces which may be maintained in each nation after the end of the period of actual disarmament under the limitations of Article 14 of this Annex, together with an estimate of the maximum arms and equipment which such forces shall be permitted to have under the limitations of that Article at the end of the period of actual disarmament.

Comment. It is proposed that on the first day after the completion of the preparatory stage, the Executive Council shall issue a public announcement that the stage of actual disarmament has begun, bringing this historic fact to the attention of all the governments and peoples of the world. On that day a series of new obligations would become binding and the arms truce would be supplemented by the progressive scaling down of all national military forces, armaments and facilities for the production of armaments.

The Executive Council would at that time already be in possession of information furnished by all the nations with respect to their military strength, and would have received a report from the United Nations Inspection Commission that all such information had been verified and was in complete order. On this basis the Council would, within two weeks after the beginning of the actual disarmament stage, publish two schedules: one listing all the existing military forces, armaments and facilities for the production of armaments of every nation in the world; and another schedule listing the existing strength, arms and equipment of all the internal police forces of every nation.

The second schedule would be accompanied by the Executive Council's estimate of the maximum strength, arms and equipment of the internal police forces which each nation would be permitted to maintain after the end of the actual disarmament stage. In making this estimate the Council would have to take into account not only the changes in population expected to take place during the actual disarmament stage but also the strict limitations imposed by Article 14 of this Annex, i.e., that the strength of the internal police forces of any nation shall not exceed two for each 1000 of its population and in no case shall exceed 500,000, and that the light weapons to which these forces would be restricted shall be kept within the kinds and limits specified in that Article.

These two schedules—of military forces and of internal police forces—and the accompanying estimate of the prospective permitted strength of the internal police forces must be published at the very beginning of the actual disarmament stage, since the figures embodied in the two schedules would serve as the basis for calculating the percentage reductions in both types of forces to be made annually during this stage, as provided for by Articles 10-12 of this Annex.

Article 10

1. During the ten-year period of the actual disarmament stage, every nation in the world shall annually reduce by ten per cent all its military forces, armaments and facilities for the production of armaments, so that at the end of the actual disarmament stage all national military forces, armaments and facilities for the production of armaments shall be abolished.

During the ten-year period of the actual disarmament stage, every nation in the world shall also annually reduce its internal police forces and their arms and equipment by ten per cent of the excess thereof over the estimated maximum which such nation is permitted to have after the end of the actual disarmament stage under the limitations of Article 14 of this Annex.

2. After the completion of at least forty per cent of the disarmament process, the General Assembly may by a vote of two thirds of all the Representatives then in office, whether or not present or voting, shorten the remainder of the actual disarmament stage by not more than half

through an increase in the percentages of the required reductions to not more than twenty per cent annually.

Comment. As provided in the over-all plan set forth in Article 2 of this Annex, it is proposed that the process of actual disarmament shall be completed in ten years, unless shortened or lengthened under the applicable provisions, and this Article 10 implements that plan.

The ten-year period of actual disarmament seems long enough to permit annual reductions of such a limited size (ten per cent) that complying nations would not be put at too great a disadvantage if a nation or group of nations should suddenly cease to disarm and the General Assembly should find it necessary to suspend further disarmament until the elimination of the situation caused by such noncompliance. At the same time this period of ten years seems short enough to ensure that the momentum and good will generated by the actual operation of the plan will not be dissipated by the time the crucial point arrives when the very last military forces of every nation must be disbanded.

It is possible, however, that the successful completion of the disarmament process during the first few years of the actual disarmament stage might bring such relief and confidence among the peoples of the world that they would demand that the tempo of disarmament be accelerated. To enable such a speed-up, paragraph 2 of this Article empowers the General Assembly, by a special majority vote of two thirds of all the Representatives then in office, to shorten the actual disarmament stage to seven years, provided that the first forty per cent of the disarmament process has been completed. On the other hand, as above noted, provision is made in Article 12 of this Annex for extending the ten-year period (but for no more than six months at a time) if it becomes absolutely essential to do so.

The disarmament plan envisaged by this Annex distinguishes sharply between *military* forces and internal *police* forces (as defined by the General Assembly pursuant to Article 8 of this Annex). As explained in the Introduction and in the General Comment on this Annex, the whole disarmament plan is based upon the premise that nothing less than *complete* disarmament will suffice. On the other hand, the practical necessity is recognized that, subject to careful safeguards, each nation shall be entitled to possess such lightly armed police forces as are strictly necessary for internal order.

The essence of the entire proposal is that the disarmament process, while it must be complete, shall proceed in such carefully guarded stages that no nation need fear the consequences of compliance. Consequently, this Article provides for the gradual but steady elimination of all military forces over a ten-year period. They would be reduced annually by ten per cent, and after ten years no nation would be allowed to maintain any military forces whatever. Similarly, all national armaments and facilities for the production of armaments would be gradually reduced to nothing over this same ten-year period. While most of such armaments and machines and tools for their production would be destroyed or scrapped, a small part of them would be made available for the use or equipment of the United Nations Peace Force, to be built up during the same ten-year period. The disarmament of the nations (under this Annex

1) and the building up of the world police (under Annex II) would thus proceed simultaneously and in parallel.

A slightly different procedure would be followed with respect to the internal police forces. Since every nation would be allowed to retain some such forces, a particular nation would be obliged to reduce them only if they exceeded the estimated maximum which such nation would be permitted to have at the end of the actual disarmament stage, i.e., no more than two members of such forces for each 1000 of its population and in no case more than 500,000. Similarly, the light arms at the disposal of the permitted internal police forces would be restricted to not more than one revolver or rifle for each member of these police forces and not more than one automatic rifle for each 100 members of such forces (Article 14 of this Annex). The necessary reductions would be made by the annual elimination of ten per cent of the excess strength, arms and equipment. Provisions are made later (in Article 13 of this Annex) for a final determination of the permissible strength of the internal police forces of each nation, and for such periodic changes in their permitted strength as may be necessary in view of population changes.

A nation whose internal security forces were below the authorized strength would be permitted to increase them up to that limit. However, the maximum strength set for each nation would not, of course, impose an obligation to maintain internal police forces of that strength; and if any nation did not wish for any reason to maintain internal police forces of the permitted strength, the United Nations would certainly raise no objections.

As heretofore explained, a practicable disarmament plan needs to provide not only for complete disarmament, but also for disarmament which is universal, simultaneous and proportionate.

No disarmament plan is possible, unless *all* nations are bound by it. It is obvious that if any one of the larger and stronger nations were exempted from the disarmament process, no disarmament would be feasible. But it is also true in this world of novel weapons of tremendous destructive power that even a small nation might become a menace to the peace of the world. The disarmament system must, therefore, cover *all* nations, whether they are members of the United Nations or not. Under the ratification procedure proposed in Article 110 of the revised Charter (whereby the revised Charter would not come into force until ratified by five sixths of all the nations having at least five sixths of the world's population and including each of the twelve nations having the largest populations), it is very possible, in practice, that there would actually be no nonmember nations whatever; and in any event any such nonmember nations would be few in number and relatively small in size. In case, however, there should be a few nations which chose to refrain from active membership, it is essential that they shall nevertheless be bound to refrain from violence on the same basis as the member Nations and to settle all their disputes by peaceful means; and these specific obligations are imposed by Article 2 of the revised Charter. Correspondingly, all nonmember nations must be required to observe the disarmament provisions; and to this end this Article 10, in harmony with the entire Annex, imposes the obligation to disarm upon "every nation in the world". In recognition of this obligation, para-

236

graph 5 of Article 11 of the revised Charter provides for agreements by which every nonmember nation would be brought into a special relationship with the United Nations and whereby all nonmember nations would agree to comply with the disarmament provisions of this Annex and the laws, regulations and decisions made thereunder.

The disarmament plan embodied in this Annex depends also on its *simultaneous* execution by all nations. It is obvious that no nation would be willing or could be expected to disarm ahead of the others; and therefore all necessary safeguards must be established to ensure that no nation would be put in a disadvantageous position because other nations have not executed their part of the plan at the proper time. Such safeguards are provided for by Article 12 of this Annex which empowers the Inspection Commission to approve the annual disarmament plans of each nation and thus to ensure their simultaneous execution.

The disarmament plan must further make sure that all nations will disarm *proportionately*. The diminution of military strength must be equal for all nations. No nation can be expected to disarm by a larger percentage than others; and no nation should be deprived of a main source of its military strength while other nations still retain their principal sources of strength. Thus a nation strong in nuclear weapons should not be entirely deprived of them while other nations retain a large proportion of their preponderant land armies. Similarly, a nation could not reasonably be asked to abandon its ballistic missiles while another was permitted to retain its bombing planes. This Article provides, therefore, for an annual across-the-board cut of ten per cent in *all* forces, armaments and facilities for the production of armaments. Further provisions on this subject are contained in Article 11 of this Annex.

Article 11

1. All reductions in the personnel of active and reserve military forces and in their arms, weapons, ammunition and military equipment shall be distributed in each annual period proportionately as between the major services, land, sea and air, of every nation and the main components thereof; as between the active and reserve elements of each major service and the main components thereof; and as between the units stationed in the home territory and abroad.

All reductions in the personnel of the internal police forces of every nation and in their arms, ammunition and equipment shall be distributed in each annual period proportionately as between the main components of such forces in each nation, and as between the active and reserve elements thereof, unless the Executive Council, upon the recommendation of the Inspection Commission, shall for good cause shown permit a different distribution of the reductions.

All reductions in the facilities for the production of armaments shall be distributed in each annual period proportionately as between the

237

various facilities in the territory of every nation which produce the principal categories of armaments and the main subdivisions thereof.

2. When required reductions are made in the personnel of active and reserve military forces and of internal police forces, all persons relieved from active duty in such forces or released from membership therein shall be permanently exempt from any obligation for future military duty of any description, save only such obligation as may in an extreme emergency be imposed upon them by their respective nations for service in the United Nations Peace Force pursuant to Article 43 of this revised Charter and Annex II.

3. When required reductions are made in the arms, weapons, ammunition and military equipment of active and reserve military forces and of internal police forces, all the arms, weapons and ammunition, and all the equipment suitable for military use only, which such forces are required to discard, shall be destroyed or scrapped, save only such arms, weapons, ammunition and equipment as are transferred to the United Nations Peace Force in accordance with Annex II, or to the Nuclear Energy Authority in accordance with Articles 26 and 27 of this Annex, or to the Outer Space Agency in accordance with Article 29 of this Annex, such transfer to be subject to payment of compensation as provided in Article 30 of this Annex.

4. When required reductions are made in facilities for the production of armaments, all machines, appliances and tools of any kind which are suitable for the production of military material only and which are to be discarded in order to make the necessary reductions, shall be destroyed or scrapped, save only such machines, appliances and tools as are transferred to the United Nations for use in the manufacture of military material for the United Nations Peace Force in accordance with Annex II, such transfer to be subject to payment of compensation as provided in Article 30 of this Annex.

5. Subject to the principles stated in the foregoing paragraphs of this Article, the General Assembly shall, after receiving proposals on the subject from the Inspection Commission and the recommendations of the Executive Council as to such proposals, make regulations to govern the carrying out of the reductions required by this Annex.

6. During the actual disarmament stage, all nations shall continue to observe the limitations and prohibitions set forth in Article 6 of this Annex, except that such limitations and prohibitions shall apply in each year of this stage to the lower levels of military forces, armaments and facilities for the production of armaments brought about by the application of Article 10 of this Annex. The General Assembly, upon the recommendation of the Executive Council, shall adopt regulations governing the replacement of personnel discharged because of the termina-

tion of their period of service rather than because of the required reductions under Article 10 of this Annex.

Comment. This Article supplements the preceding Article 10 of this Annex and specifies how the various reductions provided for in Article 10 shall be executed. In particular, paragraph 1 of this Article spells out the application of the principle of proportionate reduction to military forces, armaments and facilities for the production of armaments. It is clearly not sufficient to provide broadly for an annual ten per cent reduction in the military forces of the various nations, since a particular nation might, for example, simply demobilize the necessary number of foot soldiers and leave the strength of its air force and navy unimpaired. Similarly, some other nation might limit a required numerical cut to maintenance troops of its air force but keep all its pilots in the service. The obligations with respect to the reduction of weapons might also be easily evaded if a nation were permitted to divide the reduction unequally between its fighter planes and long-range bombers, or between its fissionable and fusionable weapons. A really fair and safe method of reduction requires, therefore, that each nation must reduce in an equal manner the personnel of each major service (land, sea and air), and also of each major component thereof, as well as each major category of weapons. Similar rules should be applied to internal police forces and to the facilities for the production of armaments. Reductions of the same proportionate size should be made, for instance, in each nation's capacity to produce various types of guns, tanks, airplanes, warships or nuclear weapons. Here again, identical cuts should be made in the capacity to produce various categories of these weapons, e.g., with respect to guided and ballistic missiles, separate cuts would be necessary in the capacity for the production of short-, medium- and long-range missiles. Moreover, this principle of proportionate reductions would need to be applied uniformly to troops stationed in the home territory and abroad. For example, if in a given year the ground forces of a particular nation should consist of 500,000 men of whom 100,000 were stationed abroad, a ten per cent reduction of 50,000 in that year would have to be divided in such a way as to ensure that 40,000 be discharged from the forces stationed in the home territory and 10,000 from those stationed abroad.

Paragraphs 2-5 of this Article deal with the implications of reductions in various components of a nation's military strength. Thus reductions in the personnel of military forces and of internal police forces would result in the permanent exemption from national military service of persons relieved from active duty or released from membership in military reserve. No new recruits could be inducted, except to replace personnel discharged not because of the reduction but because of the termination of the period of service for which they had volunteered or had been drafted. To prevent possible abuses in this field, the General Assembly would be empowered to make regulations governing such replacements. There is also the remote possibility that former members of national armed forces or new recruits might be drafted by their respective nations to serve in the United Nations Peace Force in case of an extreme emergency, pursuant to Article 43 of the revised Charter and Annex II.

When arms or military equipment suitable for military use only are discarded by military or internal police forces in order to make a required reduction, they would be destroyed or scrapped in accordance with regulations on the subject to be adopted by the General Assembly. On the other hand, the temporary replacement of arms or equipment not yet subject to reduction, but which have been discarded because of obsolescence, would be permitted under special regulations to be issued by the General Assembly under Article 6 of this Annex.

In order to avoid unnecessary waste, discarded arms and equipment which are immediately needed for the United Nations Peace Force or which could be put in storage for its use in case of emergency, would not be destroyed but would be transferred to the United Nations. All nuclear weapons, except those which would be placed in the custody of the United Nations Nuclear Energy Authority for the possible use of the United Nations Peace Force, would also be destroyed, and all the nuclear materials contained in these dismantled weapons would be transferred to the Nuclear Energy Authority, which would allocate them to peaceful uses in accordance with the provisions of Chapter V of this Annex. All rockets, satellites and spacecraft for which no license had been issued by the Outer Space Agency would be transferred to that Agency which would provide for their peaceful use, in accordance with the provisions of Chapter VI of this Annex.

Since most facilities for the production of armaments could be used for other purposes, it is not proposed to destroy them when they become subject to reduction. But all the machines, appliances and tools which are suitable for the production of military material only would be removed from such facilities and destroyed or scrapped. If, however, they were needed for equipping the United Nations Peace Force, such machines, appliances and tools, instead of being destroyed, would be transferred to the United Nations which, at the end of the actual disarmament stage, would alone have the right to manufacture any armaments or military equipment whatever.

The execution of the provisions of this Annex would require from time to time the issuance of additional rules for the guidance of national governments, of private individuals (e.g., owners of facilities for the production of armaments) and of the United Nations Inspection Service. Accordingly, whenever the Inspection Commission might find it necessary, it would submit to the General Assembly, through the Executive Council, a report on the subject, on the basis of which the Assembly could adopt further regulations.

Paragraph 6 of this Article provides for the extension to the actual disarmament stage of the provisions in Article 6 of this Annex which relate to various limitations and prohibitions against increases by direct or indirect means in the military strength of any nation.

Article 12

1. During the first month of each of the ten years of the actual disarmament stage, every nation in the world shall submit to the Inspection

Commission a detailed plan for a ten per cent reduction within that year of all its military forces, armaments and facilities for the production of armaments, and wherever necessary such plans shall include proposals for adjustments in particular cases in which an exact ten per cent reduction is technically impossible. This plan shall also contain proposals for the reduction, if necessary, of its internal police forces and their arms and equipment by ten per cent of the excess thereof, if any, over the maximum which such nation is permitted to have after the end of the actual disarmament stage under the limitations of Article 14 of this Annex.

2. During the second month, the Inspection Commission shall approve the plan of each nation or direct its modification in so far as the Commission may deem necessary in order to ensure that the plan complies with the regulations made by the General Assembly under Article 11 of this Annex and that the reductions by all nations shall, to the utmost practicable extent, be simultaneous and proportionate.

3. If any nation is dissatisfied with any modification made by the Inspection Commission of its own plan or is dissatisfied with the plan of any other nation as accepted or modified by the Commission, it may appeal to the Executive Council during the first ten days of the third month. The Council shall decide all such appeals before the end of the third month, and shall have the authority to approve or modify the contested plan; its decisions shall be final.

4. During the following six months, the plan of each nation, as so approved or modified, shall be fully carried out; and the United Nations Inspection Service shall supervise and verify the execution of all such plans through inspection by Inspectors of the Inspection Service acting with the authority and subject to the limitations provided for in Articles 18 to 24 of this Annex. During this six-month period, the Inspector-General shall make monthly reports to the Inspection Commission as to the progress of the required reductions and the verification thereof; and during the last week of the six-month period, he shall make a final report to the Commission as to the over-all results. The Inspection Commission shall forthwith consider all such reports of the Inspector-General; and if the Inspector-General has reported that any nation has failed to carry out any required reduction or has placed any obstacle in the way of verification, the Commission shall consider what measures shall be taken. If the Commission determines that any such failure or obstacle is serious, it shall immediately present a special report to that effect to the Executive Council, stating whether or not in the Commission's judgment the failure or obstacle is so serious as to prejudice the execution of the entire disarmament plan.

In addition to such special reports, if any, the Inspection Commission shall during the tenth month make a general report to the Executive

Council concerning the execution of the required reductions, including the opinion of the Commission as to whether the over-all results have been reasonably satisfactory.

5. The Executive Council shall forthwith consider all reports of the Inspection Commission; and if the Commission has determined that there has been any serious failure on the part of any nation to carry out any required reduction, or that any nation has placed any serious obstacle in the way of verification by the Inspection Service, the Council shall consider what measures shall be taken. If the Council accepts the conclusion of the Commission that such failure or obstacle is so serious as to prejudice the execution of the entire disarmament plan, the Council shall take such interim action as it is authorized to take pursuant to Article 34 of this Annex and shall immediately present a special report on the subject to the General Assembly for possible action by it under that Article.

In addition to such special reports, if any, the Executive Council shall during the eleventh month make a general report to the General Assembly, which report shall include the conclusions of the Council as to the adequacy of the performance by all the nations of their obligation to carry out their approved reduction plans and as to the adequacy of the verification of such performance.

If the Executive Council concludes that such performance or verification is so unsatisfactory as to prejudice the execution of the entire disarmament plan, it shall so state and shall recommend that the coming into operation of the next annual reduction ought to be postponed for a period not exceeding six months. If, however, the Council concludes that such performance and verification are reasonably satisfactory, it shall so state; and the Council shall then decide and announce that the next annual reduction shall begin on schedule, subject only to a resolution of the General Assembly under paragraph 6 of this Article disagreeing with such decision of the Council.

6. If the Executive Council has presented a special report to the General Assembly informing it that there has been a serious failure on the part of any nation to carry out a required reduction or that any nation has placed a serious obstacle in the way of verification by the Inspection Service, the Assembly shall deal with the matter as soon as possible, and shall have authority to take such action under Article 34 of this Annex as it may deem necessary. If the Assembly is not then in session, a special session thereof shall be convoked immediately.

In any event, the General Assembly shall in the twelfth month consider the general report of the Executive Council; and, if necessary, a special session shall be convoked for the purpose.

If the Executive Council has decided that the next annual reduction shall come into operation on schedule, that decision shall be deemed final unless before the end of the twelfth month the General Assembly shall disagree with the decision of the Council and by resolution specifying its objections postpone the next annual reduction, which postponement shall in no case exceed six months.

If, however, the Executive Council has recommended that the next annual reduction ought to be postponed, the General Assembly shall by resolution approve or disapprove that recommendation. If the recommendation of the Council for a postponement is approved, the Assembly shall in its resolution determine the duration of the postponement, which postponement shall in no case exceed six months. If the recommendation of the Council for a postponement is disapproved, the Assembly shall in its resolution direct that the next annual reduction shall come into operation on schedule.

7. In the event of the postponement of any annual reduction, the question whether that postponed reduction shall come into operation during the year following the period of postponement shall be considered by the General Assembly in advance of the date on which the period of postponement is to end. The Executive Council shall report to the Assembly whether the conditions which led to the postponement have been remedied and the Assembly in the light of such report shall decide whether the next annual reduction shall come into operation during the year following the period of postponement or whether another postponement, not exceeding six months, is necessary. In case more than one postponement is necessary, a similar procedure shall be followed in each instance, but the period of postponement shall in no case exceed six months.

Comment. To ensure simultaneous execution by all the nations of the world of the annual ten per cent reduction of: (1) their military forces, armaments and facilities for the production of armaments and (2) any excess of their internal police forces over the authorized maximum, this Article calls for the submission by every nation of detailed plans for the required reductions and provides that the Inspection Commission shall pass upon all such plans and either approve them or direct their modification.

More specifically, the proposal is that during the first month of each of the ten years of the actual disarmament stage, every nation in the world shall submit to the Inspection Commission its detailed plan specifying how it intends to carry out the reductions required during that year. Each yearly plan would necessarily contain a detailed list of the military units which the particular nation proposes to disband or reduce, of the armaments which it proposes to discard and of the facilities for the production of armaments which it proposes to dismantle; and also a detailed proposal for reducing any excess of its internal police forces. During the second month of each year of the actual disarmament stage, the Commission would carefully examine these national plans and verify that the proposed cuts for that year have been

243

properly apportioned among all the services and their major components, and among the various categories of armaments and types of facilities for the production of armaments.

The Inspection Commission, having received and examined the plans of all the nations, would then be responsible for seeing to it that the reductions were carried out in such a way that all the major nations would disband or scrap similar forces, armaments and facilities at the same time. Thus the Commission, under its authority to modify national plans "in order to ensure . . . that the reductions by all the nations shall, to the utmost practicable extent, be simultaneous and proportionate", would, for example, synchronize the plans of the principal naval nations so that each would scrap the same proportion of its fleet on the very same day. The Commission could also modify any other features of national plans in order to carry out a reduction proposed by a nation in a more proportionate manner as, for example, by directing the elimination of certain units of that nation's military strength different from those specified in its particular national plan. To prevent any misuse of this power of modification by the Commission, provision is made for appeals to the Executive Council by any nation which is dissatisfied either with any modification made by the Commission in that nation's own plan or with the plan of any other nation as accepted or modified by the Commission. The decisions of the Executive Council on such appeals would be final.

It is assumed that the Inspection Commission would direct that the annual reductions shall not be delayed to the last possible day and that they shall be carried out gradually during the six months following the final approval of the plan for each disarmament year. It is also assumed that the Commission would require all major acts of scrapping large quantities of arms and equipment to be performed in the presence and under the supervision of United Nations Inspectors and that other reductions would be verified by the Inspectors through examinations of official records and inspections on the spot. Such inspections would, it is assumed, be conducted not only in the military establishments and facilities for the production of armaments listed in the arms census, but also in other establishments and facilities which, though not listed in the arms census, could easily be used for military purposes. Chapter IV of this Annex defines in some detail the proposed powers of the Inspectors in this field and provides guarantees against their abuse.

If serious difficulties should arise during any annual reduction period and any nation should either fail to carry out a required reduction or prevent adequate verification of the fulfillment of its obligations with respect thereto, the Inspection Commission would be required immediately to notify the Executive Council which could either itself apply sanctions to the extent that it is authorized to do so by Chapter VII of the revised Charter and by Article 34 of this Annex, or refer the matter to the General Assembly for alternative or further action.

If, however, everything went smoothly, the general report of the Inspection Commission, to be submitted to the Executive Council in the tenth month of each year of actual disarmament, would certify the satisfactory fulfillment of the required reductions. Ordinarily, the Council would approve this report in the eleventh month of each disarmament year and announce the commencement on schedule of the next annual reduction. Nevertheless, the right is reserved to the General Assembly to change this decision during the twelfth month by a special resolution. Assuming, however, that the Assembly agrees with the decision of the Council, the Commission and all national authorities would be able at the close of each reduction year to start work on the detailed plans for the next annual reduction.

It is possible, of course, that the Executive Council, either on the advice of the Inspection Commission or on its own initiative, might decide that the performance by some nation or nations of their obligation to reduce, or the verification of the process of reduction by the United Nations Inspection Service, had been so unsatisfactory as to prejudice the execution of the entire disarmament plan. In such event, the Council could recommend a postponement of the next annual reduction, but under no circumstances for more than six months. Moreover, since even a brief postponement would be a serious matter, it is proposed that any postponement could come into effect only by a special resolution of the General Assembly.

Before the end of any period of postponement, the Executive Council would be required to present a report to the General Assembly concerning the improvement, or otherwise, of the situation which led to the postponement. In the light of that report, the Assembly would determine either that everything is now in order and that the next annual reduction shall come into operation at the end of the period of postponement, or that some further postponement is necessary. A similar procedure is provided for at the end of each period of postponement, any postponement whatever being always limited to a maximum of six months. Thus the Assembly would have to consider anew at frequent intervals the matter of any postponed reduction, and even if one or more postponements were necessary, there would be constant pressure to remedy the causes of the delay and to proceed as soon as possible with the disarmament process.

CHAPTER III

GENERAL PROVISIONS FOR THE MAINTENANCE
OF COMPLETE DISARMAMENT

Article 13

1. On the first day after the end of the actual disarmament stage, the Executive Council shall announce that all national military forces, armaments and facilities for the production of armaments have been abolished, and shall proclaim the termination of the actual disarmament stage and the beginning of the period of complete disarmament.

2. Within ten days thereafter, the Executive Council shall publish a schedule listing the maximum strength of the internal police forces which may be maintained in each nation under the limitations of Article 14 of this Annex, together with the kind and amount of arms and equipment which such forces shall be permitted to have under the limitations of that Article. This schedule shall govern until the Council shall publish a new schedule subsequent to the first world census taken under Article 9 of this revised Charter.

3. The Executive Council shall, within three months after the population figures are available from the first world census and within three months after the population figures are available from each subsequent world census, publish a revised schedule listing for every nation the maximum permissible strength of the internal police forces which may be maintained in that nation and the permissible arms and equipment of those forces. Each such schedule shall govern until the next schedule is published.

4. In case the strength of the internal police forces of any nation, or the amount of their arms or equipment, exceeds the strength or amount listed in the applicable schedule published by the Executive Council, such excess shall be removed by the nation concerned within six months after the publication of such schedule.

Comment. The plan contemplates that in normal course all nations would be completely disarmed ten years after the beginning of the actual disarmament stage. If the General Assembly should use its power under paragraph 2 of Article 10 of this Annex to shorten the actual disarmament period, the moment of complete disarmament might arrive at the end of the seventh, eighth or ninth year of that period. On the other hand, that final moment might be somewhat delayed, if some serious difficulties should lead the Assembly to order one or more postponements pursuant to Article 12 of this Annex.

Whenever the historic moment arrives, the Executive Council would be required formally to proclaim it. The actual disarmament stage would then have ended and the period of complete disarmament would have begun. From that point on, no nation could legally possess any *military forces* whatever (it being understood that the lightly armed and strictly limited forces which may be retained for internal order only are not deemed to be military forces), or any armaments or facilities for the production of armaments.

Within ten days after the beginning of the period of complete disarmament, the Executive Council would publish a definitive schedule listing for each nation the maximum permissible strength, arms and equipment of the internal police forces of that nation. This final schedule would replace the provisional estimate made at the beginning of the actual disarmament stage pursuant to Article 9 of this Annex; and like that estimate, this final schedule would be based upon the principle that the strength of the internal police forces of any nation shall not exceed two for each 1000 of its population and in no case may exceed 500,000. Because of population changes which could not be foreseen at the time of the estimate ten years previously, the final schedule at the end of the actual disarmament stage would almost necessarily differ from the estimate made at the beginning of that stage, with consequent changes in the strength of the internal police forces permitted in the various nations. Similarly, a new schedule would be published after the first world census to be taken within ten years after the coming into force of the revised Charter and after each of the subsequent world censuses to be taken at ten-year intervals (Article 9 of the revised Charter).

Article 14

After the termination of the actual disarmament stage and the beginning of the period of complete disarmament:

a. No nation shall maintain any military forces whatever; and no nation shall have any internal police forces in excess of two for each 1000 of its population and in no case exceeding 500,000, the permissible number for each nation to be determined in the successive schedules to be published by the Executive Council pursuant to Article 13 of this Annex.

b. No nation shall allow any military training whatever either under government or private direction; and no nation shall allow any training of its internal police forces except such training as is appropriate to internal police duties and is permitted under the regulations adopted by the General Assembly pursuant to Article 8 of this Annex.

c. No nation shall possess any military weapons or equipment whatever. No nation shall allow the possession by its internal police forces of any arms or equipment except of the types permitted by the regulations adopted by the General Assembly pursuant to Article 8 of this Annex; and in no case shall the number of revolvers and rifles combined exceed one for each member of the internal police forces, the number of automatic rifles one for each 100 members of such forces, and the ammunition supplies 100 rounds per rifle or revolver and 1000 rounds per automatic rifle. No nation shall allow the possession by any public or private organization or individual of any military equipment whatever or of any arms except such small arms as are reasonably needed by duly licensed hunters or by duly licensed individuals for personal protection.

d. No nation shall produce or allow the production of any military weapons or equipment whatever, or of tools for such production, and no nation shall produce or allow the production of any light arms except: (1) to supply the light arms, ammunition and equipment which its internal police forces are allowed to have; (2) for sale to other nations of permissible light arms, ammunition or equipment needed by their internal police forces; and (3) such small arms as are required to meet the reasonable needs of duly licensed hunters or of duly licensed individuals for personal protection, either in the nation where such arms are produced or elsewhere.

e. No nation shall permit any research directed toward the invention of new military weapons or the improvement of existing military weapons, including the utilization for military purposes of any nuclear materials.

f. No nation shall produce or allow the production of any explosives except in so far as the General Assembly may authorize their production for use in mining, agricultural and other industries of that nation, or for sale for similar purposes in other nations.

g. No nation shall construct or allow the construction of any ship or airplane containing any feature which would facilitate the adaptation of such ship or airplane to military purposes.

h. No nation shall prepare or allow the preparation of its heavy industry (including its tool-manufacturing industry) for the production of armaments of any description (including arms, weapons, ammunition, explosives and military equipment of any kind) or of tools for such production.

i. No nation shall prepare or allow the preparation of any plant for the production of chemical or biological weapons.

j. No nation shall possess or allow the possession of any special nuclear materials, or of substantial quantities of radioactive materials, except to the extent that the General Assembly may authorize such possession for research, industrial, commercial or other nonmilitary purposes, and subject to the licensing requirements of Article 16 of this Annex and to such limitations as may be determined by the Assembly pursuant to Articles 23 and 26 of this Annex.

k. No nation shall operate or allow the operation of facilities for the processing of materials which might enter into the production of

248

special nuclear materials, or facilities for the processing of special nuclear materials themselves, or facilities for the production of radioactive materials in substantial quantities, or facilities using any such materials for research, industrial, commercial or other nonmilitary purposes, except when licensed pursuant to Article 16 of this Annex, and only in such manner and subject to such limitations as may be determined by the General Assembly pursuant to Articles 23 and 26 of this Annex.

l. No nation shall possess or allow the possession of any rockets, satellites or spacecraft, except to the extent that the General Assembly may authorize such possession for research, industrial, commercial or other nonmilitary purposes, and subject to the licensing requirements of Article 16 of this Annex and to such limitations as may be determined by the Assembly pursuant to Article 29 of this Annex.

m. No nation shall operate or allow the operation of facilities for the production of rockets, satellites or spacecraft, except when licensed pursuant to Article 16 of this Annex, and only in such manner and subject to such limitations as may be determined by the General Assembly pursuant to Article 29 of this Annex.

Comment. Once disarmament is completed, not only would all national military forces be abolished, but also all national military *activities* would be prohibited. At this point there should come into effect a comprehensive set of safeguards to ensure against the revival of any national military activities whatever. Under Article 6 of this Annex a similar set of prohibitions is proposed to take effect forthwith on the coming into force of the arms truce and to cover the sixteen-month period of the arms truce; and, under paragraph 6 of Article 11 of this Annex, that set of prohibitions would apply also during the ten-year period of the actual disarmament stage. This Article 14 continues in force in identical or modified form various of the prohibitions provided for in Articles 6 and 11 of this Annex, but adds some new prohibitions. The purpose is to have in effect during the period of complete disarmament as comprehensive a set of permanent safeguards against rearmament as possible.

All national governments would be obligated both themselves to observe this new set of permanent prohibitions and to enforce them against all organizations and individuals within their jurisdiction. The United Nations Inspection Service would verify the compliance by every nation with these provisions; and various measures of enforcement would be available against violators, whether governments or individuals.

It being always understood that the permitted internal police forces would not be deemed to be military forces, the maintenance of any military forces whatever by any nation would, by subparagraph (a) of this Article, be completely forbidden. This prohibition would apply to military forces of all kinds, including para-military organizations. Consequently, by subparagraph (b) no military training whatsoever would be permitted except, of course, the limited type of training required for the members of the internal police forces.

Subparagraph (c) would wholly prohibit the possession of any military arms or equipment, except that internal police forces would be allowed to possess certain light arms, ammunition and equipment of the types authorized by Article 8 of this Annex. This subparagraph (c), however, contains definite restrictions on the number of the principal arms which internal police forces could possess, e.g., no more than one automatic rifle for each 100 members of such forces. The prohibition against the possession of arms would extend to all private individuals and organizations, except that some small arms would be allowed for hunting and personal protection only.

In order to place all nations on an equal basis, it is important to abolish not only all military forces (land, sea and air) and all stocks of military weapons, but also to abolish the advantage possessed by nations having well-developed armament industries. In consequence, it is necessary to prohibit entirely the manufacture of all military weapons and equipment, whether by public or private industry. The only arms manufacture which could remain would be for the production of the light arms permitted to the internal police forces, and of small arms for hunting or personal protection. And even this permitted production would be strictly limited to the amounts required by the internal police forces, hunters, etc., of the country of production, or for export to satisfy similar needs abroad (subparagraph d).

It would obviously be inconsistent with the regime of total national disarmament to permit any nation to engage in or allow any effort to invent new weapons or improve existing weapons; and consequently subparagraph (e) prohibits any such military research.

Since modern explosives can easily be converted into dangerous weapons, production of explosives should also be restricted to the minimum necessary for usual purposes, such as mining, road building, etc.; and subparagraph (f) covers this subject.

In a world in which all naval vessels and military airplanes have been abolished, there would be an ever-present danger that nonmilitary ships and airplanes could suddenly be converted to military purposes. And because this danger is especially great with respect to airplanes, proposals have been made by various governments that all airplanes should be internationalized. While it does not seem practicable to obtain consent to so drastic a proposal, everything possible should be done to prevent the conversion of these non-military means of transportation into tools of war. It is proposed, therefore, to keep a close watch over the construction of all ships and airplanes, and the United Nations Inspection Service would be empowered to conduct periodic inspections not only of shipyards and airplane factories, but also of all ships and airplanes which might be easily adapted to military use. With these considerations in mind subparagraph (g) prohibits the construction of any ship or airplane containing any feature designed for adaptation to military purposes.

Since it is important to destroy the ability to make war at its inception rather than to attempt to curtail an already developed war potential at the last moment, it is not enough merely to prohibit the actual manufacture of armaments. It is necessary to go a further step down the production scale by prohibiting (subparagraph h) the advance adaptation of heavy industry to the production of military items; in particular the military adaptation of the tool-manufacturing industry.

For similar reasons precautions need to be taken against the too easy adaptation of chemical and biological production facilities to military production; and subparagraph (i) contains a separate prohibition on this subject.

Special safeguards are also necessary with respect to "special nuclear" and radioactive materials which can be easily converted for use in weapons of tremendous destructive power. It seems imperative, therefore, that all such materials shall come into the custody of the United Nations as soon as they reach a stage at which, subject only to final processing, they can be incorporated in nuclear weapons. As stated in Article 5 of this Annex, the term employed to describe materials which have reached this stage is "special nuclear materials". By subparagraph (j) of this Article 14 the possession of any such "special nuclear materials" by any government or by anyone other than the United Nations itself would be permitted only if they are already in use or are about to be used for research, industrial, commercial or other nonmilitary purposes. Correlative provision is made in Chapter V of this Annex for the transfer to a proposed new organ, to be called the United Nations Nuclear Energy Authority, of all "special nuclear materials" which are not immediately needed for such nonmilitary purposes.

To this end it is proposed that the United Nations, through its Nuclear Energy Authority, shall acquire by purchase at a fair price the full ownership of these excess materials; this ownership, however, to be subject to a strict obligation (pursuant to the provisions of Chapter V of this Annex) to make the materials available as speedily as circumstances permit for research, industrial, commercial or other nonmilitary uses under such stipulations and arrangements as would ensure against their diversion to military use. The enforcement of the prohibition against any unauthorized national or private possession of any "special nuclear materials" would constitute one of the chief functions of the United Nations Inspection Service; and the allotment for nonmilitary use of these materials would constitute the most important function of the Nuclear Energy Authority.

The danger of diversion for military purposes of nuclear and radioactive materials from facilities producing them or utilizing them for nonmilitary purposes is so great that for some years after the so-called Baruch Plan of 1946 the actual *ownership* by the United Nations of all such materials and facilities was considered by many as the only safe solution. But if very careful safeguards are provided in the shape of: (a) wide distribution of such facilities throughout the globe, (b) a strict system of United Nations supervision, and (c) a strong world military force (the United Nations Peace Force), it is believed that outright ownership by the United Nations may be safely dispensed with. The feasibility of this approach will necessarily depend to a large extent upon the effectiveness of the supervision system. It is not enough in respect of these dangerous facilities and materials merely to provide for periodic inspection or even for continuous inspection by the most competent inspectors. Supplementing all such inspections, it will be advisable to have a system enabling persons appointed by the United Nations actually to participate in the operation and management of the facilities on various levels.

Articles 23 and 26 of this Annex give, therefore, to each nation (or even to

251

each facility producing or using "special nuclear materials") a choice among three options: (1) to close the facilities entirely; (2) to lease them to the United Nations; or (3) to make an agreement with the United Nations which would authorize personnel of the United Nations Inspection Service or of the United Nations Nuclear Energy Authority, or of both, to participate in the management and operation of the facility. It would be provided that unless an agreement satisfactory to the United Nations is concluded within a period to be specified by the General Assembly, the dangerous facility shall not be built, and, that if it is already in existence, it shall either be closed and dismantled or transferred to the United Nations under a long-term lease.

It is to be expected that most nations owning such facilities (or the private owners thereof) would prefer to reach an agreement with the United Nations authorizing the Inspection Service or the Nuclear Energy Authority, or both, to appoint properly qualified persons to take part in the management and operation of any such dangerous facility. While some standard clauses would doubtless be embodied in all such agreements, these agreements would necessarily differ, depending on the size of the facility, the type of activity conducted therein and the danger of diversion from it of "special nuclear materials" or radioactive materials. Such agreements could provide, for example, that representatives of the Inspection Service or the Nuclear Energy Authority be permitted to participate, without vote, in all meetings of the board of directors (if any) of the facility and of any other group responsible for the formulation of policy or the conduct of the principal activities of that facility. In most cases, such agreements would also authorize the assignment to the facility of properly qualified persons selected by the Inspection Service or the Nuclear Energy Authority (scientists, engineers, accountants, etc.), with the right actually to participate in the operation of the facility or in the research conducted therein. The management of the facility would be obliged to treat these United Nations appointees in the same way as its other employees, to provide for them mutually satisfactory positions within the facility, and to give them free access to all parts of the facility. During their assignment to a particular facility, these persons would be subject to local regulations and to rules established by the management of the facility, unless such regulations or rules should conflict with their duties as United Nations employees. Besides the ordinary duties assigned to these persons by the management of the facility, they would be obliged to make regular reports to the Nuclear Energy Authority; to assist the Inspectors of the United Nations Inspection Service in the inspection of the particular facility; and to give immediate notice to the Nuclear Energy Authority and the Inspection Service of any unauthorized diversion of "special nuclear" or radioactive materials. These special appointees, when assigned to a national or private facility, would continue to be paid by the United Nations; but the facility benefiting from their services would be required to pay to the United Nations an amount equivalent to the value of their services, in accordance with regulations on the subject to be enacted by the General Assembly (paragraph 4 of Article 23 of this Annex).

Where the danger of diversion of "special nuclear" or radioactive materials is especially great, the agreement between the United Nations and the management of the facility would authorize the United Nations to appoint guards to be stationed around-the-clock at all the important locations, with the right to take any necessary action to prevent any unauthorized removal of such materials (paragraph 3 of Article 23 of this Annex).

Besides the above-mentioned specific prohibitions and safeguards under Articles 23 and 26 of this Annex, general provision is made in subparagraph (k) of this Article 14 that no dangerous facility may be operated by any nation or private person except in a manner and subject to limitations determined by regulations issued by the General Assembly. Thus the Assembly might provide for special accounting procedures, constructional changes in the facility to make diversion of "special nuclear" and radioactive materials more difficult, and for such other safeguards as experience might prove to be advisable (paragraphs 2 and 5 of Article 23 of this Annex).

The sum of all the above safeguards may seem formidable, but it is believed that no less rigorous a system will suffice to give reasonable assurance against the diversion of these deadly materials to military purposes. Rigorous as they are, these safeguards fall short of the plan for complete *ownership* of all nuclear facilities contemplated by the Baruch Plan of 1946 and by the later majority report of the United Nations Atomic Energy Commission. The conception governing the plan here proposed in respect of nuclear and radioactive materials is to find a middle way between a plan which, while ideally "foolproof", would not be realizable in practice, and a plan which, while readily acceptable, would not in practical operation give sufficient assurance against diversion. It is believed that the proposed plan should be both acceptable and effective.

It is necessary to provide special safeguards also in respect of rockets, satellites and spacecraft. Their possession and production would, under subparagraphs (1) and (m) of this Article 14, be prohibited except when licensed by the Outer Space Agency.

Article 15

After the termination of the actual disarmament stage and the beginning of the period of complete disarmament:

1. Every nation shall annually submit to the Executive Council in form prescribed by that Council a certificate signed by the chief executive of each such nation to the effect that neither the government of that nation nor, so far as known to that government, any person within the territory of that nation is engaging in any activity prohibited by Article 14 of this Annex and that both the government and, so far as known to that government, all such persons are fulfilling in good faith all the requirements of this Annex for the maintenance of complete disarmament.

2. Every nation shall annually supply to the Inspector-General, pursuant to a questionnaire furnished by him, the following information:

a. The manpower strength, organization, composition and disposition of its internal police forces.

253

b. The location and description of all installations utilized by its internal police forces for training and quartering.

c. The location, kind and quantity of all arms, ammunition and equipment possessed by or at the disposal of its internal police forces.

d. The location, description and rate of current output of all facilities within its territory engaged in the production of any light arms, ammunition or equipment of the sort permitted for internal police forces, or of any small arms permitted for hunting and personal protection, or of tools for any such production.

e. The location, description and rate of current output of all facilities within its territory engaged in the production of explosives of the sort permitted for mining, agricultural and other industries.

f. The number, kind, home ports or home airfields of all ships and airplanes capable of adaptation to military use, owned or operated by it or its nationals.

g. The location, description and rate of current production of all shipyards and airplane plants within its territory.

h. The location, description and rate of current production of all heavy industry plants within its territory (including all plants of the tool-manufacturing industry) which are capable of easy adaptation to the production of armaments of any description (including arms, weapons, ammunition, explosives and military equipment of any kind) or of tools for such production.

i. The location, description and rate of current production of any plant within its territory which is capable of easy adaptation to the production of chemical or biological weapons.

j. A description of all extensive surveys and explorations conducted within its territory for the purpose of discovering new sources of any raw materials which might enter into the production of special nuclear materials.

k. The location, type and estimated content of deposits within its territory which are known to contain substantial amounts of raw materials which might enter into the production of special nuclear materials.

l. The location, type, amount and stage of processing of all raw materials within its territory which might enter into the production of special nuclear materials and which have been removed from their place of deposit in nature; of all special nuclear materials; and of all materials which have been made radioactive by artificial means.

m. The location, description and rate of current output of all mines within its territory which are engaged in the mining of raw materials which might enter into the making of special nuclear materials.

n. The location, description and rate of current output of all facilities of any kind within its territory which are engaged in the processing of raw materials which might enter into the making of special nuclear materials; or in the processing of special nuclear materials themselves; or in the production of auxiliary materials which might be employed in the process of making special nuclear materials or nuclear weapons, such as graphite, heavy water, beryllium, lithium and cobalt; or in the production of radioactive materials in substantial quantity.

o. The location and description of all laboratories or other facilities within its territory which are concerned with the study of nuclear energy.

p. The location and description of all facilities within its territory which are utilizing any special nuclear materials or substantial quantities of radioactive materials for research, industrial, commercial or other nonmilitary purposes.

q. The number, kind and location of all rockets, satellites and spacecraft within its territory or which are owned or operated by it or its nationals.

r. The location, description and rate of current output of all facilities within its territory engaged in the production of rockets, satellites and spacecraft, or of tools for such production; and the location and description of all facilities within its territory which are equipped for the launching of rockets, satellites and spacecraft.

Comment. In the territory of each nation, its own governmental authorities would have co-ordinate responsibility with the United Nations for the execution of the disarmament plan. It seems proper, therefore, to require that the government of every nation should present annually to the United Nations a certificate, signed by its chief executive (head of state, prime minister or other person actually in executive charge of the government), testifying that neither that government nor, to its knowledge, any person in its territory is engaged in any activity prohibited by this Annex. The obligation to submit this annual certificate should make the chief executives of the nations of the world very conscious of their duty to see to it that all the requirements of this Annex for the maintenance of disarmament are fulfilled in good faith. If one of them should himself violate any provision of this Annex, or tolerate a violation thereof by others, he would be faced at the end of the year with a painful choice between refusing to submit the prescribed certificate and thus clearly indicating that something is wrong in his country, or submitting a false certificate and facing the severe penalties which would presumably be prescribed therefor by the General Assembly under Article 11 of the revised Charter. The duty to submit the certificate should, therefore, have a strong moral influence in obtaining a satisfactory compliance with the provisions for the maintenance of complete disarmament once it is achieved.

To facilitate the task of the United Nations Inspection Service, every nation would also be obliged to submit annually to the Inspector-General detailed information on its internal police forces, and on materials and facilities within its territory which could be easily used or adapted for military purposes. Information would have to be submitted, in particular, with respect to materials which might enter into the production of "special nuclear materials" and facilities engaged in the production of such materials, and with respect to rockets, satellites and spacecraft and facilities engaged in producing them. If a government should fail to transmit the required information or should submit untrue information, it would be the duty of the United Nations to take such enforcement measures under Chapter VIII of this Annex, either against the government concerned or the delinquent individual, as might be deemed appropriate in view of the seriousness of the offense.

Article 16

1. After the termination of the actual disarmament stage and the beginning of the period of complete disarmament, every nation shall obtain a special license from the Inspector-General for:

a. The operation of every installation or training camp at which are stationed more than 100 of the personnel of its internal police forces.

b. The operation of every depot in which is stored any substantial quantity of the light arms, ammunition and equipment permitted for the use of its internal police forces.

c. The operation by it or by any public or private organization or individual of any facility within its territory engaged in the production of any light arms, ammunition or equipment of the sort permitted for internal police forces, or of any small arms permitted for hunting and personal protection, or of tools for any such production.

d. The operation by it or by any public or private organization or individual of any facility within its territory engaged in the production of explosives of the sort permitted for mining, agricultural and other industries.

e. The operation by it or by any public or private organization or individual of any plant within its territory which is easily adaptable to the production of chemical or biological weapons.

f. The operation by it or by any public or private organization or individual of any mine within its territory containing any substantial quantity of raw materials which might enter into the production of special nuclear materials, or of any mill or dump within its territory containing any substantial quantity of such raw materials.

g. The operation by it or by any public or private organization or individual of any facility within its territory engaged in the processing of raw materials which might enter into the production of special nuclear materials.

h. The operation by it or by any public or private organization or individual of any facility within its territory engaged in the processing of any special nuclear materials, or of radioactive materials in substantial quantities.

i. The possession within its territory by it or by any public or private organization or individual of any substantial quantity of raw materials which might enter into the production of special nuclear materials and which have been removed from their state of deposit in nature; or of any special nuclear materials; or of any substantial quantity of radioactive materials.

j. The construction or operation by it or by any public or private organization or individual of any facility within its territory in which it is intended to use any special nuclear materials, or substantial quantities of radioactive materials, for research, industrial, commercial or other non-military purposes or in which such materials are actually being used.

k. The operation by it or by any public or private organization or individual of any facility within its territory engaged in the production of auxiliary materials which might be employed in the process of making special nuclear materials or nuclear weapons, such as graphite, heavy water, beryllium, lithium and cobalt.

l. The conduct by it or by any public or private organization or individual of any research or developmental activity within its territory relating to the use for peaceful purposes of nuclear energy.

m. The possession or operation by it or by any one of its nationals, whether individuals or organizations, of any rockets, satellites or spacecraft.

n. The construction or operation by it or by any public or private organization or individual of any facility within its territory engaged in the production of rockets, satellites or spacecraft, or of tools for such production; or in the launching of rockets, satellites or spacecraft.

o. The conduct by it or by any public or private organization or individual of any other activity within its territory which the General Assembly has determined to be of sufficient importance for the maintenance of complete disarmament as to require a special license.

2. Every public or private organization or individual conducting or wishing to conduct any activity required to be licensed under paragraph 1 of this Article shall so inform the government of the nation within whose territory such activity is being or would be conducted, with the request that the government of such nation shall obtain the necessary license on his or its behalf; and no such public or private organization or individual shall conduct any such activity until the required license has been obtained.

3. No nation shall conduct or allow the conduct of any activity mentioned in paragraph 1 of this Article unless the required license has first been obtained.

4. Such licenses shall be issued or refused in accordance with standards and procedures to be established by regulations to be adopted by the General Assembly after receiving a report on the subject from the In-

spection Commission and the recommendations of the Executive Council as to such report. In adopting such regulations the Assembly shall be guided by the principle that their purpose is to aid in providing assurance that none of the activities required to be licensed shall be conducted in a manner endangering the maintenance of complete disarmament.

5. If the Inspector-General should refuse to grant a license, the nation making the application, or the public or private organization or individual on whose behalf the application was made, shall have the right to appeal to the Inspection Commission, and the right to appeal from a decision of the Commission to the United Nations regional court within the jurisdiction of which is included the territory of the nation which made the application in question. The Inspector-General shall have the right to appeal from a decision of the regional court to the International Court of Justice; and the nation which made the application in question shall have the same right of appeal, on its own behalf or on behalf of the public or private organization or individual for whom it made the application. The public or private organization or the individual on whose behalf the application was made shall have the right to appeal from a decision of the regional court to the International Court of Justice to the extent permitted by the laws enacted by the General Assembly pursuant to Part D of Annex III. In case of any such appeal to the International Court of Justice, the decision of that Court shall be final.

Comment. Effective supervision of potentially dangerous activities which, if misused, could lead to clandestine rearmament, can be considerably aided by means of a thorough licensing system. While the licenses would be issued by the United Nations Inspection Service, the conception is that the respective national governments should have the primary responsibility for seeing to it that all the activities within their territories requiring a license are duly licensed.

For such a system, there are several distinct advantages: (a) the United Nations would thus be relieved from the tremendous administrative task of dealing directly with the many thousands of applicants for licenses; (b) since this task would be assumed by the governments of the respective nations, opposition on the ground of excessive intrusion by a supranational authority would be reduced; (c) the respective national governments, through having the obligation to see to it that licenses are actually obtained for all the activities within their territories requiring a license, would normally have a greater sense of moral responsibility for the effective supervision of potentially dangerous activities than they would have if the licensing system were administered solely by an outside authority; and (d) by imposing this duty upon the respective national governments, any nation neglecting to see to it that organizations or individuals engaged in activities requiring licenses actually obtain them would itself be subject to rebuke or sanctions in addition to the sanctions which could be imposed upon the organizations or individuals failing to conform to the licensing requirements.

On the other hand, the licensing system would also impose direct responsibility for operating without a license upon the organizations and individuals required to be licensed, so that they could be directly penalized for failure to comply with the licensing system.

Still further, such a licensing system would facilitate the administrative task of inspection by defining the class of activities deemed to be potentially most dangerous and therefore subject to a more rigid system of inspection than other activities whose operation would be potentially less dangerous.

The main activities subject to license are defined in this Article 16 itself, and the General Assembly is empowered to issue regulations defining the standards and procedure for the issuance of licenses. To prevent any abuse of this licensing power, a nation should have the right of appeal either on its own behalf or on behalf of the applicant against any refusal of the Inspector-General to grant a license. Such an appeal would first be made to the Inspection Commission from whose decision an appeal could be made to the nearest United Nations regional court (to be established under Part D of Annex III). Provision is also made for a final appeal by either side to the International Court of Justice. Similar rights of appeal would also be granted to any organization or individual on whose behalf a nation has made the application, except that the final right of appeal to the International Court of Justice could be restricted by the General Assembly to cases of importance (as authorized by paragraph 7 of Part D of Annex III).

Under this Article 16 it would be a violation of law to conduct any activity requiring a license without such license. And in case of discovery by the United Nations Inspection Service or otherwise that such an activity is being conducted without a license, enforcement action is provided for, pursuant to Chapter VIII of this Annex, against the delinquent person and the responsible nation.

Article 17

1. The United Nations Inspection Service shall verify the compliance by every nation with the prohibitions contained in Article 14 of this Annex, the accuracy and completeness of the information required to be furnished by every nation under Article 15 of this Annex and the observance by every nation of the licensing requirements of Article 16 of this Annex. This verification shall be accomplished by Inspectors of the Inspection Service acting with the authority and subject to the limitations provided for in Articles 18 to 24 of this Annex.

2. The Inspector-General shall submit monthly reports to the Inspection Commission as to the progress of the verifications, and such special reports as the Inspector-General or the Inspection Commission may deem necessary. If the Inspector-General reports that any nation has violated the provisions of Article 14 of this Annex, or that any nation has failed to furnish complete and accurate information pursuant to Article 15 of this Annex, or that any nation is not observing the licensing

requirements of Article 16 of this Annex, or that any nation has placed any obstacle in the way of verification by the Inspection Service, the Commission shall consider what measures shall be taken. If the Commission determines that any such violation, failure, nonobservance or obstacle is serious, it shall immediately present a special report on the subject to the Executive Council.

In addition to such special reports, if any, the Inspection Commission shall make an annual report to the Executive Council as to the results of the verifications, which report shall include the opinion of the Commission as to whether the over-all results have been reasonably satisfactory and such proposals for the enactment of new regulations or other action as the Commission deems desirable in the light of its experience.

3. The Executive Council shall forthwith consider all reports of the Inspection Commission; and if the Commission has determined that there has been a serious violation of the prohibitions contained in Article 14 of this Annex, or a serious failure to furnish information pursuant to Article 15 of this Annex, or a serious nonobservance of the licensing requirements of Article 16 of this Annex, or that any nation has placed any serious obstacle in the way of verification by the Inspection Service, the Council shall consider what measures shall be taken. If the Executive Council accepts the conclusion of the Inspection Commission that any such violation, deficiency, nonobservance or obstacle is serious, the Council shall take such interim action as it is authorized to take pursuant to Article 34 of this Annex and shall immediately present a special report on the subject to the General Assembly for possible action by it under that Article.

In addition to such special reports, if any, the Executive Council shall make an annual report to the General Assembly, which report shall include the conclusions of the Council as to the observance of the provisions of this Annex with respect to complete disarmament and as to the adequacy of the verification thereof.

4. If the Executive Council has presented a special report to the General Assembly informing it that there has been a serious violation of the prohibitions contained in Article 14 of this Annex, or a serious failure to furnish information pursuant to Article 15 of this Annex, or a serious nonobservance of the licensing requirements of Article 16 of this Annex, or that any nation has placed a serious obstacle in the way of verification by the Inspection Service, the Assembly shall deal with the matter as soon as possible and shall have authority to take such action under Article 34 of this Annex as it may deem necessary. If the General Assembly is not then in session, a special session thereof shall be convoked immediately.

The annual reports of the Executive Council shall be considered by the General Assembly at its regular annual sessions, and the Assembly may on the basis thereof issue such directions to the Council, and through it to the Inspection Commission, as the Assembly deems necessary.

Comment. The task of verifying whether all the nations are complying with their obligations as to the maintenance of national disarmament after it has been completed (like the task of verifying the stages of the disarmament process itself under Articles 7 and 12 of this Annex), would be in the hands of the United Nations Inspection Service. While the former task would be only temporary, the task under this Article 17 would be permanent, to be performed year after year. The Inspection Service would be required to verify constantly that no prohibited activities are conducted anywhere in the world; that activities subject to license are not conducted without a license; and that all the information required to be furnished by nations and other licensees is actually furnished and is correct.

A chain of reports is provided for in order to ensure constant supervision of the whole inspection process. The Inspector-General would have to report monthly to the Inspection Commission, which in turn would report annually to the Executive Council. In turn, the Executive Council would make an annual report to the General Assembly, which would be required to consider the report at its regular annual session. In addition, the Assembly's Standing Committee on the Peace Enforcement Agencies, to be established under Article 22 of the revised Charter, would keep a permanent watch over the operation of the inspection system, and would give to the Assembly independent appraisals of the performance of the Inspection Service. If the Standing Committee should discover evidence of a dangerous evasion of the disarmament provisions, or a serious abuse by the Inspection Service of its powers, or any collusion between members of the Service and any nation or any person or organization operating a facility subject to license, it would have authority to have the Assembly called into special session under Article 20 of the revised Charter (see Article 4 of this Annex). The Assembly would then have to consider the matter forthwith and could take such enforcement action, pursuant to Article 34 of this Annex, as it might deem necessary.

On the other hand, if the Inspection Service should uncover a violation with respect to the maintenance of complete disarmament, and if the Inspection Commission deemed such a violation serious, the Commission would immediately present a special report to the Executive Council. The Council, if it agreed that the violation was serious, would take the necessary interim measures and would immediately submit the question to the General Assembly, which if not then in session, would be specially convoked for that purpose. The Assembly in such a case would have full authority to order enforcement action under Chapter VII of the revised Charter, including action by the United Nations Peace Force (Article 34 of this Annex).

❊ ❊ ❊

In summary, it will be seen that the purpose of the above Chapter III (Articles 13-17) is to provide an extremely comprehensive system to ensure

261

that once national armaments have actually been eliminated they will so remain. When the successful abolition of national armaments is an accomplished fact and confidence grows in the permanence of complete disarmament, the fears and tensions of the former regime of competitive armaments could be expected to abate.

CHAPTER IV

THE INSPECTION PROCESS — AUTHORITY AND LIMITATIONS

Article 18

1. With the authority and subject to the limitations provided for in this Chapter, the United Nations Inspection Service shall have direct responsibility for and direct supervision over the fulfillment by all the nations and all individuals of their obligations under this Annex with respect to all phases of disarmament, including the arms census, the arms truce, the successive annual reductions during the actual disarmament stage and the subsequent maintenance of complete disarmament.

2. Upon the recommendation of the Executive Council or upon its own initiative, the General Assembly shall adopt such laws and regulations as it may deem necessary to ensure the efficacy of the United Nations inspection system and at the same time to protect nations and individuals against any abuses. Such laws and regulations shall embody the principles stated in the following Articles of this Chapter.

3. The General Assembly shall enact such laws as it may deem necessary to punish violations by members of the Inspection Service of the laws and regulations which have been adopted under paragraph 2 of this Article.

Comment. Both the effective execution of the disarmament plan and the successful maintenance of complete disarmament, once achieved, would largely depend upon the impartiality and efficiency of the United Nations Inspection Service. In respect of impartiality, Article 4 of this Annex establishes the necessary safeguards. It provides, for instance, various limitations upon the number of nationals of any nation who may serve in the Inspection Service and ensures that the Inspection Commission will not be dominated by the larger nations. This Chapter IV supplements those provisions by careful regulation of the actual conduct of the inspection process. On the one hand, it defines the powers which may be exercised by the members of the Inspection Service; on the other hand, it protects national and private interests against possible abuse of power by the Service.

Only a few guiding principles concerning the inspection process should be stated in this Chapter IV itself. The necessarily detailed regulations governing this process would be adopted by the competent organs of the United Nations. Paragraph 2 of this Article 18 would empower the General Assembly to enact laws and regulations on the subject, either on its own initiative or

263

upon the recommendation of the Executive Council. Such regulations would presumably delegate to the Council the power to implement them and allow the Inspection Commission to issue such additional administrative instructions as it might deem necessary.

In respect of possible derelictions of duty by members of the Inspection Service—such as abuse of authority or corruption—contrary to laws or regulations adopted by the General Assembly, the Assembly would be empowered by paragraph 3 of this Article to impose appropriate penalties. The trial of any such offenses would, pursuant to Part D of Annex III, be in the regional courts of the United Nations. On the other hand, offenses which members of the Inspection Service might commit against the domestic law of the respective nations would be triable in the courts of those nations, except that a member of the Service would be entitled to limited immunity under Annex VI with respect to his official acts.

It should be clearly understood that the principles stated in this Chapter IV and in the regulations enacted thereunder apply to all phases of disarmament, not only to the arms census, the arms truce and the process of actual disarmament, but also to the maintenance of complete disarmament once it has been accomplished.

Chapters II and III of this Annex prescribe in a general manner the functions to be performed by the Inspection Service during these various phases, while Chapter IV specifies more precisely how these functions are to be exercised.

Article 19

1. The Inspectors of the United Nations Inspection Service shall have complete freedom of entry into, movement within and egress from the territory of every nation. They shall have the right to use all communication and transportation facilities available within each nation to the extent necessary for the effective exercise of their functions. Their United Nations *laissez-passer* shall be accepted as valid travel documents by the authorities of all nations, and, with respect to them, such authorities shall either dispense with visas or issue long-term visas without charge.

2. If a nation because of some special circumstances objects to the presence in its territory of a particular Inspector, the Inspector-General, if he finds the complaint justified, shall recall such Inspector from that territory as soon as possible. If the Inspector-General finds the complaint unjustified, the objecting nation may appeal to the Inspection Commission, which shall decide whether the Inspector shall be recalled.

3. In conducting inspections, the Inspectors shall have due regard for all rights of personal privacy and private property, taking into consideration the laws and customs of the respective nations to the fullest extent consistent with the effective discharge of their duties.

4. Neither the United Nations nor its Inspectors nor other personnel shall use or disclose any confidential or private information which is

acquired in the course of inspection and which is unrelated to the accomplishment and maintenance of disarmament.

5. The United Nations shall be liable to pay just compensation for any damage unnecessarily caused by its Inspectors or other personnel of the Inspection Service in the exercise of their functions. The conditions of such liability and the procedures for fixing the amount of such damages shall be determined by the General Assembly.

Comment. Since the members of the United Nations Inspection Service should have complete freedom of movement, no restrictions should be put on their right to enter the territory of any nation, to travel therein and to leave it. Moreover, since ordinary immigration restrictions could not be applied to them, they should be entitled to enter any nation on the basis of their special travel documents (the United Nations *laissez-passer*). They should not be required to obtain visas for each trip, and arrangements should be made for exempting them from visas or for granting them in advance long-term visas to all nations of the world. It is also important that the Inspectors shall have the right to use all means of communication and transportation available in the nation under inspection and shall be free to communicate with their headquarters, without any interference or censorship.

It is possible, however, that a nation might have objections to the presence within its territory of a particular Inspector. If, for instance, an Inspector should publish a statement criticizing in immoderate language the government or people of a nation on grounds unrelated to the control of disarmament, that nation might wish to ask his recall as soon as possible. But care must be taken to prevent a sabotaging of the inspection process through the untimely recall of too many Inspectors, and consequently the Inspector-General would be authorized to accede to a request for recall only if he deems it justified by the facts of the case. If, however, the Inspector-General should disagree with a nation as to the recall of a particular Inspector, the aggrieved nation would have the right to appeal to the Inspection Commission.

In the conduct of inspections, the Inspectors would, of course, be required to observe the limitations imposed by this Annex and the regulations enacted thereunder. In particular, they would be required to pay due respect to all rights of personal privacy and private property, taking into consideration the laws and customs of the nations in which they are working in so far as consistent with the efficient discharge of their duties. Other guarantees against abuses by personnel of the United Nations are provided for in the proposed Bill of Rights, set forth in Annex VII. Moreover, as provided in Article 18 of this Annex, the Inspectors would be subject to penalties imposed by regional courts of the United Nations for derelictions in connection with their duties.

Special precautions are needed to prevent disclosure by the United Nations or its Inspectors and other personnel of any confidential or private information acquired through the inspection process. Only if such information is closely related to the accomplishment or maintenance of disarmament would it be permissible to disclose it in an official document of the United Nations or during the meetings of one of the organs of the United Nations. No other information, e.g., relating to new industrial processes, could be legally disclosed under any circumstances, and special penalties would presumably be imposed for a violation of this injunction.

If some property or interests of a nation or public or private organization or individual should be unnecessarily damaged in the course of an inspection or in consequence of the improper conduct of an Inspector or other personnel, the United Nations should be liable to pay just compensation. It would be the function of the General Assembly to enact appropriate laws defining the conditions of such liability and the procedures to determine the amount of compensation due to the injured entity or person.

Article 20

1. During the preparatory stage and the actual disarmament stage and until the establishment of the licensing system provided for in Article 16 of this Annex, all installations, plants, laboratories and other facilities and places of every description which have been reported in the arms census provided for in Article 5 of this Annex, shall be completely open to inspection by United Nations Inspectors who shall be entitled to enter them without hindrance at any time upon presentation of their credentials, in order to verify the accuracy and completeness of the information furnished by the respective nations pursuant to Article 5 of this Annex, the observance of the arms truce inaugurated under Article 6 of this Annex and the execution of the plan for complete disarmament pursuant to Articles 10 to 12 of this Annex.

2. After the establishment of the licensing system provided for by Article 16 of this Annex, all facilities, establishments and places in which activities licensed under that Article are conducted, shall be completely open to inspection by United Nations Inspectors who shall be entitled to enter them without hindrance at any time upon presentation of their credentials, in order to ascertain whether the state of complete disarmament provided for in Chapter III of this Annex is being fully maintained.

3. In addition, periodic inspections of the following shall, subject to the limitations provided in Article 21 of this Annex, be conducted by United Nations Inspectors:

a. Of all ships and airplanes capable of adaptation to military use in order to make sure that they do not contain any feature which would facilitate their adaptation to military purposes.

b. Of all shipyards and airplane plants in order to make sure that they do not construct any ship or airplane containing any feature which would facilitate the adaptation of such ship or airplane to military purposes.

c. Of all heavy industry plants (including all plants of the tool-manufacturing industry) which are capable of easy adaptation to the production of armaments of any description or of tools for such production, in order to make sure that they have not been actually adapted to such production.

d. Of all areas containing substantial deposits of raw materials which might enter into the production of special nuclear materials.

The Executive Council shall determine from time to time how often such periodic inspections are to be conducted. Within the limits thus determined, the United Nations Inspection Service may conduct the periodic inspections at any time of its own choosing.

4. The United Nations Inspectors shall have authority:

a. To examine central and local, governmental and private records relating to any licensed activity or any facility, establishment or area which is subject to periodic United Nations inspection, including records relating to personnel, financing, consumption of raw materials and of heat and electricity, and distribution of finished products.

b. To check the consistency of these records with the situation on the spot.

c. To question central and local governmental officials, and the managers and employees of any facility or establishment subject to inspection, concerning any matter relevant to compliance with this Annex.

5. Any person having any information concerning any violation of this Annex or of any law or regulation enacted thereunder shall immediately report all such information to the United Nations Inspection Service. The General Assembly shall enact regulations governing the granting of rewards to persons supplying the Inspection Service with such information, and the provision of asylum to them and their families.

6. No nation shall penalize directly or indirectly any person or public or private organization supplying information to the United Nations with respect to any violation of this Annex.

Comment. This Article envisages two basic types of inspection: (1) inspection at any time of facilities, establishments and places in which are conducted activities with especially dangerous potentials; and (2) periodic inspection of certain types of airplanes and ships, and of certain other facilities and areas. It should here be noted that the United Nations Inspection Service would also be entitled, under Article 22 of this Annex and subject to its limitations, to conduct inspections by aerial surveys; and under Article 21 of this Annex and subject to its limitations, to conduct special inspections of facilities and places not ordinarily subject to inspection, either by consent or upon a showing to a United Nations regional court of reasonable cause to believe or suspect a violation of this Annex.

During the preparatory stage and the actual disarmament stage (a twelve-year period unless shortened or lengthened), it seems very necessary that the United Nations inspection system shall extend broadly to all those installations, facilities and activities which would have been reported in the arms census called for by Article 5 of this Annex. This is important because the carrying out of the disarmament process can only proceed on the basis of confidence that every nation is fully complying with the step-by-step requirements; and to provide that confidence, it is essential that the inspection be unhindered and thorough. On the other hand, when the process of actual disarmament has been completed, so that no national military forces or arms-producing facilities would any longer exist, it would be possible with safety somewhat to restrict the scope of the inspections.

Accordingly, paragraph 1 of this Article gives broad authority during the twelve-year period of the disarmament process itself to inspect at will each and every installation, facility, etc. that has been reported in the arms census; while after the actual disarmament stage has been completed and when the licensing system has been set up, the unrestricted inspection process would be limited by paragraph 2 to licensed activities.

With regard to all the places thus made subject to unhindered inspection at will, Inspectors would have the right to enter merely upon presentation of credentials. A refusal to permit entry by an Inspector into any such place could be considered a serious violation of the provisions of this Annex and might even lead to enforcement measures under Chapter VIII of this Annex.

Where the danger of evasion is less serious, periodic inspections should suffice. The Executive Council would determine within what periods (e.g., annually, semi-annually or quarterly) such periodic inspections shall be conducted, taking into account, on the one hand, the necessity of preventing violations and, on the other hand, the need to protect the establishments subject to inspection against too frequent interference with their day-to-day operations. After the Council has decided in general terms as to the frequency of periodical inspections for various types of facilities, the Inspection Service could order an inspection of a particular facility at any time within the permitted limits.

The Inspectors should be permitted not only to enter a facility but also to examine its records and to check their consistency with the situation on the spot. They should be given access also to governmental records, e.g., in order to make certain that no armaments expenditures are hidden under some other name in a nation's budget. Since also some of the facilities producing special nuclear materials would require large amounts of heat and electricity, the Inspectors should be allowed to check consumption records of heat and electricity and to investigate all facilities consuming them in more than ordinary amounts. They should have the right to question both governmental officials and the management and personnel of any plant as to any possible violations; and for the protection of anyone giving information, it is proposed in paragraph 5 to prohibit the imposition of any penalty by reason of any such cooperation in the enforcement of disarmament. Authority is also given to provide rewards to persons supplying the Inspection Service with information relative to the violation of any disarmament provisions and, if necessary, to make arrangements for safe asylum in another country for informants and their families.

Article 21

1. Before each periodic inspection under Article 20 of this Annex, the United Nations Inspection Service shall give notice to the nation concerned, and that nation may, if it so desires, or shall, if requested by the Inspection Service, send a liaison representative (or several of them, if agreed to or requested by the Inspection Service) to accompany and assist the Inspectors. The liaison representatives shall see to it that the Inspectors receive the cooperation of national officials and other persons concerned, and that they be granted such freedom of movement and access as is necessary for the proper supervision of the execution of this Annex or of the regulations enacted thereunder by the General Assembly. In no case shall the liaison representatives delay or restrict, or permit other nationals to delay or restrict, the Inspectors in the prompt, safe and efficient performance of their functions; but if a liaison representative considers that an act about to be performed by an Inspector is not authorized by this Annex or the laws or regulations enacted thereunder, he may call the matter to the attention of his government which may request the United Nations regional court within the jurisdiction of which is included the place where the act complained of is to be performed to issue an injunction.

2. Periodic inspections shall ordinarily be conducted only after reasonable notice. But in exceptional circumstances, where the purpose of the inspection might be defeated through removal or concealment or otherwise if advance notice were given, the United Nations Inspection Service may conduct the inspection without notice, provided that it has first obtained a special authorization from the United Nations regional court within the jurisdiction of which is included the place where the inspection is to be conducted. Such an authorization may require the Inspection Service to invite a liaison representative of the nation concerned to accompany the Inspectors.

3. Inspection of places, facilities or records other than those specifically made subject to inspection by this Chapter may be conducted with the written approval of a duly authorized national official in the case of publicly owned or controlled places and facilities, or, in the case of privately owned places and facilities, with the consent of the management thereof or, if such consent be withheld, with the written approval of a duly authorized national official. The requirements of paragraph 1 of this Article with respect to notice and liaison representatives shall apply also to inspections under this paragraph. In exceptional circumstances, however, a special authorization may be obtained by the United Nations Inspection Service from the United Nations regional court within the jurisdiction of which is included the place where the inspection is to be conducted to conduct such an inspection without approval or consent or notice to anyone. Such an authorization may require the Inspection

269

Service to invite a liaison representative of the nation concerned to accompany the Inspectors.

4. Special authorizations for the exceptional inspections provided for in paragraphs 2 and 3 of this Article shall be issued by a United Nations regional court only when the United Nations Inspection Service shows to the court reasonable cause to believe or suspect that there exists within the areas or premises sought to be entered and inspected:

a. any activity which should have been reported by a nation in its reply to the arms-census questionnaire provided for by Article 5 of this Annex, but which has not been so reported;

b. any activity prohibited by this Annex;

c. any material the possession of which by nations or persons is prohibited under this Annex;

d. any activity requiring a license under this Annex, but with respect to which no license has been obtained;

e. any material the possession of which is required to be licensed under this Annex, but with respect to which no license has been obtained;

f. any evidence that a violation of this Annex or of any law or regulation adopted thereunder has occurred, is occurring or is threatened.

5. The special authorization shall describe, so far as practicable, the area or premises authorized to be entered and inspected, and shall specify the manner in which the inspection shall be conducted. It may authorize the United Nations Inspectors to take temporary custody of property which they believe to be possessed by any nation or person in violation of this Annex or of any law or regulation adopted thereunder.

Comment. While there should be no limit on inspection of licensed facilities, it seems desirable to provide special guarantees against abuses of the inspection process in relation to: (a) the inspection of facilities subject only to periodic inspection; and (b) the inspection of places which are not ordinarily subject to inspection at all. Somewhat different guarantees are appropriate in these two types of situations.

Periodic inspections should usually be preceded by an adequate notice to the nation concerned, specifying the place and time of the proposed inspection. If the nation thus notified so desires, or if the United Nations Inspection Service so requests, one or more liaison representatives appointed by that nation should accompany the Inspectors on their mission. The function of such liaison representatives would be a dual one. On the one hand, they would watch over the conduct of the Inspectors and be entitled to complain to appropriate organs of the United Nations if a particular Inspector should overstep the bounds of his authority. On the other hand, they would assist the Inspectors in the performance of their duties, facilitate their trips in unfamiliar surroundings, help in establishing contact with local officials and the management of the facility to be inspected, remove obstacles in the path of the inspection, and in general smooth out the difficulties inherent in the novel process of international inspection of national or private facilities. They would have to see to it that the Inspectors are granted all necessary freedom of movement and sufficient access to all places subject to inspection, and that the Inspectors are enabled to perform their functions safely and without delay or friction.

In no case would the liaison representatives be permitted to delay or restrict the progress of the inspection, and they would be duty bound to prevent other persons from delaying or restricting the activities of the Inspectors. If, however, a liaison representative believes that a particular act of an Inspector is not authorized by this Annex or the laws or regulations adopted thereunder, he would presumably point this out to the Inspector or his immediate superior. And if the Inspector should deem it necessary to perform that act despite such warning, the liaison representative could bring the matter to the attention of his government which might request the nearest United Nations regional court (to be established under Part D of Annex III) to issue an injunction. Until such an injunction was issued, the Inspector could continue his inspection; but if his action were found to be unauthorized by this Annex I, or the laws or regulations adopted thereunder, the United Nations would be liable for damages caused thereby (in accordance with paragraph 5 of Article 19 of this Annex). The regulations of the Inspection Service should provide also for the adequate discipline of Inspectors who take steps unauthorized by this Annex or any laws or regulations of the United Nations (see paragraph 3 of Article 18 of this Annex).

It is conceivable that, if advance notice is given to a nation concerned, a periodic inspection would not always guarantee the absence of a violation; for instance, if tools for making prohibited armaments could easily be removed from a heavy industry plant. In such a case an inspection without notice is provided for, on condition that the Inspector in charge of the desired inspection obtains a special authorization from the nearest United Nations regional court. A specially authorized inspection of this sort would be conducted not only without notice, but also without a liaison representative from the nation concerned, except when the regional court has made the authorization conditional upon an invitation for a liaison representative to accompany the Inspectors. For example, liaison representatives might be necessary to ensure the safety of the inspecting group, or to help it in obtaining access to a particular area or plant. To facilitate the assignment of a liaison representative in such emergency cases, each nation might be required by regulation to furnish to the Inspection Service at stated intervals a list with names and addresses of the liaison representatives designated by it and resident in the vicinity of the facilities subject to periodic inspection. Upon receiving a special authorization from the regional court, the Inspector in charge of the particular inspection would select one of the liaison representatives on the list and request him to accompany the inspecting group, without giving any warning to the facility to be inspected. The feasibility of such an arrangement would, however, depend to a large extent on restrictions that would need to be placed on the freedom of communication of the liaison representative thus selected; and in many instances it would doubtless be preferable for the regional court to authorize a special inspection of this sort without any accompanying liaison representative.

However extensive the system of licensing and of periodic inspection, an adequate inspection process cannot be limited solely to the places which are licensed or which are made subject to periodic inspection. Still other places must be inspected from time to time in order to ensure that prohibited activities are not conducted therein. Ordinarily inspections of this latter sort should take place only by consent of the management, or if such consent is refused, by permission of a properly authorized national official. In some cases national laws would doubtless provide for the issuance of such permits. If, however, such a consent or permission is not obtainable, or if a prior notice to the nation concerned is deemed inadvisable, the Inspector in charge of the particular inspection should be entitled to apply for a special authorization to the nearest United Nations regional court. As in the case of a specially authorized periodic inspection, the regional court could in such case also require that the inspecting group be accompanied by a liaison representative of the nation concerned.

In all such applications to a regional court, either for a periodic inspection without notice, or for an inspection of places or facilities not ordinarily subject to inspection, the applying Inspector would be required to satisfy the court that there is reasonable cause to suspect a violation. It is also proposed that the court, in any such authorization, shall describe, so far as practicable, the place to be inspected and shall specify the manner in which the inspection is to be conducted. The court could also authorize the Inspector in charge to take temporary custody of any property found in the place to be inspected when the mere possession of such property is prohibited, or when the Inspector believes it will be used for a prohibited purpose.

Article 22

1. The United Nations Inspection Service shall be entitled to conduct periodic aerial surveys to supplement other methods of inspection. Such periodic surveys shall be conducted in accordance with general regulations to be adopted by the General Assembly, after receiving a report on the subject from the Inspection Commission and the recommendations of the Executive Council as to such report. The Council shall determine from time to time how often such periodic surveys are to be conducted, provided that no more than three periodic surveys of any particular part of the territory of any nation shall be conducted in any year. Within the limits thus determined, the Inspection Service may conduct the periodic surveys at any time of its own choosing. Any nation concerned shall receive adequate notice of every periodic aerial survey, and shall have the right to send one observer on each survey flight.

2. In exceptional circumstances, when the Inspection Service deems an aerial survey advisable in addition to the periodic surveys permitted under paragraph 1 of this Article, or believes that the purpose of a

survey would be defeated if advance notice were given, the Inspection Service may conduct a survey without notice provided that it has first obtained a special authorization from the United Nations regional court within the jurisdiction of which is located the area to be surveyed. Such authorization shall, however, be granted only upon a showing to the court that there is reasonable cause to believe or suspect that there exists within the area to be surveyed an activity prohibited by this Annex or by any law or regulation adopted thereunder.

3. Copies of photographs taken during any aerial survey shall be furnished to the nation concerned upon its request. No such photographs may be made available to any other nation or published without the consent of the nation concerned, except that in so far as they may constitute evidence of a violation of this Annex or of any law or regulation adopted thereunder, they may be used as such evidence.

Comment. According to available scientific information, aerial surveys would constitute a useful method of supplementing other methods of inspection, since telltale signs of unauthorized activities could often be discovered from the air more easily than on the ground, and since an aerial survey permits a quick survey of a large area at a relatively small expense and with the use of only a few highly qualified persons.

Two types of aerial survey are envisaged by this Article: periodic aerial surveys to be conducted on a routine basis; and special surveys to be conducted in exceptional circumstances.

While routine surveys should be conducted as often as necessary, nations should at the same time be protected against constant flights by United Nations survey planes over the length and breadth of their territories. This Article 22 therefore establishes a limit on the annual number of periodic survey flights by providing that no more than three such surveys shall be conducted in any year with respect to any particular area. Subject to this limitation, the Executive Council would determine from time to time how often these periodic aerial surveys shall be conducted; it might, for instance, determine that in a particular year only one complete survey is necessary, while in another year it might wish to utilize this power of inspection to the full by authorizing three complete surveys. The programming of each periodic survey would be left to the Inspection Service, but it might be expected that regulations enacted by the General Assembly would require the Inspection Service to treat all nations equally, without any discrimination as to the length and quality of surveys, except as might be justified by the respective sizes of their territories and the configuration of the terrain.

Ordinarily, the nation concerned would receive an adequate notice of each periodic survey flight and would be entitled to send an observer on it. But a United Nations regional court would, on request of the Inspection Service, have the power to authorize a flight without notice, if there were reason to believe that such a flight would help to locate an unauthorized activity or facility. Such special surveys would not be considered as substitutes for the routine periodic surveys, but might be conducted apart from and in addition to the regular surveys authorized for a particular year. The constitutional limitation of three surveys per year would not apply to these special surveys.

Proper safeguards are necessary with respect to photographs taken during an aerial survey. This Article, therefore, provides that no such photographs shall be published or made available to any other nation without the consent of the nation concerned, except when the photographs constitute evidence of a violation of this Annex or of a law or regulation adopted thereunder. It is also provided that copies of all photographs taken must be furnished to the nation concerned upon its request. This requirement would, of course, in no way limit the right of the Inspection Service on its own motion to bring any photographs to the attention of the nation concerned, pointing out any places which appear to require further investigation on the spot; nor would it limit the Inspection Service's right to conduct any such investigation directly, subject, however, to the limitations contained in this Chapter.

Article 23

1. The General Assembly may, after receiving proposals on the subject from the Inspection Commission and the recommendations of the Executive Council as to such proposals, prescribe that, in addition to the general information supplied by all the nations pursuant to the provisions of this Annex, any public or private organization or individual licensed under Article 16 of this Annex shall supply to the Inspector-General, pursuant to a questionnaire furnished by him, such special information as may in the opinion of the Inspector-General facilitate the conduct of inspections.

2. The General Assembly may, after receiving proposals on the subject from the Inspection Commission and the recommendations of the Executive Council as to such proposals, prescribe that any public or private organization or individual licensed under Article 16 of this Annex shall adopt such special accounting procedures approved by the Inspector-General as may in the opinion of the Inspector-General facilitate the conduct of inspections.

3. The General Assembly may, after receiving joint proposals on the subject either from the Inspection Commission and the United Nations Nuclear Energy Commission to be established under Chapter V of this Annex, or joint proposals from the Inspection Commission and the Outer Space Commission to be established under Chapter VI of this Annex, and the recommendations of the Executive Council as to such proposals, adopt general regulations prescribing that United Nations Inspectors or special United Nations guards shall be stationed in any category of facilities or establishments reported under Article 5 of this Annex or licensed under Article 16 of this Annex, whenever the Assembly shall find that with respect to that category of facilities or establishments there is: special danger of any prohibited production of arms, weapons, ammuni-

tion, explosives or military equipment; or special danger of diversion of special nuclear materials or of materials which might enter into the production of such materials; or special danger of any prohibited production or launching of rockets, satellites or spacecraft. Any such regulations shall apply without discrimination to all facilities within a particular category wherever situated.

4. The General Assembly may, after receiving joint proposals on the subject either from the Inspection Commission and the Nuclear Energy Commission, or joint proposals from the Inspection Commission and the Outer Space Commission, and the recommendations of the Executive Council as to such proposals, enact regulations prescribing that with respect to certain categories of facilities or establishments required to be licensed under Article 16 of this Annex no license shall be granted, unless the nation or public or private organization or individual applying for such license shall enter into an agreement with the Inspection Service or the Nuclear Energy Authority or the Outer Space Agency, or with any combination of them, authorizing them to appoint properly qualified persons to take part in the management and operation of the facility or establishment in question. These regulations shall determine: the number and qualifications of the persons to be appointed under such agreements, it being understood that their number and qualifications may differ for various categories of facilities; the relations between the persons appointed by the United Nations and the management of the facility or establishment; the extent to which the persons thus appointed shall be subject to local regulations; the duties of such persons toward the United Nations; the compensation to be paid them by the United Nations and the method to be adopted for calculating the amount to be paid to the United Nations for their services by the facilities or establishments in which they are stationed. Any such regulations shall apply without discrimination to all facilities within a particular category wherever situated.

5. The General Assembly may, after receiving proposals on the subject from the Inspection Commission and from the Nuclear Energy Commission and the recommendations of the Executive Council as to such proposals, prescribe such special safeguards as it may deem necessary for:

a. The extracting or processing of raw materials which contain, besides other raw materials, any substantial amount of raw materials which might enter into the production of special nuclear materials.

b. The production, storage, transfer, transportation, import or export: of the light arms, ammunition and equipment, the production of which is permitted under Articles 8 and 14 of this Annex; of any raw materials which might enter into the production of special nuclear materials; of any special nuclear materials; and of any materials made artificially radioactive.

c. The production, storage, transfer, transportation, import or export of special equipment and materials (such as ball bearings, gyroscopes, mass spectrometers, diffusion barriers, gas centrifuges, electromagnetic isotope separation units, graphite, heavy water, beryllium, lithium, cobalt and rocket fuels) which might be employed in the making of armaments of any description, in making special nuclear materials or nuclear weapons, or in equipping rockets, satellites or spacecraft.

d. The operation of facilities having features of size and design or construction or operation which, in combination with their location or production or consumption of heat or electricity, make them peculiarly adaptable by conversion for the processing of special nuclear materials, or for the production of radioactive materials in substantial quantities.

6. The General Assembly shall, after receiving proposals on the subject from the Inspection Commission and from the Nuclear Energy Commission and the Outer Space Commission, and the recommendations of the Executive Council as to such proposals, define any terms used in this Annex which in the judgment of the Assembly require definition. In particular, it shall determine from time to time:

a. What weapons shall be considered as "nuclear, biological, chemical and other weapons of mass destruction"; what materials shall be considered as "special nuclear materials" or as "raw materials which might enter into the production of special nuclear materials"; and what facilities shall be considered as facilities "engaged in the production of arms, weapons, ammunition, explosives, or military equipment of any kind, or of tools for such production", or as facilities "engaged in the mining or processing of raw materials which might enter into the production of special nuclear materials", or as facilities "using any such materials for research, industrial, commercial or other nonmilitary purposes", or as facilities for the "production of rockets, satellites and spacecraft", or as facilities for the "launching of rockets, satellites and spacecraft."

b. What amounts of light arms, ammunition and equipment, or of radioactive materials, shall be considered as "substantial" quantities thereof.

c. What categories of ships or airplanes shall be considered as "containing any feature which would facilitate the adaptation of such ship or airplane to military purposes".

d. What categories of heavy industry shall be considered as "capable of easy adaptation to the production of armaments".

e. What plants shall be considered as plants "capable of easy adaptation to the production of chemical or biological weapons".

Comment. An underlying conception of this entire Annex is that the responsibility both for the accomplishment and the maintenance of complete disarmament shall, to the greatest possible extent, be assumed by the national governments of the respective nations. It is to this end that various provisions of this Annex define and regulate the obligations of national governments to see to it that all public and private organizations and individuals within their respective territories faithfully comply with the provisions of this Annex and the regulations enacted thereunder.

As a further safeguard, however, it is desirable that organizations and individuals shall have a direct obligation to the United Nations to observe the provisions of the disarmament plan. Accordingly, previous Articles of this Annex and this Article 23 authorize the General Assembly to enact special regulations which shall apply not only to the national governments themselves, but also directly to certain public or private organizations or individuals engaged in activities required to be licensed.

For example, by the terms of this Article 23 (paragraphs 1 and 2) the General Assembly is authorized to prescribe that operators of any facilities licensed under Article 16 of this Annex shall furnish certain data to the Inspector-General and shall adopt special accounting procedures needed to facilitate the conduct of inspections.

This Article further provides (paragraph 3) that when the General Assembly finds that there is special danger of illegal production in any category of facilities licensed under Article 16 of this Annex, or of the diversion of potentially dangerous materials therefrom, it may provide that Inspectors, or especially qualified guards, be regularly stationed in such places. In order, however, that these extra precautions shall not be applied in a discriminatory manner as between particular countries, provision is made that any such special measures must apply equally to all facilities, wherever situated, within the particular category as to which the General Assembly deems the special safeguards necessary.

The various careful safeguards envisaged in this Annex should be sufficient to provide every reasonable assurance against clandestine rearmament, except that still further precautions ought to be taken with respect to some facilities with especially dangerous potentials, such as those engaged in the production or launching of rockets, satellites or spacecraft, or in the actual processing or utilization of the "special nuclear materials" suitable for nuclear weapons. To the latter group belong, in particular, most of the facilities engaged: in the treatment or refining of raw materials which might enter into the production of "special nuclear materials"; or in the production of "special nuclear materials" themselves, or of radioactive materials in substantial quantities; or in the use of such materials for research, industrial or other nonmilitary purposes. It is not enough to require that these especially dangerous facilities must be operated under license and be open to constant inspection. Neither is it sufficient to assign to such facilities special guards or permanent Inspectors. In some, if not all of such facilities, a still further safeguard is advisable. It is proposed, therefore, to institute in these particular facilities an additional system of supervision by specially qualified persons actually participating in the operation and management of the facilities on various levels. A nation or a public or private organization or individual wishing to operate a facility of this especially dangerous character would not be given the necessary license except under an agreement with the United Nations Inspection Service or the United Nations Nuclear Energy Authority, or the United Nations Outer Space Agency, or with any combination of them, authorizing it or them to appoint as many persons as the Inspection Commission or the Nuclear Energy Commission or the Outer Space Commission deems necessary to the managerial and operational staff of the facility in question. Again, it is important not to discriminate between facilities situated in different countries, although it may be necessary to adopt different rules for different types of facilities or for facilities of different size. While some measure of discretion must be left to the Inspection Commission, the Nuclear Energy Commission and the Outer Space Commission, proper uniformity would be provided by the detailed regulations on this subject to be adopted by the General Assembly under paragraph 4 of this Article.

These regulations might provide, for instance, that one or more persons appointed by the Inspection Commission, or by the Nuclear Energy Commission or the Outer Space Commission shall be permitted to take part in the meetings of the board of directors or other group responsible for the conduct of the principal activities of the particular potentially dangerous facility. While such persons should be permitted to participate, on a footing of equality, in the meetings of such a board or group, and should be entitled to receive or have access to all the information available to the other members thereof, it does not seem necessary to give them a veto over the decisions of the board or group, or even to permit them to take part in voting thereon. They should be entitled, however, to participate in the discussions of such a board or group, in order to be able to warn the other members thereof that some particular decision or activity would or might be incompatible with the disarmament regulations of the United Nations, and to report to the Inspector-General and the Nuclear Energy Commission or the Outer Space Commission, any such decision or activity.

An agreement of this sort with respect to a potentially dangerous facility might also authorize properly qualified members of the Inspection Service, or of the Nuclear Energy Authority's or the Outer Space Agency's staff to participate in the actual operation of the facility, whenever the Inspection Commission or the Nuclear Energy Commission or the Outer Space Commission deemed it necessary. Thus a scientist might be assigned to assist in the research conducted in the facility, an engineer might take part in the construction of a new atomic reactor or a new spacecraft, and an accountant might be put in charge of an especially important accounting division of the facility. Once a member of the Inspection Service, or of the staff of the Nuclear Energy Authority or the Outer Space Agency, was appointed to the staff of such a facility, he should be treated as one of its staff and should have corresponding rights and obligations, except when the special agreement with the Inspection Commission, or with the Nuclear Energy Commission or the Outer Space Commission, establishes some necessary difference, e.g., by according him access to records and to parts of the facility which are not accessible to other employees. These United Nations members of the staff would also have the additional obligation to present periodic and, when necessary, emergency reports to the Inspector-General, and to the Nuclear Energy Commission or the Outer Space Commission, and—as persons familiar with local conditions—

to assist the regular United Nations Inspectors in the inspection of the facility in which they are working. To ensure necessary independence for members of the Inspection Service or the personnel of the Nuclear Energy Authority or the Outer Space Agency assigned to a facility, it should be provided that they will continue to be paid by the United Nations, although it seems proper that the owners of the facility shall recompense the United Nations for the actual value of their services.

The General Assembly should also have authority to prescribe safeguards concerning various aspects of the production, storage, transfer, transportation, import and export of some particular kinds (enumerated in paragraph 5 of this Article 23) of potentially dangerous materials. On the basis of experience, it may be necessary to devise new methods of indirect supervision of various potentially dangerous activities in order to ensure the efficiency of the inspection process and the fulfillment by all authorities and persons concerned of their obligations under this Annex. As with all the other safeguards of this Annex, the purpose is to provide as sure a guarantee as possible that any violation of the provisions of the Annex will be detected at an early stage and remedied before assuming too dangerous proportions.

The final paragraph of this Article 23 authorizes the General Assembly to define from time to time certain key terms used in this Chapter and in other parts of the Annex. The most important is the power to define what weapons should be considered to be "nuclear weapons" or "other weapons of mass destruction", and what materials should be considered to be "special nuclear materials". While at present "special nuclear materials" are limited to those containing uranium, plutonium or thorium, it may be necessary, with the progress of nuclear science, to broaden the definition to include other important materials. In this connection it may be noted that the Protocol of the Western European Union on control of armaments, signed at Paris on 23 October 1954, defines "atomic weapons" as follows:

"(a) An atomic weapon is defined as any weapon which contains, or is designed to contain or utilize nuclear fuel or radioactive isotopes and which, by explosion or other uncontrolled nuclear transformation of the nuclear fuel, or by radioactivity of the nuclear fuel or radioactive isotopes, is capable of mass destruction, mass injury or mass poisoning.

"(b) Furthermore, any part, device, assembly or material especially designed for, or primarily useful in, any weapon as set forth under paragraph (a), shall be deemed to be an atomic weapon.

"(c) Nuclear fuel as used in the preceding definition includes plutonium, Uranium 233, Uranium 235 (including Uranium 235 contained in Uranium enriched to over 2.1 per cent by weight of Uranium 235) and any other material capable of releasing substantial quantities of atomic energy through nuclear fission or fusion or other nuclear reaction of the material. The foregoing materials shall be considered to be nuclear fuel regardless of the chemical or physical form in which they exist."

Article 24

Appropriate measures pursuant to Article 34 of this Annex shall be taken if a nation shall try to prevent the conduct of an inspection or aerial survey especially authorized by a United Nations regional court or shall in any other manner place any serious obstacle in the way of the United Nations Inspectors.

Comment. It is obvious that if any nation should place serious obstacles in the way of the United Nations Inspectors, it would be a matter of great concern, requiring prompt measures. To this end, as will be seen in Article 34 of this Annex, the General Assembly would have wide powers to correct such a situation, and certain emergency measures could be taken by the Executive Council subject to the limitations of paragraph 2 of Article 39 of the revised Charter.

280

CHAPTER V

UNITED NATIONS NUCLEAR ENERGY AUTHORITY

General Comment. The proposed United Nations Nuclear Energy Authority is intended to fulfil a dual purpose: (a) to supplement the work of the United Nations Inspection Service by supervising certain critical stages in the production and distribution of special nuclear materials, i.e., of materials which might enter into the making of nuclear weapons, whether fissionable or fusionable (as defined pursuant to Articles 5 and 23 of this Annex); and (b) to promote to the greatest possible extent the utilization of nuclear energy for peaceful purposes.

In the latter respect, the Nuclear Energy Authority would exercise all the functions of the International Atomic Energy Agency, established in 1956; but the proposed Authority would have broader powers than the Agency and larger resources at its disposal.

The main functions of the International Atomic Energy Agency are:

(1) To encourage and assist research on the practical application of atomic (nuclear) energy for peaceful uses.

(2) To receive from member nations such "special fissionable" (nuclear) materials as the members of the Agency deem it "advisable" to transfer to the Agency.

(3) To establish and administer safeguards designed to ensure that "special fissionable" materials and equipment and information made available by the Agency will not be used "in such a way as to further any military purpose".

(4) To distribute the "special fissionable" materials in its possession in such a way as not to allow concentration of large amounts of such materials in any one country or region of the world.

(5) "To acquire or establish any facilities, plant and equipment useful in carrying out its authorized functions, whenever the facilities, plant and equipment otherwise available to it in the area concerned are inadequate or available only on terms it deems unsatisfactory."

(6) To allocate its resources in such a manner as to secure "the greatest general benefit in all areas of the world, bearing in mind the special needs of the under-developed areas in the world."

All these functions of the International Atomic Energy Agency are clearly compatible with the functions of the United Nations Nuclear Energy Authority as proposed in this Annex I.

It is believed, however, that the structure and powers of the Agency have much to be desired. For example, the Agency has supervisory powers only over activities within nations which receive "special fissionable" materials from it and not over activities within other nations which might be the principal producers of nuclear materials. Moreover, the Agency's principal organs—a General Conference of all the members and a large Board of Governors—would seem to be too cumbersome for effective direct supervision of the Agency's many functions; and since the relation of the Agency to the United Nations does not seem entirely clear it seems likely that the United Nations would not have sufficient control over the Agency's activities.

While it might be possible to amend the statute of the Agency in such a way as to empower it to exercise the additional functions necessary to ensure complete control of *all* nuclear materials, it seems wiser to establish a new authority of wider scope and directly within the framework of the revised Charter, and to transfer to that authority all the functions of the Agency.

Another possible alternative would be to continue the Agency within its authorized field of activity and to assign to a new United Nations authority only those functions which are so closely connected with the disarmament plan that they can best be carried out by an organ subject to direct United Nations control. It seems, however, that it would be more efficient and less wasteful of available personnel and financial resources if all responsibilities and functions with respect to the control of nuclear energy were assigned to a single authority rather than to overlapping and perhaps competing administrative units.

Accordingly, it is proposed that when the United Nations Nuclear Energy Authority comes into being, arrangements be made to merge the International Atomic Energy Agency with the new Authority and to transfer to the Authority all the personnel and assets of the Agency (see Article 26 of this Annex).

Article 25

1. There shall be a United Nations Nuclear Energy Authority which shall be under the direction and control of a United Nations Nuclear Energy Commission.

2. The Nuclear Energy Commission shall consist of five persons, none of whom shall be a national of any of the nations then having fifteen or more Representatives in the General Assembly; nor a national of any nation which has one of its nationals on the Military Staff Committee or the Inspection Commission; and no two of whom shall be nationals of the same nation. The members of the Nuclear Energy Commission shall be appointed by the Executive Council, subject to confirmation by the Assembly. The first members of the Nuclear Energy Commission shall be appointed by the first Executive Council within two months after the election of the Council by the General Assembly pursuant to Article 110 of this revised Charter. The terms of office of the first members of the Commission shall begin on the same date and shall expire, as designated by the

Council at the time of their appointment, one at the end of one year, one at the end of two years, one at the end of three years, one at the end of four years and one at the end of five years from that date; later appointments shall be made for terms of five years. The Executive Council shall have general supervision over the Nuclear Energy Commission and may from time to time issue such instructions to it as the Council deems necessary. The Executive Council shall also have authority to remove any member of the Nuclear Energy Commission whenever the Council deems it necessary.

The General Assembly, through its Standing Committee on the Peace Enforcement Agencies provided for in Article 22 of this revised Charter, shall watch over the carrying out by the Nuclear Energy Commission and the Executive Council of their responsibilities under this Chapter and other provisions of this Annex. The Standing Committee shall be entitled to obtain from the Commission and the Council all relevant information and shall make such investigations as it may deem necessary or as the Assembly may request it to make. If in the judgment of the Standing Committee a situation exists which requires the convoking of a special session of the Assembly, it shall be entitled in accordance with Article 20 of this revised Charter to request the Secretary-General to convoke such special session.

3. A General Manager shall be the administrative head of the staff of the Nuclear Energy Authority subject to the direction and control of the Nuclear Energy Commission. The General Manager shall not be a member of the Nuclear Energy Commission, nor a national of any nation which at the time of his appointment has one of its nationals on the Nuclear Energy Commission, nor a national of the nation whose national is then serving as the Inspector-General of the United Nations Inspection Service, nor a national of any of the nations then having fifteen or more Representatives in the General Assembly. The General Manager shall be appointed by the Nuclear Energy Commission for a term of six years, subject to confirmation by the Executive Council. The first General Manager shall be appointed by the first Nuclear Energy Commission, subject to confirmation by the first Executive Council, within two months after the appointment of the first Nuclear Energy Commission. The Nuclear Energy Commission shall have authority to remove the General Manager whenever the Commission deems it necessary.

4. The staff of the Nuclear Energy Authority shall be appointed by the General Manager, subject to regulations concerning qualifications, tenure, compensation and other conditions of service to be adopted by the General Assembly after receiving proposals therefor from the Nuclear Energy Commission and the recommendations of the Execu-

tive Council as to such proposals. Such regulations shall include provisions for the following:

a. That all members of the staff of the Nuclear Energy Authority shall be selected on the basis of their competence, integrity and devotion to the purposes of the United Nations.

b. That they shall make a solemn declaration that they will perform their functions impartially and conscientiously.

c. That they shall not seek or receive instructions from any government or other authority external to the United Nations.

d. That they shall refrain from any conduct which might reflect on their position as international officials.

e. That they shall receive fully adequate pay and allowances together with fully adequate retirement pensions after loyal and reasonably long service, all such compensation and pensions to be free from all taxation.

f. That they shall be recruited on as wide a geographical basis as possible.

g. That with respect to those members of the staff who are to perform duties requiring special scientific and technical qualifications, the number of nationals of any nation shall be limited to not more than four per cent of the total number of such scientific and technical members of the staff.

Comment. The new problems of world security created by the discovery of nuclear fission and fusion cannot be exclusively dealt with by an inspection system. On the one hand, the great potentialities for industrial and other peaceful uses of nuclear energy obviously preclude the abolition or even the curtailment of facilities for its production and utilization. On the other hand, the easy convertibility of materials used for peaceful purposes into materials from which nuclear weapons may be made requires that special precautions be taken with respect to those materials. It does not seem wise to burden the United Nations Inspection Service with too many duties in this field; and it, therefore, seems desirable to place all necessary safeguards in respect of nuclear energy which are not closely related to inspection, in the hands of a special world authority. This is here designated as the United Nations Nuclear Energy Authority, the proposed functions of which are defined in the succeeding Articles of this Chapter.

With respect to the composition and direction of this Nuclear Energy Authority, it is proposed to adopt all the safeguards which apply to the United Nations Inspection Service. The explanations concerning these safeguards made in the comment on Article 4 of this Annex apply equally to this Article 25. These safeguards are intended to provide the maximum assurance that the Nuclear Energy Authority, like the Inspection Service, shall not be dominated by any nation or group of nations, and that the highest standards of competence and integrity will be achieved by the staff of the Authority.

Article 26

1. The United Nations Nuclear Energy Authority shall have the following functions and powers in order to promote the use of nuclear energy for peaceful purposes and to assist in the prevention of the use of nuclear energy for any military purpose:

a. To acquire for a just compensation and take into its custody all special nuclear materials in the world which, in its judgment, are not needed for immediate use for research, industrial, commercial or other nonmilitary purposes.

b. To supervise the production of special nuclear materials and the distribution of facilities for such production, and also the distribution of special nuclear materials themselves, all to the extent necessary to prevent a dangerous concentration of such facilities and materials in any country or region.

c. To establish its own research laboratories and facilities for the utilization of nuclear energy for scientific, industrial, commercial and other nonmilitary purposes, and to assist nations, public or private organizations or individuals in the establishment of adequate research laboratories and facilities for the utilization of nuclear energy for such purposes.

d. To assume the responsibilities of the International Atomic Energy Agency and for that purpose to acquire such of the assets and employ such of the personnel of the Agency as the General Assembly may authorize.

e. To cooperate with the United Nations Inspection Service in the supervision of licensed facilities and establishments, in accordance with the provisions of Article 23 of this Annex.

f. To conduct, or arrange for the conduct of, surveys and explorations to discover new sources of any raw materials which might enter into the production of special nuclear materials.

2. During the actual disarmament stage provided for in Articles 9 to 12 of this Annex, every nation in the world shall annually reduce all stocks of special nuclear materials situated in its territory which are not in actual use for research, industrial, commercial or other nonmilitary purposes by ten per cent (or if the actual disarmament stage is shortened pursuant to paragraph 2 of Article 10 of this Annex, by such larger annual percentage as is appropriate to the shortened period); and all such reductions shall be distributed proportionately as between the principal types of these materials. All the materials which any nation is required to discard in order to make such reductions shall be transferred to the Nuclear Energy Authority, subject to compensation therefor as provided in Article 30 of this Annex. During the actual disarmament stage, the Authority may authorize transfer of these materials to a laboratory or facility duly reported under Article 5 of this Annex if

285

proper safeguards have been established to ensure that these materials will be used only for research, industrial, commercial or other nonmilitary purposes; and after the termination of the actual disarmament stage, the Authority may authorize the transfer of these materials to a laboratory or facility duly licensed under Article 16 of this Annex.

3. The General Assembly shall, after receiving proposals on the subject from the Nuclear Energy Commission and the recommendations of the Executive Council as to such proposals, establish maximum annual quotas for the total world production, and for the production within each nation, of raw materials which might enter into the production of special nuclear materials, of special nuclear materials themselves and of radioactive materials. The first of such maximum annual quotas shall be established by the Assembly at least two months before the beginning of the ninth month of the preparatory stage provided for in Articles 2 to 8 of this Annex and shall take effect on the first day of that month, except in case of a suspension under paragraph 3 of Article 5 of this Annex in which case the quotas shall take effect on the first day after the end of the suspension period. In each year thereafter the Assembly shall establish the quotas for the ensuing year at least two months prior to the beginning of such ensuing year. Such quotas shall not exceed by more than ten per cent the estimated annual needs for each category of these materials for use in research, industrial, commercial and other nonmilitary activities. The Nuclear Energy Commission shall assign maximum annual quotas for the production of raw materials which might enter into the production of special nuclear materials as between the principal areas containing significant deposits of such raw materials, subject to the principle that comparable known deposits throughout the world shall be depleted proportionately to the end that so far as possible no nation's known deposits shall be drawn upon to a greater extent than the known deposits of any other nation, and pursuant to such other standards as may be established by the General Assembly. The Nuclear Energy Commission shall also assign maximum annual quotas for the production of special nuclear materials and radioactive materials to each facility duly licensed to produce such materials.

4. All special nuclear materials and all radioactive materials which are produced under paragraph 3 of this Article and are not needed for immediate use for research, industrial, commercial or other nonmilitary purposes, shall be transferred to the Nuclear Energy Authority, subject to compensation therefor as provided in Article 30 of this Annex and in accordance with regulations to be adopted by the General Assembly after receiving proposals on the subject from the Nuclear Energy Commission and the recommendations of the Executive Council as to such proposals.

5. The special nuclear materials and radioactive materials acquired

by the Nuclear Energy Authority under paragraphs 2 and 4 of this Article shall be either kept by it in safe storage, or used by it in its own laboratories or facilities, or transferred to laboratories or facilities licensed for the use of such materials for research, industrial, commercial or other nonmilitary purposes, subject to such conditions as the General Assembly may from time to time prescribe in general regulations.

6. The Nuclear Energy Authority shall arrange for such a geographical distribution of the stocks of materials acquired under paragraphs 2 and 4 of this Article as will minimize the risk that any nation or group of nations might achieve a military advantage by the seizure of stocks situated within a particular territory or region; and, to this end, such arrangements shall provide that not less than five per cent or more than ten per cent of the total United Nations stock of these materials shall be situated in any one of the regions provided for in paragraph 9 of this Article.

7. In order to ensure a wide distribution of facilities for the production of special nuclear materials and radioactive materials, the Nuclear Energy Authority either shall itself build and, with the consent of the nation concerned, operate facilities for the production of these materials in the territories of nations which do not possess sufficient facilities of this sort, or shall assist those nations in the building and operation of such facilities. The Nuclear Energy Authority shall aim at such a distribution of these facilities as will minimize the risk that any nation or group of nations might achieve a military advantage by utilizing the output of facilities situated in a particular territory or region for the production of nuclear weapons. After a period of adjustment to be determined by the General Assembly but which in no case shall exceed ten years after the end of the actual disarmament stage, all facilities for the production of special nuclear materials and radioactive materials shall be distributed among the various regions of the world provided for in paragraph 9 of this Article in accordance with the principle that not less than five per cent or more than ten per cent of the total productive capacity of all such facilities shall be concentrated in any one of such regions.

8. The Nuclear Energy Authority shall also promote the utilization of nuclear energy for scientific, industrial, commercial and other nonmilitary purposes, and for that purpose the Authority either shall itself build and operate the necessary laboratories and experimental facilities, or shall assist nations, or public or private organizations or individuals in the building and operation of such laboratories or experimental facilities. In addition, in order to ensure a wide distribution of facilities making use of nuclear energy for scientific, industrial, commercial and other nonmilitary purposes, the Authority either shall itself build and

operate such facilities in such of the regions provided for in paragraph 9 of this Article as do not possess sufficient facilities of this sort, or shall assist in the building and operation of such facilities in those regions; but in no case shall such facilities be built or operated by the Authority in the territory of any nation without that nation's consent, and in no case shall such facilities be operated by the Authority for more than ten years after their completion. The Nuclear Energy Authority shall aim at such a distribution of all these laboratories and facilities as will minimize the risk that any nation or group of nations might achieve a military advantage by seizing the special nuclear materials or radioactive materials which are contained in any such laboratories or facilities. After a period of adjustment to be determined by the General Assembly but which in no case shall exceed ten years after the end of the actual disarmament stage, all laboratories and facilities utilizing nuclear energy for peaceful purposes shall be distributed among the various regions of the world provided for in paragraph 9 of this Article in accordance with the principle that not less than five per cent or more than ten per cent of the total amount of the materials available in the world for such purposes shall be contained in laboratories or facilities situated in any one of such regions.

9. The General Assembly shall during the first three months of the first year of the actual disarmament stage make an initial delineation of not less than eleven or more than twenty regions of the world for the purposes of paragraphs 6, 7 and 8 of this Article, thereby assigning each nation to a particular region. This initial delineation shall be revised by the Assembly during the first year following the completion of the first world census provided for in Article 9 of this revised Charter, and in the first year following the completion of each subsequent world census. In making these delineations, the Assembly shall observe the principles that no nation shall be divided between two or more regions, that every nation which is entitled to thirty Representatives in the Assembly shall constitute a separate region and that no region shall have a population of less than 150 million.

10. The Nuclear Energy Authority shall adopt appropriate measures to assure the internal and external security of its facilities, laboratories and stockpiles, and shall employ for that purpose either its own guards or units of the United Nations Peace Force assigned to it, or both. The Authority shall institute and maintain the most rigorous accounting procedures and an effective system of continuous supervision in order to prevent any diversion of materials acquired by it or produced or utilized in its facilities.

11. The Nuclear Energy Authority shall make all necessary arrangements with the Inspection Service to assign properly qualified members

of the staff of the Authority to take part in the management and operation of facilities and establishments with respect to which agreements for such participation have been concluded pursuant to paragraph 4 of Article 23 of this Annex.

12. The Nuclear Energy Authority shall make all necessary arrangements to discover new sources of any raw materials which might enter into the production of special nuclear materials, and for that purpose either shall itself conduct surveys and explorations, or arrange with any nation, public or private organization or individual for the conduct of such surveys and explorations. The General Assembly shall, after receiving proposals on the subject from the Nuclear Energy Commission and the recommendations of the Executive Council as to such proposals, adopt regulations for the conduct of such surveys and explorations. The Assembly shall also establish procedures for dealing with possible complaints by any nation alleging abuse by the Nuclear Energy Authority of its power to conduct these surveys and explorations.

13. Appropriate measures pursuant to Article 34 of this Annex shall be taken if a nation shall to any serious extent fail to conform to the provisions as to quotas contained in this Article.

Comment. As stated in the General Comment on this Chapter V, the proposed United Nations Nuclear Energy Authority is intended to assume all the functions of the International Atomic Energy Agency with respect to promoting the world-wide use of nuclear energy for peaceful purposes. The proposed Authority, supplementing the work of the United Nations Inspection Service, would also have important responsibilities with respect to supervising the production and distribution of all materials which might enter into the making of nuclear weapons.

Various functions of the necessary supervision would be performed by the Inspection Service under the previous Chapters of this Annex, but other functions could be more effectively exercised by the proposed Nuclear Energy Authority. This assignment to the Authority of certain supervisory functions would also have the advantage of providing a cross-check on the efficacy of the Inspection Service and of avoiding too large a concentration of power in the hands of the Inspection Service.

In order to enable the Nuclear Energy Authority not only to promote the utilization of nuclear energy for peaceful purposes, but also to aid in the prevention of any unauthorized military use of nuclear energy, it is proposed to assign the following five principal functions or powers to the Authority:

1. The temporary custody of all special nuclear materials before their allotment to laboratories and facilities requiring them for scientific, industrial, commercial or other nonmilitary purposes.

2. The supervision of certain steps in the production and distribution of special nuclear materials, in particular through the administration of a system of quotas for various categories of materials and facilities.

3. The promotion of the use of nuclear energy for peaceful purposes both through research in its own laboratories and facilities and through assisting national and private efforts in this field.

4. The supervision, jointly with the Inspection Service, of certain facilities producing or utilizing nuclear materials.

5. The conduct of surveys and explorations in order to discover new sources of raw materials which might enter into the production of special nuclear materials.

The Nuclear Energy Authority would have another important function quite apart from promoting the use of nuclear energy for peaceful purposes and the prevention of its use by any nation for military purposes, i.e., the function of providing the United Nations Peace Force with nuclear weapons in the possible, even if remote, event that the General Assembly might find it unavoidable to permit the use of such weapons against a nation which has first actually used or threatened to use nuclear weapons. The proposed functions of the Authority in this regard are, however, set forth separately in the following Article 27, this Article 26 being confined to the Authority's functions in respect of the peaceful use of nuclear energy and the prevention of any national use of such energy for any military purpose.

The first function of the Nuclear Energy Authority under the present Article, i.e., its custodial function, would at first be rather extensive, but would probably diminish in importance after the inauguration of a proper system of production and distribution quotas. During the period of actual disarmament and for some time thereafter, the Authority would need to have custody of all the stockpiles of nuclear materials suitable for nuclear weapons accumulated during the armaments race. For if confidence is to prevail that no considerable amounts of such materials are being concealed, they must be impounded by the Authority in safe custody until they can be properly allocated to peaceful purposes. How long this custodianship would continue would mainly depend on the speed at which the industrial use of nuclear energy is developed. Only small amounts of nuclear materials might be required for scientific purposes; but in view of the prospects for the extensive use of these materials in power plants and transportation, it might be possible for the Authority to distribute quickly even very large stocks of nuclear materials which would come into its custody through the dismantling of nuclear weapons. If, however, considerable delay should occur in the large-scale utilization of these materials, the transition period might be much longer and the custodial responsibilities of the Authority correspondingly greater. In any case, the custodial function would continue even after the Authority's initial stockpile had been distributed, since new nuclear materials would constantly become available.

In order to prevent new production from exceeding the requirements for peaceful purposes, it is proposed to establish a system of quotas to ensure that the production does not exceed the demand for industrial and other nonmilitary purposes by more than ten per cent. This margin of ten per cent is proposed in order to obviate a possible shortage of nuclear materials for peaceful uses because of erroneous estimates. The Nuclear Energy Authority

290

would assign most of the new production directly to the chief industrial and commercial consumers, but would still need to purchase and provide custody for those materials which could not be immediately directed into consumption channels and also for any excess production resulting from the ten per cent margin.

Both during the initial period of large stockpiles and later, the Nuclear Energy Authority would need to establish careful safeguards to ensure that no nation can achieve a military advantage by seizing the stockpiles of special nuclear materials resulting from the dismantling of nuclear weapons and which are in the temporary custody of the Authority. It is essential that even a group of nations acting in concert shall not be able to achieve such an advantage, and the necessary safeguards must, therefore, apply not only to particular territories, but also to whole regions. To this end it is proposed that not less than five per cent or more than ten per cent of the total amount of special nuclear materials in the temporary custody of the United Nations shall be situated in any region of the world, and that the General Assembly shall from time to time determine which areas of the world shall be included in not less than eleven or more than twenty "regions" to be delineated for this purpose by the Assembly.

The second principal function of the Nuclear Energy Authority would be to administer a system of production quotas: (a) of raw materials which might enter into the production of special nuclear materials; (b) of the special nuclear materials themselves; and (c) of radioactive materials. As a first step the Nuclear Energy Commission would assist the General Assembly in the determination of the production quotas for the world as a whole and for each producing nation. The Commission would then allocate proportions of the global and national quotas thus determined among the principal producing areas and facilities, and would supervise the observance of the quotas so as to prevent a dangerous accumulation in any particular nation or region of materials suitable for nuclear weapons. In allocating quotas to principal areas containing significant deposits of raw materials which might enter into the production of special nuclear materials, the Commission would be required to follow the principle that comparable deposits throughout the world shall be depleted proportionately, thus avoiding so far as possible the exhaustion of deposits in some regions of the world, while large deposits remain in other regions. As new deposits were discovered, the quotas for various nations and areas would be revised, taking into account the size of the new deposits. Similarly, the Commission would assign separate production quotas to each facility engaged in the various stages of the processing of special nuclear materials and of radioactive materials. The Inspection Service would assist the Commission in the supervision of the quota restrictions, and special powers with respect to supervision over the transfer and transportation of potentially dangerous materials would doubtless be granted to the Inspection Service by the regulations to be enacted by the General Assembly under paragraph 5 of Article 23 of this Annex. If, however, additional controls became necessary, the Assembly would have power to prescribe them.

In determining the quotas for the processing of special nuclear materials after the beginning of the period of complete disarmament, account would need to be taken of the fact that the then existing processing facilities would probably be distributed in a very uneven fashion among the nations of the world. To achieve proportionate equality, it might even be necessary to close some facilities temporarily and to reopen them only after a better balance has been achieved. In order that such a balance may be reached as soon as possible, it seems necessary to empower the Nuclear Energy Authority to build or assist in building new facilities for the processing of special nuclear materials in those areas of the world where no such facilities then exist or where they have much smaller capacity than in other areas. Such facilities could be built either by the Authority itself, or by nations or public or private organizations or individuals with the assistance of the Authority, both with respect to technical matters and financing. Moreover, with the consent of the nation in whose territory the new facility has been built, the Authority could actually operate the facility, either permanently or until sufficient local technicians became available. Before such facilities built by the Authority were turned over to local management and operation, and also if agreements were made for assistance in building new facilities or rebuilding old ones, proper arrangements would be necessary to enable adequate supervision of such facilities by the Inspection Service or the Nuclear Energy Authority through participation in management and operation, in accordance with paragraph 4 of Article 23 of this Annex. The purpose of a building program of this sort would be to bring about the eventual distribution of these potentially dangerous facilities around the world in such a way that not less than five per cent or more than ten per cent of the world's total productive capacity would be located in any one region. From that point on, the Authority would limit its expansion program to the building of only such facilities as might be necessary to satisfy a growing demand for nuclear and radioactive materials. The building of any such new facilities would, of course, need to be done in such a way as not to disturb the required balance between the various regions of the world.

The third proposed function of the Nuclear Energy Authority is to promote the *utilization* of nuclear energy for peaceful purposes. To this end, the Authority would be empowered to engage directly in research aimed at finding new and better ways of utilizing nuclear energy for the common good of all mankind. The Authority could also stimulate and assist national and private research in this field. To accomplish this research aim, the Authority would be authorized to build and operate its own laboratories and experimental facilities and assist nations, public and private organizations and individuals in the building and operation of their own laboratories and experimental facilities. In addition, the Authority would be empowered to build and operate or to assist in the building and operation of such plants as may be needed for the practical utilization of nuclear energy for the production of electric power or other industrial or commercial purposes, provided however: (a) that no such plant shall be built or operated by the Authority without the consent of the nation concerned; and (b) that any such operation by the Authority shall be only of a temporary character, in no case

292

exceeding ten years. With regard to all its activities to promote the utilization of nuclear energy for peaceful purposes, the guiding principle is laid down that there shall be no excessive concentration either of experimental or production facilities in any nation or region. It is to this end that the Authority is directed to take such steps as are necessary to arrange the division of facilities as equally as may be among the various regions of the world. The effect would be, on the one hand, to lessen the possibility that any nation or group of nations could obtain a military advantage by seizing a large part of the world's stockpile of these dangerous materials suitable for easy utilization in military weapons. On the other hand, such a distribution of facilities all over the world would spread the benefits of the atomic age to all nations and help to diminish those great discrepancies in standards of living between various peoples which constitute an underlying danger to the peace of the world.

The fourth function of the Nuclear Energy Authority would be to cooperate with the Inspection Service in the managerial and operational *supervision* of facilities engaged in the production or utilization of special nuclear materials. As has been explained in the comment on Articles 14 and 23 of this Annex, this type of supervision would take the place of the original American proposal (the so-called Baruch Plan) for complete United Nations *ownership* of all dangerous facilities. The personnel of the Nuclear Energy Authority would be specially qualified to take part in this method of supervision, and it is to be expected that the regulations adopted by the General Assembly under paragraph 4 of Article 23 would provide for the proper division of supervision under that paragraph between the Authority and the Inspection Service. Thus another cross-check would be provided on the efficacy of various inspection and supervision methods of the Inspection Service and the Authority.

The fifth function of the Nuclear Energy Authority would be to conduct, or arrange for the conduct of, surveys and explorations to discover new sources of any raw materials which might enter into the production of special nuclear materials. Ordinarily such surveys would be made by the national governments themselves or by public or private organizations or individuals. But if the Authority considers that no adequate surveys have been made in a particular area and cannot find anybody willing to make an adequate survey, the Authority should be entitled to conduct a survey directly and to send its own survey group to the area in question. The General Assembly would have the power to regulate the conduct of such surveys or explorations, and would also be authorized to adopt suitable procedures for dealing with complaints against any possible abuses on the part of the Authority.

As in other instances of possible serious violations of the disarmament plan, it would be necessary to take prompt and effective measures if any nation should attempt to evade the important restrictions imposed by this Article on the production of dangerous materials. Under Article 34 of this Annex the General Assembly would have wide powers to deal with such a situation and the Executive Council would be granted limited power to take temporary emergency measures.

Article 27

1. The United Nations Nuclear Energy Authority shall have the following functions and powers in respect of nuclear weapons:

a. To conduct research and experiments and development work in the military application of nuclear energy.

b. To have custody of such stocks of nuclear weapons as, pursuant to decisions of the General Assembly, are set aside during the actual disarmament stage for the possible use of the United Nations Peace Force.

c. To produce, to the extent authorized by the General Assembly, new nuclear weapons for the possible use of the Peace Force.

d. To make available to the Peace Force such nuclear weapons as the General Assembly may authorize in the circumstances and under the conditions set forth in Article 4 of Annex II.

2. Upon the recommendation of the Executive Council or upon its own initiative, the General Assembly shall:

a. Adopt regulations governing the conduct by the Nuclear Energy Authority of research and experiments and of development work in the military application of nuclear energy.

b. Decide what portion of the stocks of nuclear weapons which are discarded by the nations during the actual disarmament stage pursuant to Article 11 of this Annex shall be placed in the custody of the Nuclear Energy Authority for the possible use of the United Nations Peace Force pursuant to Article 4 of Annex II.

c. Decide whether and to what extent the Nuclear Energy Authority shall engage in the production of new nuclear weapons for the possible use of the Peace Force.

3. The transfer of nuclear weapons to the Nuclear Energy Authority shall be subject to the payment of compensation as provided in Article 30 of this Annex.

Comment. The functions of the Nuclear Energy Authority covered by this Article relate to the potential arming with nuclear weapons of the United Nations Peace Force, which under the plan would possess a monopoly of military power after the completion of national disarmament. The plan contemplates that, while the Peace Force would not be regularly equipped with nuclear weapons, it could be provided with such weapons only if and when the Assembly has formally declared that nuclear weapons have been actually used either against a nation or against the United Nations itself or that such use is imminently threatened (Article 4 of Annex II). In order, however, to provide the most careful safeguards with respect to such possible use even in that extreme contingency, it is proposed that *all* nuclear weapons shall be in the custody of a nonmilitary agency—the Nuclear Energy Authority—until the General Assembly specifically directs that one or more nuclear weapons be released to the Peace Force for use in such contingency.

This custodianship by the Nuclear Energy Authority would apply both to existing nuclear weapons discarded by the nations during the actual disarmament stage and placed by the General Assembly in the custody of the Nuclear Energy Authority and to new nuclear weapons which the Authority might be empowered by the Assembly to produce. It should be emphasized that even the Assembly itself would have no power to authorize the turning over of nuclear weapons to the Peace Force except under the above-mentioned extreme contingency that nuclear weapons had actually been used or were about to be used either against a nation or nations, or in a revolt against the United Nations itself.

The reason why it seems essential that the world police force—the United Nations Peace Force—shall have the potential capacity to use nuclear weapons is that it seems impossible to devise any system of inspection which can afford an *absolute* guarantee that no nuclear weapons will be concealed during the disarmament period or that no such weapons whatever will be clandestinely produced thereafter. And the reason why it seems necessary to make possible the production of new nuclear weapons for the use of the Peace Force is that, although all national and private military research would be prohibited after the period of complete disarmament has begun, it is always possible that secret and undiscovered research might lead to the invention of new nuclear weapons of even greater destructive power than those impounded from previous national stocks. It is important, therefore, to authorize the Nuclear Energy Authority to conduct research in the military application of nuclear energy and to produce weapons based on that research, so that in case of necessity the Peace Force could, if properly authorized by the General Assembly, be equipped with no less powerful weapons than those which might conceivably be developed by clandestine effort.

It should be noted that the conception of entrusting both the custody and possible production of these weapons of mass destruction to a nonmilitary authority follows the precedents embodied in the United States Atomic Energy Acts of 1946 and 1954 and in similar legislative acts of other countries. The effect would be to enable the Peace Force to suppress any possible aggression through the use when absolutely necessary of the most modern and destructive weapons while, on the other hand, providing strict safeguards against any possible attempt of the Peace Force to usurp power.

295

CHAPTER VI

UNITED NATIONS OUTER SPACE AGENCY

General Comment. Recent technological developments have made possible the first explorations of outer space. Rockets and satellites are already moving through outer space, and in the not too distant future manned space stations and manned spacecraft may well become a reality.

The General Assembly of the United Nations has already recognized "the common interest of mankind in outer space" and "the common aim that outer space should be used for peaceful purposes only." In 1958 it appointed a committee to study: (a) the "activities and resources of the United Nations . . . relating to the peaceful uses of outer space"; (b) the "area of international co-operation and programmes in the peaceful uses of outer space which could appropriately be undertaken under United Nations auspices"; (c) the "future organizational arrangements to facilitate international co-operation in this field within the framework of the United Nations"; and (d) the "nature of legal problems which may arise in the carrying out of programmes to explore outer space." In 1959 the General Assembly expressed the desire "to avoid the extension of present national rivalries into this new field", and established a new Committee on the Peaceful Uses of Outer Space to make further studies on the subject.

It is generally recognized that the exploration and exploitation of outer space present one of the greatest challenges to the ability of the human race to cooperate for the common good. From the very beginning this vast new area will require an orderly coordination by an international agency. Since in 1960 no vested rights as yet exist in this field, the powers of such an agency can be made broader than those of agencies existing in other fields where prior rights and privileges form an obstacle to the extension of international jurisdiction.

It is proposed, therefore, to establish a United Nations Outer Space Agency which will have two principal objectives: (a) to ensure that outer space is used for peaceful purposes only; and (b) to promote to the fullest possible extent exploration and exploitation of outer space for the common benefit of all mankind.

Under the over-all authority of the General Assembly and the Executive Council, the Outer Space Agency would exercise the following functions:

1. To possess and operate its own rockets, satellites and spacecraft and to licence, through the Inspector-General, the possession and operation of rockets, satellites and spacecraft by nations, organizations and individuals.

2. To supervise the departure into space of both manned and unmanned rockets, satellites and spacecraft.

3. To promote international cooperation in the study of the problems of outer space.

4. To conduct research with respect to the development of new rockets, satellites and spacecraft.

5. To supervise the use of rockets, satellites and spacecraft for various peaceful purposes, such as astronomy, meteorology and communication.

6. To take all measures necessary to prevent the use of outer space for military purposes by any nation and to keep other organs of the United Nations informed of any violation of the prohibition against the use of outer space for military purposes.

7. To exercise in the name of the United Nations any control which it may be advisable and possible to exercise over the moon or any other planet or body within the solar system which may be reached by any spacecraft from earth, and to preclude the exercise of any such control by any nation or group of nations.

Article 28

1. There shall be a United Nations Outer Space Agency which shall be under the direction and control of a United Nations Outer Space Commission.

2. The Outer Space Commission shall consist of five persons, none of whom shall be a national of any of the nations then having fifteen or more Representatives in the General Assembly; nor a national of any nation which has one of its nationals on the Military Staff Committee, the Inspection Commission or the Nuclear Energy Commission; and no two of whom shall be nationals of the same nation. The members of the Outer Space Commission shall be appointed by the Executive Council, subject to confirmation by the Assembly. The first members of the Outer Space Commission shall be appointed by the first Executive Council within two months after the election of the Council by the General Assembly pursuant to Article 110 of this revised Charter. The terms of office of the first members of the Commission shall begin on the same date and shall expire, as designated by the Council at the time of their appointment, one at the end of one year, one at the end of two years, one at the end of three years, one at the end of four years and one at the end of five years from that date; later appointments shall be for terms of five years. The Executive Council shall have general supervision over the Outer Space Commission and may from time to time issue such instructions to it as the Council deems necessary. The Executive Council shall also have authority to remove any member of the Outer Space Commission whenever the Council deems it necessary.

3. The General Assembly, through its Standing Committee on the Peace Enforcement Agencies provided for in Article 22 of this revised Charter, shall watch over the carrying out by the Outer Space Commission and the Executive Council of their responsibilities under this Chapter and other provisions of this Annex. The Standing Committee shall be entitled to obtain from the Commission and the Council all relevant information and shall make such investigations as it may deem necessary or as the Assembly may request it to make. If in the judgment of the Standing Committee a situation exists which requires the convoking of a special session of the Assembly, it shall be entitled in accordance with Article 20

of this revised Charter to request the Secretary-General to convoke such special session.

4. A Managing Director shall be the administrative head of the staff of the Outer Space Agency subject to the direction and control of the Outer Space Commission. The Managing Director shall not be a member of the Outer Space Commission, nor a national of any nation which at the time of his appointment has one of its nationals on the Outer Space Commission, nor a national of either of the two nations whose nationals are then serving as the Inspector-General of the United Nations Inspection Service and the General Manager of the United Nations Nuclear Energy Authority, nor a national of any of the nations then having fifteen or more Representatives in the General Assembly. The Managing Director shall be appointed by the Outer Space Commission for a term of six years, subject to confirmation by the Executive Council. The first Managing Director shall be appointed by the first Outer Space Commission, subject to confirmation by the first Executive Council, within two months after the appointment of the first Outer Space Commission. The Outer Space Commission shall have authority to remove the Managing Director whenever the Commission deems it necessary.

5. The staff of the Outer Space Agency shall be appointed by the Managing Director subject to regulations concerning qualifications, tenure, compensation and other conditions of service to be adopted by the General Assembly after receiving proposals therefor from the Outer Space Commission and the recommendations of the Executive Council as to such proposals. Such regulations shall include provisions for the following:

a. That all members of the staff of the Outer Space Agency shall be selected on the basis of their competence, integrity and devotion to the purposes of the United Nations.

b. That they shall make a solemn declaration that they will perform their functions impartially and conscientiously.

c. That they shall not seek or receive instructions from any government or other authority external to the United Nations.

d. That they shall refrain from any conduct which might reflect on their position as international officials.

e. That they shall receive fully adequate pay and allowances together with fully adequate retirement pensions after loyal and reasonably long service, all such compensation and pensions to be free from all taxation.

f. That they shall be recruited on as wide a geographical basis as possible.

g. That with respect to those members of the staff who are to perform duties requiring special scientific and technical qualifications, the number of nationals of any nation shall be limited to not more than four per cent of the total number of such scientific and technical members of the staff.

Comment. While the United Nations Inspection Service would exercise various functions with respect to the production, possession and operation of rockets, satellites and spacecraft (as provided in Articles 5, 6, 14, 15, 16 and 23 of this Annex), it seems desirable to concentrate the principal functions in this field in a separate agency combining the functions of supervision and development.

It is proposed, therefore, to establish a United Nations Outer Space Agency, the composition and functions of which are defined in Articles 28 and 29 of this Annex.

The provisions of this Article 28 in respect of the composition, direction and supervision of this new agency are similar to those relating to the United Nations Inspection Service and the United Nations Nuclear Energy Authority (Articles 4 and 25 of this Annex). Careful safeguards are established in order to provide the maximum assurance that the Outer Space Agency, like the Inspection Service and the Nuclear Energy Authority, shall not be dominated by any nation or group of nations. It is also proposed to establish high standards of competence and integrity for the staff of the Agency. The explanations concerning these safeguards and standards which are contained in the comment on Article 4 of this Annex apply equally to this Article 28.

Article 29

1. The General Assembly shall, after receiving proposals on the subject from the Outer Space Commission and the recommendations of the Executive Council as to such proposals:

a. Define the boundary between outer space and airspace.

b. Issue regulations concerning all aspects of navigation in, and other uses of, outer space for peaceful purposes.

c. Issue regulations governing the possession and operation by the Outer Space Agency and by nations, or public or private organizations or individuals, of rockets, satellites or spacecraft.

2. The United Nations Outer Space Agency shall have the following functions and powers in order to promote the exploration and use of outer space for peaceful purposes and to assist in the prevention of the use of outer space for any military purpose:

a. To possess and operate rockets, satellites and spacecraft to the extent necessary to supervise the use of outer space for peaceful purposes only.

b. To license, through the Inspector-General, the possession, testing and operation of rockets, satellites and spacecraft by nations, or public or private organizations or individuals, to the extent authorized by regulations adopted by the General Assembly.

c. To cooperate, in accordance with the provisions of Article 23 of this Annex, with the United Nations Inspection Service in the supervision of licensed facilities and establishments.

d. To control the departure into outer space of unmanned rockets, satellites and spacecraft in order to ensure that they will be used for peaceful purposes only.

e. To control the use of rockets, satellites and spacecraft for scientific meteorological, communication, inspection and other peaceful purposes.

f. To ensure that manned flights into outer space are conducted only by members of the staff of the Outer Space Agency or by persons who first obtain, through the Inspector-General, a special license from the Agency for such flights.

g. To serve as a world center for the collection and dissemination of information on outer space and to promote international cooperation in the study of the problems of outer space.

h. To conduct research and experiments and development work with respect to the production, use and operation of rockets, satellites and spacecraft.

i. To take all measures necessary to prevent the use of outer space for military purposes by any nation and to prevent the use of force or threat of force in or from outer space, and to report immediately to the Executive Council and to the General Assembly upon any serious violation of the provisions of this Chapter or of any regulations enacted thereunder.

j. To exercise in the name of the United Nations any control which it may be advisable and possible to exercise over the moon or any other planet or body within the solar system which may be reached by any spacecraft from earth, and to prevent the exercise of any such control by any nation or group of nations.

2. Before the end of the sixth month of the preparatory stage provided for in Articles 2 to 8 of this Annex, the General Assembly shall, after receiving proposals on the subject from the Outer Space Agency and the recommendations of the Executive Council as to such proposals, determine which types of rockets, satellites and spacecraft may be launched and operated exclusively by the Outer Space Agency and which may be launched and operated for nonmilitary purposes by nations, or public or private organizations or individuals, subject to conditions specified in a license to be issued in each case by the Outer Space Agency through the Inspector-General.

3. During the actual disarmament stage provided for in Articles 9 to 12 of this Annex, every nation in the world shall annually reduce all stocks of rockets, satellites and spacecraft situated in its territory for which no license has been issued by the Outer Space Agency by ten per cent (or if the actual disarmament stage is shortened pursuant to paragraph 2 of Article 10 of this Annex, by such larger annual percentage as is appropriate to the shortened period); and all such reductions shall be distributed proportionately as between the principal types of these outer space vehicles. All the rockets, satellites and spacecraft which any

nation is required to discard in order to make such reductions shall be transferred to the Outer Space Agency, subject to compensation therefor as provided in Article 30 of this Annex.

4. All the rockets, satellites and spacecraft acquired by the Outer Space Agency under paragraph 3 of this Article or produced in its own facilities shall be either kept by it in safe storage or used for research, exploration or other nonmilitary purposes, subject to such conditions as the General Assembly may from time to time prescribe in general regulations.

5. The Outer Space Agency shall arrange for such a geographical distribution of its stock of rockets, satellites and spacecraft and of its facilities for their production and launching, as will minimize the risk that any nation or group of nations might achieve a military advantage by the seizure of stocks or facilities situated within a particular territory or region; and to this end, such arrangements shall provide that not less than five per cent or more than ten per cent of the total of these space vehicles or facilities for their production or launching shall be situated in any one of the regions provided for in paragraph 9 of Article 26 of this Annex.

6. The Outer Space Agency shall adopt appropriate measures to assure the internal and external security of its facilities and stockpiles, and shall employ for that purpose either its own guards or units of the United Nations Peace Force assigned to it, or both.

7. The Outer Space Agency shall make all necessary arrangements with the United Nations Inspection Service to assign properly qualified members of the staff of the Agency to take part in the management and operation of facilities and establishments with respect to which agreements for such participation have been concluded pursuant to paragraph 4 of Article 23 of this Annex, and in the operation of rockets, satellites or spacecraft with respect to which licenses have been issued by the Agency to nations, public or private organizations or individuals.

8. The Outer Space Agency may be authorized by the General Assembly to equip some of its rockets, satellites or spacecraft for police duty in outer space or for military action; provided that no military action shall be taken by the Agency without prior authorization of the Assembly, or of the Executive Council in the circumstances defined in paragraph 2 of Article 39 of this revised Charter, except in self-defense against an armed attack on its facilities, bases, vehicles or military units.

9. Appropriate measures pursuant to Article 34 of this Annex shall be taken if a nation shall to any serious extent fail to conform to the provisions of this Article or place any serious obstacle in the way of the Outer Space Agency.

Comment. As stated in the General Comment on this Chapter VI, the proposed Outer Space Agency would have a variety of functions with respect to the

301

promotion of the exploration and exploitation of outer space for peaceful purposes and the prevention of the use of outer space for military purposes. These various functions are carefully defined in this Article 29.

It is proposed to assign to the Outer Space Agency the following principal functions:

1. To assist the General Assembly in the issuance of regulations concerning the definition of outer space, navigation in outer space, and possession and operation of rockets, satellites or spacecraft.

2. To control the use of outer space for peaceful purposes only through the licensing of rockets, satellites or spacecraft operating therein, through the supervision of the use actually made of these rockets, satellites and spacecraft, and through the operation of its own rockets, satellites and spacecraft.

3. To conduct such research with respect to rockets, satellites and spacecraft as may be needed to keep the Agency in the forefront of technical knowledge on the subject.

4. To promote international cooperation in the study of the manifold problems of outer space.

5. To take such measures as it may deem necessary to prevent the use of outer space for military or aggressive purposes, and to call to the attention of the General Assembly and the Executive Council all cases of such prohibited use.

6. To prevent disputes relative to the occupation and control of the moon or any other planet or body within the solar system which may be reached by any spacecraft from earth by having the Agency take over any control which may be advisable and possible as soon as any such bodies are reached by any such spacecraft.

It cannot be expected that all these functions would be exercised by the Outer Space Agency from the beginning, but sufficient flexibility must be provided to enable the Agency to keep up with the rapid growth of man's conquest of space. At the beginning, the Agency would take over all those national establishments for the exploration of outer space which are determined by the General Assembly to be so dangerous from the military point of view as to require their operation by the Agency. Other establishments would be subject to license by the Outer Space Agency, to be issued in each case through the Inspector-General and in cooperation with the Inspection Service. In proper cases, the Agency would be authorized to assign members of its staff to facilities producing or launching rockets, satellites or spacecraft. The members of its staff might also join the crews operating rockets, satellites or spacecraft and take part in expeditions exploring space. In this way they would be able to see to it that these space vehicles are not used for military purposes and would be able to take over newly discovered extraterrestrial bodies in the name of the United Nations.

While the rockets, satellites and spacecraft which would be at the disposal of the Outer Space Agency would be primarily used for peaceful exploration, some of them might be equipped for policing outer space and a few of them would even be adapted for military use in case of a serious emergency which should require the use of outer space weapons. Such use would have to be strictly limited and would require in each case a special authorization of the General Assembly or, in an emergency case, of the Executive Council.

CHAPTER VII

FINANCIAL PROVISIONS

Article 30

1. The expenses of the United Nations Inspection Service, of the United Nations Nuclear Energy Authority and of the United Nations Outer Space Agency shall be borne by the United Nations.

2. The General Assembly shall determine the salaries and allowances of the members of the Inspection Commission, the Inspector-General, the members of the Nuclear Energy Commission, the General Manager of the Nuclear Energy Authority, the members of the Outer Space Commission and the Managing Director of the Outer Space Agency. The Assembly shall also, after receiving a report on the subject from the Inspection Commission, determine the salary scales of the staff of the Inspection Service; after receiving a report on the subject from the Nuclear Energy Commission, determine the salary scales of the staff of the Nuclear Energy Authority; and after receiving a report on the subject from the Outer Space Commission, determine the salary scales of the staff of the Outer Space Agency.

3. The annual budget of the Inspection Service shall be prepared by the Inspector-General, subject to the approval of the Inspection Commission. The annual budget of the Nuclear Energy Authority shall be prepared by the General Manager of the Authority, subject to the approval of the Nuclear Energy Commission. The annual budget of the Outer Space Agency shall be prepared by the Managing Director of the Agency, subject to the approval of the Outer Space Commission. All these budgets shall be submitted to the General Assembly for action pursuant to the procedure provided for in Annex V.

4. The United Nations shall promptly pay just compensation for all arms, weapons, ammunition and equipment, and for all machines, appliances and tools for the production of military material, which are transferred to the United Nations under Article 11 of this Annex, and for all special nuclear materials and weapons which are transferred to the United Nations under Articles 11, 26 and 27 of this Annex, and for all rockets, satellites and spacecraft, which are transferred to the United Nations under Article 29 of this Annex; and the United Nations shall pay equitable rent for the laboratories, facilities and other properties used by the Inspection Service, the Nuclear Energy Authority and the Outer Space Agency. The compensation or rent to be paid under the

previous sentence during the actual disarmament stage may be paid out of funds borrowed by the United Nations for that purpose as well as out of current funds of the United Nations; but the compensation or rent to be paid after the end of the actual disarmament stage shall be paid entirely out of current funds of the United Nations.

5. Subject to such regulations as the General Assembly may adopt, the United Nations shall charge appropriate fees for the various services performed under this Annex, including the issuance of licenses, and shall receive adequate compensation or rent for the special nuclear materials sold or leased to nations, public or private organizations or individuals for research, industrial, commercial or other nonmilitary purposes.

6. In case of a dispute as to whether the compensation paid or offered by the United Nations is just, or whether the rent paid or offered by the United Nations is equitable, the private owner of the property in question, or the nation which owns such property or within which such property is situated acting on its own behalf or on behalf of the private owner of such property as the case may be, may submit the dispute for decision to the United Nations regional court within the jurisdiction of which such property is situated. If either the United Nations or the private owner of the property in question or the nation which owns such property or in the territory of which such property is situated is dissatisfied with the decision of the regional court, any of them shall have the right to appeal to the International Court of Justice; except that in the case of a private owner, such right shall be subject to any legislation which may be enacted by the General Assembly pursuant to Part D of Annex III. In the case of such an appeal to the International Court of Justice, the decision of that Court shall be final.

Comment. Although the main provisions relative to the finances and budget of the United Nations are contained in Annex V, it is advisable to include a few additional provisions on the subject in this Annex. Thus paragraph 1 of the above Article makes it clear that the United Nations shall bear the considerable expense of the United Nations Inspection Service, of the United Nations Nuclear Energy Authority and of the United Nations Outer Space Agency, in the same way that it bears the expenses of the various other organs and agencies of the United Nations.

The annual budget of the Inspection Service would be prepared by the Inspector-General, subject to the approval of the Inspection Commission; the annual budget of the Nuclear Energy Authority by its General Manager, subject to the approval of the Nuclear Energy Commission; and the annual budget of the Outer Space Agency by its Managing Director, subject to the approval of the Outer Space Commission. The budgets thus prepared would be examined under the provisions of Annex V by the Standing Committee on Budget and Finance of the General Assembly to be established pursuant to Article 22 of this revised Charter; and these budgets would be subject to final scrutiny, amendment and adoption by the Assembly itself.

The General Assembly would also determine from time to time the salaries and allowances of the chief officers of the Inspection Service, the Nuclear Energy Authority and the Outer Space Agency and of the members of the Inspection Commission, the Nuclear Energy Commission and the Outer Space Commission, which would respectively control them. The Assembly would have like authority to determine the salary scales of the other personnel of the Inspection Service, the Nuclear Energy Authority and the Outer Space Agency; but it seems wise to require recommendations as to these salaries from the Commissions in charge of these agencies.

A financial problem for the United Nations in the field of disarmament, including nuclear-energy control, might result from the transfer to the United Nations during the actual disarmament stage of considerable quantities of arms and other valuable military equipment, and of large quantities of "special nuclear materials" and of rockets, satellites and spacecraft. Certain nations might perhaps be willing to make this transfer to the United Nations without compensation, but other nations and nearly all private organizations and individuals would doubtless require just and prompt compensation. This compensation might involve large sums, and since during the early years of the actual disarmament stage the United Nations might not have adequate revenues for this purpose, provision should be made for borrowing the necessary funds. In later years, however, it should be possible to provide the amounts needed for such compensation in the annual budgets of the United Nations, especially since much of the outgo for this purpose would probably be balanced by receipts derived from the sale or lease for research, industrial and other nonmilitary purposes of special nuclear materials from the United Nations stockpile.

In order to enable the United Nations to lease such buildings and real estate as would be necessary for the offices, laboratories and other facilities of the Inspection Service, Nuclear Energy Authority and the Outer Space Agency, provision is made for the payment of equitable rents.

It is also provided that any dispute as to the adequacy of such compensation or rent may be submitted for decision to the nearest United Nations regional court established under Part D of Annex III, from which decision an appeal could be taken to the International Court of Justice.

305

CHAPTER VIII

ENFORCEMENT MEASURES AGAINST INDIVIDUALS, ORGANIZATIONS AND NATIONS

Article 31

The General Assembly shall, pursuant to Article 11 of this revised Charter, enact laws defining what violations of this Annex or of any law or regulation enacted thereunder, either by individuals or by private organizations, shall be deemed to be offenses against the United Nations; and shall also enact laws prescribing the penalties for such offenses and providing for the apprehension of individuals accused of serious offenses, for the trial of accused individuals or organizations and for the enforcement of penalties.

Comment. The enforcement measures envisaged in this Chapter cover two classes of possible violations: (1) violations which are individual acts only not involving any government and which can adequately be dealt with by the admonition or prosecution of individuals; and (2) violations which involve the government of a nation and which can adequately be dealt with only by representations to or sanctions against the government concerned. Articles 31 and 32 of this Annex deal with the former category, Article 34 with violations involving governments and Article 33 with both categories.

It is reasonable to assume that in most instances the government of a nation in whose territory a violation occurs would not be involved in it and that such violations could be adequately dealt with by prompt action against the individuals responsible for them. If, for example, the United Nations Inspection Service should discover that an individual scientist, not licensed by the United Nations, has without the knowledge of his government been experimenting with nuclear material, proper steps could be taken directly against him, and his government need not in any way be involved in the proceedings. Similar direct action could be taken against a private organization, such as a corporation manufacturing prohibited arms without the knowledge of its government. On the other hand, if a nation, as represented by its government, should make it impossible for the Inspection Service to conduct inspections in its territory, measures would need to be taken under Article 34 of this Annex even including, in a very serious case, action by the United Nations Peace Force against the offending nation.

The above Article 31 relates to the class of violations by individuals or private organizations which do not involve a national government. Since it is obviously inappropriate in a constitutional instrument to attempt a definition of all possible violations and to prescribe the penalties therefor, the General

306

Assembly would have broad authority under this Article and Article 11 of the revised Charter to enact the necessary laws on those subjects. The Assembly would also be authorized to prescribe the procedures for the trial of all persons charged with violations and for the enforcement of penalties; and also to make provision for the apprehension of individuals accused of serious offenses. The purpose is to provide an effective and just system for applying the principle of individual responsibility. Such a system must include adequate guarantees against abuse, and it is to be noted that all the safeguards embodied in the United Nations Bill of Rights (Annex VII) would apply to any prosecutions under this Article.

Article 32

1. If the Inspector-General determines that a particular violation of this Annex or of any law or regulation enacted thereunder is of a character that can be adequately dealt with by action against an individual or private organization, and considers that such violation is due only to error, negligence or other cause which makes prosecution of the violation unnecessary, he shall call on the individual or organization concerned to remedy the violation within a fixed period; and if the violation is duly remedied, no further action shall be taken.

2. If, however, the violation is not promptly remedied, or if the Inspector-General determines that the particular violation ought to be prosecuted, he shall notify the Attorney-General of the United Nations, appointed under Part D of Annex III. If the Attorney-General agrees that the violation notified to him by the Inspector-General constitutes an offense defined in laws enacted pursuant to Article 11 of this revised Charter or Article 31 of this Annex, he shall institute appropriate proceedings, and shall arrange for the apprehension when necessary of the alleged violator, and for such provisional measures as may be required to prevent the continuance of any alleged violation.

Comment. This Article deals with the procedure to be followed in case of a violation by an individual or private organization.

It would be the function of the Inspection Service to detect such violations and the duty of the Inspector-General to decide what action should be taken in each case. If the Inspector-General should consider that a particular violation is due only to error, negligence or other minor cause, he is directed merely to warn the individual or organization concerned and, if necessary, to require the cessation of the prohibited activity within a fixed period. If such a violation were remedied in accordance with the order of the Inspector-General, no further action would, of course, be necessary.

If, however, the violator should persist in the violation, or if the Inspector-General should consider that the violation is of so serious a character that it ought to be prosecuted in accordance with the laws enacted by the General Assembly, it would be his duty to refer the matter to the prosecuting authority of the United Nations, namely, the Attorney-General of the United

Nations to be appointed pursuant to Part D of Annex III. The Attorney-General would then be responsible for the final decision as to the necessity for penal proceedings and the place where they should be instituted; and also as to whether an accused individual should be arrested, and whether provisional measures should be taken to prevent the continuance of the alleged illegal activity.

Article 33

1. The Inspector-General shall have authority to suspend or revoke any license issued by him to any nation or public or private organization or individual pursuant to Article 16 of this Annex, if he finds that the licensee has violated the terms of the license or any provision of this Annex or of any law or regulation enacted thereunder.

2. In case of the suspension or revocation of a license by the Inspector-General, the licensee, whether such licensee is a nation, a public or private organization or an individual, shall have the right to appeal to the Inspection Commission, and the right to appeal from a decision of the Commission to the United Nations regional court within the jurisdiction of which is included the territory of the nation to which or through which the license in question was issued. The Inspector-General shall have the right to appeal from a decision of the regional court to the International Court of Justice; and any nation which is itself a licensee or through which a license has been issued, shall have the same right of appeal on its own behalf or on behalf of the licensee for whom it obtained the license. An individual licensee or a licensee which is a public or private organization shall also have a right to appeal from a decision of the regional court to the International Court of Justice to the extent permitted by the laws enacted by the General Assembly pursuant to Part D of Annex III. In the case of any such appeal to the International Court of Justice, the decision of that Court shall be final.

Comment. The purpose of this Article is to enable the Inspection Service to exercise effective control over all the potentially dangerous activities for which a license is required under Article 16 of this Annex, including activities conducted by a nation itself and activities conducted by individuals or organizations within its territory. To this end the Inspector-General would be empowered to suspend or revoke any license if he makes a finding that the licensee has violated either the terms of the license or some specific provision of this Annex or any law or regulation enacted thereunder. This authority should operate as a powerful deterrent to any prohibited activity either of the nation itself or of the licensees sponsored by that nation, and should constitute a highly effective sanction supplementing the other sanctions provided in this Annex.

It is to be assumed that the power merely to suspend would be used in the case of less serious violations, the power of revocation being reserved for violations of the most serious character. In consequence of either a suspension or revocation, the licensee would be required completely to cease the licensed activity; might be deprived of all materials the possession of which requires a license; and might even be obliged to close all or part of the plant in which the licensed activities were being conducted. In view of these serious consequences to the licensee, it is important to provide safeguards against possible abuse of the Inspector-General's authority in this respect.

It is accordingly proposed to give any licensee (whether a nation, or public or private organization, or individual) an unqualified right to appeal from an order of the Inspector-General to the Inspection Commission in the first instance, and a further unqualified right to appeal to a United Nations regional court if dissatisfied with the Commission's decision. In respect of final appeals to the International Court of Justice, it is proposed that the Inspector-General shall have this right without qualification and also any nation, either on its own behalf as licensee or on behalf of a licensee for which the nation obtained a license. With regard, however, to appeals to the International Court by individuals or organizations, it seems necessary to qualify the right of appeal by limiting such right to cases where an appeal is permitted by laws enacted by the General Assembly under Part D of Annex III. Such laws should prohibit appeals by individuals and organizations in cases where the nation which obtained the license for the licensee has itself undertaken an appeal on behalf of the licensee. They might also, like the laws governing the jurisdiction of the United States Supreme Court, give the International Court itself considerable discretion as to what appeals of this character it would entertain. The purpose is to provide for every reasonable right of appeal and yet to relieve the International Court from a possible undue buden.

Article 34

1. If the Inspector-General determines that a particular violation of this Annex or of any law or regulation enacted thereunder is of a character that cannot be adequately dealt with by action against an individual or private organization, but is a violation by a nation itself or by a public agency or organization for which the government of a nation is directly or indirectly responsible, the procedure provided for in this Article shall be followed.

2. If the Inspector-General considers that such a violation is due only to negligence, error or improper action of subordinate authorities or officials and does not constitute a deliberate act of the government of the nation concerned, he shall call on that government to remedy the violation within a fixed period; and if the violation is duly remedied, no further action shall be taken.

3. If, however, a violation of the minor kind mentioned in paragraph 2 is not promptly remedied, or if there is a too frequent repetition of such minor violations, or if several such violations occur simultaneously, or if the Inspector-General considers that a particular violation is serious, or that there is an imminent threat of a serious violation, he shall immediately notify the Inspection Commission.

4. If a nation considers that any provision of this Annex or of any law or regulation enacted thereunder has been violated by another nation, or that any such violation is threatened, it may make a complaint to the Inspection Commission.

5. Any nation whose compliance with this Annex or with any law or regulation enacted thereunder may have been subjected to public criticism, shall be entitled to present to the Inspection Commission a request for an investigation.

6. When the Inspection Commission receives a notification, complaint or request pursuant to paragraphs 3, 4 or 5 of this Article, it shall invite the nation whose compliance with this Annex or with any law or regulation enacted thereunder has been questioned to supply the Commission with all information and explanations which may be useful. The Commission shall also invite any complaining nation, any other interested nation and any organization or individual deemed likely to have useful information to supply such information to the Commission; and no nation shall penalize directly or indirectly any nation, organization or individual supplying information to the Commission upon such request. The Inspection Commission may also order a special investigation on the spot under the supervision of one or more of its members; and the Commission shall order such investigation if requested by the nation whose compliance has been questioned. The limitations on the inspection process provided for in Articles 18 to 23 of this Annex shall not apply to a special investigation conducted under this paragraph.

7. The Inspection Commission shall prepare as soon as possible a reasoned report on the result of any such special investigation, taking into account the explanations, if any, supplied by the nation whose compliance has been questioned. If the report does not represent the unanimous opinion of the members of the Commission, any member shall be entitled to present a separate report.

8. All such reports of the Inspection Commission shall be immediately communicated to the Executive Council, to the General Assembly and to all the nations. They shall be made public as soon as possible.

9. No nation shall take, or allow to be taken, any measures restricting the publication within its territory of any such report of the Inspection Commission; nor shall any nation penalize directly or indirectly any individual or organization responsible for such publication.

10. If the Inspection Commission finds that no violation of this Annex or of any law or regulation enacted thereunder has occurred, it shall so state in its report. Any nation which disagrees with such a finding shall have the right to have the Executive Council consider the matter and, if the Council approves the finding, to bring the case to the International Court of Justice for final decision.

11. If, however, the Inspection Commission finds that a violation has occurred, it shall call upon the nation concerned to remedy the violation within a fixed period; and if the violation is duly remedied, the Commission shall so state in a special report. Any nation which disagrees with any such special report shall have the right to have the Executive Council consider the matter and, if the Council approves the special report, to bring the case to the International Court of Justice for final decision.

12. If the nation whose compliance has been questioned disagrees with a finding of the Inspection Commission that it has committed a violation, it shall have the right to have the Executive Council consider the matter and, if the Council approves the finding, to bring the case to the International Court of Justice for final decision. Pending the judgment of the Court upon any such appeal, the General Assembly (or the Executive Council in the circumstances defined in paragraph 2 of Article 39 of this revised Charter) may take such action under paragraph 13 of this Article as it may deem necessary to remedy the situation, unless the Court shall make an order enjoining such action, in whole or in part, during the Court's consideration of the appeal.

13. If a violation is not remedied within the period fixed by the Inspection Commission, the Commission shall immediately notify the Executive Council which shall forthwith submit the situation to the General Assembly if then in session; and the Assembly shall take such action under Chapter VII of this revised Charter as it may deem necessary to ensure compliance with this Annex. If the Assembly is not then in session, the Council shall take such interim measures as are authorized by paragraph 2 of Article 39 of this revised Charter, provided that the Council shall simultaneously request the Secretary-General to convoke a special session of the Assembly; the Assembly shall approve, modify or revoke the interim measures taken by the Council and may direct such further action under Chapter VII of this revised Charter as it deems necessary to ensure compliance with this Annex.

14. The procedures prescribed in the preceding paragraphs of this Article shall also be followed in cases of violations in which action has been taken in the first instance not by the Inspection Commission but by the Nuclear Energy Commission pursuant to Chapter V of this Annex, or by the Outer Space Commission pursuant to Chapter VI of this Annex. In such cases, the powers conferred by this Article upon the Inspection Com-

mission shall be exercised by the Nuclear Energy Commission or the Outer Space Commission, as the case may be.

Comment. This Article deals with the procedure to be followed in case of a violation by a nation or by a public agency or organization for which the government of a nation is directly or indirectly responsible.

If in such a case the Inspector-General is informed of a violation of this Annex or of any law or regulation enacted thereunder, he shall first determine whether such violation can be remedied by action against an individual official. If the Inspector-General determines that such a remedy will be inadequate (e.g., because the violation is of such scope that it would not have been committed without governmental cognizance or assistance), he would call upon the government of the nation concerned to remedy the violation within a fixed period. This step should be sufficient whenever the violation is due to negligence, error or improper action of subordinate officials (e.g., of a governor of a remote province who refuses to permit an inspection of his district). And if such violation were remedied in pursuance of the warning, no further action would be necessary, and no publicity need be given to the case.

If, however, the situation were not remedied within the period fixed by the Inspector-General, he would be required immediately to notify the Inspection Commission and send it all available information on the subject. The Inspector-General would also be required to send such a notification to the Inspection Commission, whenever there is a series of minor violations in a particular nation which seem to fall into a dangerous pattern, or when he believes that an actual or threatened violation is in itself of a serious character. Any such situation could also be brought before the Inspection Commission by any nation which had reason to believe that another nation had either actually violated the provisions of this Annex (or of any law or regulation enacted thereunder) or was about to commit such a violation. There is the further possibility that a nation might feel that its good faith was being questioned, as by a smearing press campaign, despite the fact that no official complaint had been brought against it; and in such case the nation concerned could request an investigation by the Inspection Commission to prove that the accusations were unfounded.

In any one of these cases, the Inspection Commission would be required to gather all available information. It would, moreover, be authorized to conduct a special investigation on the spot; and would be required to conduct such an investigation if requested by the nation whose compliance has been questioned. The investigating group would have complete freedom of movement in the territory of the nation which has been accused of a violation, and could not be hampered by the restrictions imposed by Chapter IV of this Annex on the ordinary activities of the Inspection Service; for example, the investigating group would not need to obtain a special court authorization for a search of suspected premises.

On the basis of the information received and of its own special investigation, the Inspection Commission would be required to draw up a report, which would be communicated to all concerned and widely publicized. The pressure of public opinion could thus be focused on the situation, and might well convince a nation which had been found guilty of a violation that it should bow to the verdict and remedy the situation within the period fixed by the Commission. Provision is also made that if the accused nation still feels that it is not guilty, it may appeal to the Executive Council and then to the International Court of Justice for a reconsideration of the case. It is further provided, however, that such an appeal shall not preclude any action necessary to remedy the situation, unless the Court should enjoin such action pending disposition of the appeal.

While affording every fair protection to an accused nation, it is necessary to ensure that the Inspection Commission does not too readily accept the nation's explanations. Provision is therefore made that any nation which believes that the Commission has erroneously exonerated the accused nation shall be entitled to appeal to the Executive Council, and from the decision of the Council to the International Court of Justice, the decision of which shall be final.

When a nation has been finally found guilty of a violation, the General Assembly (or in certain circumstances the Executive Council) would be empowered to decide what steps shall be taken to remedy the violation. Under Articles 41 and 42 of the revised Charter, these measures could include severance of diplomatic relations with the violator, or economic sanctions, and in extreme cases action by the United Nations Peace Force. If time permitted, the decision as to such disciplinary measures would be for the General Assembly. But under emergency conditions the Executive Council could direct interim measures in the first instance, all such decisions of the Council, however, to be promptly reviewed by the Assembly, which would either confirm, modify or revoke any such interim measures (Article 39 of the revised Charter).

Similar procedures would be followed in matters falling within the jurisdiction of one of the two other Commissions which would be responsible for the enforcement of the provisions of this Annex. Both the Nuclear Energy Commission and the Outer Space Commission would have the same powers in their special fields as would be possessed by the Inspection Commission under this Article. It could be expected that these several Commissions would cooperate in the performance of their duties under this Article, thus avoiding unnecessary duplication.

The various measures described above should be sufficient to ensure prompt and adequate enforcement of the disarmament plan against all possible violators, irrespective of size or strength. While it is believed that all these measures must be provided for, it can reasonably be expected that the more drastic of them would seldom or never need to be employed. An efficient and imaginative inspection system should enable the United Nations to discover any threat of a serious violation at an early stage, when warnings or, at most, limited enforcement measures should suffice to remove the danger.

ANNEX II

THE UNITED NATIONS PEACE FORCE

General Comment. This Annex contains a detailed plan for a world police force, to be called the United Nations Peace Force and to consist of two components, i.e., a full-time standing force with a strength of not less than 200,000 or more than 600,000 and a Peace Force Reserve with a strength of not less than 600,000 or more than 1,200,000. The standing force would be distributed throughout the world in its own bases and would include highly trained, mobile units ready to move at short notice; while the Reserve would be composed of partially trained individual reservists subject to call for service with the standing force in case of need.

These forces would not be composed of national contingents but of individual volunteers recruited from all the nations and with careful safeguards against any undue proportion from any nation. Within the above limits, the strength of the standing component and of the Reserve would be annually fixed by the General Assembly. All the expenses of the Peace Force would be borne by the United Nations pursuant to appropriations by the Assembly; and the Assembly would enact all necessary laws, within the limits of this Annex, governing the recruitment, pay, organization, administration, discipline, training, equipment and disposition of both components.

The general control of the Peace Force would rest with the Executive Council; while the immediate direction, both of the standing force and the Reserve, would be in the hands of a Military Staff Committee of five persons appointed from the smaller nations.

The General Assembly alone (except for temporary emergency action by the Executive Council) could order enforcement action by the Peace Force, any such action to be limited to measures absolutely essential to prevent or suppress violent aggression or serious defiance of the authority of the United Nations. Elaborate safeguards would be provided to prevent the use of the Peace Force for any other purpose.

This plan rests on two basic assumptions. The first is that, in order to provide the nations of the world with adequate protection, a permanent and indisputably effective supranational force must be provided to take the place of national armaments.

It is true, as already stressed, that the problem of maintaining peace calls for more than national disarmament and a world police, and that workable world institutions are also required to enable peaceful change and to mitigate excessive economic disparities between different regions of the world. Nevertheless, the importance of a reliable world police as an absolutely indispensable element of world order cannot be exaggerated,— just as an adequate and respected police force is essential to the maintenance of order in a large city. It has been well said that "in every civilized community the members contribute toward the maintenance of a police force as an arm of law and order" and "only the society of nations has failed to apply this rudimentary principle of civilized life." The purpose of this Annex II is to apply that principle to the problem of world order through a detailed and practical plan.

The second basic assumption is that it would not be feasible to maintain an adequate world police force unless national disarmament is not only universal but also complete. While a world police force can and should be moderate in numbers, it must be strong enough to provide reliable protection against any foreseeable violation of world peace; and it would be clearly impracticable to maintain a world force of sufficient strength to supply the necessary confidence if any considerable national military forces remained in existence. For example, if we assume that in 1960 the strength of all national military forces on full-time duty is about fifteen million men, a reduction even by four fifths to three million would still make it impossible, as a practical matter, to maintain a world police that would unquestionably be superior to some possible military alliance. Theoretically it might seem feasible to reduce national military forces by nine tenths or more, to a point where even a strong alliance would not threaten a world police. In practice, however, it would probably be easier to agree on a complete elimination of national armaments than on a reduction to a very small fraction. And even if it were possible to reduce all the national forces of the world to one million men, the suspicion would still remain that they could be easily expanded and become dangerous in this age of new and appalling weapons. The practical fact is, therefore, that the problem of maintaining a world force capable of preventing or suppressing all international violence becomes manageable only under a regime of complete national disarmament.

With these considerations in mind, the proposed Annex I calls for absolutely complete national disarmament, thus making it practicable to provide in this Annex II for a United Nations military force sufficiently powerful promptly to suppress any threat to the world's peace. At the same time Annex II contains careful safeguards against the danger that any such world police force might itself threaten to dominate the world.

It is proposed that the United Nations Peace Force shall be built up parallel with and proportionate to the process of national disarmament and would thus attain its full strength at the end of the ten-year period of actual disarmament called for by Annex I. That strength would be determined from time to time by the General Assembly, but the Assembly would be required to observe the constitutional limitation that the strength of the standing component of the Peace Force shall not be less than 200,000 or more than 600,000 and of the Peace Force Reserve not less than 600,000 or more than 1,200,000. Only in the possible event of an extreme emergency, and if the General Assembly should determine that it was essential to exceed the ordinary maximum limits, would the Assembly have authority to enlarge the Peace Force for the period of the extreme emergency only beyond the maximum total limit of 1,800,000.

The members of the Peace Force would normally be recruited by voluntary enlistment only; and the Peace Force would ordinarily do its own recruiting.

In case, however, of an extreme emergency when the ordinary maximum limits had been raised, the United Nations could seek the aid of the member Nations in bringing the strength of the Peace Force to the temporarily authorized higher level. In such event, the Assembly could assign quotas of recruits to be raised for the Peace Force by the respective nations. But even in this case, the member Nations would be required to fill their quotas by voluntary enlistment if possible, and to employ a compulsory draft only in the last resort.

To ensure against domination of the Peace Force by any nation or group of nations, it is proposed that the number of nationals of any nation serving in the Peace Force shall at no time exceed three per cent of the total strength of the Peace Force, except that this limit would be five per cent during a possible time of extreme emergency. On the other hand, no nation could be required to furnish recruits, even in an extreme emergency, to a number which would make the number of its nationals in the Peace Force exceed one per cent of the population of such nation.

For the maintenance of a successful world police force, it is all-important that it shall command the confidence and respect of the people of the world. Just as an effective police force of a great city—whether it be London, Moscow, New York or Tokyo—needs the confidence and, if possible, the liking of the people, the same is no less true of a police force for the world.

This objective is explicitly stated in paragraph 2 of Article 1 of this Annex II in the words: "In the recruitment and organization of the United Nations Peace Force, the objective shall be to constitute and maintain a force which will be composed of individuals with exceptional qualifications, which will command the respect of all the peoples and be fully adequate to the task of safeguarding the peace of the world."

Accordingly, this Annex includes a careful set of provisions designed to ensure that the Peace Force shall be well adapted to its vital task.

Obviously the most important single factor in obtaining "respect" for a world police is the quality of its personnel. This will depend primarily on the physical, mental and moral qualifications of those who volunteer, on care in selection, on adequate pay and good living conditions while in service, on proper retirement allowances, and on the excellence of the officer corps. Therefore, while the General Assembly would have considerable discretion in enacting the "basic laws" for the organization of the Peace Force, it would be required to observe a number of Charter provisions on these points.

As to terms of service, the proposal is that for the standing component it shall be not less than four or more than eight years, as determined by the General Assembly, the purpose being to ensure that the personnel shall be highly trained. To ensure continuity and stability, re-enlistments of "especially well-qualified personnel" are also provided for; but, in order to have a continuous inflow of new recruits, it is proposed that the number of re-enlistments in a particular year shall not exceed three quarters of those whose first terms of service expire during that year or one half of those whose second terms of service expire during that year.

The proposed service terms for reservists are somewhat wider, i.e., not less than six or more than ten years, as fixed by the General Assembly. This

316

difference is made, because as distinguished from the standing component, the Peace Force Reserve would consist merely of individual reservists, partially trained and living at home. They would be obliged to undergo not less than four or more than eight months basic training during the first three years of their period of service and thereafter would be required to take additional training aggregating not less than four or more than eight months. Except when in training, or when called to active duty (which could be only in case of grave emergency), they would live at home pursuing their regular vocations. Their arms would be kept at the various bases throughout the world at which units of the standing component were stationed. Their uniforms, however, would presumably be kept at home and might well be worn on occasions of ceremony such as United Nations Day, commemorating the anniversary of the coming into force of the 1945 Charter, or the equally significant anniversary of the coming into force of the revised Charter.

In respect of age limitations, the proposed maximum limit for initial enlistment in either component is twenty-five so as to make sure that, combined with the re-enlistment limitation, both the standing component and the Reserve would be mainly composed of young and vigorous men (and women, since a small percentage of both components would presumably consist of women).

With regard to compensation, there would be a specific requirement that the pay and allowances of the standing component shall be "fully adequate" and that there also must be "fully adequate retirement allowances" after "loyal and reasonably long service." As to the Reserve it would be provided that they shall receive "fair compensation" in return for "their obligation to hold themselves in readiness" and that when in training or on active duty, they shall receive "full pay and allowances on the same basis as members of the standing component."

The independence and prestige of the Peace Force would also be promoted by the proposed provision that members of the standing component shall have the right at the termination of their service to settle in any nation of their own choice if they have been honorably discharged after two full periods of enlistment.

The question of an officer corps of the highest possible standard is of prime importance. The methods whereby the officers would be selected, trained, promoted and retired must of necessity be left to the General Assembly. One requirement is, however, provided for, namely that there shall be "adequate opportunity" for the selection of highly qualified men from the ranks as officer candidates. As an encouragement for the enlistment of men of high quality, this provision is deemed essential.

Besides having the highest possible quality of personnel, the Peace Force should be equipped with excellent and up-to-date weapons. Moreover, in order to have a high degree of mobility so that the units of the standing component could be promptly concentrated, the Peace Force should be provided with fully adequate aircraft for troop transportation. Initially both components would be largely equipped by taking over arms and equipment discarded by national forces during the process of stage-by-stage disarmament. In later years, however, the Peace Force would need to be provided with newly manufactured arms and equipment; and to this end provision is made for their direct manufacture by the United Nations in its own plants under the management of a separate agency to be known as the United Nations Military Supply and Research Agency. The functions of this Agency would include research in new weapons and equipment, in order that the Peace Force shall at all times be equipped in the most modern manner.

Another distinct set of provisions would provide strict safeguards to prevent subversion of the Peace Force either by external or internal influences. These safeguards would include the following provisions:

1. Units of the Peace Force shall be composed to the greatest possible extent of nationals of different nations and no unit exceeding fifty in number shall be composed of nationals of a single nation.

2. Units of the Peace Force shall be stationed in military bases leased and controlled by the United Nations itself; these bases to be located in easily defensible places (such as islands and peninsulas), and all to be located in the territories of the smaller nations, i.e., the nearly ninety nations which would be entitled to less than fifteen Representatives in the General Assembly.

3. The standing component of the Peace Force shall be distributed in such a way that not less than five per cent or more than ten per cent of its total strength would be stationed in any one of the eleven to twenty regions of the world to be delineated for that purpose by the General Assembly.

4. The immediate direction of the Peace Force would not be in the hands of a single person, but would be entrusted to a committee of five persons all of whom would be nationals of the smaller nations—the Military Staff Committee. Only if action by the Peace Force had been ordered by the General Assembly, or in case of an emergency by the Executive Council, could commanders for its land, sea and air components and regional commanders, or in exceptional circumstances a temporary Commander-in-Chief, be appointed by the Executive Council; and their terms would expire at the end of the particular operation.

5. The Military Staff Committee would be under the general control of the Executive Council; and the General Assembly, through its Standing Committee on the Peace Enforcement Agencies, would exercise a close watch over the carrying out by the Military Staff Committee and the Executive Council of their responsibilities.

With regard to authority to order action by the Peace Force, care has been taken to limit such authority solely to the civilian authorities of the United Nations, i.e., the General Assembly itself or the Executive Council. Action by the Council would, however, be authorized only if the Assembly is not in session and special circumstances require immediate action, and there would be the additional safeguard that if the Council orders any such action, it must forthwith summon the Assembly in special session. These strict requirements would not, of course, prejudice the right of the Peace Force to defend itself in case of a possible direct attack against it.

Besides these safeguards as to authorizing any sort of action by the Peace Force, further safeguards are proposed as to the nature and extent of such action. In this regard, it is proposed that in ordering any action by the Peace Force to prevent or remove a threat to the peace, to suppress an act of aggression or to ensure compliance with the revised Charter, the General Assembly (or in case of an emergency the Executive Council) would be required to limit any such action to measures absolutely necessary to accomplish the desired end. For instance, in the event of threats to the peace of a minor sort, a mere demonstration by a few naval or air units of the Peace Force might well suffice to stop any further unlawful activity. Stronger measures would be required only in case of an actual aggression or serious resistance to United Nations authority; and even then any unnecessary destruction of life or property would be forbidden.

The solution proposed for the equipment of the Peace Force with nuclear weapons and their possible use is that the Force shall not be normally equipped with nuclear weapons at all, but that such weapons shall be held in reserve in the custody of the Nuclear Energy Authority, never to be used save by the order of the General Assembly itself and then only if such weapons have actually been used against the United Nations or such use is imminently threatened. While it would be possible to equip a world police force with these weapons of mass destruction so that it could crush forthwith any aggression by ruthless action, this is deemed no more consistent with the purpose of the Peace Force than it would be to equip a city police force with weapons which might tempt it to suppress a riot by the slaughter of thousands of citizens.

The Peace Force would, therefore, be so organized and equipped as to operate with the absolute minimum of force and destruction. On the other hand, while the possibility remains, as it would remain under the most effective inspection system, that somewhere or somehow nuclear weapons could be secretly concealed or manufactured, it seems necessary to make such counter-weapons available to the Peace Force in case of absolute need. The proposed precautions whereby these nuclear weapons would not ordinarily be in the possession of the Peace Force at all, but would be in charge of the Nuclear Energy Authority, subject only to release by order of the General Assembly itself, are intended to provide the maximum possible assurance against the misuse of these weapons.

During the period of actual disarmament (normally ten years) when the Peace Force would not as yet have achieved its full strength, the United Nations might perhaps need additional military forces if an emergency should arise. Since some national military forces would still exist during all of that period until the very end thereof, it is proposed to impose upon each member Nation the interim obligation to make available to the United Nations one tenth of the gradually diminishing strength of its military forces as they exist from time to time during the actual disarmament stage. The possible employment of such national contingents would be subject to various safeguards; and the General Assembly would have power to adopt laws and regulations to provide further guarantees that these forces would only be called upon and used for proper purposes.

By virtue of these carefully integrated measures, the United Nations should be able to suppress any attack by nation against nation or any possible revolt against its own authority with a minimum of destruction, either of life or

319

property. At the same time, it is believed that the careful safeguards established in this Annex II would be sufficient to reduce to a minimum any risk that the Peace Force itself might seek to endanger the freedom of the world.

The probable cost of the United Nations Peace Force is obviously a matter of interest and importance. It would, of course, depend largely on the authorized strength from time to time of the standing component which might vary, as determined by the General Assembly, between the constitutional minimum of 200,000 and the maximum of 600,000. If, however, we assume a midway figure of 400,000, some reasonably accurate estimates are possible on the basis of an assumed over-all per capita cost for all items,—pay, pensions, housing, clothing, food, transportation, equipment, etc. The corresponding cost per man in 1959 for the approximately 2,500,000 men in the military forces of the United States was about $16,000 per man; and, while this may seem a high figure, it is probably a fair estimate for a world police force of very high quality and stationed, as it would be, in all parts of the world.

On this assumption, the annual cost for a 400,000 standing component of the Peace Force would be roundly $6.4 billion, to which must be added the cost of the Peace Force Reserve. If we make a similar assumption that the Reserve would be maintained at a strength of 900,000, i.e., midway between the constitutional minimum and maximum of 600,000 and 1,200,000, and if we take an assumed average of about $2500 per man, and add active-training expenses for, say, 100,000 reservists each year, we would have a total annual cost for the Reserve of roundly $2.7 billion.

On this basis the total annual cost of the Peace Force would be slightly more than $9 billion,—an amount believed to be reasonable for a world police of very high quality and of an assumed strength of 400,000 on full-time duty with 900,000 reservists. If the actual strength were at the minimum of 200,000 and 600,000 for the two components, the estimated cost would be correspondingly less; on the other hand, correspondingly more if the two components were maintained at their constitutional maximum strength.

While a cost of, say, $9 billion for a world police force may seem formidable, it is to be remembered that this cost would be many times offset by the complete elimination of all national military forces, the total expense of which in 1960 is estimated at not less than $100 billion.

* * * * *

A United Nations Peace Force organized and restricted as envisaged by this Annex should give to the peoples of the world that assurance of protection which would enable them to accept with confidence the idea of complete national disarmament.

The proposed text of Annex II covering the organization, maintenance, command, etc. of this Peace Force now follows. While no detailed comment follows each of the eight Articles, it is believed that their intent and interrelation are adequately explained in the foregoing General Comment.

320

CHAPTER I

BASIC PRINCIPLES

Article 1

1. In order to make available to the United Nations effective means for the enforcement of universal and complete national disarmament, for the prevention and removal of threats to the peace, for the suppression of acts of aggression or other breaches of the peace, and for ensuring compliance with this revised Charter and the laws and regulations enacted thereunder, an independent United Nations military force shall be established to be called the United Nations Peace Force.

2. In the recruitment and organization of the United Nations Peace Force, the objective shall be to constitute and maintain a force composed of individuals with exceptional qualifications, which will command the respect of all the peoples and be fully adequate to the task of safeguarding the peace of the world.

3. The United Nations Peace Force shall in no case be employed to achieve objectives inconsistent with the Purposes and Principles of this revised Charter.

CHAPTER II

ORGANIZATION AND FUNCTIONS

Article 2

1. The United Nations Peace Force shall consist of two components: a full-time, standing force and a reserve force composed of partially trained individual reservists subject to call. The term "United Nations Peace Force" or "Peace Force" shall be deemed to include both components; the term "standing component" shall be deemed to mean the full-time, standing force; and the term "Peace Force Reserve" or "Reserve" shall be deemed to mean the reserve force. The United Nations Peace Force shall be recruited and organized in accordance with the provisions of this Chapter.

2. The General Assembly shall annually determine the strength of the standing component and of the Peace Force Reserve for the next fiscal year, provided that, except in case of extreme emergency declared by the Assembly pursuant to Chapter III of this Annex, the strength of the standing component shall be not less than 200,000 or more than 600,000, and the strength of the Reserve shall be not less than 600,000 or more than 1,200,000.

3. The United Nations Peace Force shall be organized step by step in accordance with the following plan:

a. Before the end of the third month of the preparatory stage provided for in Annex I, the Executive Council shall appoint the first members of the Military Staff Committee, in accordance with and subject to the limitations of Article 47 of this revised Charter. The terms of office of the first members of the Military Staff Committee shall begin on the same day and shall expire, as designated by the Council at the time of their appointment, one at the end of one year, one at the end of two years, one at the end of three years, one at the end of four years and one at the end of five years from that date; later appointments shall be for terms of equal lengths for all members of the Committee, to be determined from time to time by the Council, but in no case shall they exceed five years.

b. Before the end of the first year of the preparatory stage, the General Assembly shall, after receiving a report on the subject from the Executive Council, and in accordance with the objective set forth in paragraph 2 of Article 1 of this Annex and subject to the other principles and limitations set forth in this Annex, adopt the basic laws necessary to provide for the organization, administration, recruitment, discipline, training, equipment and disposition of both the standing and the reserve components of the Peace Force.

c. During the second year of the preparatory stage, the Military Staff Committee shall make all necessary preparations for the recruitment and training of both components of the Peace Force, and shall organize the administrative staff necessary for that purpose.

d. When the Executive Council has announced the beginning of the period of actual disarmament pursuant to Article 9 of Annex I, the Military Staff Committee shall proceed to the recruitment within the next year following such announcement of: (1) the first ten per cent of the strength of the standing component as then authorized by the General Assembly, and (2) the first ten per cent of the strength of the Peace Force Reserve as then authorized by the Assembly. Thereafter, the standing component and the Reserve shall be increased by ten per cent of their respective authorized strengths during each new annual period for the reduction of national military forces pursuant to Articles 10 and 12 of Annex I. The recruitment of the standing component and of the Reserve shall thus be carried on parallel with and proportionate to the process of national disarmament and shall be completed simultaneously with the completion of the actual disarmament stage; and the recruitment of both components shall be correspondingly accelerated if the General Assembly should shorten the actual disarmament stage in accordance with paragraph 2 of Article 10 of Annex I.

4. The members of both components of the United Nations Peace Force shall ordinarily be recruited wholly by voluntary enlistment. The General Assembly shall have no power to enact any compulsory draft law; and no nation shall apply any sort of compulsion to require its nationals or persons resident in its territory to enlist in either component of the Peace Force, except under the circumstances set forth in Article 43 of this revised Charter and subject to the limitations set forth in Chapter III of this Annex.

5. The members of both components of the United Nations Peace Force shall be selected on the basis of their competence, integrity and devotion to the purposes of the United Nations. At the time of initial enlistment they shall be not more than twenty-five years of age.

6. The members of both components of the United Nations Peace Force shall make a solemn declaration of loyalty to the United Nations, in a form prescribed by the General Assembly. They shall not seek or receive instructions from any government or other authority external to the United Nations. They shall refrain from any conduct which might reflect on their position as members of the Peace Force responsible only to the United Nations.

7. The term of service of members of the standing component of the United Nations Peace Force shall be not less than four or more than eight years, as determined from time to time by the General Assembly. The Assembly shall provide for the re-enlistment of especially well-qualified personnel, but the number of re-enlistments in any year shall not exceed three quarters of those whose first terms of service expire during that year or one half of those whose second terms of service expire during that year.

8. The term of service of members of the Peace Force Reserve shall be not less than six or more than ten years, as determined from time to time by the General Assembly. They shall receive basic training of not less than four or more than eight months during the first three years of their term of service, and during the remainder of their term of service additional training of not less than four or more than eight months, as determined from time to time by the Assembly.

9. The officers of both components of the United Nations Peace Force shall be selected, trained, promoted and retired with a view to ensuring an officer corps of the highest possible quality; and adequate opportunity shall be provided for the selection as officer candidates of highly qualified men from the rank and file.

10. The members of the standing component of the United Nations Peace Force shall receive fully adequate pay and allowances together with fully adequate retirement pensions after loyal and reasonably long service. The members of the Peace Force Reserve, when in training or on active duty, shall receive full pay and allowances on the same basis as members of the standing component, and when not in training or on active duty shall receive fair compensation in return for their obligation to hold themselves in readiness. All such pay and other compensation, including retirement pensions, shall be free from all taxation.

11. A member of the standing component of the United Nations Peace Force after being honorably discharged therefrom following at least two full enlistment periods, shall be entitled to choose freely the nation in which he and his dependents desire to establish residence, and he and his dependents shall be entitled to acquire the nationality of that nation if they are not already nationals thereof.

12. The members of both components of the United Nations Peace Force shall be recruited on as wide a geographical basis as possible, subject, except in an extreme emergency as provided in Article 7 of this Annex, to the following limitations:

a. That the number of nationals of any nation (including any non-self-governing or trust territory under its administration) serving at any one time in either component shall not exceed three per cent of the then existing total strength of such component.

b. That the number of nationals of any nation (including any non-self-governing or trust territory under its administration) serving at any one time in any of the three main branches of either component (land, sea and air) shall not exceed three per cent of the then existing strength of such main branch.

c. That the number of nationals of any nation (including any non-self-governing or trust territory under its administration) serving at any one time in the officer corps of either of the three main branches of either component shall not exceed three per cent of the then existing strength of the officer corps of such main branch.

d. That not less than five per cent or more than ten per cent of the members of either component of the Peace Force shall be nationals of the nation or nations constituting any one of the regions delineated under paragraph 9 of Article 26 of Annex I.

13. Units of the United Nations Peace Force shall be composed to the greatest possible extent of persons of different nationality and, to this end, no unit exceeding fifty in number shall be composed of nationals of a single nation (including any non-self-governing or trust territory under its administration).

14. The standing component of the United Nations Peace Force shall be stationed at military bases of the United Nations, which shall be so distributed around the world as to facilitate prompt action by the standing component in case such action is directed by the General Assembly, or the Executive Council in the circumstances defined in paragraph 2 of Article 39 of this revised Charter. No such base shall be situated within the territory of any nation which has fifteen or more Representatives in the General Assembly. All the remaining territory of the world shall be divided by the Assembly into not less than eleven or more than twenty regions for the purpose of the disposition among them of the standing component of the Peace Force. Not less than five per cent or more than ten per cent of the total strength of the standing component shall be stationed in bases located in any one of the regions so delineated, except when the Peace Force has been duly called upon to take action to maintain or restore international peace or to ensure compliance with this revised Charter and the laws and regulations enacted thereunder. All such military bases shall be located to the greatest extent possible on islands or peninsulas, or in other easily defensible positions.

15. The military bases of the United Nations shall be obtained by the United Nations from or with the assistance of the respective nations in the territories of which it is desired to locate the bases. Such bases shall be acquired on long-term leases, by agreement if possible and otherwise by condemnation with just compensation; provided that no such base shall be located in the territory of a nonmember nation without the consent of its government; and further provided that the United Nations shall not, except with the consent of the government concerned,

acquire an area exceeding one tenth of one per cent of the territory of any nation or an area in any nation exceeding three per cent of the total area of all such bases throughout the world.

The General Assembly shall adopt regulations governing the selection of the military bases and the payment of just compensation in the form of equitable rentals therefor. In case of a dispute as to whether the rent paid or offered by the United Nations is equitable, the private owner of the property in question, or the nation which owns such property or within which such property is situated acting on its own behalf or on behalf of the private owner of such property as the case may be, may submit the dispute for decision to the United Nations regional court within the jurisdiction of which such property is situated. If either the United Nations or the private owner of the property in question or the nation which owns such property or in the territory of which such property is situated is dissatisfied with the decision of the regional court, any of them shall have the right to appeal to the International Court of Justice; except that in the case of a private owner, such right shall be subject to any legislation which may be enacted by the General Assembly pursuant to Part D of Annex III. In the case of such an appeal to the International Court of Justice, the decision of that Court shall be final.

16. The United Nations Peace Force shall not possess or use any biological, chemical or other weapons adaptable to mass destruction, save only such nuclear weapons as it may be specially authorized by the General Assembly to possess and use pursuant to Article 4 of this Annex; but the Peace Force may possess and use all other weapons to the extent authorized and provided for by the Assembly. The Peace Force shall acquire its initial arms and equipment (including airplanes and naval vessels) through the transfer to it of arms and equipment (including airplanes and naval vessels) discarded by national military forces during the period of actual disarmament pursuant to paragraph 3 of Article 11 of Annex I. Any further arms and equipment (including airplanes and naval vessels) subsequently needed by the Peace Force shall be produced by the United Nations in its own production facilities. These production facilities shall be administered by a separate agency of the United Nations, which shall be called the United Nations Military Supply and Research Agency and shall be established pursuant to legislation to be enacted by the General Assembly. Such production facilities shall be initially equipped with machines, appliances and tools discarded during the period of actual disarmament pursuant to paragraph 4 of Article 11 of Annex I; and any further machines, appliances and tools subsequently needed for these production facilities shall be manufactured by the United Nations in its own plants, to be administered by the Military Supply and Research Agency. The requirement contained in the preceding two sentences that the production of arms and equipment (in-

cluding airplanes and naval vessels), and of machines, appliances and tools for their manufacture shall be confined to the production facilities and plants of the United Nations itself, shall not apply if and when the General Assembly shall have declared the existence of an extreme emergency pursuant to Chapter III of this Annex.

17. The United Nations Military Supply and Research Agency shall, to the extent authorized and provided for by the General Assembly, engage in research related to the development of new military weapons or the improvement of existing weapons of the kind which the United Nations Peace Force is permitted to have; and also in research relative to methods of defense against the possible illegal use of nuclear, biological, chemical or other weapons adaptable to mass destruction.

18. The stocks of arms and equipment of both components of the United Nations Peace Force shall be located in the military bases of the United Nations. The facilities of the United Nations Military Supply and Research Agency for the production of arms and equipment (including airplanes and naval vessels), its facilities for the production of machines, appliances and tools for the production of arms and equipment, and its facilities for research, shall also be located in the military bases of the United Nations or in areas leased by the United Nations for this purpose, such leases to be subject to the provisions and limitations of paragraph 15 of this Article. The Peace Force and the Military Supply and Research Agency respectively shall, subject to the approval of the Executive Council, arrange for such a geographical distribution of these stocks and facilities as will minimize the risk that any nation or group of nations might achieve a military advantage by the seizure of stocks or facilities situated in a particular territory or region; and to this end, such arrangements shall provide that not less than five per cent or more than ten per cent of the total amount of these stocks and not less than five per cent or more than ten per cent of the total productive capacity of these facilities shall be concentrated in any one of the regions provided for in paragraph 14 of this Article.

19. The United Nations Peace Force shall, to the extent authorized and provided for by the General Assembly, possess and operate rockets, satellites and spacecraft for reconnaissance and police purposes. Special precautions shall be taken pursuant to paragraph 18 of this Article to distribute the stocks of such rockets, satellites and spacecraft, and the facilities for launching them, around the world in such a manner as will minimize the risk that any nation or group of nations might achieve a military advantage by the seizure of the stocks or facilities situated in any particular region.

20. The United Nations Peace Force shall, to the extent authorized and provided for by the General Assembly, employ civilian personnel for the performance of all such services and functions as do not need

to be performed by military personnel; but such civilian personnel shall not be deemed to be members of the Peace Force.

21. The expenses of the United Nations Peace Force and of the United Nations Military Supply and Research Agency shall be borne by the United Nations. The General Assembly shall determine the compensation and allowances of the Military Staff Committee; and after receiving a report on the subject from that Committee and the recommendations of the Executive Council as to such report, shall determine the pay and allowances of the personnel of the Peace Force. The annual budget of the Peace Force shall be prepared by the Military Staff Committee, subject to the approval of the Executive Council. The annual budget of the Military Supply and Research Agency shall be prepared by the management of that Agency subject to the approval of the Executive Council. Both budgets shall be submitted to the General Assembly for action pursuant to the procedure provided for in Annex V. No appropriation for the use of the Peace Force or the Military Supply and Research Agency shall be made for a longer term than two years.

Article 3

1. The General Assembly shall have authority from time to time to amend the basic laws adopted pursuant to subparagraph (b) of paragraph 3 of Article 2 of this Annex and to enact such laws and regulations, additional to such basic laws, as it may deem necessary for the organization, administration, recruitment, discipline, training, equipment and disposition of the United Nations Peace Force; provided that all such amendments and new laws and regulations shall be in accordance with and subject to the principles and limitations set forth in this Annex.

2. Subject to such laws and regulations and subject to the general control of the Executive Council, the Military Staff Committee shall have the immediate direction of the United Nations Peace Force. The Executive Council may from time to time issue such instructions to the Military Staff Committee as the Council deems necessary.

3. The Military Staff Committee shall submit monthly reports to the Executive Council and such special reports as the Military Staff Committee may deem necessary or as the Council may call for.

4. The General Assembly, through its Standing Committee on the Peace Enforcement Agencies provided for in Article 22 of this revised Charter, shall watch over the carrying out by the Military Staff Committee and the Executive Council of their responsibilities under this Annex. This Standing Committee shall be entitled to obtain from the Military Staff Committee and the Council all relevant information and shall make such investigations as it may deem necessary or as the Assembly may request it to make. If in the judgment of the Standing Com-

mittee a situation exists which requires the convoking of a special session of the Assembly, it shall be entitled in accordance with Article 20 of this revised Charter to request the Secretary-General to convoke such special session.

Article 4

1. In accordance with Article 46 of this revised Charter, advance plans for possible action by the United Nations Peace Force to maintain or restore international peace or to ensure compliance with this revised Charter and the laws and regulations enacted thereunder, shall be made by the Executive Council with the assistance of the Military Staff Committee.

2. When action by the standing component or by both components of the Peace Force has been directed by the General Assembly pursuant to Articles 37, 40, 42 or 43 of this revised Charter, or if action by the standing component has been directed by the Executive Council in the circumstances defined in paragraph 2 of Article 39 of this revised Charter, the Military Staff Committee shall be responsible for the final preparation and execution of the plans for such action, subject to the general control of the Executive Council.

3. When action by only a part of the standing component of the Peace Force has been directed by the General Assembly, or by the Executive Council in the circumstances defined in paragraph 2 of Article 39 of this revised Charter, the Council may, with the advice of the Military Staff Committee, appoint regional commanders and commanders of the land, sea and air elements; and when action by the whole standing component has been directed, the Council, if it deems such appointment essential, may also appoint a Commander-in-Chief. All such commanders shall be appointed by the Executive Council for terms not exceeding the period of the actual operation in the particular situation; and they shall be removable at any time by the Council.

4. No action by the United Nations Peace Force pursuant to Articles 37, 40, 42 or 43 of this revised Charter shall be permitted without prior authorization of the General Assembly, or of the Executive Council in the circumstances defined in Article 37 or in paragraph 2 of Article 39, respectively, of this revised Charter, but this provision shall not impair the inherent right of the Peace Force to take strictly necessary measures of self-defense in case of an armed attack on its bases, ships, or airplanes, or on its personnel stationed outside its bases.

5. Any action by the United Nations Peace Force pursuant to Articles 37, 40, 42 or 43 of this revised Charter shall be limited to such operations as are strictly necessary to maintain or restore international peace or to ensure compliance with this revised Charter and the laws and regu-

329

lations enacted thereunder, and any unnecessary destruction of life or property shall at all times be avoided. If in case of a large-scale violation which cannot be dealt with by more limited means it should be deemed absolutely essential to destroy or damage an inhabited locality, the inhabitants shall be given sufficient warning so that they may evacuate it in time. Whenever possible, and in particular when action is being taken to forestall rather than suppress a breach of the peace or a violation of this revised Charter or of the laws or regulations enacted thereunder, any use of force shall be preceded by naval or air demonstrations, accompanied by a warning that specified further measures will be taken if the breach or violation does not cease. When a violation consists of the operation of prohibited or unlicensed installations, establishments or facilities, the action of the Peace Force shall be confined to the occupation unless the destruction of such installations, establishments or facilities (including plants supplying them with heat and electricity and the main lines of communications in their vicinity) is absolutely essential to prevent a continuance of the illegal operation.

6. The United Nations Peace Force shall in no event employ nuclear weapons except when the General Assembly: (a) has declared that a nuclear weapon has actually been used either against a nation or against the United Nations itself or that there is a serious and imminent threat that a nuclear weapon will be so used; (b) has declared that nothing less than the use of a nuclear weapon or weapons by the Peace Force will suffice to prevent or suppress a serious breach of the peace or a violent and serious defiance of the authority of the United Nations; and (c) has authorized the United Nations Nuclear Energy Authority to transfer to the Peace Force one or more nuclear weapons. When the occasion for the use or possible use of a nuclear weapon or weapons by the Peace Force has ceased, or when the General Assembly so directs, any nuclear weapon or weapons so transferred to the Peace Force shall be forthwith returned to the Nuclear Energy Authority.

7. The United Nations Peace Force shall in no case use rockets, satellites or spacecraft in its military operations except when the General Assembly has declared that nothing less than the use of such weapons by the Peace Force will suffice to prevent or suppress a serious breach of the peace or a violent and serious defiance of the authority of the United Nations.

8. The United Nations Peace Force, when taking action pursuant to Articles 37, 40, 42 or 43 of this revised Charter, shall be entitled to pass freely through the territory of any nation and to obtain from any nation such assistance with respect to temporary bases, supplies and transport as may be needed by it. The General Assembly shall enact laws regulating the extent of such assistance and the payment of just compensation therefor.

9. Upon the termination of any action by the United Nations Peace Force pursuant to Articles 37, 40, 42 or 43 of this revised Charter, the Peace Force shall be withdrawn as soon as possible to its bases.

Article 5

1. The members of the United Nations Peace Force and its civilian employees, together with their dependents, shall be entitled to all the privileges and immunities provided for in Annex VI.

2. The United Nations shall have exclusive criminal and disciplinary jurisdiction in respect of the members of the Peace Force, its civilian employees and the dependents of such members and employees in any area which the United Nations has leased for the use of the Peace Force within the territory of any nation. The General Assembly shall enact laws defining the offenses committed in any such area by any member of the Peace Force or by any civilian employee or any dependent of such member or employee, prescribing the penalties therefor, and providing for the apprehension, trial and punishment of any such member of the Peace Force, or civilian employee or dependent who is accused of any such offense. If a person so accused is found outside any such area, the authorities of the nation in which such person is found shall assist in his apprehension and in removing him to the area in which the alleged offense was committed.

3. Other criminal and civil jurisdiction in respect of members of the United Nations Peace Force and its civilian employees and their dependents, shall be exercised by the national authorities having jurisdiction in respect of the acts and omissions, transactions or relations in question in accordance with international law, except as such jurisdiction may be modified by agreement between the United Nations and the respective nations. The General Assembly may, however, in case of an apparent gross denial of justice by any nation to any member of the Peace Force, or civilian employee thereof, or to any of their dependents, provide by law for an appeal by the United Nations or the person concerned to the United Nations regional court within the jurisdiction of which the apparent denial of justice has occurred. If either the United Nations or the person or nation concerned is dissatisfied with the decision of the regional court, any of them shall have the right to appeal to the International Court of Justice; except that in the case of the person concerned, such right shall be subject to any legislation which may be enacted by the General Assembly pursuant to Part D of Annex III. In the case of such an appeal to the International Court of Justice, the decision of the Court shall be final.

331

CHAPTER III

ENLARGEMENT IN CASE OF GRAVE OR EXTREME EMERGENCY

Article 6

1. If the General Assembly, pursuant to paragraph 1 of Article 43 of this revised Charter, shall have declared the existence of a grave emergency, it shall call all or part of the United Nations Peace Force Reserve to active duty pursuant to the following procedures and subject to the following limitations:

a. If such call to active duty is for less than all of the Peace Force Reserve, members of the Reserve shall be called to duty in proportion, as nearly as may be, to the number of nationals of the respective nations then enrolled in the Reserve.

b. The period of active duty required under any such call shall not exceed the period of the grave emergency, and no member of the Reserve shall be obliged to serve after the expiration of the term of service for which he has been originally enrolled pursuant to paragraph 8 of Article 2 of this Annex.

2. If the General Assembly shall have declared the existence of a grave emergency pursuant to paragraph 1 of Article 43 of this revised Charter and if at that time the authorized strength of the standing component of the Peace Force is below its constitutional limit of 600,000 or the authorized strength of the Peace Force Reserve is below its constitutional limit of 1,200,000, the Assembly may increase the authorized strength of the standing force to 600,000 or of the Reserve to 1,200,000 or of both to these limits. The Assembly may authorize such increase or increases whether or not it has then called to active duty part or all of the Peace Force Reserve, and if any such increase or increases shall be authorized, the Assembly may call upon the member Nations to assist in the recruitment of either or both components to the increased strength.

Article 7

1. If the General Assembly, pursuant to paragraph 2 of Article 43 of this revised Charter, shall have declared the existence of an extreme emergency and shall have directed an increase of the strength of the Peace Force beyond the maximum combined strength of 1,800,000 for

both components as provided in paragraph 2 of Article 2 of this Annex, the Assembly shall direct the member Nations to cooperate with the United Nations in obtaining the needed additional personnel; provided that such increase shall be made pursuant to the following procedures and subject to the following limitations:

a. The quota of new recruits which any member Nation (including any non-self-governing or trust territories under its administration) may be directed to obtain shall not exceed a number which when added to the number of nationals of such nation (including any non-self-governing or trust territories under its administration) then serving in the Peace Force would make the total number of the nationals of such nation (including any non-self-governing or trust territories under its administration) exceed five per cent of the total strength of the Peace Force at that time.

b. The quota of new recruits which any member Nation (including any non-self-governing or trust territory under its administration) may be directed to obtain shall not exceed a number which when added to the number of nationals of such nation (including any non-self-governing or trust territory under its administration) then serving in the Peace Force would exceed one per cent of the population of such nation (including any non-self-governing or trust territory under its administration).

c. Persons recruited for the Peace Force under this Article shall be obtained by voluntary enlistment, but any member Nation which fails promptly to raise its quota shall adopt the necessary compulsory measures to enable it to fill its quota.

d. Personnel of the United Nations Peace Force recruited for the period of the extreme emergency under this Article shall not be required to serve beyond the period of the extreme emergency as declared by the General Assembly and shall be demobilized and returned to their nations of origin (or to a nation of their own choice, if accepted by that nation) as soon as possible after the end of the extreme emergency.

2. In accordance with Article 44 of this revised Charter, and subject to the procedures and limitations contained in paragraph 1 of this Article, the General Assembly shall adopt in advance regulations in respect of the aid to be furnished by member Nations in obtaining recruits for the Peace Force under this Article. These regulations shall establish standards in respect of age, education and physical condition to be applied by member Nations in supplying recruits under this Article.

3. In accordance with Article 45 of this revised Charter, the member Nations shall adopt in advance such internal legislation and administrative measures as may be necessary to assure prompt and effective compliance by them with the regulations adopted under paragraph 2 of this Article.

CHAPTER IV

TRANSITIONAL ARRANGEMENTS

Article 8

1. Each member Nation shall designate as available to the United Nations during the period of organization of the United Nations Peace Force one tenth of its military forces as they exist from time to time during such period. Such period shall be deemed to begin with the ninth month of the preparatory stage provided for in Article 2 of Annex I and to terminate at the end of the third month of the last year of the actual disarmament stage provided for in Article 10 of Annex I. During that period one fourth of the forces thus designated shall be maintained in a state of immediate readiness for military action under the direction of the United Nations.

2. If the General Assembly considers that the economic measures provided for in Article 41 of this revised Charter would be inadequate or have proved to be inadequate to maintain or restore international peace or to ensure compliance with this revised Charter and the laws and regulations enacted thereunder, and that the United Nations Peace Force has not yet reached sufficient strength to deal with the situation, the Assembly shall direct such action by part or all of the national forces which have been designated pursuant to paragraph 1 of this Article as it may deem necessary. Such action shall be taken within the limitations of Article 4 of this Annex.

3. The General Assembly shall have authority to enact such laws and regulations as it may deem necessary for the strategic direction, command, organization, administration and disposition of the national forces designated pursuant to paragraph 1 of this Article when action by any such national forces has been directed pursuant to paragraph 2 of this Article.

334

ANNEX III

THE JUDICIAL AND CONCILIATION SYSTEM OF THE UNITED NATIONS

Comment. This Annex would consist of four Parts: (A) a proposed revision of the Statute of the International Court of Justice which now constitutes the only Annex to the 1945 Charter; (B) a new Statute for the World Equity Tribunal called for by paragraph 1 of Article 93 of the revised Charter; (C) a new Statute for the World Conciliation Board called for by paragraph 2 of revised Article 93; and (D) a new Statute for the regional courts of the United Nations called for by paragraph 3 of revised Article 93.

The broad purpose of this Annex is to provide for the judicial and quasi-judicial institutions of the United Nations requisite for the maintenance of the rule of law in the field of war prevention. It is proposed to accomplish this through the establishment of institutions and machinery for the adjustment or adjudication of disputes between nations of a sort likely to endanger peace; and also by providing institutions and machinery for the application both to individuals and nations of the Charter and laws of the United Nations in respect of the maintenance of peace.

With regard to the adjustment or adjudication of all dangerous international disputes, a comprehensive plan is proposed. This includes the grant to the existing International Court of Justice of compulsory jurisdiction in certain categories of legal disputes; the creation of an entirely new tribunal—the World Equity Tribunal—to deal with nonlegal disputes; and the creation of a new conciliation agency—the World Conciliation Board—to deal through conciliation and mediation with any international disputes whether of a "legal" or "nonlegal" character.

In respect of the enforcement of United Nations law, it is proposed to establish a system of United Nations regional courts subordinate to the International Court of Justice, in order to provide adequate machinery for dealing with offenses against the Charter or laws of the United Nations and adequate safeguards against possible abuse of power by any organ or official of the United Nations itself.

International disputes. It is impossible to predict what particular method, or combination of methods, will be most suitable for dealing in a peaceful manner with some particular controversy between nations. In one case the dispute may primarily involve questions which are susceptible of decision on legal principles and by strictly judicial proceedings,—for example, a boundary dispute depending on the interpretation of some ancient treaty or a dispute involving principles of international law concerning the treatment of aliens. It is proposed that in such instances the General Assembly (or the Executive Council by delegated authority from the Assembly) could order the disputing nations to submit to the final and enforceable judgment of the

335

International Court of Justice. In other instances, however, the dispute might primarily involve various political questions such as those involved in the complex Arab-Israeli controversy, so that a peaceful solution would require the decision of various "nonlegal" questions as much or more than the adjudication of any "legal" issue. Accordingly, in order to equip the United Nations to deal authoritatively with disputes of this character, the World Equity Tribunal, as described below, would be established.

Finally, it is proposed to create a World Conciliation Board, constituted and empowered as described below, whose function would be limited to mediation and conciliation and which could deal at any stage with international controversies of any sort.

Through a comprehensive and flexible system of this character, it is intended to provide suitable means for the adjustment or adjudication of *any and all* international controversies likely to endanger peace, and to eliminate once and for all any reasonable excuse for resort to violence on the ground that the United Nations lacks machinery and power to deal effectively with serious international controversies.

Enforcement of United Nations law. Along with the machinery for dealing with international disputes, it is intended, through the proposed system of United Nations regional courts, to provide effective tribunals throughout the world for the interpretation and application of the Charter, of the laws and regulations of the United Nations in respect of disarmament and of the other provisions for the prevention of war. It is also intended to provide adequate judicial safeguards against possible abuse of power by any United Nations agency and for the observance of the guarantees of the proposed Bill of Rights (Annex VII).

The system of United Nations regional courts would be supplemented by the creation of the office of Attorney-General of the United Nations and by the maintenance of a United Nations civil police force. The Attorney-General would have general responsibility for the prosecution in the regional courts of alleged offenses by individuals and private organizations against the Charter and the laws and regulations of the United Nations; while the civil police force (not to exceed 10,000 in number) would assist the Inspection Service in the detection of violations of the disarmament provisions, would investigate other possible violations of the Charter and the laws and regulations enacted thereunder and would be responsible for the apprehension of alleged offenders. The civil police force would be under the general direction of the Attorney-General.

Outline. The texts of the four Parts of this Annex remain to be drafted, but their main features would be as follows:

A. The Statute of the International Court of Justice

It is proposed to make the following principal changes in the present Statute:

1. The judges of the Court would be elected, not by concurrent action of the General Assembly and the Security Council, as at present, but by the General Assembly alone, from a list of candidates prepared by the Executive Council on the basis of nominations received from the members of the highest

courts of justice of member Nations, from national and international associations of international lawyers and from professors of international law. The Council shall present three candidates for each vacancy.

2. To ensure greater independence for the judges of the Court, the judges would be elected not for nine-year terms, as provided by the present Statute, but for life. This life tenure would, however, be subject to the possibility of dismissal if, in the unanimous opinion of his colleagues, a judge is no longer able properly to perform his functions or, as now provided, has in their unanimous opinion "ceased to fulfil the required conditions" of his tenure.

3. In contrast to the provision of the present Statute that "only states may be parties in cases before the Court", access to the Court would also be granted: (a) to the United Nations; (b) to its specialized agencies; (c) to regional international organizations when authorized by the General Assembly; and (d) to individuals and private and public organizations in certain cases of appeal from the regional courts of the United Nations (see paragraph 7 of Part D, below).

4. The jurisdiction of the Court (which, apart from special agreement, is merely optional under the present Statute) would be made compulsory with respect to the following categories of disputes between any nation and the United Nations, between two or more nations, between one or more nations and one or more international organizations and between two or more international organizations:

a. any dispute relating to the interpretation or application of the revised Charter (including all the Annexes thereto);

b. any dispute relating to the constitutionality of any law, regulation or decision made or adopted under the revised Charter (including all the Annexes thereto), and any dispute relating to the interpretation or application of any such law, regulation or decision;

c. any dispute relating to legal questions involved in an international dispute or situation if the General Assembly (or the Executive Council, when acting in the matter pursuant to authority from the Assembly) should decide that the continuance of that dispute or situation is likely to endanger the maintenance of international peace and security and should direct that such legal questions be submitted to the Court pursuant to Article 36 of the revised Charter;

d. any dispute relating to the interpretation or application of the constitutions of specialized agencies;

e. any dispute relating to the interpretation or application of treaties and other international agreements or instruments registered with the Secretariat of the United Nations under Article 102 of the revised Charter;

f. any dispute relating to the validity of a treaty or other international agreement or instrument, or of a constitution or law of any member Nation, which is alleged to be in conflict with the revised Charter (or with any law or regulation enacted thereunder);

g. any other dispute where recourse to the Court against the United Nations is specifically provided for in the revised Charter (including all the Annexes thereto) or in any law or regulation enacted thereunder.

5. The International Court of Justice would retain all its jurisdiction under

treaties and conventions, and under declarations made pursuant to paragraph 2 of Article 36 of the present Statute of the Court, as such jurisdiction exists at the time the revised Charter comes into force.

6. The International Court of Justice would also hear appeals from decisions of the regional courts of the United Nations in those cases in which such appeals are permitted by laws enacted by the General Assembly pursuant to paragraph 7 of Part D.

7. The International Court of Justice would have a general power of supervision over the administration of the regional courts.

8. The judgments of the International Court of Justice would be enforceable by measures to be adopted by the General Assembly under paragraph 2 of Article 94 of the revised Charter.

B. *The Statute of the World Equity Tribunal*

It is proposed to establish a new organ of the United Nations—the World Equity Tribunal—for dealing with disputes which are not primarily of a legal nature. By this is meant disputes which, while they may have some incidental legal aspect, involve questions which cannot be satisfactorily resolved on the basis of applicable legal principles. As pointed out in the comment on Article 36 of the revised Charter, many current international disputes are of this character and require adequate procedures to ensure their settlement. These procedures are set out in paragraphs 4-10 of revised Article 36, which should be read together with the Statute of the proposed World Conciliation Board (see Part C, below) as well as that of the World Equity Tribunal.

The Statute of the World Equity Tribunal would contain the following basic provisions:

1. The Tribunal would be composed of fifteen persons, whose character, experience and reputation would furnish the best assurance of impartiality and breadth of view. No two of them could be nationals of the same nation, and at least ten of them must have had more than twenty years of legal experience as judges, teachers of law or practicing lawyers.

2. The members of the Tribunal would be elected by the General Assembly from a list of persons nominated by the member Nations upon the recommendation of a committee in each member Nation which shall include representatives of the principal judicial tribunals and legal associations, and of leading academic, scientific, economic and religious organizations. In selecting the members of the Tribunal, the General Assembly would be required to pay due regard to their geographical distribution in order that in the Tribunal as a whole all the principal regions of the world would be fairly represented.

3. To ensure the independence of the members of the Tribunal, they would be elected for life, subject, however, to the possibility of dismissal if, in the unanimous opinion of his colleagues, a member is no longer able properly to perform his functions or has ceased to fulfil the required conditions of his tenure.

4. The Tribunal would have authority to deal only with disputes or situations involving the United Nations, the specialized agencies of the United Nations, nations, and non-self-governing or trust territories.

338

5. The Tribunal would have jurisdiction in respect of disputes or situations referred to it by voluntary agreement, as follows:

a. under a special agreement concluded between all the nations or international organizations concerned;

b. under a bipartite or multipartite treaty providing in advance for the reference of certain categories of questions to the Tribunal, provided that the particular question referred to the Tribunal falls within the categories enumerated in the treaty;

c. under unilateral declarations applicable to certain categories of questions, provided that all the nations concerned have made such declarations with respect to the category to which the particular question referred to the Tribunal belongs.

The agreement, treaty or declaration providing for the jurisdiction of the Tribunal could empower it either to make recommendations without binding force or to render a binding decision; and if the parties agreed to be bound by the decision of the Tribunal, it would be enforceable by the same measures as a judgment of the International Court of Justice, i.e., in accordance with paragraph 2 of Article 94 of the revised Charter.

6. Under certain conditions, the World Equity Tribunal would also have jurisdiction without regard to the agreement of those involved in the dispute or situation. This jurisdiction could be conferred by the General Assembly pursuant to Article 36 of the revised Charter with respect to any questions which in the judgment of three fifths of all the Representatives in the Assembly: (a) cannot be satisfactorily decided on the basis of applicable legal principles; and (b) relate to a dispute or situation the continuance of which is likely to endanger the maintenance of international peace and security. If the Assembly should in this way refer a dispute or situation to the Tribunal, the Tribunal would conduct public hearings and make all necessary investigations.

Thereafter, the Tribunal could adopt such recommendations as it deems reasonable, just and fair for the solution of the whole dispute or situation, or of particular questions involved therein, which had been referred to the Tribunal; provided that the recommendations are approved by a two-thirds majority of all the members of the Tribunal.

Recommendations of the Tribunal (pursuant to Article 36 of the revised Charter) would become binding on all concerned only after they had been approved in their entirety by the General Assembly by a three-fourths majority vote of all the Representatives, including two thirds of the Representatives then in office from the member Nations entitled to fifteen or more Representatives in the Assembly; provided that the resolution of the Assembly approving the recommendations had included a finding that the dispute or situation was likely to continue unless the recommendations of the Tribunal were carried out and that such continuance would constitute a serious danger to peace.

In case of any failure to comply with the recommendations of the Tribunal when so approved by the Assembly, the Assembly would be authorized to enforce them by means of economic and military sanctions, pursuant to paragraph 3 of Article 94 of the revised Charter, i.e., in a manner corresponding to that provided for the enforcement of judgments of the International Court of Justice in paragraph 2 of the same Article.

C. The Statute of the World Conciliation Board

It is proposed to establish a new organ of the United Nations—the World Conciliation Board—whose function it would be to help in bringing about mutually acceptable agreements between nations which become involved in disputes or situations dangerous to peace.

The Statute of the Board would contain the following basic provisions:

1. The Board would be composed of five persons, whose character, experience and reputation would furnish the best assurance of impartiality and breadth of view.

2. The members of the Board would be elected in the following manner:

a. There would be established a World Conciliation Panel, composed of persons highly qualified to serve as international mediators or conciliators. Each nation would appoint one such person to serve on the Panel for four years and until the appointment of his successor.

b. The World Conciliation Panel would meet before the first session of the first General Assembly elected under the revised Charter and every four years thereafter before the first session of each newly elected Assembly. At each of these meetings, the Panel would nominate from their own number fifteen candidates for membership on the World Conciliation Board, these nominees to be chosen with due regard to geographical distribution as well as individual qualifications.

c. The first General Assembly elected under the revised Charter would at the beginning of its first session elect five members of the Board from among the fifteen nominees to serve during the four-year term of that Assembly and until the election of their successors; and each subsequently elected Assembly would at the beginning of its first session similarly elect the five members of the Board from the list of fifteen nominees submitted by the Panel. In electing the members of the Board, the Assembly would be required to pay due regard to their geographical distribution in order to give representation to the main regions of the world. Members of the Board would be eligible for renomination and re-election.

3. When the Board is dealing with a dispute or situation, any nation which is party to such dispute or is concerned in the situation would, unless one of its nationals is then a member of the Board, have the right to request that the member of the World Conciliation Panel appointed by that nation be added to the Board during the consideration of such dispute or situation. If the Board should consider that in a dispute or situation referred to it, the interests of a non-self-governing or trust territory are specially affected, the Board would be required to request the Trusteeship Council to appoint a properly qualified person resident in such territory to represent the interests of the territory. Any member of the Panel thus temporarily added to the Board would have the right to participate, without vote, in the deliberations of the Board.

4. The Board would have authority to deal only with disputes or situations involving the United Nations, the specialized agencies of the United Nations, nations and non-self-governing or trust territories.

340

5. The Board would have authority to seek the settlement of disputes or situations referred to it:

a. under a special agreement concluded between all the nations or international organizations concerned;

b. under a bipartite or multipartite treaty providing in advance for the reference of certain categories of questions to the Board, provided that the particular question referred to the Board falls within the categories enumerated in the treaty;

c. under unilateral declarations applicable to certain categories of questions, provided that all the nations concerned have made such declarations with respect to the category to which the particular question referred to the Board belongs;

d. pursuant to a decision of the General Assembly or the Executive Council, under paragraph 4 of Article 36 of the revised Charter, that the continuance of the particular dispute or situation is likely to endanger the maintenance of international peace and security, that the dispute or situation involves questions which cannot be satisfactorily resolved on the basis of applicable legal principles, and that the dispute or situation as a whole or certain questions involved therein are suitable for consideration by the Board.

6. In the fulfillment of its functions, the Board would have authority: to appoint one or more individuals, preferably but not necessarily from the membership of the World Conciliation Panel, to mediate in the particular dispute or situation; to make such investigations as the Board may deem necessary to establish the facts and to clarify the issues; to hold such private or public hearings as the Board may deem best; and to use such other means to bring the nations concerned to a mutually acceptable agreement as the Board may deem appropriate.

7. If an agreement should be reached under the auspices of the Board, the Board would so report to the General Assembly and would submit to it the text of the agreement. If, however, no agreement should be reached within six months from the date on which a particular dispute or situation was submitted to the Board, or within such other period as the nations concerned might agree to, the Board would present to the Assembly a report containing a summary of the Board's efforts.

D. The Statute of the Regional Courts of the United Nations

It is proposed to establish United Nations regional courts, inferior to the International Court of Justice, for the trial of individuals and private organizations accused of violating the revised Charter or any law or regulation enacted thereunder. These regional courts would also be authorized to deal with other matters specifically provided for in the various Annexes, some of which are mentioned below.

The Statute for these courts would contain the following basic provisions:

1. The General Assembly would be required to establish not less than twenty or more than forty regional courts and to delineate the regions in which they would have jurisdiction.

2. Each regional court would be composed of three to nine judges, depend-

ing on the probable number of cases to be brought before it. Three judges would constitute a quorum, except that the General Assembly could authorize the performance of certain functions by single judges.

3. The judges would be appointed by the Executive Council from a list of qualified persons prepared by the International Court of Justice, the appointments to be subject to confirmation by the General Assembly. Not more than one third of the judges of any regional court could be nationals of the nations included in the region of the court's jurisdiction, and no two judges of any regional court could be nationals of the same nation.

4. The judges would be appointed for life, subject only to the possibility of dismissal if, in the opinion of two thirds of all the judges of the International Court of Justice, a judge is no longer able properly to perform his functions or has ceased to fulfil the required conditions of his tenure.

5. Each regional court, in addition to regular sessions at its seat, would be required to hold periodical sessions in the capital or other principal city of each of the nations included in the region.

6. The jurisdiction of the regional courts would include:

a. the trial of individuals and private organizations accused of offenses against the revised Charter or any law or regulation enacted thereunder;

b. the issuance, under Articles 21 and 22 of Annex I of the revised Charter, of authorizations for the conduct, without notice, of periodic inspections and of aerial inspections, and of authorizations for the inspection of places and facilities other than those specifically made subject to inspection by Annex I;

c. the consideration of appeals against decisions of the Inspector-General refusing the grant of a license under Article 16 of Annex I, or suspending or revoking a license under Article 33 of that Annex;

d. the determination, in case of dispute, of the amount of compensation or rent payable by the United Nations under Article 104 of the revised Charter, Article 30 of Annex I and Article 2 of Annex II;

e. the issuance, under Article 21 of Annex I, of injunctions against performance by the Inspection Service of acts not authorized by Annex I or by laws or regulations enacted thereunder;

f. any other matter where access to a regional court by nations, public or private organizations or individuals is specifically provided for in the revised Charter (including any Annex thereto) or in any law or regulation enacted thereunder.

7. The General Assembly would be authorized to enact laws specifying the categories of cases in which appeals from decisions of the regional courts to the International Court of Justice would be allowed. It would be provided that these laws must permit appeals when it appears to at least one third of the judges of the International Court of Justice: (a) that a decision of a regional court may be inconsistent with a prior decision of the same issue of law by the International Court of Justice or by another regional court; (b) that a regional court may have wrongly decided a question involving the interpretation of the Charter of the United Nations; (c) that a regional court may have exceeded its jurisdiction; (d) that a regional court may have deprived a person of a right or privilege guaranteed by the Bill of Rights (Annex VII); or (e) that a regional court may have made a fundamental

error resulting in a serious denial of justice. These laws should also give considerable discretion to the International Court of Justice as to what appeals by public or private oganizations or individuals it would entertain so that the Court could limit such appeals to cases in which an important legal issue seemed to be involved. But no appeal by a public or private organization or individual should be allowed in case of the denial, suspension or revocation of a license under Articles 16 and 33 of Annex I, if the nation which applied for such a license on behalf of an organization or individual has itself undertaken an appeal to the Court on behalf of such an organization or individual.

8. The General Assembly would be empowered to enact laws prescribing the procedures to be followed in apprehending an accused individual, in trying individuals and private organizations, and in enforcing the penalties.

9. The prosecution of alleged offenses committed by individuals and private organizations would be in the hands of an Attorney-General of the United Nations, to be appointed by the Executive Council, subject to confirmation by the General Assembly. Assistant Attorneys-General of the United Nations would be assigned to each regional court and, except in extraordinary circumstances, cases would be brought before the regional court within whose territorial jurisdiction the alleged offense was committed.

10. The General Assembly would be required to establish a civil police force of the United Nations, the functions of which would be: to aid the Inspection Service in the detection of violations of the disarmament provisions in Annex I; to investigate other actual or threatened offenses against the revised Charter or any law or regulation enacted thereunder; and to apprehend individuals accused of having committed such violations. This civil police force would be under the general direction of the Attorney-General of the United Nations. The General Assembly would be empowered to enact such laws and regulations as it might deem necessary for the organization, recruitment, discipline, training, equipment, compensation, administration and authority of this United Nations civil police force, subject to the limitation that the strength of the force shall not exceed 10,000.

11. The Attorney-General of the United Nations would be required to make arrangements with national authorities for:

a. assistance to the civil police force in the apprehension of persons accused of having committed offenses against the revised Charter and the laws and regulations enacted thereunder;

b. the detaining of such persons pending trial or pursuant to a judgment of a United Nations regional court;

c. the collection, for the account of the United Nations, of fines imposed by a judgment of a United Nations regional court.

12. Except where proper arrangements have been made with national authorities for the detention of offenders, they would be detained in United Nations houses of detention. Buildings would be leased by the United Nations for this purpose, or special buildings might be built on land leased to the United Nations.

13. Except to the extent that arrangements have been made with national authorities for the collection of fines for the account of the United Nations, the General Assembly would be required to enact laws providing for the

direct collection of fines imposed by regional United Nations courts, by United Nations court marshals appointed by the Attorney-General, and defining the circumstances in which the marshals would be permitted to sequester property in order to satisfy a judgment of a United Nations court.

* * * * *

Through the institutions and measures above described, it is believed that the following purposes would be fulfilled: (1) there would exist tribunals of the highest independence and authority to which any nation could resort, for the settlement of any international dispute whatever, thus removing any excuse for war or the threat of it by reason of any such dispute; (2) adequate means would be provided for dealing by due process of law with possible violators of the revised Charter and the laws and regulations enacted thereunder; and (3) adequate safeguards and appropriate remedies would be provided against possible abuse of power by any organ or official of the United Nations.

As already stressed, we must, in order to achieve genuine peace, have more than disarmament and more than an effective world police. We must also have well-established world tribunals to which the nations can resort with confidence for the decision or adjustment of their disputes. As Annex I provides for complete, universal and enforceable disarmament and Annex II for a world police force, this Annex III would provide the tribunals of justice which constitute another great essential for world peace.

344

ANNEX IV

THE WORLD DEVELOPMENT AUTHORITY

Outline. Pursuant to Articles 7 and 59 of the revised Charter, it is proposed to establish a new organ of the United Nations, to be called the World Development Authority. Its purpose would be to provide efficient means to carry out one of the basic objectives of the United Nations as stated in the Preamble of the present Charter, namely, to promote "the economic and social advancement of all peoples".

The Statute of this proposed World Development Authority would contain the following provisions:

1. The Authority would be under the direction and control of a World Development Commission consisting of five persons to be appointed by the Economic and Social Council, subject to confirmation by the General Assembly. The members of this Commission would be appointed for terms of five years, their terms to be so arranged that one member would be appointed every year. No two members of the Commission could be nationals of the same nation and they would be selected with due regard to equitable geographical distribution.

2. The Economic and Social Council would have general supervision over the World Development Commission in a manner corresponding to the proposed power of the Executive Council to supervise the Inspection Commission, the Nuclear Energy Commission and the Outer Space Commission. This supervisory power of the Economic and Social Council would include authority to remove any member of the World Development Commission and to issue such instructions to the Commission as the Council might deem necessary.

3. The chief administrative officer of the World Development Authority would be a Director-General, to be appointed by the World Development Commission subject to confirmation by the Economic and Social Council.

4. The Economic and Social Council, with the advice of the World Development Commission, would from time to time formulate the immediate objectives and priorities of the World Development Authority subject to such policy directives as the General Assembly might adopt. Within the framework of these directives, objectives and priorities, it would be the function of the Commission to decide upon particular applications for grants and loans from the Authority.

5. The principal means whereby the World Development Authority would fulfil its purpose of promoting "the economic and social advancement of all peoples" would be grants-in-aid or interest-free loans (either to governments or to public or private organizations) for economic and social projects deemed indispensable to "the creation of conditions of stability and well-being" (Article 55 of the present Charter); in particular for such projects as railways, roads, ports, dams and irrigation, power stations, schools, hospitals and housing.

345

No loans or grants could, however, be made in respect of projects for which adequate financing could be obtained through other channels, either private or public.

6. The funds of the World Development Authority would be provided from the general budget of the United Nations as annually adopted by the General Assembly. The proposed budget of the Authority would in the first instance be prepared by its Director-General and would then be passed upon by the World Development Commission and submitted to the Economic and Social Council. When approved by that Council and after scrutiny by the Standing Committee on Budget and Finance, the budget would go to the General Assembly for final approval.

The amount which could be appropriated for the World Development Authority would, of course, be subject to the general restriction that the total revenue to be raised by the United Nations in any particular year could not exceed two per cent of the estimated gross world product in that year (Annex V).

Comment. The proposal to establish a World Development Authority is based on the premise that genuine and stable peace can be maintained only if all the nations of the world can be assured that everything possible is being done to ameliorate their worst economic and social ills. Should the General Assembly use generously its power to allocate to the World Development Authority a large proportion of the two per cent of the estimated gross world product which may be raised in any year by the United Nations, it should be possible for the Authority to grant sufficient aid to the most underdeveloped areas of the world. In this way it might well be possible even within a generation to remove the danger to peace caused by the immense economic disparity between those areas and the more industrialized parts of the world.

It must be remembered that a world population of nearly 3.5 billion persons must be assumed for 1970; and that, even with considerable economic improvement in the world's underdeveloped areas, most of that vast number will still continue to be inadequately fed, clothed and housed, and without adequate educational and health facilities.

The gap in living standards between the people of the industrialized West and of the so-called underdeveloped areas of the world is truly appalling. With a population of nearly 180,000,000 in 1960 and an estimated gross national product in 1960 of about $500 billion, the approximate per capita product of the inhabitants of the United States is nearly $2800. By contrast, the per capita national product of the approximately 500,000,000 people of India and Pakistan in 1960 is usually estimated at about $80; and of the 640,000,000 people of China at about $70. With due allowance for differences in price levels, it is therefore plain that the gap between the material standard of life of the average inhabitant of the United States and that of the average inhabitant of India, Pakistan and China is tremendous. The difference between the living standards of these nations and the standards of various industrialized nations other than the United States, while less extreme, is also very great.

It seems perfectly clear that when facts such as these are available to nearly everyone in the world and when the possibility exists for making tremendous improvements in the standard of life of the underdeveloped areas, this condition of affairs will be found intolerable. It is a condition which, unless much alleviated, will continue to be an underlying source of danger to the world's peace.

When we speak of "underdeveloped" areas, it hardly needs saying that reference is made solely to *material* underdevelopment,—since it is obvious that various of the peoples who are obliged to live at the lowest economic level are quite as advanced in cultural and spiritual values as those which have the highest standards of living. Nevertheless, this fact makes it no less abnormal and unhealthy that in the modern world there should be so great a gap in material welfare between the people of the industrialized West and vast populations in Asia, the Middle East, Africa and Latin America.

In these circumstances, it is plain that even if so considerable an annual sum as $25 billion is made available through a World Development Authority to improve the economic condition of most of the world's people, this would be by no means an excessive amount. Looking ahead even a few years from 1960, this sum would need to be applied in aid of at least two billion persons, on which assumption it would amount to no more than about $12 per person per annum; or, in terms of families with an average of five members, about $60 per annum per family. On this basis, even the maximum amount that could be expended through the proposed World Development Authority seems rather less than more than could be advantageously spent in the interest of world stability and peace.

The example of a relatively small-scale effort to lift up a nation's material standards will show how moderate would be an expenditure of the supposed $25 billion per annum for the welfare of so vast a number as two billion people.

In Israel, since its establishment as an independent state in 1948, there has been expended purely for the economic benefit of its people (as distinguished from military purposes) certainly not less than $100 million per annum of funds from outside the country, i.e., an amount which, assuming an average population of 1,600,000 in the 1948-59 period, comes to at least $60 per annum per inhabitant, or $300 per annum for a family of five. If a corresponding amount of capital from other nations had been spent for the benefit of the people of India and Pakistan, which had an average population of about 450 million during the same ten-year period, the amount expended would have been about $27 billion per annum for those countries alone.

Since the estimated annual $60 per capita for Israel has proved no more than enough to meet the development needs of that nation, can it be doubted that $12 per capita of outside funds could be usefully employed each year in aid of areas with even more urgent needs?

It is believed, therefore, that the World Development Authority should have at its disposal not less than $25 billion per annum for use in mitigating the disparity between the standards of living of the economically underdeveloped areas of the world and those of the industrialized areas. Such an expenditure would by no means be wholly a matter of altruism on the part of the industrialized West, since a marked betterment in the living standards of the economically underdeveloped nations would stimulate trade in both raw materials and industrial products to the benefit of all nations. And while it is true that the initial burden of financing this work of the World Development Authority would mainly rest upon a few of the richer nations, it could be expected that after a relatively short period of economic growth the circle of nations contributing to the budget of the Authority would be greatly enlarged. Moreover, it should never be forgotten that the funds needed for the Authority would be more than offset by the savings from universal and complete disarmament and would, therefore, not constitute an additional burden on any nation which before disarmament maintained any substantial military force.

Consequently, assuming total and complete disarmament, the proposed program appears to be not only desirable but also feasible; and Annex V presents a detailed plan whereby the necessary funds could be reliably provided.

348

ANNEX V

THE REVENUE SYSTEM OF THE
UNITED NATIONS

Main features. The purpose of this proposed Annex is to supplement Article 17 of the revised Charter with detailed provisions for an adequate and effective revenue system of the United Nations.

The complete text of the Annex remains to be drafted, but its main features would be as follows:

1. There would be a grant to the United Nations of adequate powers to raise, through collaborative arrangements with the member Nations, sufficient and reliable revenues to assure the effective fulfillment of its enlarged responsibilities; but this grant would be subject to strict safeguards and limitations.

2. The scope of the revenue powers and the methods for their exercise would be carefully delimited in a detailed plan which would provide in particular for a limit on the total budget of the United Nations in any year of two per cent of the estimated gross world product in that year.

3. The formula for the apportionment of the total budget would be based upon the ability to pay of the people of the member Nations, with the limitation, however, that the amount to be contributed by the people of any member Nation in any year shall not exceed two and one half per cent of the estimated gross national product of that nation in that year.

4. Provision would be made for the establishment in each member Nation of a United Nations fiscal office, the functions of which would be: (a) to receive the taxes of those in that nation who, under national laws enacted for the purpose, have been made liable to pay taxes to the United Nations; and (b) to transmit the sums so received to the central treasury of the United Nations.

5. All the member Nations would undertake to place their tax-collecting machinery at the disposal of the United Nations for the collection and turning over to the United Nations of the taxes levied in their respective territories which are to go to the United Nations, in order that the revenue of the United Nations shall be received by it without the creation of any large tax-collecting organization of its own.

6. Provision would be made whereby the administrative work of obtaining the payment to the United Nations of the amounts due to it from the people of each member Nation would be made the function of that nation, including the investigation and penalization of defaults on the part of its inhabitants.

7. The United Nations would have a carefully defined borrowing power, subject to an upper limit whereby the amount of United Nations debt outstanding at the end of any year could not exceed five per cent of the gross world product as estimated for that year, save only in case of grave emergency.

8. The plan would also define the authority of the General Assembly in

this field and the limitations thereon; such limitations to include, in addition to the above limits on the maximum amount to be raised in any year and on the maximum debt, a general limitation that revenue may be raised or money borrowed only to meet the expenses of the United Nations for purposes within its constitutional authority.

9. Detailed provisions would define the procedures and establish the machinery: for the preparation and adoption by the General Assembly of the yearly budgets of the United Nations; for the supervision of expenditures; and for the assignment of quotas among the member Nations and the arrangements for their fulfillment. The proposed Standing Committee on Budget and Finance of the General Assembly (Article 22 of the revised Charter) would assist the Assembly in these matters.

Maximum limit on annual budgets. As above noted, a principal feature of this revenue plan would be an *over-all limit* on the amount which could be raised for the United Nations in any year, to be measured by a percentage of the estimated gross world product from year to year. The proposed percentage is two per cent of the world's gross product (total value of all goods produced and services rendered) as estimated by the Standing Committee on Budget and Finance. For example, if the value of the world's gross product in 1980 were estimated at $2600 billion, the maximum budget of the United Nations in that year would be $52 billion.

This limit of two per cent of the estimated gross world product, which would determine the maximum amount of revenue which could be raised for the United Nations in any one year, has two purposes. On the one hand, it is intended to ensure that the strengthened United Nations could not aggrandize itself by making too severe a levy on the resources of the member Nations. On the other hand, the purpose is to ensure the capacity of the United Nations to raise sufficient funds for the effective discharge of its new and vital functions.

Apportionment of annual budgets. The proposed formula and procedure for the apportionment of the yearly budgets among the member Nations upon the broad principle of *ability to pay* would be as follows:

a. The gross national product of each member Nation for the next fiscal year, i.e., the calendar year, would be estimated by the Standing Committee on Budget and Finance; and the Standing Committee would also estimate the average population of each member Nation during that year.

b. From this estimated gross national product of each member Nation a "per capita deduction" would be made equal to an amount arrived at by multiplying the estimated population of such nation by a sum fixed from time to time by the General Assembly, which sum shall be not less than fifty or more than ninety per cent of the estimated average per capita product of the people of the ten member Nations having the lowest per capita national product.

c. The amount arrived at for each member Nation by this process would be known as the "adjusted national product", and the proportion of the total

350

United Nations budget to be supplied by the people of a particular member Nation would be ascertained by the relation between the "adjusted national product" of that nation and the sum of the "adjusted national products" of all the member Nations.

d. It would be provided, however, that the people of any member Nation shall not be required to supply in any year more than two and one half per cent of the estimated gross national product of that nation in that year.

To illustrate: Let us assume that the budget in question is for the year 1980, that the revised Charter has come into force at the end of 1969, so that it has been in effect for ten years and that every nation in the world is a member Nation. Let us also assume that during these ten years two great operations have been carried out: (1) that following the one-year transition period and the two-year preparatory stage, the complete disarmament of all the nations has been accomplished in the minimum period of seven years contemplated by the plan; and (2) that, parallel with the disarmament process, the organization of the United Nations Peace Force has been completed.

Let us further assume that the total population of the world (estimated at nearly 2,900,000,000 early in 1960) has increased in the twenty years through December 1979 by about 55 million per annum, i.e., by some 1100 million, to about 4,000,000,000; that the estimated gross world product for 1980 is $2600 billion (about $650 per person); and that the estimated average per capita product for 1980 of the ten nations with the lowest per capita product is $100.

Let us now assume: (a) that the General Assembly has adopted for 1980 an over-all budget of $36 billion (i.e., $16 billion less than the maximum $52 billion budget which it could adopt); and (b) that the Assembly has fixed $70 per capita (midway between the minimum of $50 and the maximum of $90) as the "per capita deduction" to be made in arriving at the "adjusted national product" of each nation.

On these assumptions, the practical effect of the plan can be illustrated by a comparison of its application to the United States, on the one hand, and to Pakistan on the other.

Let us assume that the average population of the United States in 1980 is estimated at 240 million and that its estimated gross national product for 1980 is $800 billion, or about $3300 per capita (as against about $500 billion in 1960, or about $2800 per capita); and that the corresponding estimates for Pakistan in 1980 are for a population of 135 million and a gross national product of $13.5 billion, i.e., $100 per capita. On the basis of the assumed $70 "per capita deduction" as fixed by the General Assembly, the amount to be deducted from the estimated gross national product of the United States would be $16.8 billion, leaving $783.2 billion as its "adjusted national product"; and the deduction for Pakistan would be $9.45 billion, leaving $4.05 billion as its "adjusted national product". If every nation in the world had ratified the revised Charter, the total of the deductions for all the nations would be $280 billion ($70 x 4 billion persons) leaving $2320 billion ($2600 billion less $280 billion) as the "adjusted world product". The quota of the United States for the assumed $36 billion 1980 budget would therefore be 783.2/2320, or approximately 34 per cent of $36 billion, i.e., about $12.2 billion; and the quota of Pakistan would be 4.05/2320, or approximately .175 per cent of $36 billion, or about $63 million.

At first glance this discrepancy may seem very great but, on analysis, will be found to do no more than reflect in an equitable manner the ability to pay of the people of the United States and of Pakistan. It may also be noted that the quota of the United States at $12.2 billion would be far below the permissible maximum of $20 billion, i.e., two and one-half per cent of its estimated gross national product for 1980 of $800 billion.

No excuse is needed for the careful and elaborate character of this plan, since it is of the utmost importance that the burden of raising the revenues of the strengthened United Nations shall be so equitably distributed as to command general acceptance.

Procedures for the preparation, submission and adoption of annual budgets. The procedure for the *preparation* (including the apportionment) of each annual budget would be as follows, taking as an example the supposed budget for 1980 and assuming that there are no nonmember nations:

a. All the various organs and agencies of the United Nations would be required to submit their respective budgets for the next fiscal year (the calendar year) at least eleven months before the beginning of that year, i.e., by February 1, 1979 in respect of the 1980 budget. The Executive Council would submit a budget for its own expenses and for the United Nations Peace Force; the Inspection Commission for the United Nations Inspection Service; the Nuclear Energy Commission for the Nuclear Energy Authority; the Outer Space Commission for the Outer Space Agency; the Economic and Social Council for its own expenses, for the World Development Authority and all the specialized agencies; and so on.

b. These separate budgets would in the first instance be submitted to the Secretary-General who would transmit them, together with a budget for the Secretariat itself, to the Standing Committee on Budget and Finance.

c. The Standing Committee on Budget and Finance would then scrutinize the requested budgets and would discuss them with the various organs and agencies for which the funds are asked.

d. Simultaneously, the Standing Committee on Budget and Finance would make estimates of the gross national product of every nation for 1980, after notice to and consultations with the government of each nation, and would thus arrive at an estimate of the total gross world product for 1980.

e. Following this scrutiny of the requests and the making of these estimates, the Standing Committee on Budget and Finance would formulate its recommendations as to the amounts required by the various organs and agencies in 1980, and would report a total recommended budget to the General Assembly. In so doing the Standing Committee would, of course, make sure that the total recommended budget did not exceed the constitutional maximum of two per cent of the estimated gross world product in 1980.

f. With relation to the apportionment between the nations of the total recommended budget, the Standing Committee on Budget and Finance

352

would proceed as follows: It would first estimate the average population of each member Nation during 1980; would determine the "adjusted national product" for each nation on the assumption that the "per capita deduction" as last approved by the General Assembly would be continued; and would in this way determine the "adjusted world product" and each nation's percentage share therein. The Standing Committee would then calculate provisionally the amount to be supplied from each nation in order to pay its share of the revenue needed to cover the recommended budget; would hold discussions with each nation as to the method of payment to be adopted by that nation, including the taxes to be used for this purpose and the share of such taxes which would be assigned to the United Nations. Upon the basis of these estimates, calculations and discussions the Standing Committee would formulate its recommendations as to the apportionment of the proposed total budget among the various nations and as to the method of payment to be used by each nation.

The procedure for the *submission* of each annual budget (again taking 1980 as the example) would be as follows:

a. The Standing Committee on Budget and Finance would prepare a full report to the General Assembly containing its recommendations not only as to the amount of the proposed budget (including the division thereof among the various organs and agencies) but also as to the apportionment of the proposed budget among the nations and the proposed methods of payment by the people of each nation.

b. The Standing Committee would be required to submit such report to the General Assembly not later than two months before the convening of the annual session of the Assembly, i.e., at least two months before the third Tuesday in September. Thus in the supposed case of the budget for 1980, the Standing Committee's report would be submitted by July 18, 1979, i.e., two months before the third Tuesday in September 1979 (i.e., September 18, 1979).

The procedure for the *adoption* of each annual budget would be as follows:

a. The General Assembly, upon its convening on the third Tuesday of September, would be required to give priority to the discussion of the report of the Standing Committee on Budget and Finance and to vote upon the recommendations of that report as soon as reasonably possible. In accordance with Article 17 of the revised Charter and a further special provision to be included in this Annex V, these budgetary votes would require the approval of a majority of all the Representatives then in office, including a majority of the Representatives from the member Nations which would have the ten largest quotas of the budget then being voted upon.

b. The General Assembly, having debated and voted upon the report of the Standing Committee and having adopted the whole budget for the ensuing year by the required special majority, would refer the budget as finally approved back to the Standing Committee on Budget and Finance.

c. The Standing Committee would then make the final deteminations as to the "adjusted national product" of each nation in the light of any change in the "per capita deduction" which may have been made by the General Assembly; and the Standing Committee would thus determine each nation's *proportionate share* in the final budget. On this basis the Standing Committee would then finally calculate and determine the *actual amount* to be supplied by the people of each nation toward the budget as adopted by the General Assembly and would make an agreement with the government of each nation as to the manner of payment.

Through these procedures it should be possible, except in the most exceptional circumstances, to give careful consideration to each annual budget and for the General Assembly to dispose of it well ahead of the budget year in question, e.g., as to the supposed 1980 budget by, say, December 1, 1979.

Limitations on revenue sources. Apart from the procedures for the preparation and adoption of the annual budgets and for determining the amount of the contributions thereto from the people of each member Nation, this proposed revenue plan would also limit the *available revenue sources*. This would be done by enumerating the specific *national taxes* which could be made available to the United Nations while, at the same time, providing for a large degree of choice to each member Nation as to one or more of the specified taxes to be employed by it in order to meet the revenue quota allotted to the people of that nation.

The proposal is that each member Nation would assign to the United Nations in whole or in part one or more of the following revenue sources:

a. All or part of the income taxes assessed by any member Nation under its own laws on individuals and corporations. (For example, by the nation's own decision, ten, twenty or thirty per cent of any such income taxes could be made payable to the United Nations in the particular year.)

b. All or part of national excise taxes on motor vehicles, gasoline, liquor or tobacco, or any other excise tax that a particular nation might offer in addition or substitution. (For example, all or part of the liquor taxes due to a member Nation could in a particular year be made payable to the United Nations.)

c. All or part of a member Nation's export and import duties.

Each member Nation would determine for itself which of the enumerated national taxes shall be assigned to the United Nations in whole or in part; and unless the taxes so assigned would be plainly inadequate to cover the quota from the particular member Nation, the United Nations would be obliged to accept the choice made by it.

Since the assignment by the member Nations of particular taxes or portions thereof would necessarily be based upon estimates as to their adequacy to fulfil the respective national quotas, there would obviously be surpluses or deficiencies from year to year. Provision would therefore be made for crediting any surplus from a particular nation against its quota for the following year; or, on the other hand, for adding the amount of the deficiency to its quota for the following year.

The practical working of the proposed revenue plan can best be envisaged by a concrete example.

354

Let us assume that, as above mentioned, the General Assembly has voted a United Nations budget for 1980 of $36 billion and that the quota to be furnished by taxpayers in the United States has been fixed at the above-mentioned $12.2 billion.

Upon these assumptions it would be for the Congress of the United States to choose what national taxes collectible in 1980 should be assigned in whole or part to the United Nations, in order to ensure fulfillment of the $12.2 billion quota for that year.

The choice would lie between individual and corporate income taxes; excise taxes of any sort, including those on motor vehicles, gasoline, liquor and tobacco; and customs duties. The assignment could be of part or all of the estimated collections from these taxes in any combination, provided only that the plan chosen appeared adequate to supply the required $12.2 billion.

For instance, if in 1980 the United States had in effect a system of individual and corporate income taxation similar to that of 1960, a natural and convenient choice would be to assign to the United Nations a proportion of these taxes. Thus, assuming a total yield in 1980 from these particular taxes of no more than $61 billion (as compared with an estimated $68.2 billion in 1960-61), the assignment of only one fifth thereof would suffice to cover the $12.2 billion quota.

Let us assume this to have been done and examine how the actual process of collecting the $12.2 billion could most conveniently be carried out.

The United States, with all other member Nations, would have pledged itself to collaborate in the effective maintenance of the United Nations revenue system and to adopt appropriate laws and regulations to that end. Pursuant to this pledge, the United States would, by Congressional action, provide that in the supposed year of 1980 each individual and corporate income taxpayer shall pay to the United Nations one fifth of his or its liability, the other four fifths to be paid in the usual way into the treasury of the United States. In this manner, the legal liability to make the required payments to the United Nations would be established *under the domestic law* of the United States.

As to mechanics, the natural procedure would be to direct each income taxpayer, after computing his or its liability, to draw two checks, one to the order of the United Nations for one fifth of his total liability, and the other to the order of the United States revenue collector for four fifths of the liability; and then to send the checks in the very same envelope to the collector. In this way the United States collector would know whether the amount due to the United Nations had been received and he would then forward the check drawn to the order of the United Nations to the fiscal office of the United Nations located in the United States. The Internal Revenue Service of the United States would then proceed in the usual way to audit the taxpayer's return and would call attention to any deficiency. One fifth of any such deficiency would, when paid, be forwarded to the United Nations fiscal office; or, if a refund resulted, the United Nations would be required to pay back one fifth of the refund.

In the event, presumably rare, that a taxpayer duly paid his liability to the

United States but neglected to remit the one fifth for the United Nations, it would be the administrative duty of the tax collecting system of the United States to remind the delinquent and to follow up the collection.

In case of violation of the tax laws and regulations, the United States would in virtually all cases have a mutual interest with the United Nations to uncover and prosecute the offense. While the offending taxpayer would almost necessarily have defrauded the United Nations as well as the United States, the offense would be against a national law of the United States whereby the taxpayer would have a no less binding obligation to pay one fifth of his liability to the United Nations than to pay the other four fifths to the United States itself. It would, therefore, be the proper function and duty of the government of the United States to investigate and prosecute any such violations; and it would not be necessary for the United Nations to enact penal laws against tax delinquents or to prosecute them in United Nations courts. Nor would it be necessary for the United Nations to have any tax-collecting organization of its own, save only its fiscal office in each member Nation to receive and remit amounts collected in that nation for the United Nations.

The above illustration relates only to income taxes, where it is perhaps easiest to perceive how a feasible and effective system can be devised without any necessity for a United Nations tax bureaucracy. However, it should not be difficult to work out corresponding methods whereby all or part of certain excise taxes assigned to the United Nations would be set aside by the manufacturers of motor vehicles, cigarettes, etc. and remitted through the regular tax systems of the member Nations to the United Nations fiscal offices.

Through a plan of this sort providing for the *collaborative* use of the tax-collecting machinery of each member Nation, there is every reason to suppose that the United Nations can be provided with substantial and reliable revenue.

The need for large and reliable United Nations revenue. The proposed maximum permissible budget (two per cent of the estimated gross world product) may seem high by comparison with the relatively small expenses of the United Nations in 1947-59 when they have averaged less than $500 million per annum, including the budgets of all affiliated agencies and all special emergency funds. But measured with relation to the new tasks of the strengthened United Nations and in comparison with the vast savings resulting from complete national disarmament, this figure seems moderate indeed. By such disarmament there would be lifted from the world's shoulders a burden which in 1960 will be not less than $100 billion (for the maintenance of some fifteen million men in uniform, with their equipment and reserves), or about twice the maximum revenue of $52 billion which, on the above estimates, could be raised for the new United Nations in 1980.

In the case of the United States, there would be totally eliminated from the Federal budget immense military expenses which in 1960-61 will amount to about $46 billion out of a total budget of about $80 billion. Even if we assume that by 1980 the general expenses of government had increased as much as $41 billion through large new expenditures for the nation's economic and social welfare (for such purposes as highways, conservation of natural resources and aid to education), the 1980 Federal budget would not be more than $75

356

billion. In view of the expected increase in the gross national product of the United States from about $500 billion in 1960 to $800 billion in 1980, such a budget of $75 billion would be less than 10 per cent of the estimated gross national product for 1980, as compared with the 16 per cent of the gross national product that will be absorbed by the 1960-61 Federal budget. Similar beneficial savings and results would accrue to many other peoples where, relatively speaking, the present military burden is even more oppressive than for the United States.

In view of this tremendous economic relief to the whole world, even the proposed maximum United Nations budget could not be considered a serious burden, since the net result of the whole plan for disarmament and enforceable world law would be greatly to lessen the tax burden and considerably to improve the living standards of all the world's people.

It may be asked what good use the United Nations could make of so large a sum as might be collected within the constitutional limit of two per cent of the estimated gross world product, if the General Assembly should exercise its right to vote a maximum budget.

The answer is found by analysis of the above-supposed United Nations budget of $36 billion for the year 1980. One must first estimate the irreducible or, so to speak, mandatory requirements. These include the support of: the United Nations Peace Force; the General Assembly; the Executive Council; the Inspection Service; the Nuclear Energy Authority; the Outer Space Agency; the judicial and conciliation system (including the International Court of Justice, the United Nations regional courts, the World Equity Tribunal and the World Concilation Board); the Trusteeship Council; and the Economic and Social Council with its various affiliated agencies, such as the World Health Organization and the United Nations Food and Agriculture Organization.

The United Nations Peace Force would be the major item among these, since (as estimated in detail in the General Comment to Annex II) its annual cost, including the Peace Force Reserve, might well run to $9 billion. The combined expense of the other organs and agencies might well come to $2 billion, making a total, *without* the World Development Authority, of, say, $11 billion.

Could the World Development Authority usefully employ any such annual sum as the remaining $25 billion in its task of improving the economic and social welfare of all the people of the world? For the reasons set forth in the comment on Annex IV, it is believed that the Authority certainly could expend such a sum to the world's great advantage; and that expenditures of this order would be in the enlightened self-interest of those nations most highly developed in an economic sense.

The borrowing power. While it is expected that this revenue plan would ordinarily provide the United Nations with sufficient funds, it seems prudent to provide also for a borrowing power to meet unexpected contingencies. But, as in the case of the revenue-raising power, this borrowing power should be subject to careful safeguards. Accordingly, a constitutional debt limit is proposed whereby the maximum United Nations debt at the end of any year could not exceed five per cent of the estimated gross world product for that year, except in a grave emergency declared by the General Assembly pursuant to Article 43 of the revised Charter.

The purpose of this limitation on the borrowing power, like the limitation of two per cent of the gross world product on the revenue-raising power, is to strike a sound balance which, on the one hand, will prevent extravagance, and, on the other hand, will enable a strengthened United Nations to have reasonably adequate revenues for the fulfillment of its responsibilities.

* * *

Summary. The rationale of this revenue plan is: (1) that for the support of the strengthened United Nations a reliable system for the raising of large sums —of the order of $30-$50 billion per annum—is absolutely essential; (2) that it is equally essential to avoid the creation of a large United Nations tax-collecting bureaucracy and, therefore, that the taxation machinery and personnel of the respective member Nations must be employed; (3) that in respect of financial support there should be a direct relation between the people of the world community and the world organization which exists to safeguard world peace; (4) that there should be the maximum degree of autonomy in the choice of methods, nation by nation, for furnishing the necessary financial support; and finally (5) that these purposes can be reconciled and accomplished by a carefully devised plan of *collaboration* between the United Nations and the member Nations of the sort therein described.

358

ANNEX VI

PRIVILEGES AND IMMUNITIES

Outline. It is believed wise to define in constitutional form, through a special annex, the basic principles governing the difficult and controversial problem of the privileges and immunities which should be enjoyed by the United Nations itself, its officials and other persons connected with it. The text of this Annex remains to be drafted, but its main features are outlined below.

The provisions here proposed are based, to a large extent, upon the Convention on the Privileges and Immunities of the United Nations adopted by the General Assembly on February 13, 1946; upon the agreement of June 26, 1947, between the United Nations and the United States regarding the headquarters of the United Nations; and upon similar conventions governing the privileges and immunities of the specialized agencies of the United Nations, the Council of Europe, the North Atlantic Treaty Organization, the Western European Union, and the European Coal and Steel Community.

The proposals are as follows:

A. *Privileges and Immunities of the United Nations Itself*

1. The United Nations and all its property shall enjoy immunity from every form of legal process except in so far as in any particular case the United Nations has waived such immunity.

2. The premises of the United Nations shall be inviolable. The property of the United Nations shall be immune from search, requisition, confiscation, expropriation or any other form of interference, whether by executive, administrative, judicial or legislative action.

3. The archives of the United Nations, and all documents belonging to it or held by it, shall be inviolable.

4. The United Nations, its income and properties shall be exempt:

(a) from all taxes, except that the United Nations will not claim exemption from taxes or dues which are no more than charges for public utility services;

(b) from all customs duties on imports and exports in respect of articles imported or exported by the United Nations for its official use, including arms, equipment and supplies for the use of the United Nations Peace Force and materials and equipment for the use of the United Nations Nuclear Energy Authority and the Outer Space Agency; and from all prohibitions and quantitative restrictions in respect of such imports and exports;

(c) from all customs duties, prohibitions and restrictions, on imports and exports in respect of its publications.

5. No censorship shall be applied to the official correspondence or other official communications of the United Nations.

6. The United Nations shall have the right to use codes, and to despatch

and receive its correspondence by courier or in sealed bags, which shall have the same privileges and immunities as diplomatic couriers and bags.

7. The United Nations shall have the right to establish and operate in the territory of each nation one long-range, all-purpose radio station, and such additional special broadcasting facilities as may be required by the United Nations Inspection Service for the proper performance of its functions.

8. The area in which is located the headquarters of the United Nations and all areas owned by or leased to the United Nations shall be under the exclusive control and authority of the United Nations; and the United Nations shall have the power to make laws and regulations applicable in the headquarters area and in such other areas, and to establish tribunals for the application and enforcement of such laws and regulations. No officials of any nation shall enter the headquarters area or other areas under United Nations control to perform any official duties therein except with the consent of the Secretary-General or of the United Nations official in charge of the area in question.

9. The United Nations shall be entitled to display the United Nations flag in its headquarters area and in all other areas owned by or leased to the United Nations, and on its vehicles, vessels and aircraft.

B. Privileges and Immunities of Representatives in the General Assembly

1. No administrative or other restrictions shall be imposed on the free movement of Representatives in the General Assembly to and from the meetings of the General Assembly, or its committees or subcommittees, or to and from the meetings of any other organ of the United Nations of which they are members or in the proceedings of which they have been invited to participate.

2. Representatives in the General Assembly shall be immune from official interrogation by any national authority and from arrest and all legal process in respect of words spoken or written or acts performed or votes cast by them in the exercise of their functions.

3. While attending the sessions of the General Assembly or meetings of committees and subcommittees of the Assembly or of other organs or committees or agencies of the United Nations, the Representatives in the General Assembly shall enjoy:

(a) immunity from personal arrest or detention, except when a Representative is found in the act of committing an offense against the domestic law of any nation or of attempting to commit such an offense or when the General Assembly has waived the immunity;

(b) immunity from inspection or seizure of their personal baggage;

(c) inviolability for all papers and documents;

(d) such further privileges and immunities as are enjoyed by members or the national legislative body of the nation in which these privileges or immunities are claimed.

These privileges and immunities shall also apply when Representatives are travelling to and from the place of meeting of the General Assembly, or its committees or subcommittees or of any other organs or committees or agencies of the United Nations of which they are members or in the proceedings of which they have been invited to participate.

4. Representatives shall, in the matter of customs and exchange control, be accorded:

(a) by the governments of their own nation, the same facilities as those accorded to members of the national legislative body of the nation when travelling abroad on official duty;

(b) by other governments than their own, the same facilities as those accorded by such governments to members of foreign legislative bodies travelling on official duty.

5. Privileges and immunities are granted to Representatives in the General Assembly not for the personal benefit of the individuals themselves, but to safeguard the independent exercise of their functions. The Assembly shall have the right and the duty to waive the immunity of any Representative in any case where, in its opinion, the immunity would impede the course of justice and can be waived without prejudice to the interests of the United Nations.

C. Privileges and Immunities of Officials of the United Nations

1. The General Assembly shall enact regulations specifying what categories of officials shall be entitled to the privileges and immunities provided for in this Section C. The Secretary-General shall communicate to all nations the names of the officials included in these categories.

2. Officials of the United Nations belonging to the categories specified pursuant to paragraph 1 of this Section C shall:

(a) be immune from all legal process in respect of words spoken or written and all acts performed by them in their official capacity;

(b) be immune, together with members of their immediate families residing with them and dependent on them, from immigration restrictions and alien registration and fingerprinting;

(c) be accorded the same facilities in respect of currency or exchange restrictions as are accorded to diplomatic personnel of comparable rank;

(d) have the right to import free of duty their furniture, effects and private motor vehicles at the time of first arrival to take up their posts in the nation in question, and, on the termination of their functions in that nation, to re-export such furniture, effects and vehicles free of duty.

3. Officials of the United Nations belonging to the categories specified pursuant to paragraph 1 of this Section C shall be exempt from all national and local taxation on the salaries and emoluments paid to them by the United Nations.

4. The General Assembly shall have authority to determine to what extent various categories of employees of the United Nations, including members of the United Nations Inspection Service, members of the staff of the United Nations Nuclear Energy Authority and the Outer Space Agency, members of the United Nations Peace Force and members of the United Nations civil police, other than those belonging to the categories specified pursuant to paragraph 1 of this Section C, shall be entitled to some or all of the privileges and immunities provided for in this Section C.

5. In addition to the privileges and immunities provided for in paragraphs

2 and 3 of this Section C, the Secretary-General and the Under Secretaries-General of the United Nations, the Inspector-General, the General Manager of the United Nations Nuclear Energy Authority, the Managing Director of the Outer Space Agency and the Director-General of the World Development Authority; the members of the Military Staff Committee, of the Inspection Commission, of the Nuclear Energy Commission, of the Outer Space Commission, and of the World Development Commission; and such other officials of the United Nations as may be specified by the General Assembly, shall be accorded in respect of themselves and the members of their immediate families residing with them and dependent on them, all the privileges and immunities, exemptions and facilities normally accorded to diplomatic envoys.

6. Privileges and immunities are granted to officials of the United Nations in the interest of the United Nations and not for the personal benefit of the individuals themselves. The Secretary-General shall have the right and the duty to waive the immunity of any official in any case where, in his opinion, the immunity would impede the course of justice and can be waived without prejudice to the interests of the United Nations. In the case of the Secretary-General and of other principal officials mentioned in paragraph 5 of this Section C, the Executive Council shall have the right to waive immunity.

7. The General Assembly shall enact laws establishing procedures for the settlement of disputes involving any official of the United Nations whose immunity has not been waived in accordance with the provisions of paragraph 6 of this Section C.

8. The privileges and immunities provided for in this Section C shall be accorded by a nation to those officials of the United Nations who are nationals of that nation on the same basis as to those who are not its nationals.

D. Privileges and Immunities of Permanent Observers at the United Nations Headquarters

1. Each nation may, if it wishes, have an observer at the headquarters of the United Nations for the purpose of liaison with the Secretariat of the United Nations.

2. These observers, their families and official staff, shall enjoy the privileges and immunities ordinarily accorded by the nation in the territory of which the headquarters area of the United Nations is situated to diplomatic envoys accredited to that nation, their families and official staff.

3. These privileges and immunities are subject to waiver by the government of the nation whose national is concerned in accordance with rules governing the waiver of diplomatic immunities.

E. Privileges and Immunities of United Nations Resident Commissioners

1. The Secretary-General of the United Nations shall, subject to confirmation by the Executive Council, appoint a United Nations Resident Commissioner to every member Nation. They shall reside in the capitals of the member Nations to which they are respectively accredited, shall maintain liaison with the governments of such nations and coordinate the activities of the United Nations in those nations.

2. These Resident Commissioners, their families and official staff, shall enjoy the privileges and immunities ordinarily accorded by the nation in the capital of which they reside to diplomatic envoys accredited to that nation, their families and official staff.

3. These privileges and immunities are granted in the interest of the United Nations and not for the personal benefit of the individuals themselves. The Secretary-General shall have the right and duty to waive the immunity granted by this Section E in any case where, in his opinion, the immunity will impede the course of justice and can be waived without prejudice to the interests of the United Nations.

F. Privileges and Immunities of Other Persons Entitled to Attend United Nations Meetings

No nation shall impose any impediments on the transit of the following persons to and from places in which a United Nations meeting is being held:

(a) representatives of the press, or of radio, television, film or other information agencies, who have been accredited by the United Nations;

(b) representatives of nongovernmental organizations with which arrangements for consultation have been made pursuant to Article 71 of the revised Charter;

(c) other persons especially invited by the United Nations to come to a particular meeting.

G. General Provisions

1. The United Nations shall cooperate at all times with national and local authorities to facilitate the proper administration of justice, ensure the observance of police regulations and prevent any abuse in connection with the privileges and immunities provided for in this Annex.

2. If a nation considers that there has been an abuse of any privilege or immunity granted by or under this Annex, consultations shall be held between that nation and the United Nations to determine whether any such abuse has occurred and to formulate such procedures as may be necessary to prevent the repetition of any abuses found to have occurred.

3. The General Assembly shall adopt regulations prescribing the procedure to be followed when a nation considers that any person entitled to privileges and immunities under this Annex has abused them to such an extent as to warrant his being called upon to leave the territory of the nation concerned.

4. The General Assembly shall adopt regulations concerning the issuance of a United Nations *laissez-passer* to any person entitled to privileges and immunities provided for in Sections B, C and E of this Annex. Such a *laissez-passer* shall be recognized and accepted as a valid travel document by the authorities of all the nations. Applications for visas (where required) from the holders of United Nations *laissez-passer*, when accompanied by a certificate that they are travelling on the business of the United Nations, shall be dealt with as speedily as possible.

5. The General Assembly shall enact laws defining the responsibility of the

United Nations for damage caused by United Nations officials. Such laws shall provide:

(a) that the officials themselves shall not be responsible toward third parties for any damage caused by acts performed by them in their official capacity and within the limits of their authority;

(b) that the United Nations shall make reparation for any damage caused by its officials in circumstances referred to in paragraph (a) above;

(c) that any official of the United Nations shall be personally responsible to an injured party for any damage caused by acts not connected with his official duties which, while performed by such official in his official capacity, were outside the limits of his authority;

(d) that the United Nations shall make reparation for any damage caused by its officials in circumstances referred to in paragraph (c) above, if the injured party is unable to obtain reparation from the responsible official and if a United Nations regional court deems such reparation equitable.

6. The General Assembly shall enact laws establishing procedures for dealing with claims arising under paragraph 5 above and such other claims as may arise out of other acts of the United Nations, such as contracts concluded by it with its own officials and other persons. These procedures shall ensure to the extent possible that the immunity of the United Nations from legal process does not result in an injustice to any person or nation.

Comment. The general purpose of this Annex is, on the one hand, to safeguard the independence of the United Nations by protecting it against national acts which might hamper the exercise of its authority, restrict the proper activities of its officials or prejudice the independence of the Representatives in the General Assembly. On the other hand, the purpose is to accomplish this objective with a due regard to the need of the nations to have their laws respected and with proper safeguards against abuse of the privileges and immunities granted by this Annex.

ANNEX VII

BILL OF RIGHTS

General Comment. The purposes of this Annex are: (a) to provide assurance that the United Nations, even when greatly strengthened in accordance with the proposals of this book, would still be an organization of strictly limited powers in no way comparable, for example, to a federation of very wide powers such as the United States of America; and (b) to provide assurance against the violation by the strengthened United Nations of certain fundamental individual rights.

The former purpose would be fulfilled through an explicit reservation whereby all powers not delegated by the revised Charter to the United Nations by express language or clear implication would be reserved to the respective nations (including any nonmember nations) or to their peoples. And the latter purpose would be accomplished by a set of provisions whereby the United Nations would be forbidden to deny or impair certain specified individual rights which are, or should be, universally recognized as fundamental rights of man.

With regard to the proposed reservation of nongranted powers, it can, indeed, be argued that since the United Nations could have no sound claim to any powers except such as are plainly delegated in the revised Charter, there is no occasion or necessity for a reservation of this sort. But just as it seemed wise to the framers of the Ninth and Tenth Amendments to the Constitution of the United States to make the limitation of powers doubly sure by an express reservation of all powers not delegated by the constitutional document, it seems wise in a revised Charter to include a similar reservation, but in even more explicit form.

The content and language of the proposed reservation are naturally influenced to some extent by the Ninth and Tenth Amendments to the Constitution of the United States because the basic purpose is the same, namely, to provide assurance against the assumption by a newly created authority of powers not intended to be conferred upon it. Nevertheless, the problem is somewhat different in that, in the case of the United States, the Constitution submitted for ratification after the historic convention of 1787 envisioned a genuine central government not only "to form a more perfect union, establish justice, insure domestic tranquility, provide for the common defense" but also to "promote the general welfare, and secure the blessings of liberty to ourselves and our posterity",—all as proclaimed in the Preamble to that Constitution. In harmony with these wide purposes, the powers granted to the Federal Government of the United States under its original Constitution were correspondingly broad.

On the other hand, the purposes of the strengthened United Nations, as proposed in this book, would be far more modest and restricted and its powers correspondingly more limited. Thus the new United Nations would

365

have no *authority* (as distinguished from the right to recommend) in such matters as international commerce and travel, or in respect of a world currency, or in respect of various other subjects analogous on the world scene to powers expressly granted to the government of the new United States by the Constitution of 1787. On the contrary, as often stressed in this book, the authority of the proposed new United Nations would be carefully restricted to certain matters *directly* related to the prevention of war.

It follows that the reservation provision in a Bill of Rights for the United Nations should recognize this basic difference and consequently should be more definite and more strict than Articles Nine and Ten of the United States Constitution. And while it is true that in the body of the revised Charter itself (paragraph 1 of Article 2) there is an explicit reservation of this character, it seems best to repeat this reservation verbatim as the first article of the proposed Bill of Rights.

With regard to the proposed prohibitions and guarantees required for the protection of certain basic individual rights, it is assumed that these should certainly include guarantees of the right of fair trial, in respect of which there should be specific mention of the following: (a) the right to a speedy and public trial of any person accused by the United Nations of a violation of the revised Charter or of any law or regulation enacted thereunder; (b) the right of any person so accused to be informed in advance of trial of the specific charge made against him; (c) the right to be confronted with the witnesses against him; (d) the right of compulsory process to obtain witnesses in his favor; (e) the right to engage counsel of his own choice; (f) the right not to be compelled to give testimony against himself; (g) the right to have an interpreter; and (h) the right to communicate with his own government and to have a representative of that government present at his trial.

There should also be a guarantee against double jeopardy, that is to say against being tried twice for the same alleged offense against the United Nations; and also a prohibition against any *ex post facto* law of the United Nations, that is to say against any law making criminal an act which was not criminal at the time the act occurred or increasing the penalty for a criminal act after its occurrence.

Provisions should also be included against excessive bail and any cruel or unusual punishment, including excessive fines; and the death penalty should be specifically prohibited. In addition, a remedy should be provided against unreasonable detention through a provision securing the right of any person detained for any alleged violation of the revised Charter or of any law or regulation enacted thereunder to be brought without undue delay before an appropriate United Nations judicial tribunal to determine whether there is just cause for his detention.

Unreasonable searches and seizures should also be forbidden, subject to the proviso that this prohibition shall not prejudice searches and seizures clearly necessary or advisable for the enforcement of complete disarmament.

Finally, it should be provided that the United Nations shall not restrict or interfere with freedom of conscience or religion; freedom of speech, press or expression in any other form; freedom of association and assembly; or freedom of petition.

366

As in the case of the proposed general reservation of powers, it can be argued that since the revised Charter would contain nothing which could be fairly construed as authorizing the United Nations to interfere with any of these rights, it is superfluous to provide specific constitutional guarantees in this regard. But here again, as when the first eight amendments to the Constitution of the United States were adopted, it seems wise to make doubly sure by providing certain explicit safeguards.

In studying the proposed text of these specific guarantees, the reader is asked to remember that the authors' purpose, while stating the essentials, is also to avoid cumbersome and perhaps dangerous overelaboration through attempting to specify in detail every variety of right (e.g., every form of expression) to be protected. In this connection it is assumed that under the amended Statute of the International Court of Justice (see Annex III) that tribunal in the exercise of its jurisdiction to interpret the revised Charter and to declare void any law, regulation or decision conflicting with the revised Charter as so interpreted, would gradually build up a body of world constitutional law in respect of the scope and application of the provisions of the Bill of Rights. And this consideration, together with certain express or clearly implied powers of the General Assembly to define offenses and afford remedies, makes it seem the more advisable to state certain of the guarantees in broad language, leaving it for the judicial and legislative branches to interpret and apply them reasonably and justly.

A good example is the broad and even sweeping language in which it is proposed to forbid the United Nations to "restrict or interfere" not only with freedom of speech and press, but also with "freedom of expression in any other form." Taken with complete literalness this language could be construed to prevent the penalization of even the most extreme written or verbal incitement to rebel against even the most basic provisions of the revised Charter and would, for example, permit anyone to advocate with impunity open and armed rebellion against the prohibition of the national manufacture of nuclear weapons. In practice, however, it is assumed that a "rule of reason" would prevail, that the General Assembly could and would enact legislation penalizing extreme incitement of this sort and that, if reasonably drafted, the International Court of Justice would uphold the validity of such legislation. With these considerations in mind, it seems best not to encumber a United Nations Bill of Rights with various provisos and exceptions which, however carefully drafted, might not cover all contingencies.

It should be emphasized that all the proposed provisions are limitations or guarantees in respect of action by the *United Nations only*. While it may be argued that the revised United Nations ought also to guarantee certain fundamental rights against violation by any member Nation, the authors have not deemed this practicable or wise. To do so would involve the enactment of United Nations legislation against various customs and practices still acceptable in various countries. It would also involve very difficult questions as to access to the courts of the United Nations in order to assert rights alleged to have been violated by a particular nation, and as to the enforcement within a particular nation of decisions by courts of the United Nations which might conflict with the laws and mores of that nation. For all these reasons, it seems wiser to restrict the constitutional prohibitions and guarantees to the actions of the United Nations itself, leaving to the future the consideration of any further extension of such constitutional safeguards.

This view does not, of course, imply that the United Nations should not promote the protection of human rights through recommendations and nonbinding pronouncements, such as the Universal Declaration of Human Rights of 1948. Moreover, the very existence of a United Nations Bill of Rights could be expected to contribute to the improvement of national protection of human rights and fundamental freedoms, since this Bill of Rights would serve as a standard which national governments would find it difficult to ignore.

A question may fairly be raised as to the propriety of the use of the term "Bill of Rights" as applied to this Annex upon the ground that this term would be more properly used as applicable to a set of provisions safeguarding certain fundamental rights and freedoms against infringement by the member Nations of the United Nations themselves. However, the authors prefer the American usage in which the term "Bill of Rights" was originally applied to the first ten Amendments to the Constitution of the United States, i.e., to reservations and prohibitions upon the central authority only, as distinguished from its constituent parts—just as the Bill of Rights herein proposed would apply only to the strengthened United Nations itself rather than to its member Nations.

Much more could be usefully said by way of comment upon the purposes and particular provisions of a Bill of Rights for a strengthened United Nations. But, as in the case of other parts of this book, the objective is not always to present an exhaustive explanation, but rather to make definite proposals in order to stimulate study and discussion out of which an eventual consensus can develop.

At the risk of repetition, it is again emphasized: (a) that it is wise and desirable to make it *constitutionally* clear that the scope of the new United Nations shall extend no further than those minimum enumerated powers that are necessary to prevent the nations from "murdering each other"; and (b) that it should be made equally clear by *constitutional* guarantees that the strengthened world organization to maintain peace shall, under no circumstances, deny or impair certain basic individual rights.

In short, the broad purpose of this proposed Annex VII is to give assurance to the governments and peoples of the world that, by strengthening the United Nations to the extent necessary to maintain peace, they would not be establishing a "superstate" and would be safe against usurpation of power or oppression by the strengthened world organization.

The proposed text is as follows:

Article 1

As provided by paragraph 1 of Article 2 of this revised Charter, there are reserved to all nations or their peoples all powers inherent in their sovereignty, except such as are delegated to the United Nations by this revised Charter, either by express language or clear implication, and are not prohibited by this revised Charter to the nations.

Article 2

The United Nations shall not, through any law, regulation or decision enacted, adopted or made by the General Assembly, the Executive Council or any other organ or agency, or in any other manner:

a. Restrict or interfere with freedom of conscience or the free exercise of religion; or with freedom of speech, press or expression in any other form; or with freedom of association and assembly; or with freedom of petition.

b. Deny or impair the right of any person detained for any alleged violation of this revised Charter or of any law or regulation enacted thereunder to be brought without undue delay before an appropriate judicial tribunal of the United Nations for a determination as to whether just cause exists for his detention, or deny or impair the right of any such person to be released from detention if such tribunal determines that there is no just cause therefor.

c. Deny or impair the right of any person accused of a violation of this revised Charter or of any law or regulation enacted thereunder to a speedy and public trial; or the right of any person so accused to be informed at the time of the accusation against him, in a language which he understands and in detail, of the nature and cause of the accusation; or the right of any person so accused to be confronted at his trial with the witnesses against him; or the right of any person so accused to have adequate time and facilities for his defense and to have compulsory process to obtain witnesses in his favor; or the right of any person so accused to defend himself in person or through legal assistance of his own choice and, if necessary, to have an interpreter at any stage of the proceedings against him; or the right of any person so accused to communicate with his own government and to have a representative of that government present at his trial.

d. Deny or impair the right of any person accused of a violation of this revised Charter or of any law or regulation enacted thereunder not to be compelled to testify against himself or to confess guilt.

e. Require excessive bail or inflict any cruel or unusual punishment, including any excessive fines; and in particular the death penalty shall not be imposed for any offense against the United Nations.

f. Twice put in jeopardy any person for the same alleged offense against the United Nations; nor shall any person be held guilty of any offense against the United Nations on account of any act or omission which

369

did not constitute an offense at the time when it occurred, or be subjected to any greater penalty than was prescribed for the offense at the time the act or omission occurred.

g. Carry out any unreasonable searches or seizures provided that this prohibition shall not be deemed to prevent such searches and seizures as are authorized by this revised Charter for the enforcement of universal and complete disarmament.

INDEX

(The references are to pages.)

371

Cyprus, 30
Czechoslovakia, Soviet position in, 103

Damage
  caused by Inspectors, 265-266, 271
  by United Nations officials, 363-364
Declarations accepting the jurisdiction
  of International Court of Justice, 101, 338
  of World Conciliation Board, 341
  of World Equity Tribunal, 339
Demonstrations, military, 116, 319, 330
Diffusion barriers, safeguards concerning, 276
Diplomacy, xv, xlv, lii
Disarmament
  by stages, xvi, xxiv, 207-208, 215, 233-245
  Commission, 63
  complete, xi-xiii, xv-xix, xxiii-xxvi, xxviii-
    xxix, xxxiii, xxxvi-xxxvii, xli, xliii-xlvi,
    xlix-liv, 1, 5, 10, 33, 36, 40-42, 89, 120,
    203, 206-207, 214, 227, 232-233, 315,
    320-321, 344, 351, 370
  maintenance of, 246-262
  comprehensive, xi, li
  "foolproof", xxix
  laws and regulations, 36, 41-42, 212, 218-
    220, 226-227, 232-233, 238-240, 255,
    257-259, 263-264, 272-279, 283-284,
    286, 289, 291, 293-294, 298-299, 302,
    304, 306-307, 336
  partial, xlix, 206
  plan, xxiv-xxix, xliii, 1, 7-8, 10, 36, 41-42,
    63-64, 75, 79-80, 93, 128, 159, 193-194,
    203, 207, 282
    actual disarmament stage, xxiv-xxvi, xxix,
      xlv, 206-207, 211, 215, 229-247, 249,
      263-264, 266-268, 285-286, 300, 319,
      323, 351
    Annex containing, 206-313
    applicability to individuals, 15, 43-45,
      212, 256, 258-259, 306-309, 312
    application to trust territories, 161-162
    certificate of compliance with, 253, 255
    enforcement of, xix, xxiii, 5-6, 8, 11, 36,
      46-47, 63-64, 79-80, 212-213, 218-
      220, 229, 231, 242, 244, 256, 259-
      261, 268, 279-280, 289, 293, 301, 306-
      313, 321, 367
    maintenance of complete disarmament,
      xxii, 246-264
    observance of, 7, 10, 13, 39, 46-47, 208,
      228, 231
    preparatory stage, xxiv-xxv, 207-208,
      215-233, 266-268, 286, 300, 322-323,
      351
    punishment of violations of, 38, 40, 45,
      212, 306-313
    questionnaires, 220-224, 226, 230, 233,
      253-256, 270
    serious noncompliance with, 222-224,
      226-232, 242, 260-261, 280, 293, 310-
      313
    temporary postponement, xxiii, xxv,
      xxvii, 222-232, 242-243, 245, 286
    total, see complete

Disarmament (cont.)
  plan (cont.)
    violations of, xxviii, xxxv, 37, 40, 78, 212-
      213, 231, 255, 269-270, 336, 343-344;
      reporting of information on, 267-268
    practical prospects for, xliii-liii
    proportionate, xvi, xxiv, xxvi, 207-208,
      214, 237-240, 244
    proposals, British and Soviet, xi-xii
    savings from, xxxix, xlviii, 348, 356-357
    simultaneous, xvi, xxvi, 207, 214, 237,
      241, 243
    universal, xiii, xv-xvi, xxv-xxvi, xxxiii,
      xxxvi-xxxvii, xliii-xliv, 10, 36, 40-42,
      120, 203, 214, 227, 236, 321, 344, 370
    See also Armaments; Arms
Disputes
  agreement to refer to United Nations, 109-
    110
  investigation of, 93-94
  legal, xxxiii-xxxv, 91, 96-98, 100-101, 103-
    104, 175-176, 335-337
  likely to endanger peace, xxxiii, xxxv, 90-
    91, 96-109, 179, 337, 339, 341
  local, 129-131
  nonlegal, xxxiii-xxxv, 96-106, 175, 177, 179,
    335, 338-339, 341
  of concern to United Nations, 92
  participation of parties to, 86-88
  prevention of aggravation of, 107-108
  settlement of, xii, xv-xvi, xxvi, xxxiii-xxxviii,
    xliv, 5-8, 10, 33, 40, 81-82, 89-110, 112-
    113, 128-131, 212, 335-341, 344
  submission of to General Assembly or Ex-
    ecutive Council, 35-36, 94-95
Domestic jurisdiction, no interference in matters within, xvii, xix, xxii, 7-8, 10-11, 105-
  106, 132

Economic
  advancement, xxxvi-xxxviii, 4, 11, 132-133,
    136, 141-142, 152-155, 160, 171, 345,
    347-348, 357-358
  assistance to underdeveloped countries, xvi,
    xxxvi-xxxvii, 132, 345-348, 357
  burden of the arms race, xlviii
  conditions, disparities in, xvi, 40, 346
  field, cooperation in, 6, 49, 133-134, 147
  information, 152-154
  obstacles to disarmament, xlv
  organizations, 338
  problems caused by sanctions, 126-127
  reports, 133, 142, 144, 153-154
  sanctions, xxxiv, xxxvi, 42-43, 115, 180,
    212, 313, 334, 339
  studies, 142
  systems, no change sought in, 11
Economic and Social Council, xlii, 49, 63,
  79, 174, 184, 186, 202
  authority to request advisory opinions, 180
  commissions of, 147, 149
  composition, xxiii, 63, 136-141
  control over World Development Author-
    ity, xxxvi-xxxvii, 136, 141, 345-346

Facilities (cont.)

    for producing arms, 214, 221, 223-226, 230, 234-235, 237-240, 243, 246; for United Nations Peace Force, 326-327

    for use of nuclear materials, 209-210, 222, 248-249, 255, 257, 276-279, 285, 287, 290, 292-293

Financing

    by World Development Authority, 345

    of United Nations, xxxvii-xxxix, 49, 52-54, 58, 64, 132, 135, 143-144, 203, 349-358

    private, 346

    public, 346

Fingerprinting, exemption from, 361

Food and Agriculture Organization, xlii, 49, 135, 357

Force

    prohibition of use, xvi, 3, 7, 10, 37, 40, 89, 92

    rule of, 40

    threat of, 37, 40

    See also Aggression, Violence

Formosa, 103

France

    assent to Charter amendments, 196

    attack on Egypt, 119

    consent needed for Charter revision, xviii

    dispute with United Kingdom, 100

    member of Security Council, 66

    participation in transitional security arrangements, 192-193

    population, 30

    ratification of Charter by, 200, 203

    representation: in the General Assembly, 27; on Executive Council, xxii, 72; on Trusteeship Council, 169

    trust territories under administration of, 150

Freedoms

    from fear, 207

    fundamental, promotion of, 3, 6, 49, 133, 142, 155, 367-368

    protection against United Nations, xl, 365-370

    See also Human rights

General Assembly

    assistance to by Economic and Social Council, 144

    authority

        to appoint the Secretary-General, 183

        to approve budgets, xxxviii-xxxix, 52-54, 134, 143-144, 295-296, 328, 346, 349-358

        to confirm appointments, xxiv, xxviii, xxxvi, 123-124, 217, 220, 282, 342-343, 345

        to deal with disputes, 8, 10, 35-36, 50, 55, 57, 90-110, 112-113

        to declare extreme emergency, 119, 322, 327, 332-333

        to delineate regions, xxx, 67, 72, 210, 288, 291, 318, 325, 341

        to determine quotas for nuclear mate-

General Assembly (cont.)

    authority (cont.)

        rials, 286, 291-292

        to direct action by national forces, 319 334

        to discharge Councils and Committees, xxii, 55, 62, 65, 69-70, 74, 82-83, 139-141, 167-168

        to discuss, 35-36, 40, 46-47, 153-154

        to elect members of other organs, xxii-xxiv, xxxiv, 35-36, 55, 58, 60-64, 66-69, 71-73, 137-141, 164-169, 336, 338, 340

        to enforce the disarmament plan, xxii, 8, 36, 212, 228-229, 231, 242, 244, 260-261, 279-280, 289, 293, 301, 306-307, 311, 313, 367

        to enforce judgments of International Court of Justice, xxxiv, 50, 55, 57, 96, 101, 178-180, 338

        to enforce recommendations of World Equity Tribunal, xxxv, 8, 10, 50, 55, 57, 99, 103, 105, 178-180, 339

        to legislate, xii, xix, xxii, xlii, 8, 10, 34-35, 52-55, 57, 120-121, 176, 185, 190-191, 211-212, 218-220, 225-226, 232-233, 238-241, 253, 257, 259, 263-264, 272-279, 283-284, 286, 294, 298-303, 306-307, 314, 316, 319, 322, 326-328, 333-334, 337, 342-343, 361-364, 367

        to maintain peace, xix, xxii-xxiii, xli-xlii, 35-36, 55, 57, 75-76, 111-122, 334

        to order action by Peace Force, xxxvi, 43, 80, 116-120, 212, 313-314, 318-319, 329-330

        to permit use of nuclear weapons, xxxi-xxxii

        to raise revenue, 8, 10, 52-54, 57-58, 346

        to recommend, xxii, 8, 11, 35-36, 40-41, 47-50, 57, 132, 145

        to refer questions to International Court of Justice, xxxiii, 13-14, 50, 91, 96-98, 100-101, 180, 335-337

        to refer questions to World Conciliation Board, 50, 91, 96-98, 100-104, 109

        to refer questions to World Equity Tribunal, 8, 10, 50, 91, 97-106, 109, 179, 339

        to remove the Secretary-General, 183

        to request advisory opinions, 13-14, 91, 101, 180-182

        to supervise other organs, xxii-xxiii, xxxii, 35, 75-77, 136, 145, 345-346

        to suspend rights of member Nations, 16, 55-56

        to waive immunities, 361

        with regard to expulsion of members, 16, 55-56

        with respect to admission to membership, 13-14, 55

        with respect to disarmament, xxii-xxiii, xxv, 36, 39-42, 208, 211-212, 217, 219-220, 222-232, 238, 240-245, 257-

377

Military
  activities, prohibitions against, 247-253
  advantages of seizure of nuclear materials, etc., to be minimized, 287-288, 291, 293, 327
  bases, xxvii
  forces, national
    abolition of, xii, xxiv-xxvii, xlix-l, 5, 9-10, 41, 206-208, 214, 232-241, 243-244, 246-250, 315, 320
    census of, 221, 223
    prohibition of increase, 225-226
    schedule of, 234
    use by United Nations during actual disarmament stage, 306, 334
  forces of the United Nations. *See* Peace Force
  installations, 220, 230
  profession, influence of, xliv-xlv, lii
  training, 208, 216, 232-233, 247, 249, 317, 320, 322-324, 328
Military Staff Committee
  appointment, 123-124, 322
  composition, xxxii, 60, 64, 123-124, 282, 314, 318
  establishment, 122
  functions, 122-124, 314, 318, 322-323, 328-329
  immunities, 362
  removal of members of, 123-124
  reports by, 328
  supervision of, by General Assembly and Executive Council, xxxii, 123-125, 314, 318, 328-329
  terms of office, 322
Military Supply and Research Agency, 318, 326-327
Mines, 221, 254, 256
Missiles
  ballistic, xxvi-xxvii, xlvi-xlvii, 225, 237, 239
  guided, 239
Moon, control over, 211, 297, 300, 302
Morocco
  attainment of independence by, 151
  nationality decrees in, 100
Moscow Declaration, 192

National product
  adjusted, 137, 141, 350-351, 353
  gross, xxiii, xxxix, 349-353
  per capita, xxi, xxxix, 141, 350-351, 353
Nations
  ability to pay, 203, 349-352
  admission to United Nations, 12-14
  application of world law to, xvi-xvii
  constitutions and laws in conflict with Charter, 188, 337
  economic development, xxxvi-xxxviii, 4, 11, 132-133, 141-142, 152-155, 160, 171, 345, 357-358
  equality of, 3, 5-6, 9, 25, 56, 133, 203
  friendly relations among, 5, 49, 133
  "have" and "have not", xii
  independent, xviii, xx, 12-14, 26, 72, 150-

Nations *(cont.)*
  independent *(cont.)*
    151, 199, 205; list of, 28-29
  information to be supplied by, 220-224, 228, 230, 234, 253-255, 274, 277
  jurisdiction, 331. *See also* Domestic jurisdiction
  legislation to be enacted by, 121-122, 333
  maintenance of law and order in, xi, xv-xvi, 40-41, 206-207, 232, 235
  mutual assistance, 126
  neutral, li-lii
  obligations, 6-11, 38-39, 46, 49-50, 78-79, 107, 116, 125-126, 133, 178, 185, 222, 225-227, 234, 236-241, 247-250, 253-258, 333
  participation in discussions: of the Economic and Social Council, 147-149; of the Executive Council, 85-88
  peace-loving, 14
  political independence, use of force against, 7
  protection against abuse, 175, 209, 220, 263-264, 269-272, 289, 293, 337
  prospective, 30
  representatives from, 20-34
  responsibility for licenses, 256-259
  reserved powers of, xvii, xix, xxxix-xl, 2, 6, 9, 365-369
  right to economic relief, 126-127
  tax-collecting machinery of, xxxviii, 349
  territorial integrity, 7
  violations of disarmament plan by, xxviii, xxxvi, 212, 306, 308-313
  See also Nonmember Nations
Nauru, 150
Negotiation, settlement of disputes by, xxxv, 89, 91-92, 100, 102
Netherlands
  population, 30
  representation on Trusteeship Council, 169
  self-governing territories, 151
Neutral nations, li-lii
New Guinea, 150
New Zealand
  representation on Trusteeship Council, 169
  trust territory under administration of, 150
Nigeria, 30
Nonmember Nations
  agreements with the United Nations, xxvi, 39-40, 46-47
  bases in territories of, 325
  obligations of, xvi, xviii-xix, xxvi, 7, 9-10, 13, 39-40, 46-47, 93, 99, 236-237
  participation in discussions: of Economic and Social Council, 147-149; of Executive Council, 87-88
  parties to Statute of International Court of Justice, 176
  status of, xviii-xix, 10
  submission of disputes: to International Court of Justice, 181-182, 337; to United Nations, 94-95
Non-self-governing territories, 150-154

Non-self-governing territories *(cont.)*
  access of: to World Conciliation Board, 340; to World Equity Tribunal, 338
  advancement, 21, 33, 151-153, 169-171
  authority of General Assembly over, 51-52, 152-154, 169-171
  categories, 150-151
  citizens, 14-15
  declaration regarding, 150-154
  election of their Representatives: to Economic and Social Council, xxiii, 138-141; to Executive Council, xxiii, 67-70, 72-74; to Standing Committees of the General Assembly, 60-62, 64-65
  information from, 153-154, 170-172
  membership in Trusteeship Council, 164-169
  participation in discussions: of Economic and Social Council, 148-149; of Executive Council, 85-86
  periodic visits to, 70
  petitions from, 170
  recruits from, 333
  representation: in General Assembly, xx, 20-21, 23-25, 30, 34; in General Conference, 197, 199; on committees, 60-62, 64-65; on World Conciliation Board, 340
North Atlantic Treaty Organization, 359
Nuclear age, xliv
Nuclear energy
  control of, 36, 41, 209-211, 281-302, 305
  promotion of peaceful use of, 210, 281, 287-288, 290, 292-293
  study of, 222, 255, 292
Nuclear Energy Authority, xxvii-xxviii, 18, 64, 279, 299, 305, 359
  custody of nuclear weapons, xxxi-xxxii
  expenses, xxxvii-xxxviii, 53, 303-305, 352, 357
  functions and powers of, xxvii, 209-212, 238, 251-252, 275-276, 281-305, 319, 330
  General Manager, xxviii, 283, 298, 303-304, 362
  staff, xxvii, 283-284, 303, 361
Nuclear Energy Commission, xxvii-xxviii, 71, 274-276, 278, 311-313, 345, 352
  composition, 61, 64, 282-284
  functions, 285-295
Nuclear materials
  accounting procedures for, 253, 274, 277
  compensation for, 211, 303-305
  danger of diversion of, xxvii, 252-253, 275, 277
  definition, 210, 221, 276, 279
  facilities for production, 209-210, 221-223, 249, 254-256, 268, 276-279, 285, 287, 290, 292-293
  facilities for utilization, 209-210, 222, 249, 255, 276-277, 285, 287, 290, 292-293
  from dismantled weapons, 240, 285-286, 290
  nonmilitary use, xxvii, 225, 227, 248, 251, 255, 277, 281, 285-293, 305
  purchase by United Nations, xxvii, 251

Nuclear materials *(cont.)*
  quotas for production, 210, 286, 289-292
  raw materials which might enter into production, 221, 254, 256, 267, 276-277, 285-286, 289-291, 293
  special, 210, 221-223, 225, 227, 249, 251-257, 275-277, 279, 281, 285-293, 305
Nuclear war, xlvi-xlvii
Nuclear weapons, xxvi, xxix, xlvi-xlvii, 44, 206, 209-211, 237, 239, 326
  census, 221
  compensation for, 211, 238, 286, 303
  custody, xxxi, 211, 240, 290, 295, 319
  definition, 276, 279
  destruction, 238
  limitations on use of by United Nations, xxxi-xxxii, 210-211, 294-295, 319, 326, 330
  materials for making, 222, 230, 275-276, 279, 281, 284
  production of new, 290, 294-295
  research on, 211, 248, 294-295
  tests, 225
  transfer to Nuclear Energy Authority, 238, 240, 294-295

Offenses
  against United Nations, xxxv-xxxvi, 37-38, 43-45, 211-212, 259, 306-313, 335-336, 342-344. *See also* United Nations Charter, violations
  by civilian employees of Peace Force, 331
  by dependents of members of Peace Force, 331
  by Inspectors, 263-264, 271
  by members of Peace Force, 331
  by Representatives in the General Assembly, 360
  Draft Code, 44
Oil, access to, 103
Optional clause, 101. *See also* International Court of Justice, compulsory jurisdiction
Order, internal, maintenance of, xi, xv-xvi, 40-41, 206-207, 232, 235
Orders, of government or superior, 38, 44-45
Organization of American States, 181
Organizations
  academic, 338
  economic, 338
  legal, 337-338
  nongovernmental: arrangements for consultation with, 149; representatives of, access to United Nations Headquarters, 363
  private: access of to International Court of Justice, 258-259, 308-309, 337; activities requiring license, 256-259, 275; assistance to, by Nuclear Energy Authority, 287, 292; conduct of surveys by, 289; information to be supplied by, 274, 277; loans to, 345; offenses by, 37, 43-44, 211-212, 261, 306-309, 336, 341-343; publishing United Nations reports, 310

381

Peace Force *(cont.)*
    safeguards against national domination,
        xxx, 318, 324-325, 332-333
    standing component, xxix-xxxi, 118, 120-
        122, 162, 207, 314-318, 320, 322-324,
        329, 332
    strategic direction, 123-124
    strength, xxx, xxxvii, 315, 320, 322, 332
    supplies for, 330
    terms of service, xxxi, 316-317, 324, 332-
        333
    tools for the production of arms for, 238,
        240, 326-327
    transportation for, xxx-xxxi, 317, 330
    tyranny-proof, xxxi, 125, 318
    use of nuclear weapons by, xxxi-xxxii, 210-
        211, 294-295, 319, 326, 330
    See also Police
Peaceful change, xxxiii, 49-50, 91, 314
Penalties
    for non-payment of taxes, 356
    for publishing United Nations reports pro-
        hibited, 310
    for violations of world law, xii, xxxvi, 38,
        40, 45, 212, 259, 265-266, 306-309,
        331, 343-344, 366, 369
Per capita deduction, xxxix, 350-351, 353
Permanent Court of International Justice
    advisory opinion, 100
    Statute, 175
Petitions
    freedom of, 366, 369
    from non-self-governing and trust terri-
        tories, 169-170
Philippines, 151
Plutonium, 210, 279
Poland, Soviet position in, 103
Police
    internal, xvi, xxv, xxix, xxxiii, 42, 128, 206-
        207, 214, 216, 221, 225, 227, 232-241, 243,
        246-250, 253-256
    United Nations civil, xxxvi, 38, 45, 336, 343
    world, xii, xvi, xix, xxv, xxix-xxxiii, xxxvi, 40,
        42, 89, 203, 207, 218, 236, 251, 314-334,
        344
    See also Peace Force
Political
    advancement of non-self-governing terri-
        tories, 152-155, 160, 171
    field, cooperation in, 49
    information, 153-154
    questions, 91, 100, 102-106, 336
    systems: no basis for rejection of new mem-
        bers, 14; no reform sought in, 11
Popular vote, for Representatives in General
    Assembly, 23-24, 32
Population
    of member Nations, 28-29; and apportion-
        ment of expenses, 350-353
    relation to representation in General As-
        sembly, 25-30
    world, xviii, xxi, 29, 72, 200, 202, 346, 351
Portugal, 169
Power politics, xlv

Press, representatives of, access to United
    Nations headquarters, 363
Property of the United Nations. *See* United
    Nations, property
Property, private
    compensation for owner, 189-190, 303-305,
        326
    due regard for, 264-265
    sequestration of, 344
    unnecessary destruction prohibited, 330
Provisional measures. *See* Measures, provisio-
    nal
Puerto Rico, 30, 151

Quantitative restrictions on imports and ex-
    ports, 359
Quemoy, xlviii, 103
Questionnaire
    arms census, 220-224, 226, 230, 233, 270
    during complete disarmament period, 253-
        256
    trusteeship, 171-172

Radioactive materials
    as components of weapons, 279
    possession and production, 221-222, 248-
        249, 251-257, 276-277, 286-287, 291
Regional
    agencies, 91, 102, 129-131, 180-181, 337
    arrangements, 77, 91, 102, 129-131
    courts, xxviii, xxxv-xxxvi, xl, 38, 45, 175,
        177-178, 189-190, 209, 212, 258-259,
        265, 267, 269-273, 304-305, 308-309,
        326, 331, 335-337, 341-344, 357
    distribution of: facilities for production or
        utilization of nuclear materials, 210, 287-
        288; nuclear materials in United Nations
        custody, 210, 281, 287, 291; Peace Force,
        xxx, 318, 325
    subcommittees of Military Staff Committee,
        124
    subgroups for elections to Executive Coun-
        cil, 67-68, 72
Rent, equitable, to be paid by United Nations,
    303-305
Reports
    by Executive Council, 50-51, 75-77, 219,
        229-231, 242-243, 245, 260-261
    by Inspection Commission, xxv, xxviii, 219,
        222-224, 228-231, 241-242, 244-245,
        257-258, 260-261, 272, 310-312
    by Member Nations, 49-50, 127, 133-134,
        144, 153-154, 170-171
    by Military Staff Committee, 328
    by Secretary-General, 184
    by specialized agencies, 144
    by Trusteeship Council, 170
    by United Nations organs, 51
    by World Conciliation Board, 97, 102, 341
Representation in General Assembly, weight-
    ed, xx-xxi, 25-31
Research
    by United Nations, 210-211, 285, 290, 292-
        295, 318, 327

Research *(cont.)*
   licensing of, 257
   nuclear, 210, 285-287, 290, 292
   participation by United Nations scientists in, 209, 278
   restrictions on military, 225, 227, 248, 250
Revenue system. *See* United Nations
Rhodesia and Nyasaland, Federation of, 30
Rivers, international, 103, 158
Rocket-launching facilities, xlvii, 222, 255, 257, 276
Rockets, 211, 222, 225, 227, 249, 253, 255-257, 275-277, 296, 299-303, 305, 327, 330
Romania, Soviet position in, 103
Ruanda-Urundi, 150
Russia, *See* Soviet Union

Samoa, Western, 150
San Francisco Conference, 4, 205
Sanctions
   against individuals, xxviii, xxxvi, 15, 37-38, 43-45, 306-309
   against member Nations, xxiii, xxviii, xxxvi, 7-8, 10, 37, 42-43, 80, 111-127, 178-180, 244, 311, 313, 339
   diplomatic, 42, 115, 180, 212, 313
   economic, xxxiv, xxxvi, 42-43, 115, 180, 212, 313, 334, 339
   general regulations on, 37, 41-43, 120-121
   national legislation on, 121-122
   none for recommendations, 50
   See also Enforcement measures; Peace Force
Satellites, space, 211, 222, 225, 227, 249, 253, 255, 257, 275-277, 296, 299-303, 305, 327, 330
Searches, unreasonable, prohibited, 366, 370
Secretariat of the United Nations, 18, 183-186
   appointment of members, 185-186
   budget, xxxvii, 352
   independence, 185
   privileges and immunities, 361-362
Secretary-General of the United Nations, 12, 14, 59, 111, 200-202, 205, 217, 283, 298, 311, 329, 352, 360-363
   appointment of, 183
   functions and powers, 183-185
   privileges and immunities, 362
Security arrangements, transitional, 192-194
Security Council, xxxiv, 14-16, 18, 35-36, 40, 47-48, 50-51, 55, 58-59, 177-181, 183-184, 336
   abolished, xxii, xlii, 18, 48, 70-71
   composition, 66, 71
   decisions, 46, 78
   functions and powers, 14-16, 35-36, 38, 40, 75-77, 79
   maintenance of peace by, 40, 50-51, 111-131
   permanent members, xxiii
   President, 85
   primary responsibility for peace, 40, 48, 52, 71, 75
   procedure, 83-85

Security Council *(cont.)*
   settlement of disputes by, 91-95, 107, 109
   subsidiary organs, 84
   voting in, xxiii, 80-81
   See also Veto
Seizures, unreasonable, prohibited, 366, 370
Self-defense, xvi, 37, 92, 127-128, 301, 318, 329
Self-determination of peoples, 5, 133
Self-government, 151-152, 155
Ships
   adaptable to military purposes, 225, 227, 248, 250, 254, 266-267, 276
   of the Peace Force, attack upon, 329
   flag of United Nations, 360
   for Peace Force, 326-327
Shipyards, periodic inspection, 250, 254, 266
Singapore, 151
Situations
   adjustment, 5, 35-36, 49, 90-110, 113, 338-341
   investigation, 93-94, 339, 341
   likely to endanger peace, xxxv, 8, 50, 90-92, 96-108, 339, 341
Social
   field, cooperation in, 5-6, 49, 133-134, 141-142, 147
   information, 153-154
   progress, promotion of, 3-4, 40, 132-133, 136, 141-142, 152-155, 160, 171, 345-346, 357
   studies, 142
   systems: no basis for rejection of new members, 14; no reform sought in, 11
Somalia, 30, 150
South-West Africa, 150
Sovereign immunity, 38, 44
Sovereignty, 6, 9, 56, 72, 82, 203, 369. *See also* Nations, reserved powers of
Soviet Union
   assent to Charter amendments, 196
   consent needed for Charter revision, xviii, xli
   disarmament proposals, xi-xii, l-li
   domination of Eastern Europe by, xlviii, 103
   member of Security Council, 66
   participation in transitional security arrangements, 192-193
   population, 56
   ratification of Charter by, 200, 203
   representation: in General Assembly, xxi, 27; on Executive Council, xxii, 72
   voting power, xx, 25, 56
Space. *See* Outer space
Spacecraft, 211, 222, 225, 227, 249, 253, 255-257, 275-278, 296, 299-303, 305, 327, 330
Spain, 169
Specialized agencies, 49, 170, 181
   access of: to International Court of Justice, 337; to World Conciliation Board, 340; to World Equity Tribunal, 338
   agreements with, 134-135, 143

Specialized agencies *(cont.)*
assistance to, 145
budgetary arrangements with, 53-54, 133-134, 143-144
coordination of activities, 135
establishment of new agencies, 134-135
funds for, 49, 53-54, 132, 135, 352, 356-357
immunities, 359
interpretation of constitutions, 337
participation in deliberations of Economic and Social Council by, 149
reports by, 144
Spectrometers, safeguards concerning, 276
States. *See* Nations
Status quo, dissatisfaction with, 89. *See also* Peaceful change
Straits, international, United Nations administration of, 103, 158, 160
Strategic areas, 51-52, 158-163
Submarines, xlvii
Sudan, 151
Suez Canal, 103-104, 161
Superior's orders, 38, 44-45
Surinam, 151
Syria, 150

Taiwan, 103
Tanganyika, 150
Taxes
compensation and pensions of United Nations personnel free from, 218, 220, 284, 361
immunity of United Nations income and property from, 359
payable to United Nations, xxxviii-xxxix, 349, 354-356
Territorial integrity, 7
Territories, non-self-governing, xx, xxiii-xxiv, 14-15, 20-21, 23-25, 30, 34, 60-62, 64-65, 67-74, 85-86, 138-141, 148-154, 164-173, 197, 199, 333, 338, 340
Terror, balance of, xv, 206
Thorium, 279
Togoland, 30, 150-151
Toynbee, Arnold, xliv
Trade, international, no regulation of, xix, xxii, 366
Transition period, xxiv, 200, 205, 208, 215, 351
Transportation
facilities: for Inspectors, 264-265; for Peace Force, 330
of nuclear materials, 275, 279
Travel, international, no regulation of, 366
Treaties
Charter prevails over, xxxiv, 187-188, 337
interpretation, xxxiv, 100, 335, 337
providing for reference of disputes: to World Conciliation Board, 341; to World Equity Tribunal, 339
registration with United Nations Secretariat, 187, 337
respect for obligations arising from, 3

Treaties *(cont.)*
validity, 183-184, 337
See also Agreements; Conventions
Tribunals
chosen by parties, 180
in United Nations headquarters and bases, 331, 360
national, 331, 336-337
of United Nations. See International Court of Justice; United Nations, regional courts; World Equity Tribunal
Truce, armed, xv
Trust territories, xx, xxiii-xxiv, 20-21, 23-25, 30, 34, 60-62, 64-65, 67-74, 85-86, 138-141, 148-149, 152, 197, 199, 333, 338, 340
administration of, 150, 155-163; by United Nations itself, 77, 158-161, 169-171
citizens, 14-15
election of their Representatives to: Economic and Social Council, xxiii, 138-141; Executive Council, xxiii, 67-70, 72-74; Standing Committees of the General Assembly, 60-61, 64-65
list, 150
membership in Trusteeship Council, 164-169
participation in discussions: of Economic and Social Council, 148-149; of Executive Council, 85-86
periodic visits to, 170
petitions from, 170
recruits from, 161-162, 333
representation in General Assembly, xx, 20-21, 23-25, 30, 34
Trusteeship agreements, 51-52, 155-160, 162, 170
Trusteeship Council, xlii, 79, 184, 186, 202
authority to request advisory opinions, 180-181
broadened authority, 152-154, 169-171
composition, xxiii-xxiv, 63, 164-169
discharge of members, 55, 65, 167-168
election of members, xxiii-xxiv, 55, 164-169
expenses, xxiv-xxxvii, 357
functions and powers, xxiv, 52, 152-154, 160-163, 169-172
meetings, 170
President, 174
principal organ of United Nations, 18
procedure, 174
questionnaire, 171-172
recommendations, 11, 170-173
reports to, 153-154, 170-172
voting in, 172-173
Trusteeship system, 51-52, 155-163
objectives, 155-156
supervision, 169-171
territories to which applicable, 156
Tunisia
attainment of independence by, 151
nationality decrees in, 100
Turkish Straits, 103, 161

Ukrainian S. S. R., 29-30

384

385